The Politics of Richard Wright

THE POLITICS OF
Richard Wright

Perspectives on Resistance

EDITED BY
Jane Anna Gordon AND Cyrus Ernesto Zirakzadeh

Copyright © 2018 by The University Press of Kentucky
Paperback edition 2020

Scholarly publisher for the Commonwealth,
serving Bellarmine University, Berea College, Centre College of Kentucky, Eastern Kentucky University, The Filson Historical Society, Georgetown College, Kentucky Historical Society, Kentucky State University, Morehead State University, Murray State University, Northern Kentucky University, Transylvania University, University of Kentucky, University of Louisville, and Western Kentucky University.
All rights reserved.

Editorial and Sales Offices: The University Press of Kentucky
663 South Limestone Street, Lexington, Kentucky 40508-4008
www.kentuckypress.com

Library of Congress Cataloging-in-Publication Data

Names: Gordon, Jane Anna, 1976– editor. | Zirakzadeh, Cyrus Ernesto, 1951– editor.
Title: The politics of Richard Wright : perspectives on resistance / edited by Jane Anna Gordon and Cyrus Ernesto Zirakzadeh.
Description: Lexington : The University Press of Kentucky, [2018] | Includes bibliographical references and index.
Identifiers: LCCN 2018021903| ISBN 9780813175164 (hardcover : alk. paper) | ISBN 9780813175171 (pdf) | ISBN 9780813175188 (epub)
Subjects: LCSH: Wright, Richard, 1908–1960—Criticism and interpretation. | Wright, Richard, 1908–1960—Political and social views. | Race in literature. | Politics in literature. | African Americans in literature. | Blacks in literature. | Politics and literature—United States—History—20th century.
Classification: LCC PS3545.R815 Z798 2018 | DDC 813/.52—dc23

ISBN 978-0-8131-7959-9 (pbk. : alk. paper)

This book is printed on acid-free paper meeting the requirements of the American National Standard for Permanence in Paper for Printed Library Materials.

Manufactured in the United States of America.

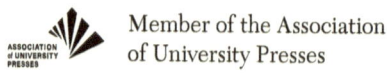

The Meaning of Protest

Between the world and me
a black boy is a native
son with a long dream
if a white man will listen.
Uncle Tom's children
were eight men, all outsiders,
fish bellies living
underground.

Pagan Spain taught us the church
was woman as mystery, a penis
the sword to butcher each other;
Black Power! we're not going
to the moon, and in Bandung
white man can't come
he's on a savage holiday.

Blossoms in a peanut field
won't bring me home;
something in the hum
of cotton is a glue
that won't hold red soil still;
ten million voices spliced
on an iron cross
between the world, and me, and you.

—Michael S. Harper

Contents

Introduction   1
    Jane Anna Gordon and *Cyrus Ernesto Zirakzadeh*

Part 1: Radical Politics

1. I Have Seen Black Hands   23
    Richard Wright
2. Wright's Afromodern Search for Political Freedom   26
    Lewis R. Gordon
3. Richard Wright and the Critique of Class Theory   45
    Cedric J. Robinson
4. Alternative Readings of Bigger Thomas   64
    Cyrus Ernesto Zirakzadeh
5. Richard Wright's Mission: Initiating a Politics of the Human   86
    Marilyn Nissim-Sabat

Part 2: Sexuality and Gender

6. Richard Wright and Black Women: Imagining the Feminine in *The Outsider*   107
    Floyd W. Hayes III
7. Masculinity, Misogyny, and the Limits of Racial Community   120
    Paul Gilroy
8. He's a Rapist, Even When He's Not: Richard Wright's Account of Black Male Vulnerability in the Raping of Willie McGee   132
    Tommy J. Curry

Part 3: Black Internationalism

9. Behind the McGee Case   155
    Richard Wright

10. Seizing Freedom with Simone de Beauvoir   159
    Lori J. Marso
11. Revisiting Richard Wright in Ghana: Black Radicalism and the Dialectics of Diaspora   181
    Kevin Kelly Gaines
12. Psychology and Black Liberation in Richard Wright's *Black Power* (1954)   198
    Dorothy Stringer

Part 4: Rhetorical Registers

13. Blueprint for Negro Writing   213
    Richard Wright
14. Floating Facts on a Sea of Emotion: The Literary Journalism of Richard Wright   224
    William Dow
15. Many Dark Mirrors in Richard Wright's *12 Million Black Voices*   247
    Perry S. Moskowitz
16. Richard Wright: The "Nature" of Politics, The "Politics" of Nature   263
    James B. Haile III

Part 5: Uncle Tom's Great-Grandchildren

17. Joe Louis Uncovers Dynamite   289
    Richard Wright
18. Notes toward a Political Economy of Life and Death: Reading Richard Wright with Frantz Fanon   293
    Abdul R. JanMohamed
19. Reading Richard Wright beyond the Carceral State: The Politics of Refusal in Black Radical Imagination   310
    Laura Grattan
20. Slavery Continued, Freedom Sought: Wright's Political Intellectual Journey   329
    Jane Anna Gordon

Acknowledgments   349
Further Reading   353
List of Contributors   359
Index   363

Introduction

Jane Anna Gordon and Cyrus Ernesto Zirakzadeh

> For my race possessed no fictional works dealing with such problems, had no background in such sharp and critical testing of experience, no novels that went with a deep and fearless will down to the dark roots of life.
> —Richard Wright, "How 'Bigger' Was Born"

> Bigger was attracted and repelled by the American scene. He was an American, because he was a native son; but he was also a Negro nationalist in a vague sense because he was not allowed to live as an American. Such was his way of life and mine; neither Bigger nor I resided fully in either camp.
> —Richard Wright, "How 'Bigger' Was Born"

> Just as a man rises in the mornings to dig ditches for his bread, so I'd work daily.
> —Richard Wright, "How 'Bigger' Was Born"

Richard Wright was a brilliant autodidact who devoted his creative energies to the question of how the descendants of enslaved Africans could live and die with dignity. Born in the first decade of the twentieth century to a sharecropper and schoolteacher in rural Mississippi, Wright lived and worked during periods of political retrenchment and radical turmoil much like the period in US life immediately following Barack Obama's presidency.

In the post-Reconstruction period, organized extralegal terror against black people became commonplace in the former Confederacy. This violent expression of a "dense ideology of [white] racial superiority" did not only push "the newly freed Negro . . . out of the United States Senate, the House of Representatives, [and] the many state legislatures."[1] Together with disenfranchisement and profound restrictions of educational and employment opportunities, it "swept [recently emancipated black people] out of the public, social, and economic life of the South."[2] Without such measures, legal abolition would have transformed the descendants of Africans kidnapped from their original homes into the numerical majority in the most fertile regions of the South. They "would have automatically controlled the richest lands of the South and with them the social, political, and economic destiny of a third of the Republic."[3] Freed black people would have controlled the lands over which they had labored for centuries while enslaved. But this potentiality of black power was systematically and brutally blocked. In its stead were arrangements designed both to shrink black hopes and to encourage their resignation before an emaciated "emancipation."

Wright's family knew such circumstances only too well. Confronting repression firsthand, they moved constantly in pursuit of basic financial stability. Except for a brief period when Wright enrolled in Hyde Park High School as an adult, his formal education ended in the ninth grade when, as valedictorian, he refused to deliver the scripted lecture.[4]

Considering the complex ways in which environments shape personalities, Wright became fascinated, during his boyhood, with those rare individuals of the Jim Crow South who refused to live by its rules. Although they were "shot, hanged, maimed, lynched, and generally hounded until they were either dead or their spirits broken," these (typically) men wanted to live and did live while they were alive in *this* world.[5] The fear and temporary backing down that they elicited from astonished white southerners, even if only for a "sweet spell," gave other black onlookers "an intense flash of pride."[6] Wright began to formulate a composite image of these rebels, which he later called "Bigger Thomas," and used it to explore the *potential* for revolutionary consciousness produced in part by the circumstances in which black people lived.

As did W. E. B. Du Bois in 1903, Wright emphasized that black people were this nation's native sons and daughters. Still, the civilization from which the "very tissue of their consciousness received its tone and timbre" sought brutally to keep them out.⁷ Wright argued that most buried what W. E. B. Du Bois called the resulting *fundamental twoness* through fierce faith in a hereafter, through tireless struggles to resurrect rights briefly tasted during Reconstruction, or through music and drink.⁸ There was only one important exception: the Biggers who openly rebelled and refused social death in order, if briefly, *to live*.

In 1927, Wright joined the chaotic mass exodus of blacks from the US South. During what scholars today call the *first* Gilded Age (with the first two decades of the twenty-first century constituting the second) and the Great Depression, Wright moved to the South Side of Chicago. Unlike Dixie, the northern city had "so much more to dazzle the mind with a taunting sense of possible achievement."⁹ Describing himself as coming into possession of his own feelings for the first time, Wright also encountered the labor movement. It offered a welcome reprieve from his intermittent work digging ditches, caring for research animals at Michael Reese Hospital, selling funeral insurance for burial societies, and periodically sorting mail at the post office. Recruited into the John Reed Club, a national literary organization of the Communist Party, and hired by the Federal Writers' Project to research the history of Illinois and of black people in Chicago, Wright began to study and write for the party's journals, *New Masses* and *International Literature*. He composed prize-winning articles on city life, including one describing black Chicagoans' reaction to the Joe Louis–Max Baer fight, which is reprinted in this volume.¹⁰

Wright realized, as he found his bearings, that the personality he had attributed to Bigger Thomas was everywhere, and it was not always or only embodied in black. Dispossessed and disinherited working-class whites in the United States, Germany, and Russia also expressed a "deep sense of exclusion" and engaged in the "tragic calculation of how much human life and suffering it would cost a man to live as a man in a world that denied him the right to live with dignity."¹¹ They also possessed "this intolerable sense of feeling and understanding so much, and yet living on a plane of social reality where the look of a world which one did not make or own struck one with a blinding objectivity and tangibility."¹² Wright described his discovery as "the pivot of [his] life" that "altered the complexion of [his] existence." He reflected, "It was as though I had put on a pair of spectacles whose power was that of an x-ray enabling me to see deeper into the lives of men."¹³ Realizing that many hopes, fears, and despairs were shared across legally defined "nations" and "races," Wright envisioned meaningful relations between American blacks and other people with "kindred consciousness."

What did the Biggers of the world all crave? According to Wright, they wished to be free, where being free involved taking meaningful responsibility with others for the shared conditions of one's life. They sought what Frantz Fanon would call being *actional*. In Wright's words, they wanted to "play a responsible role in the vital processes of the nation's life"; "to belong, to be identified, to feel that they were alive as other people were, to be caught up forgetfully and exultingly in the swing of events, to feel the clean, deep, organic satisfaction of doing a job in common with others."[14]

It struck Wright that it was through learning of the actions and feelings of men on the other side of the globe that he could grasp those of the primarily black men and women who lived beside him. For him, both Nazism and the movement of Marcus Garvey misled occupants of civilizations that offered no spiritual sustenance or "culture which could hold and claim allegiance and faith."[15] These worlds had sensitized their subjects and then left them estranged. Since what all black Bigger Thomases shared was disaffection from the black church and from African American folk culture, Wright resolved that he would take up a task unfulfilled by religious leaders and "the increasing irresolution which is paralyzing Negro middle class leadership."[16] This ambitious goal constituted his role—or, as he put it, his *social function*—as a black writer. He would use words to enlist the sympathies, loyalties, and yearnings of the millions of Bigger Thomases in every land and race, and to nurture an inclusive universalism. Black people formed its core as the restrictions on their education had most severely stunted their political voice and because the stringency of antiblack oppression had undercut and often perverted what might have been loyalty among black people. As such, Wright stated that "the conditions of life under which Negroes are forced to live in America contain the embryonic emotional prefigurations of how a large part of the body politic would react under stress."[17] The circumstances that produced both black double consciousness and its possible radical mobilization could foretell how most other human beings would respond to and could potentially liberate themselves from exploitation.

Wright left Chicago in 1937 to become the Harlem editor for the Communist newspaper *Daily Worker*, which covered topics ranging from the blues singer Lead Belly to the Scottsboro case. He also launched, with Dorothy West and Marian Minus, a short-lived journal, *New Challenge,* that was devoted to presenting black life "in relationship to the struggle against war and Fascism." His interest in Chicago never abated, however. It provided the setting for *Native Son,* a text devoted to Bigger Thomas. Published in 1940, the novel sold 215,000 copies in three weeks, was a Book of the Month Club selection, and was banned in libraries in Birmingham, Alabama. Shortly afterward, Wright and Edwin Rosskam published a photojournalistic study, *12 Million Black Voices,* about the millions of blacks who had left their rural homes in the South for the large industrialized cities in the North. Wright's candid portrayal of the material sufferings and daily indignities in northern cities prompted the Federal Bureau of Investigation to explore whether Wright's work was prosecutable under sedition statutes. Even though the government concluded that the answer was no, the FBI would continue to monitor Wright for the rest of his life.

Meanwhile, Wright's political activities multiplied. Although he served as vice president of American Peace Mobilization, which opposed American involvement in World War II, Wright openly supported the entry of the United States into the war after the Japanese attack on Pearl Harbor. The sole provider in a small family with a young infant, he was classified 3-A and was not drafted.[18] On the domestic front, he helped organize the Citizens' Emergency Conference for Interracial Unity in Harlem in response to widespread riots after the wounding of a black soldier by white police. He quietly broke from the Communist Party because of its unwillingness to confront wartime racial discrimination.[19]

Wright would engage in several historic collaborations over the course of his life. Among them, during this period, with Dr. Fredric Wertham, Wright cofounded a free psychiatric clinic in Harlem. As Frantz Fanon would in his classic *Black Skin, White Masks* (1952), Wright observed that supposedly universal psychological categories broke down when applied to colonized people:

> Extension of psychiatry to Harlem must not be confused with philanthropy, charity, or missionary work; it is the extension of the very concept of psychiatry into a new realm, the application of psychiatry to the masses, the turning of Freud upside down. The clinic has found that the most consistent therapeutic aid that it can render Harlem's mentally ill is instilling in them what Wertham calls "the will to survive in

a hostile world"; that the many Negroes sink under their loads because of hopelessness, social fear, worry, frustration, and just plain hunger.[20]

Wright concluded, as would Fanon, that the conception of a healthy black person in an antiblack world was *the happy slave*. A liberatory and anticolonial alternative would affirm the need to equip people with the ability to transform the conditions that normalized their degradation.

During this time, Wright deepened his intellectual and personal ties with numerous scholars and writers. He authored a long introduction to Horace Cayton and St. Clair Drake's classic in urban sociology, *Black Metropolis*; he served as an honorary pallbearer at the funeral of literary giant Countee Cullen; and he helped the then twenty-year-old James Baldwin win a Eugene F. Saxton Foundation Fellowship to pursue his writing. He also published a favorable review of Chester Himes's first novel, *If He Hollers Let Him Go*.

After World War II, as Wright's international reputation grew, he visited France, thanks to the help of Dorothy Norman, Gertrude Stein, and Claude Lévi-Strauss. In Paris, he met renowned anticolonial intellectuals such as Léopold Sédar Senghor, Aimé Césaire, Simone de Beauvoir, Jean-Paul Sartre, and Alioune Diop. He was present at the founding of *Présence Africaine,* a journal that would be central to debates over Pan-Africanism, anticolonial struggles in the French colonies, and the Négritude movement. When he returned to New York, he decided, partially in response to ongoing racial hostility in New York City, to move permanently to France.

He dove into the political and intellectual life of his new European home. He studied existential Marxist philosophy, met frequently with Sartre and Beauvoir, and traveled to Italy, Belgium, and England, where conversations with George and Dorothy Padmore stirred his interest in colonialism in Africa. He led, along with Sartre and Albert Camus, Rassemblement Démocratique Révolutionnaire, a group of intellectuals critical of both the Soviet Union and the United States. He began work on a screenplay about Haiti's revolutionary leader Toussaint L'Ouverture and founded and became president of the Franco-American Fellowship, which protested official US policies and opposed racial discrimination by American companies and organizations active in France.

A shift was certainly taking place. During the 1950s, Wright's popularity as a writer waned in the United States. His newest works, such as the

1953 book *The Outsider,* received mixed reviews. In France, Wright's relationships with other expatriate black Americans began to sour after the publication of "Everybody's Protest Novel," in which Baldwin criticized what he considered to be stereotypical characters and a melodramatic plot line in *Native Son.* When a film version of *Native Son* opened in January 1951 to acclaim in Buenos Aires, the US distributor cut almost thirty minutes due to pressure from New York State censors. Even the shortened version was banned in several states and received mainly negative reviews.

However, Wright's connections with the global black diaspora were growing and deepening. His relations flourished with other major black intellectuals engaged with existentialism, Pan-Africanism, and Marxism. He corresponded with Frantz Fanon and the Padmores and authored a preface to *In the Castle of My Skin,* the first novel of Barbadian writer George Lamming. Nigel Gibson and Roberto Beneduce observed that Wright's account of Bigger Thomas expressed the existential condition of "being 'hemmed in,' 'smothered,' 'imprisoned,' and 'choked' that characterize the experience of the colonized in [Fanon's] *The Wretched,* and the daily physical repression of people who are forced to live in a 'narrow world strewn with prohibitions.'"[21]

Even as new friendships and collaborations grew, Wright began to withdraw from formal public organizations and issued fewer unguarded political statements. He did so partly for reasons of self-preservation and out of fears of deportation. For example, despite his private concerns about the treatment of Algerians by the French, he avoided publicly criticizing French policies.

At the urging of the Padmores, Wright traveled to West Africa, where he met with Prime Minister Kwame Nkrumah and other members of the pro-independence Convention People's Party. Afterward, Wright hired a chauffeur and traveled by car across almost three thousand miles of Africa. He visited the Cape Coast, Christiansborg, Prampram, and slave-trading fortresses and dungeons. After returning to Europe, Wright published *Black Power,* a collection of observations on African societies and politics.

When Wright attempted to renew his US passport in 1954, State Department and FBI officials interviewed him because they were suspicious about his possible relationship to the Communist Party. Ironically, at roughly the same time, members of the black community in Paris became suspicious about Wright's participation in events cosponsored by US agencies and their fronts—for example, the conference of nonaligned nations in Bandung, Indonesia, which was partly funded by the anticommunist and US-backed Congress for Cultural Freedom. Wright himself believed that members of both the French government and the CIA were slinking at events where he spoke, such as the 1956 First Congress of Negro Artists and Writers, and inside organizations for international collaboration that he sometimes approached, such as the American Society for African Culture.

When Wright's second daughter, Rachel, fell ill with scarlet fever, Wright sought refuge in eastern Normandy, where he gardened and continued his self-imposed silence about the Algerian war of independence. He finished *Pagan Spain*, a book-length essay about his travels through Franco-ruled Spain. Another book-length essay, *White Man, Listen!*, was well received by the black US press but was criticized by other readers, including Fanon, who described Wright's perspective as superficial because, Fanon said, Wright failed to offer "down to earth" examples of the daily lives of the colonized. Fanon no doubt also rejected Wright's conclusion that black liberation required that white (rational European) man listen.[22]

After the British Home Office denied Wright the resident visa that would have enabled him to join his family in England, Wright moved into a two-room apartment in Paris. There he attempted to recover from dysentery and long-term intestinal problems. He hoped to publish a collection of his haiku, but his health was declining. In November 1960 Wright entered a clinic and shortly afterward died of a heart attack. He was cremated along with a copy of his book *Black Boy*.[23] His ashes were interred at Père Lachaise Cemetery.

Informed by the authors' knowledge of Wright's remarkable life, the following collection of essays explores Wright's unique political vision. While its center of gravity is political theory, the volume is an interdisciplinary undertaking. It draws on the expertise of specialists in political and moral philosophy and Africana literary studies. Organized into five sections, each considers a different, enduring dimension of Wright's political thinking.

The opening section is devoted to the radical spirit of Wright's political thought. Lewis R. Gordon introduces central themes concerning liberation that many of the other contributors to the volume subsequently explore. Gordon contends that Wright's work offers a historical and existentially rich window onto the suffocating world produced through the colonialism, enslavement, and racism that built Euromodernity. Exploring the exclusion of black people from the only world to which they are indigenous, Wright shows how white efforts to erode black power generate broader political impotence among humankind, undercutting the very possibility of mature responsibility. By exposing the endemic conditions in the United States—rather than individual failings in black people themselves—that produce black suffering, Wright implores readers to ask what can and should be done and, more imploringly, what I and we can *do?*

Central to Wright's answer was his lifelong creative and critical grappling with Marxism. The classic exploration of it is represented here by Cedric J. Robinson's previously published chapter on Wright. Although Wright saw capitalism as a fundamental source of slavery and unfreedom, he did not think exploited groups were just victims. They had a distinct capacity to develop visions of freedom, independent of what the church, the state, and the cultural elites declared. Maintaining a fundamentally ambivalent attitude toward modernity, Wright called for a break from the homogenized and romanticized portrayal of the proletariat common in the works of European and Euro-American Marxists that Wright thought reflected the authors' culturally specific, petit bourgeois origins. To overcome this shortcoming, Wright paid attention to ordinary black people,[24] ironically making his Marxism a more global theory through adequate consideration of how race, class, and caste developed in this hemisphere.[25]

Cyrus Ernesto Zirakzadeh explores appropriations of the fictional character "Bigger Thomas" during the Cold War. Zirakzadeh notes that three intellectual radicals—the democratic-socialist statist thinker Irving Howe; the communitarian advocate Ralph Ellison; and the cultural-politics exponent James Baldwin—used the story of *Native Son* in strikingly different ways to defend different sorts of political activism and to advance different responses to racism. Moreover, these three public intellectuals thought about Bigger in ways that differed from Wright's own reflections on the political meaning of the book. The divergent uses of Wright's artistic creation illustrate the indefinite political meaning of Bigger. The multiple uses also remind us of the wealth of symbolic resources that widely consumed popular art offers every struggle for change.

Some readers of Wright's work have criticized him for failing to portray healthy human connection or solidarity. Marilyn Nissim-Sabat, in her chapter, maintains that Wright was deeply aware that people could only live as human beings through meaningful relations with one another. This sentiment was powerfully captured in his lines: "I would hurl words into this darkness and wait for an echo; and if an echo sound, no matter how faintly, I would send other words to tell, to march, to fight, to create a sense of the hunger for life that gnaws in us all, to keep alive in our hearts a sense of the inexpressibly human." Wright understood both that the human need for solidarity ran deep and that the ability to forge it could be damaged. Without such solidarity, alienation from oneself and others would crush "Bigger" and Bigger-like characters in Chicago's South Side and globally. Wright therefore championed the healing made possible by qualitatively enlarging our lived experience of and with one another.

The second section of the book explores the challenges to forging healthy human connections across lines of gender difference. Although Wright announced in his 1940 commentary "How 'Bigger' Was Born" that he planned to compose "another novel, this time about the status of women in modern American society," he never wrote that text. Perhaps because of its absence, many women and feminist readers have criticized or ignored Wright's fiction on the grounds that the novels contain too many brutal interactions between his male and female characters and too few women characters who seem sympathetic, let alone worthy of admiration. Floyd W. Hayes III offers a synopsis of this line of criticism, with which he generally agrees. He argues that Wright wrote in this manner because he was a creature of Europatriarchy, whose male-centered narratives often treated women characters as objects or props in male-ordered worlds. Hayes concludes that even though Wright's stereotypical images of black women powerfully conveyed a black male sense of homelessness, its misogynistic expression ultimately limited Wright's political vision of black struggle.

The reprinted excerpt from Paul Gilroy's *Black Atlantic* offers an alternative interpretation of the historical context and purpose of Wright's fiction. Gilroy suggests that Wright's frank portrayal of domestic authoritarianism and violence in public and intimate relations reveals the legacies of the racially coercive Jim Crow South. Wright was not attempting to create historically abstract, idealized images of black men and women and the relations between them. Indeed, Gilroy argues, Wright's creative work included examples of black homophobia, misogyny, and other antisocial attributes that Gilroy thinks could not be attributed solely to racism.

The long-standing debate among scholars about misogyny in Wright's fiction typically confines its discussion of gender to women. The conversation thereby overlooks some of Wright's important observations about sexual politics in the United States, such as vulnerability of black males to sexual violence at the hands of both white men and white women. Tommy J. Curry explores unique forms of black male vulnerability in a discussion of Wright's impassioned response, reprinted in this volume, to the 1951 trial and execution of fellow Mississippi native Willie McGee. Curry relates Wright's defense of McGee to Wright's short story about a black man who, desperate for paid employment, cross-dresses as a female domestic worker, only to face dangerous dilemmas and humiliations more broadly shared by many black men.

Lori J. Marso opens the book's section on black internationalism by offering the kind of historically aware interpretation of Wright that Gilroy calls for.[26] According to Marso, Wright became urgently interested in the rise of anticolonial movements in Africa as well as the question of building a viable Pan-Africanism. However, he refused to assume that unity across the globe could occur automatically or easily, which has led some Pan-African advocates to question the actual depth of Wright's commitment to their project. Marso revisits Wright's unpopular 1956 speech to the Paris Congress, where he deemed many traditional, religious, and normative identities in Africa as alienating. Marso emphasizes that Wright also challenged unqualified rejections of modernity and the demands from others that he authentically embody blackness. Like Simone de Beauvoir, he wished to forge emancipatory connections through the cultivation of political bonds across black and nonblack groups that perceived the world differently.

The reprinted essay by Kevin Kelly Gaines adds to Marso's argument by noting that Wright—like his fellow black Marxist intellectuals in exile, George Padmore and C. L. R. James—rejected the myth of a transhistorical, transnational black cultural unity. All three thinkers believed that Pan-Africanism had to emerge from a shared history of oppression *and* from a critical, dialectical consciousness of the situation of blacks in the West. In contrast to Marso, Gaines argues that Wright gave pride of place to the emergent political consciousness of African people, even if some New World black people, like Wright, found some such nationalist elements to be radically foreign.

Dorothy Stringer's chapter rounds out the discussion of Wright's approach to black internationalism. Stringer explores Wright's use of Freudian psychoanalysis and the implicit psychology within African American literature. She argues that while Wright's rationalism and belief in modern progress often prompted him to question, and even condemn, the local cultures and political systems he encountered in the Gold Coast/Ghana, his emphasis on actual and historical trauma—above all, the traumas of the slave trade—also allowed him to understand daily life, quotidian relationships, and minor economic transactions as continuous with a broad history of black resistance, and as tools for projecting a different future for black people.

The book's fourth section considers how Wright's experimentation with literary modes influenced the content of his political thought. A remarkable feature of Wright's autodidacticism was the range of what he read and how he wrote. According to Cedric Robinson, Wright's broad use of literary genres enabled him to explore the complexities and subtleties of radical politics more authentically than conventional history, biography, or political tract writing would have allowed.

The section begins with William Dow's analysis of Wright's extensive work as a journalist. Dow locates Wright's journalistic essays in the company of other major African American novelists and poets, including Du Bois, Langston Hughes, Alice Childress, Zora Neale Hurston, Melvin Tolson, Nella Larsen, and Jessie Fauset. Dow argues that Wright experimented with the high modernist use of "we" to challenge who could invoke authorial authority. Meanwhile, Wright's success in combining different literary genres demonstrated how badly most conventional media outlets failed to describe nonwhite experience globally.

Dow's observations about Wright's refusal to use a conventional understanding of "we" as a method of homogenizing experience prepares us for Perry S. Moskowitz's discussion of Wright's nuanced representation of "some thirteen million people" in *12 Million Black Voices*. Moskowitz contends that in that book, Wright, working with Edwin Rosskam, constructed a series of montages that challenged simplistic assumptions about how black social realities could be comprehensively represented and documented. By counterposing distinct and often inconsistent black voices with his own narration, Wright demonstrated, as Marso also argues, that black people were in no way a naturally unified and homogeneous people. Any collective "we" had to be forged because no single voice could speak for all.

James B. Haile III continues this discussion of Wright's expansive understanding of "we." He argues that Wright's exploration of the relationship between particular physical landscapes and distinct forms of political consciousness was part of a broader tradition of African American nature writing and ecoliterature. Wright, like other African American nature authors, treated nature as a force that simultaneously envelops, nourishes, and invades the human world. His writing, including his poetry, about the natural world therefore augmented what otherwise would be a straightforward narrative about material exploitation and existential deprivation. For Wright, particular skies and horizons, waters and storms, were not simply allies of those who oppress. They also offered locations from which black people could, without mediation, foster indigenous folk culture, including practices of self-maintenance, in a way not readily available in urban, industrial settings—especially in the US North.

The book closes with a final section of three essays that consider what Wright's work can teach us about contemporary forms of resistance. Wright did not simply depict suffering. For him, the ongoing and ever-present threat of violent death curbed living expressions of freedom, but the threat also fueled and informed repertoires of response.

Building upon his earlier analysis of the short stories in Wright's anthology *Uncle Tom's Children*, Abdul R. JanMohamed reflects on Wright's gradual discovery of a close relationship among social death, physical death, and symbolic death. According to JanMohamed, Wright saw "primitive accumulation" not only as the material dispossession of the slave's world but also as the appropriation of subjectivity. For JanMohamed, this raises questions about whether a former slave can repossess psycho-political and sociopolitical components of self in Jim Crow societies that operate predominantly through the inculcation of widespread fear.

Laura Grattan argues in her chapter that today fear is frequently channeled through the bifurcation of "the citizen" and "the criminal." Building on what she frames as Wright's opting out of an existing social order—even when doing so could narrow an actor's choices—Grattan contends that Wright's sympathy toward the character Bigger Thomas can be extended to solidarity with so-called "criminals" and local experiments that attempt to resolve situations of gendered violence without recourse to policing or incarceration. As Grattan points out, such a strategy entails denying the power of the state to define and categorize human beings.

Jane Anna Gordon also explores how Wright's response to the persistence of core features of slavery after its formal abolition can be read through the lens of fugitivity. In Gordon's view, Wright was able to *steal himself away* from unfreedom in the United States, although this fell short of his normative ideal of freedom. Wright's ideal entailed bringing an end to the protracted racialized neoslavery that has marked the "postslavery" period for most black people, enabling black people to inhabit as political homes the places that they had helped to build.

Woven through this anthology is the penetrating voice of Wright himself. His 1934 poem "I Have Seen Black Hands" sets the tone for the first section on radical politics. Describing hands that, like his, are black, Wright recounts their hungry reaching for life. These hands produced riches for others and served the country through military service. When the economic tides turned, however, African Americans were left without paid employment or remuneration for their labor. What is more, they faced unfair punishment or lynching when they sought a share of the profits they had made for others. The poem culminates in a call for their hands to turn into revolting fists, joined by those of working, nonblack others.

Framing the book's section on black internationalism is Wright's 1951 editorial "Behind the McGee Case." The piece was originally written for a French audience that had protested against the planned execution of McGee. In a single sentence, Wright settles the question of McGee's innocence. He then turns to the plantation economy of Mississippi in an effort to contextualize the events of the case. According to Wright, after World War II, brutal lawlessness within the United States had become an international liability leading to a federal push to replace extralegal with legal lynching. White Mississippians, preoccupied with defending their regional power over blacks, had not anticipated that the execution of McGee would have negative global consequences. Wright assured his French readers that their agitation had an effect. It would force white Americans to think hard before staging another legal lynching, and about the price of their continued racial prejudice.

Wright's 1937 "Blueprint for Negro Writing" opens the section on Wright's style and creative use of diverse forms of rhetoric and genre. The essay explores the proper content, methods, and purpose of black writers. It is Wright's plea that Negro writers attach themselves fundamentally to the lived experience of black people, especially black workers. He further insisted that Negro writers had a moral responsibility to depict the need of black Americans for social and political revolution rather than nurturing bland acceptance of an exploitative and deadly economic and political order. This responsibility required black writers to grapple with black nationalism. Rather than treating it as autarchic, they needed to reflect critically on how black nationalism could be engaged to connect black people meaningfully with others in their search for liberation.

Kicking off the book's final section is Wright's 1935 article, "Joe Louis Uncovers Dynamite." Set in the immediate aftermath of black boxer Joe Louis's victory over then white champion Max Baer, the essay describes how, on the South Side of Chicago, thousands of black people flooded into public spaces to celebrate a moment's racial victory, an exceptional instance of black triumph over white. Taking strength from Louis's strength, spontaneously assembled masses of black people temporarily felt collectively free and invincible. Wright thought this cyclone of celebration exhibited a pent-up black folk consciousness hungry for freedom and revealed an emboldened energy that could be harnessed and channeled politically. Although soon subsiding, long-suppressed desires had been uncovered in Joe Louis's victory. This raised the question of how that agential force might be directed.

We opened this book by comparing Wright's times with the second decade of the twenty-first century of US life. Why?

In 2015, when we began work on this text, the pertinence of Wright's work was all too obvious. Even though what JanMohamed calls the "killability" of black men, women, and children was not new, the easy creation of footage documenting it certainly was. As had been the case with the widely circulated video of the brutal beating of Rodney King, however, seemingly irrefutable evidence of police wrongdoing led to prosecutions, but convictions were scarce. Behind these episodes that punctuated the news cycle was a protracted period of economic decline and stagnation that many scholars have called a second Gilded Age.[27] Among its characteristics are dramatic concentrations of wealth, extreme inequality, and brutal repression of emergent movements trying to devise protections against new forms of vulnerability. In addition, as his presidency approached its end, there was vitriolic and vindictive backlash against Barack Obama—someone who could have uniquely vindicated the country's moral character after the George W. Bush administration. Since 2015, overt public endorsements of white nationalism and racial resentment have swept the United States and the world, ushering Donald Trump into the Oval Office. All of these developments call to mind the era in which Wright wrote—another moment when dramatic global change led to a sharp rise in the appeal of fascism as a right-wing answer to domestic and international transformations.

In our political times, Wright proves an especially astute and relevant interlocutor. His explorations of how black people respond to being treated as if they *simply don't matter* anticipate the central diagnoses and concerns of the Black Lives Matter movement: that literal killing, criminalization, and mass incarceration constitute three prongs of a war against black people; that counteracting the protracted legacies of colonization and enslavement requires investing in educational and economic reconstruction that includes not only black access but black ownership; and that political power consists in the ability of all of those implicated to determine the collective conditions of their lives. We would be wise to mine Wright's prescient observations about the relationship between racist states and the appeal of fascism as we face a president who affirms his base through calls for curbing all migration from black and brown countries and who treats antifascist protestors as morally equivalent to the armed white supremacists they confront.

Wright lamented the many piecemeal approaches that aimed to suppress the revolutionary consciousness of Bigger Thomas by busying him with activities that might keep him from damaging white property. Still, Wright's desire for radical social reconstruction did not lead him to share in pessimistic refusals to affirm any constructive political engagement. Despite facing endless government investigations and repeatedly dealing with partisan intolerance, Wright neither withdrew completely from politics nor retreated behind a thick wall of dogmatism. Instead, he accepted the fundamental uncertainty of human action and remained committed to building intellectual, political, and personal bridges, even as he acknowledged that meaningful solidarities had to be forged across sharp sociopolitical divisions created by ongoing sexual and colonial forms of oppression.

For Wright, the inclusive universalism built in and from black experience would be fundamentally color-conscious or color-*seeing*. It drew on insights that emerged in black folk culture indigenous to the United States even as Wright understood that these would have to be made contemporary. Enabling Wright to pursue this complex, dialectical vision was his ability to combine a deep loyalty and belief in the necessity of collaboration with a fierce commitment to his own intellectual growth and vision, even when these put him at odds with his comrades and allies.[28]

The renowned University of Chicago urban sociologist Robert Park, a specialist in race relations, once asked Richard Wright: "How in the hell did you happen?"[29] It was a profoundly honest question that conceded the inability of existing social scientific research to explain the person of Richard Wright. Our answer is that we are fortunate that Wright *did* happen and that the time is now ripe to think with him again.

Notes

1. Richard Wright, "How 'Bigger' Was Born," available here: http://xroads.virginia.edu/~ma01/white/anthology/bigger.html.

2. Ibid.

3. Ibid.

4. As a child, when delivering lunches to railroad workers, Wright collected stray pieces of coal by the railroads to heat his family's home. Later, as an adolescent and young man, he worked as a sales clerk, at a hotel and then a movie theater, and subsequently at an optical company. He would recount these experiences in "The Ethics of Living Jim Crow."

5. Wright, "How 'Bigger' Was Born."

6. Ibid.

7. Ibid.

8. Wright also mentioned black people who through formal education became both estranged from the black masses and poised to become their official leaders.

9. Wright described Bigger's Chicago in these terms: "Then there was the fabulous city in which Bigger lived, an indescribable city, huge, roaring, dirty, noisy, raw, stark, brutal; a city of extremes: torrid summers and sub-zero winters, white people and black people, the English language and strange tongues, foreign born and native born, scabby poverty and gaudy luxury, high idealism and hard cynicism! A city so young that, in thinking of its short history, one's mind, as it travels backward in time, is stopped abruptly by the barren stretches of wind-swept prairie! But a city old enough to have caught within the homes of its long, straight streets the symbols and images of man's age-old destiny, of truths as old as the mountains and seas, of dramas as abiding as the soul of man itself! A city which has become the pivot of the Eastern, Western, Northern, and Southern poles of the nation. But a city whose black smoke clouds shut out the sunshine for seven months of the year; a city in which, on a fine balmy May morning, one can sniff the stench

of the stockyards; a city where people have grown so used to gangs and murders and graft that they have honestly forgotten that government can have a pretense of decency!" Ibid.

10. Political scientist John A. Davis would later comment that the "trouble with [Richard Wright] as an important artist is that the social scientists have undoubtedly lost an important social scientist" (see Jennifer Jensen Wallach, *Richard Wright: From Black Boy to World Citizen* [Chicago: Ivan R. Dee], 2010).

11. Wright, "How 'Bigger' Was Born."

12. Ibid.

13. Ibid.

14. Ibid.

15. Ibid.

16. Ibid.

17. Ibid.

18. Wright was fascinated by psychological warfare and tried unsuccessfully to secure a special commission in the propaganda services of the army.

19. The party also tried to control his writing, an emotionally painful struggle that Wright described in "I Tried to Be a Communist," which appeared in *Atlantic Monthly*.

20. See Richard Wright, "Psychology Comes to Harlem," *Freeworld*, no. 12 (September 1946): 49–51; and Nigel C. Gibson and Roberto Beneduce, *Frantz Fanon, Psychiatry and Politics* (London: Rowman and Littlefield International, 2017).

21. See Gibson and Beneduce, *Frantz Fanon, Psychiatry and Politics*, 18, quoting Frantz Fanon (*Wretched of the Earth*, trans. Constance Farrington [New York: Grove, 1968]), 37).

22. On this point, see Gibson and Beneduce, *Frantz Fanon, Psychiatry and Politics*, 79.

23. *Black Boy* was the published first half of his autobiography. The second half was published posthumously.

24. Wright argued that black writers should draw on existing black folklore. It was not that folklore was straightforwardly emancipatory. Its content was often internally contradictory as it also enabled people mundanely to bear the unbearable. But, for Wright, it was indigenous to and born of New World black situations, marked especially by what slavery had done to the personality of black people.

25. Unlike most of his intellectual contemporaries and certainly the people who studied them, Wright maintained a profound distrust of middle-class people and special discomfort with being around the black pseudo-bourgeoisie.

26. Nissim-Sabat's chapter also addresses Gilroy's concern when she argues that Beauvoir, through her engagements with Wright, was able to pivot away from brands of feminism rooted in resentment.

27. For discussion of this point, see Sarah Kendzior, "Ferguson in Focus: How the Tragedy of a Police Shooting Became a National Industry," *Common Reader: A Journal of the Essay*, October 30, 2015.

28. When Wright reflected on the criticisms of *Native Son* he anticipated would come from his comrades, he acknowledged that while his heart was with the collectivist and proletarian ideal, there had to be room for honesty in works of political imagination. It had been his inclination "to satisfy the claims of [his] own ideals rather than the expectations of others" that pulled him to and now put him in tension with the labor movement. In each case he was "fulfilling what [he] felt to be the laws of [his] own growth" (see Wright, "How 'Bigger' was Born").

29. Wallach, *Richard Wright: From Black Boy to World Citizen* (Chicago: Ivan R. Dee, 2010), 6.

PART 1

Radical Politics

1

I Have Seen Black Hands

I

I am black and I have seen black hands, millions and millions of them—
Out of millions of bundles of wool and flannel tiny black fingers have
 reached restlessly and hungrily for life.
Reached out for the black nipples at the black breasts of black mothers,
And they've held red, green, blue, yellow, orange, white, and purple toys in
 the childish grips of possession,
And chocolate drops, peppermint sticks, lollypops, wineballs, ice cream
 cones, and sugared cookies in fingers sticky and gummy,
And they've held balls and bats and gloves and marbles and jack-knives
 and sling-shots and spinning tops in the thrill of sport and play.
And pennies and nickels and dimes and quarters and sometimes on New
 Year's, Easter, Lincoln's Birthday, May Day, a brand new green dollar
 bill,
They've held pens and rulers and maps and tablets and books in palms
 spotted and smeared with ink,
And they've held dice and cards and half-pint flasks and cue sticks and
 cigars and cigarettes in the pride of new maturity . . .

II

I am black and I have seen black hands, millions and millions of them—
They were tired and awkward and calloused and grimy and covered with
 hangnails,

And they were caught in the fast-moving belts of machines and snagged and smashed and crushed.
And they jerked up and down at the throbbing machines massing taller and taller the heaps of gold in the banks of bosses,
And they piled higher and higher the steel, iron, the lumber, wheat, rye, the oats, corn, the cotton, the wool, the oil, the coal, the meat, the fruit, the glass, and the stone until there was too much to be used,
And they grabbed guns and slung them on their shoulders and marched and groped in trenches and fought and killed and conquered nations who were customers for what the good black hands had made,
And again black hands stacked goods higher and higher until there was too much to be used,
And then the black hands held trembling at the factory gates the dreaded lay-off slip,
And the black hands hung idle and swung empty and grew soft and got weak and bony from unemployment and starvation,
And they grew nervous and sweaty, and opened and shut in anguish and doubt and hesitation and irresolution . . .

III

I am black and I have seen black hands, millions and millions of them—
Reaching hesitantly out of days of slow death for the goods they had made, but the bosses warned that the goods were private and did not belong to them,
And the black hands struck desperately out in defense of life and there was blood, but the enraged bosses decreed that this too was wrong,
And the black hands felt the cold steel bars of the prison they had made, in despair tested their strength and found that they could neither bend nor break them,
And the black hands fought and scratched and held back but a thousand white hands took them and tied them,
And the black hands lifted palms in mute and futile supplication to the sodden faces of mobs wild in the reveries of sadism,
And the black hands strained and clawed and struggled in vain at the noose that tightened about the black throat,

I Have Seen Black Hands

And the black hands waved and beat fearfully at the tall flames that
  cooked and charred the black flesh . . .

IV

I am black and I have seen black hands
Raised in fists of revolt, side by side with the white fists of white workers,
And some day—and it is only this which sustains me—
Some day there shall be millions and millions of them,
On some red day in a burst of fists on a new horizon!

Richard Wright
June 26, 1934

Note: Originally published as "I Have Seen Black Hands," *New Masses* (1934). Reprinted courtesy of the Richard Wright Estate.

Wright's Afromodern Search for Political Freedom

Lewis R. Gordon

"I Can't Breathe," were Eric Garner's last words when he was wrenched to the ground in the choke hold of a Staten Island police officer on July 17, 2014. They summarize Richard Wright's indictment of Euromodern societies. Colonialism, enslavement, and racism create a suffocating environment in which options are so limited that reaching beyond them, even for a gasp of oxygen, is potentially life-threatening. One can "choose" to ignore such an incipient threat, but the consequences are severe. At the point when bare life is all that's left, things have proverbially gone too far.[1] This distinction between choices and options is linked to an ongoing problem in Afromodern struggles under the conditions imposed by Euromodernity—namely, the distinction between politics and rule.

Wright, however, negotiated tensions between political life and governing power with an addition: the existential challenges that racism and other forms of dehumanization posed to political life.[2] To act politically, one needs to appear, as political thinkers from antiquity through to Hannah Arendt have argued, in the social world in particular ways—for example, as a human being with a legitimate voice in public affairs.[3] Impediments to such forms of appearance raise challenges of meaning in the face of seeming futility. How could one proceed when one's actions supposedly don't matter?

Wright explored this problem of appearance through his creative and expository work as a writer. He drew on his experiences as a political organizer for the Communist Party, which he subsequently abandoned to influence the world by other means. The unfortunate consequence of that break was his eventual isolation. Compare him to the South African revolutionary Steve Bantu Biko. Though Biko drew upon similar existential and left-oriented political resources as Wright, the journey took him to Black Consciousness. This was an outward-oriented praxis whose repercussions continue to appear not only in South Africa but also many other countries, including the United States. There are ways, however, in which even Biko's efforts could be misinterpreted as a lure to isolation. His existentialism and Black Consciousness, unfortunately, were taken in certain misguided readings into directions now known as "pessimistic," especially given the tragic ending of Biko's life at the brutal hands of white interrogators during apartheid.[4] Inward and outward movements of black reflection could, however, be read beyond pessimism *and optimism* through insights into a tragic political condition and illuminating criteria that must be met in any serious, committed struggle for freedom.

Afromodernity in Euromodernity

Euromodernity emerged, as Enrique Dussel, Walter Mignolo, and many other thinkers from the Global South argue, from a series of significant events in 1492.[5] The first was the expulsion of the Moors from Grenada, one of their last strongholds in Christendom. This important event of the "Reconquest" was a harbinger of inquisitions and global expansion leading to Columbus's crew landing in the Bahamas in October, inaugurating what is aptly termed the "conquest of the Americas."[6] Colonization and the subsequent construction of a "new world" marked the transformation from Christendom into Euromodernity, from which Christians of Eurasia were transformed into Europeans, and people in the rest of the world were forced into the direction of a new nonrelation of negative terms—namely, all that is not European.

A Euromodern myth is its own completeness and universality. This presumption led to an isomorphic model of the modern and the European. In circular fashion, the consequence is straightforward. To be or become modern, one must be or become European. Likewise, not being European entails not being modern.

What, however, does it mean to be "modern" beyond being European? History offers many examples. In antiquity, many civilizations emerged as the avowed path of humankind. They all—whether in ancient Nubia, Egypt, Sumer, Mesopotamia, Babylonia, Macedonia, or Rome—offered their civilization as the exemplification of being human and the conclusion of history. To be human into the future meant to become them, because they offered the closest thing to immortality on earth: avowed eternal cities in which fame and glory would be forever remembered and, at least symbolically, lived.

For those conquered or absorbed into those empires or hegemonic states, the struggle was against what seemed like fate. They either disappeared from the unfolding story of humankind, developed the resources to overthrow the conquerors and take on the path of future existence, or hybridized with the imposed order and became a new existent capable of inhabiting the world to come. History reveals tales of different peoples who opted for or were forced into these three possibilities. The first became archaeological curiosities; the second rarely won, but when they did, they became the new narrative; and the third nearly always succeeded. Consider, for example, the transformation of the ancient Roman Empire into the Holy Roman Empire and Christendom. Those it conquered became hybrids, yielding what Jane Anna Gordon describes as a creolized, or mixed, living order.[7]

Not all conquered or colonized groups accept the notion that the future requires their elimination. Some adopt an identity of accommodation. Thus, their agency is manifested in what they adapt or reject from their conquerors. The conquered often depend on the values through which they not only make sense of their situation but also transform themselves and those around them. The well-known transformation of Rome into the Holy Roman Empire was a phenomenon of colonizer becoming like, and at times even dominated by, those colonized in many subsequent empires or hegemonic countries and peoples.

Think, for example, of the caliphates across Africa, southern Europe, and southern Asia during what is erroneously known as the "Dark Ages," and of what emerged from their new manifestation in the fifteenth century. The world of Andalusia versus Christendom offered an anthropological concept, *raza*. The concept made its way across the Atlantic into the many First Nations of its western shores. Referring to breeds of dogs, horses, and, when applied to people, Jews and Moors, the concept raised notions of metaphysical and normative belonging and exclusion. To be natural meant to be within the framework of Christian legitimacy. All others were, then, ultimately unnatural and condemned. During the Amerindian genocide in North America, the nearly such in South America, and the kidnapping of Africans amid the transformed theological economies of Christendom into the secularized theodicy of capitalism, *raza* mutated into *race* and became the anthropological grounding of Euromodernity.[8]

Many new "races" emerged in Euromodernity. Its philosophical anthropology divided the world into primitives and moderns. The former took on many manifestations of what W. E. B. Du Bois subsequently called "problems."[9] The idea behind primitiveness was that some people belonged properly to the past. They illegitimately inhabited the present because they ultimately had no place in the future. Other groups, however, never existed in the past and were entirely born from Euromodernity. Black people are an example of such. Prior to the events of the sixteenth century, Africans had no reason to refer to themselves as "black." This was an externally imposed term. Whether in the Spanish *el negro,* in the French *le noir,* or in the transformation of the Spanish term into *le nègre,* new beings of blackness indigenous to Euromodernity emerged.

A clear fallacy of this familiar history is the absence of the points of view of the people on whom Euromodernity was imposed. These peoples explored possibilities for their continued existence through resistance, creolization, and searches for meaning. A future existence—whether as hybrids, creolized subjects, or some other collective form in which their identity as a people could be maintained—meant that they could offer alternative modernities since Euromodernity demanded their future absence. For black people, such a project is Afromodernity.

Richard Wright's thought is an Afromodern response to Euromodernity's philosophical and anthropological exclusion of non-European peoples from full human membership. He identified what I call *black melancholia*.[10] This phenomenon involves the realization, by blacks, of being indigenous to a world whose claim to legitimacy is based in their exclusion. This experience happens not only within political institutions but also within other organized forms of power, including aesthetic and epistemic life.[11] An example of the latter is the Manichean readings of black intellectual production in which black intellectuals produce black things whereas white intellectuals produce "universal" offerings to humankind. The particularity of the black condition—*as particular*—connoted a special kind of failure, whereas white hegemony could remain intact. Unable to affect the universal, the particularity of black thought represented a negative term, eventually to disappear over time in the dustbin of irrelevance. Consequently, many white critics wanted Wright to regard antiblack racism as a specific problem endemic to supposed relations with blacks—a black "problem."

Wright, however, had much more in mind. When Jean-Paul Sartre asked him to explain the "Negro problem," his response was: "There is no Negro black problem in the United States. There is only a white problem."[12]

In his famous introduction to the second edition of *Native Son*, Wright offered a similar verdict. Critics who read Wright as only an informant of antiblack racism fail to see (as Floyd Hayes III argues in "Richard Wright and Black Women" and elsewhere) that he was an epochal diagnostician.[13] Wright saw how the dehumanization of black people contained an attack on humanity itself because it was an attempt to eliminate human relations from a human world. As he argued in his introduction, Bigger Thomas was the critical contradiction of a society that made it indecent for those under the heels of the system—in this case Euromodern capitalism—to live with dignity, respect, and truth.

Though there have been other modernities, Euromodernity is among those that aver a conception of the human that is marked by radical exclusion. Creolization models of new human beings have no place in a world premised on purity, a theodicy of internal value, and idolatry. The society or system becomes a god that denies what all human beings propped up as gods ultimately do: fail.

Unlike past modernities, Euromodernity is also global. This means that the future is moribund for whole groups or "races" of people, unless the paradoxical darkness in light, the matter explicit in energy and the latter explicit in the former, is embraced. Wright asks us to look beyond the light for the darkness through which distinctions make meaning possible. "Pure" light is, after all, blinding.

Read in this way, a theme emerges in Wright's critique of Euromodernity and his conceptions of Afromodernity. Instead of prescribing nihilistic aloneness, he could be interpreted as showing its limitations by taking his readers to where they wished never to go. His literary writings and some of his essays can be read in the tradition of black existentialism and Africana thought, as movements of *double consciousness*.

First, he offers the society's self-image of neatly divided, Manichean contraries: the world of the white and that of the black. The white in that world sees a seamless, consistent reality from the superior to the inferior or, at least, a self-portrait of rationality, reason, and commitment to systemic justice. The black initially sees the white's point of view. This logically means that the black presumes the problems in his or her life are functions of extrasystemic forces. As good, the white world remains intact, while the black, as outsider, has to account for the problems blacks bring to it. In short, blacks become *problems*.

Some blacks, however, realize that such a formulation is erroneous, for it effectively attributes more power to blacks than a society in which whites function as gods in fact offers. Reality intervenes. Instead of neatly divided contraries, contradictions emerge wherever *interaction* occurs. Whether Bigger Thomas in *Native Son* or Cross Damon in *The Outsider*, contradictions emerge where the two worlds *meet*.

What is hidden beneath these moments of often-violent interaction is the collapse of a systemic myth: that black suffering is an external feature of the system. Because suffering is very much "inside," as it were, the separated contraries are revealed to be myths covering the dialectical, interactive maintenance of the system through suppression.

This dialectical understanding occasions a second movement of double consciousness into what Paget Henry calls *potentiated double consciousness*.[14] The term refers to a metareflective movement in which the system receives critique as a producer of problems. This can only emerge through a transformed understanding of black people from that of systemic problems into people—human beings—who face problems of limited options from which to make meaningful choices about embodied dignity and freedom.

Put differently, Wright not only compels white readers to see what they hitherto failed or refused to see but also leads black and other readers of color to do the same. His task is to reveal lived contradictions, which means the question of agency comes to the fore. Wright thus moves beyond Vladimir Lenin's interrogative, "What is to be done?" to the very concrete, lived reality of the radically experienced, "What can I do?" pushed into the subjunctive: "What *could* I do?"

Black Consciousness, Power, and Politics

Wright challenges everyone. It doesn't follow that everyone will see him or herself in the same way, given the challenges his writings pose. Whites, after all, read black characters as *them*, not *us*. Those who dare may make a leap into what for many whites would be a source of fear and trembling—*to imagine* the points of view of black characters in Wright's fictions and essays. Such whites would, in effect, have already made an intersubjective leap of human-to-human communicative practice. What many may miss, however, is that such a leap is necessary for many *blacks*. If trapped in the first form of double consciousness, blacks as *knowing agents* would be hindered in any system that commits blacks to being incapable of knowing anything *as blacks*. The challenge, then, is to embrace blackness as an active, knowing manifestation of agency.

Moving blackness into potentiated double consciousness raises the question of black participation in the epistemic practices of societal evaluation and, crucially, power. Wright considered this combination of tasks in *Black Power*. The issue, as Mahmood Mamdani framed it in *Citizen and Subject*, is to break the Manichean divide of citizen and subject, where legitimate participation in political life belongs to the former and subjection—the condition of being ruled or governed—to the latter.[15] Reformulated: How can black people be political actors instead of objects?

The immediate answer, as black radical thinkers from Du Bois to Fanon to Biko to Angela Y. Davis have argued, is for black people to be political. To be such involves committing political action, which occurs in particular social spaces. Thinkers from Aristotle to Hannah Arendt and Jürgen Habermas have regarded such places of action as public spheres. For Arendt, in such a sphere one is *seen* and *heard*. For Habermas, that seeing and hearing is a function of communicative action. I won't belabor their differences here, as both are ultimately correct that politics requires appearance through the power and legitimacy of communication. It is thus, harkening back to Aristotle, a realm of speech.

Speech in and of itself is, however, not necessarily political. Additional elements must be brought to bear. The communicative dimensions of speech alert us to its social reality. Political activity involves the expansion of options in a social world. Politics *affects* it. Furthermore, turning away from the social world would also be a statement about politics—for example, its rejection. Such an activity would not, however, be properly political precisely because of the actor's absence or nonappearance. This is one of the reasons ancient Greeks, whose language is the source of the term "politics," used a disparaging word for people unwilling to speak in public spaces: *idiótés*. The term refers to a private person, someone not concerned with public affairs, who was for them, in a word—an idiot.

It is important not to end our etymological journey with the language of ancient Greeks. It is often overlooked that the ancient Athenians, Spartans, and Macedonians, among others, were influenced by their own ancients, most of whom were from southern shores of the Mediterranean. Going back a few millennia, we could examine the KMT/Egyptian Middle Kingdom word *idi* (deaf). Later residents of ancient Greek-speaking city-states (*poleis*) presumed that a lack of hearing entailed isolation, at least in terms of verbal speech. Sign language notwithstanding, the Hellenic view was that the deaf could not hear and thus could not participate in the discursive forms of negotiation on which the city-state depended.[16] *To choose privation*—in effect, deafness—in the public realm was, in the view of the ancient Greeks, both absurd and repugnant. It would be the abrogation of a sociopolitical responsibility and a special power.

Politics makes no sense without power. But what is power? Eurocentric archaeolinguistics point to the Latin word *potis* as its source, from which came the word "potent" as in a potentate or, in metaphysical form, an omnipotent god. Returning to Middle Kingdom Egypt, the Medu Neter word *pHty* comes to mind. It means godlike strength. We should bear in mind, however, that ancient Northeast Africans had many words for power and its achievements. Even the gods' abilities came from a source. In the *Coffin Texts*, for instance, HqAw or *heka* (origin of the word "hex") activates the *ka* (spirit or "magic"), makes reality, and the gods draw power from *heka*. All this amounts to a straightforward thesis on power as access to the means to make things happen.

With power, one changes reality. Though one could change reality with force, as when one knocks another down, one's power is limited to the physical body whose lifespan and space are small. The social world expands one's power through language and communication, and it does so over greater time than that of the lived body. The expansion of power through the resources of culture allows human beings to rival the gods (indeed, Freud refers to culture as a prosthetic god).[17] The culturally aided expansion of human power constitutes the transformation of social into political life.

Consider the meeting of blackness and power in the portrait of political action discussed thus far. In *I Write What I Like,* Biko did that with the already burgeoning concept of Black Consciousness.[18] He argued that Black Consciousness is premised on a *political* opposition to the racist state of apartheid South Africa and, by implication, to Euromodern racist states. According to Biko, the state, as an institution of power regulated by political action, faces a dilemma when it is exposed as racist. The antiblack state's aim requires the suppression of black appearance. Blackness must be not only invisible but also inaudible. For Black Consciousness to appear, then, it must seek access to the conditions of such possibility, which means a direct conflict with its suppression. It must be *heard* or, through the power of sign, *seen*. Linking blackness to politics, then, enabled Biko to conjoin blackness with speech, which means the state must attempt to rip power from the communicative practice of black and any other form of racially subordinate appearance. The racist state must, then, wage a war on what such speech signifies—*politics*.

Biko identified antiracist resistance and revolutionary practice in not only the oral expression of Black Consciousness but also its *written form*. In stating that he "writes what he likes" (or, perhaps more accurately, chooses or wishes), Biko openly asserted the political power of written expression. The racist state's repressive practices must then reach beyond the physical violence waged on protestors to the institutions they build. In his *Philosophy of Right,* Hegel referred to these phenomena as "estates," which, he argued, were best expressed in civil society, which was ultimately the market in Euromodernity. Biko was aware of this in *I Write What I Like,* but he also understood that the suppression of black estates, or group expressions of political power, required the erasure of the traces that black estates could make beyond the present into the future as an expression of Afromodernity. Such a task also required the suppression of *writing*.

Biko thus brought to the fore a core insight of Wright, who appears in and through history first and foremost as a *writer*.

An Afromodern Writer's Warning from Euromodernity

Wright understood the problem of political impotence. This is where he and Biko converge in the struggle for appearance in the Euromodern racist state. Wright diagnosed the problem of how efforts to render black political power stillborn required the erosion of political power and increased political impotence among humankind. This problem became increasingly clear during the transition from the Cold War of his time to the neoliberal and neoconservative wars of our own. He observed a tendency toward fascism wherever conditions of political appearance are undermined. The racist state is ultimately fascist because its commitments wage war on politics.

Opposing political freedom and agency, the racist state prioritizes socially stifling rule. Citizenship falls sway to subjection. One may at first imagine a limited scope of such subjection, where freedom and political life are for whites only. This could in theory offer checks and balances against the racist state's antipolitical agenda. If *whites* are truly free, they can take antiracist stances and challenge the racist state. The injunctions against such oppositional speech—and even such *thinking*—require totalitarian efforts wherein freedom becomes severely attenuated. A form of unfree or bonded freedom, such as the system of racial segregation in the United States (rationalized as natural), becomes the model. I have elsewhere described this as institutional bad faith—materialized practices and conditions in which the freedom to be free is, in effect, placed in bondage.[19] The evident contradictions are both logical and grounded in history. All racist states claim to champion freedom. Their racist commitments undermine political life and, by extension, freedom.

In his first novel, Wright offered racist states their native son; in his later one discussed here, the paradox of loss.[20] I will focus on the former and offer a brief observation of the latter.[21]

Many in the United States portray the country as a citadel of freedom. To live freely, as we have seen, requires legitimate appearance. Freedom is being able to live out in the open, as the metaphor goes, without hiddenness. Freedom also involves belonging, being at home.[22] As we have seen, a problem of Afromodernity is the emergence of blacks, beings indigenous to a world in which they—at least normatively—don't belong. In *Native Son*, Wright offers Bigger Thomas, whom he describes in his introduction to the 1940 edition as, though studied as a black man in the Chicago of the 1930s, an expression of the homeless souls of Euromodernity. Bigger's effort to live freely in the world of which he is its native son falls into the contradictions of illicit appearance—the appearance of that which should not appear—in a world premised upon white legitimation. Wright offers in his introduction a dialectical typography of Bigger from Wright's own experience.

Bigger 1 was the bully from Wright's childhood who coerced others to accede to his superiority. Bigger 2 is the black who challenged white authority and lived as he pleased, but who "was in prison the last time I heard from him," Wright confesses.[23] Bigger 3 was the proverbial "bad nigger." He took advantage of fellow blacks and defied the law. His fate was death, as expected, by police intervention. Bigger 4 was more complicated; he played with proverbial fire in his efforts to outwit whites and avoid being exploited. His fate, if he were not killed or incarcerated, was madness. Bigger 5 was another "bad nigger," but unlike Bigger 3, who persecuted other blacks, he challenged whites. Among blacks, Bigger 5 stimulated "an intense flash of pride."[24] His fate, however, was often the same as that of Bigger 3. "The Bigger Thomases," Wright reflected, "were the only Negroes I know of who consistently violated the Jim Crow laws of the South and got away with it, at least for a sweet spell. Eventually, the whites who restricted their lives made them pay a terrible price. They were shot, hanged, maimed, lynched, and generally hounded until they were either dead or their spirits broken."[25] A crucial element of Bigger Thomases is their dance with death. They seem not to be afraid of death and are thus afforded what at first looks like radical freedom. The logic, as Abdul JanMohamed argues, is peculiarly Hegelian. The bondsman *becomes a bondsman* through succumbing to his fear of death.[26]

Examining Wright's schema of Bigger Thomases, notice the following. Bigger 1 bullied blacks to submit to him and help convince him that he was superior to them. We see here a classic development of narcissism under oppressive conditions. Narcissism is a fetish of the image always resulting, as Jean Baudrillard argued, in self-deception.[27] Among oppressed peoples, there are those who buy into the Manichean logic of a world of only oppressors and the oppressed. Given that logic, the only way not to be oppressed is by oppressing others.[28] That Bigger 1 forced out of others a *statement* affirming his superiority, however, brings the logic against itself. Bigger 1 did this because he *needed* the submission of others in order to effect his posed and hoped-for superiority. This effort collapses, however, into a form of dependency. This no doubt angered Bigger 1 even more, for missing from Bigger 1's focus is the true source of his sense of inferiority—*whites*. Bigger 1 thus fails from the outset. His negative dialectic ultimately requires addressing the white world, which is why the schema inevitably leads to Biggers 2 through 5.

Biggers 2 through 5 are repressed terms in the subconscious, though sometimes reflective (as in Wright's essay) of the lives of many black people. They are manifestations of, as Frantz Fanon later argued, an urge to be "actional."[29] This leads to identification with (as with Bigger 1) *all* those who appear actional versus those whom they oppress. Wright writes: "I've even heard Negroes say that maybe Hitler and Mussolini [and more recently, the small percentage who voted for Donald Trump] are all right; that maybe Stalin is all right. They did not say this out of any intellectual comprehension of the forces at work in the world, but because they felt that these men 'did things,' a phrase charged with more meaning than the mere words imply."[30] The association of freedom with *doing*, with being actional—and the added elements of *belonging* and *being identified*—point to conditions of freedom mentioned earlier. The confusion is with doing and acting. As our discussion of the distinction between common speech and political speech indicates, doing without power cannot be actional. These movements of doing, born of frustration and premised upon a paradoxical facing of death *for the sake of life*, or at least a life worth living, suggest, as Wright argues, an expansion of Bigger as a native son of the Euromodern world. Freedom is, after all, one of the promised jewels of modern life in the face of increasingly rigorous and global devices of bondage.

Frustration and a longing to be actional (political freedom) were motifs that, for Wright, brought to the fore the dialectical struggle of freedom in the Euromodern world. Wright offered through Bigger Thomas an arch-symbol of the lives of oppressed humanity in Euromodernity: "I made the discovery that Bigger Thomas was not black all the time; he was white, too, and there were literally millions of him, everywhere."[31]

This movement is indicative, as we have seen, of potentiated double consciousness. It is a dialectical movement in which greater consciousness of wider conditions is achieved through realization of systemic contradictions. The political and existential phenomenological aspects of the analysis come to the fore here as well. Wright advances the wider understanding of consciousness *of* the conditions themselves, of the systemic impositions of limited options: "I began to feel with my mind the inner tensions of the people I met. I don't mean to say that I think that environment *makes* consciousness (I suppose God makes that, if there is a God), but I do say that I felt and still feel that the environment supplies the instrumentalities through which the organism expresses itself, and if the environment is warped or tranquil, the mode and manner of behavior will be affected toward deadlocking tensions or orderly fulfillment and satisfaction."[32]

A powerful feature of Wright's work is that Bigger Thomas is not only a mythopoetic trope of a fictional narrative. Wright chose the medium of the novel to explore the *inner life* of Bigger Thomas. The novel, in other words, shows how someone *becomes* Bigger Thomas. Even more unusual, Wright achieves this without compromising Bigger's agency. The choices Bigger makes are not the only ones he could have made. They are, however, the ones that made sense given the circumstances under which he lived. Wright's claustrophobic world is fraught with tragic symbols of destiny: the cornered rat at the beginning, who hisses and snarls; a blind woman who "sees" or at least almost saw through hearing; a drunk white woman meeting her death in the arms of a black servant; her remains in the furnace of the building where she was permitted to live but Bigger was not. The challenge of vicarious vision is established at the outset in the family's chasing a large rat around the apartment; it portends to the reader the subconscious question facing Bigger. The accidental killing of his employer's daughter asks the reader whether he or she could even imagine a verdict of Bigger's "innocence."

To face Bigger, one must see his position, imagine being in his place. That vision, however, requires an effort that many whites and some blacks are unwilling to undertake. Bigger is the contradiction of the system. This means that a failure to face Bigger entails a similar shortcoming in the system. One becomes locked into the logic of contraries instead of the dialectics of contradictions. Asserting that Bigger is outside the system has the consequence of denying the system's creation, its native son. The proverbial "black problem" is, in other words, the racist state, which, in this case, is the set of governing norms of the United States.

Wright, as is well known, studied the thought of the Danish existentialist Søren Kierkegaard. Among Kierkegaard's achievements was the art of "indirect writing."[33] Writing through pseudonyms that were known as such raised the question of what he was ultimately *doing* when he wrote. His actions alerted readers to the text and the *metatext*, where the author is brought into question. The technique of indirection is thus useful for bringing subjects into the world of dread and anxiety, since the act of reading carried with it the responsibility of interpreting what was read. The technique is also useful for confronting the world of trauma and repression. Some things are not bearable directly. Humanity needs another way. In mythic literature, this is the way of the labyrinth at the center of which waits the Minotaur.[34] Recall that the creature emerged from a tale of greed and lust. The god Poseidon loaned the Cretan King Minos the magical white bull through which wealth came to the king. Overcome by greed, Minos refused to return the bull. Minos's wife, Pasiphae, smitten by the bull, persuaded the great engineer Daedalus to fashion her a cow's costume with which to seduce the creature. She succeeded, and the result was the hideous Minotaur. Horrified, Minos commissioned Daedalus to build the labyrinth in which the creature subsequently lived and fed on victims condemned to wander through its passageways.

The image of unbridled consumption is something from which distance is needed. In *Black Skin, White Masks*, Fanon, too, uses techniques of indirection.[35] He tells a tale of hopes and failures—of language, love, and the imagination—at the intermission of which the black protagonist is driven to tears. From then onward, having washed denial away, the black faces the psychopathological reality of what happens to blacks seeking dignity in their interaction with the white world. Fanon, anticipating rationalizations such as Axel Honneth's of today and critics such as Glen Sean Coulthard, counsels against seeking recognition in racist societies.[36] Whereas Euromodernity offers resources for whites to live ethical life through dialectics of Self and Other, those in the dimension Fanon describes as "the zone of nonbeing" discover no symmetrical relationship as a basis of recognition with those "above." Located "below," to move "up" requires a preexisting recognition that is, unfortunately, sought in the quest for recognition. What this means is that from the perspective of "above," there are neither selves nor others "below." To move up is, then, an intrusion, a violation.

The unbearable truth to which these movements lead is marked by the difference of struggles among whites as opposed to conflicts between whites and blacks. The former struggles revolve around an ethical relationship demanding realignment among human beings. The latter conflicts are about *entering an ethical relationship through an expansion of the human field*. This entails recognition that there is a sphere of ethical suspension or, worse, the absence of ethics at work in the status quo. Facing such, the black must negotiate the political terrain before the ethical. The call for social transformation becomes a condition for ethical life.

It might be objected that blacks find themselves often appealed to as the moral conscience of the nation. In the United States, Martin Luther King Jr. is the most popular example. We should remember, however, that even Martin

Luther King Jr. was considered violent in his day, especially leading up to the 1964 March on Washington, DC. Consider how he is remembered as compared to Malcolm X, whose moral voice was never as a subordinate to whites. No one remembers Malcolm X as anything other than a *political* figure—and for many whites a violent one at that—even though most of, if not all, his actions were with his *words*.[37]

Wright in effect asks, in *Native Son*, for the expanded options by which Bigger would have been stillborn. What are those besides freedom to appear through words rather than being muted in a body barred from human, and by extension political, appearance?

When Wright returns to the theme of limited options and systemic idolatry in his 1953 novel *The Outsider*, the Kierkegaardian themes come to the fore. The epigraph, from Walter Lowrie's introduction to *The Concept of Dread*, reads: "Dread is an alien power which lays hold of the individual, and yet one cannot tear oneself away, nor has a will to do so; for one fears what one desires."[38] The antihero of this novel, Cross Damon, bears Euromodernity in movements from "Dread," "Dream," "Descent," and "Despair" to "Decision." Cross Damon manifests Marx's greatest fear about the so-called "lumpenproletariat" that Engels and he derided in *The Eighteenth Brumaire of Louis Bonaparte* and *The Communist Manifesto*. After killing the fascist, Cross Damon turns on the Communist. This warning about Bigger and the oxymoronic Cross Damon raises an additional consideration of the mythopoetics of Wright's characters that perhaps is best understood in classical myth and monster theory.

Let us begin with his names. Though there are many, as he adopts several over the course of the novel, "Cross" and "Damon" beg for analysis (also explored in the chapters by Cedric J. Robinson and Floyd W. Hayes III in this volume). A cross has many meanings, from geometrical intersecting signs to theological notions of bearing sin. Intersections are also crossroads, which occasion anxieties of choice. It is as creatures of choice that human beings have crosses to bear. The cross serving as a symbol of salvation in Christianity also suggests sacrifice. Yet as an adjective, it also refers to being annoyed, irritated, or vexed. Think of the angry black. The name "Damon," from the Greek *damazo*, means "to tame." As Cicero relates the myth in *De officiis*, Damon and Pythias ("to rot") were best friends. Pythias angered the tyrant of Syracuse, who imprisoned him with the sentence of death. Damon agreed to take Pythias's place in prison as he awaited execution. Pythias returned on the appointed date of his execution so his friend wouldn't bear the sentence. The Greek story had a good ending. The tyrant's cold heart was warmed by Damon's courage and Pythias's fidelity, so he pardoned him. Instead of a tyrant, Wright's Damon faces an unyielding, unjust system. A black man named "Damon" easily becomes "Demon" in a world where being born black is already a crime.

The etymology of "monster" points to the Latin *monstrum* (divine warning or omen). The related word "demonstrate," from the Latin *monstrare* (to show, to point out, or, more properly, with the prefix *de,* to show entirely), reminds us that warnings also show and reveal. In antiquity, monsters had important social functions. As divine warnings or omens, they appeared when a community lost its way. They were often articulate creatures, through whom society was forced to set things right in rituals of acknowledged responsibility. Monsters were thus also pedagogical; avoiding their counsel was catastrophic. From this perspective of monster theory, Bigger Thomas and Cross Damon offer a double critique. The first is the presentation of these "monsters" as a call for the United States to fix itself. If it ignores these warnings, the second message is evident: advancing itself as a *demon* (instead of Pythias's Damon), the country takes its place as a monster, as a warning, to the rest of humanity.[39]

Wright, however, also offers a thought on Afromodernity to blacks. The novel's ending, with Damon's dying words of suffering innocence, raises an existential paradox. Damon commits murder. But to do so, he must have a *mens rea,* an evil mind. To have that, however, he needs to be responsible for his actions. That would require him to be a man, not a child. Like Bigger, the "doers" of his world patronized him. He faced minefields along the path to live as a free human being. Bigger and Damon wanted to become people who were, in the end, men. How do they become *men?*

Fanon raises this problem in his discussion of psychopathology and *le nègre*. How is psychotherapy possible for black subjects if there is no coherent notion of a black *adult?* With adulthood comes moral responsibility. But as we saw, what Bigger actually does is irrelevant from the point of view of a legal system and civil society that treats him as guilty at birth.[40] If he is always guilty, he could never be really guilty, which collapses into a form of childlike, foreclosed innocence. To become a man, then, he must be *capable* of becoming guilty. From this reading, Cross Damon *needed* to be guilty. Dying with a sense of innocence, then, is, for him, an existential tragedy. In his dying words: "Because in my heart . . . I felt . . . I'm *innocent* . . . that's what made the horror."[41]

Wright thus offers two dimensions of alienation in Euromodernity that jeopardize freedom and the possibility of politics. The racist state is, after all, also a native son of Euromodernity. Its enemy, freedom, is thus persecuted—ironically in the name of freedom. As politics suffers from such endeavors, so, too, do political subjects. In the aching subjectivity of Afromodernity is also an imploding political life of humankind. Moribund though this portrait may be, it is also a powerful call to action. Dignity, understood as a process of mature awakening, requires growth and responsibility for which political life becomes a commitment against surrender into the self. A public world of political action is the necessary path for a future humanity now teetering on the precipice of a demonic abyss.

Notes

1. For elaboration of "bare life," see Abdul R. JanMohamed's chapter in this volume, "Notes toward a Political Economy of Life and Death: Reading Richard Wright with Frantz Fanon."

2. See Jane Anna Gordon, "Slavery Continued, Freedom Sought: Wright's Political Intellectual Journey," in this volume.

3. Hannah Arendt, *The Human Condition,* 2nd ed. (Chicago: University of Chicago Press, 1998), pt. 5.

4. For discussion of Afropessimism, see Lewis. R. Gordon, A. Menzel, G. Shulman, et al., "Critical Exchange: Afro Pessimism," *Contemporary Political Theory* (2017), https://doi.org/10.1057/s41296-017-0165-4.

5. See also Enrique Dussel, *The Invention of the Americas: Eclipse of "the Other" and the Myth of Modernity,* trans. Michael D. Barber (New York: Continuum, 1995); and Walter Mignolo, *The Darker Side of Western Modernity: Global Futures, Decolonial Options* (*Latin America Otherwise*) (Durham, NC: Duke University Press, 2011).

6. For an insightful study, see Tzvetan Todorov, *The Conquest of America: The Question of the Other,* trans. Richard Howard (New York: Harper and Row, 1984).

7. Jane Anna Gordon, *Creolizing Political Theory: Reading Rousseau through Fanon* (New York: Fordham University Press, 2014).

8. For more discussion of *raza*, see David Nirenberg, "Race and the Middle Ages: The Case of Spain and its Jews," in *Rereading the Black Legend: The Discourses of Religious and Racial Difference in the Renaissance Empires,* ed. Mar-

garet R. Greer, Walter D. Mignolo, and Maureen Quilligan (Chicago: University of Chicago Press, 2007), 71–87.

9. See W. E. B. Du Bois, *The Souls of Black Folk: Essays and Sketches* (Chicago: A. C. McClurg, 1903).

10. See Lewis R. Gordon, "Reasoning in Black: Africana Philosophy under the Weight of Misguided Reason," in *I Am Because We Are: Readings in Black Philosophy*, ed. Fred Lee Hord (Mzee Lasana Okpara) and Jonathan Lee (Amherst: University of Massachusetts Press, 2016), 281–93.

11. See, for example, Lewis R. Gordon, "Black Aesthetics, Black Value," *Public Culture* 30, no. 1 (2018): 19–34.

12. Ronald Hayman, *Sartre: A Biography* (New York: Carroll and Graf, 1987), 220–21.

13. Floyd W. Hayes III, "Richard Wright and Black Women: Imagining the Feminine in *The Outsider*," in this volume; and Floyd W. Hayes III, "The Concept of Double Vision in Richard Wright's *The Outsider*," in *Existence in Black: An Anthology of Black Existential Philosophy*, ed. Lewis R. Gordon (New York: Routledge, 1997), 181.

14. Paget Henry, "Africana Phenomenology: Its Philosophical Implications," in *Journeys in Caribbean Thought: The Paget Henry Reader*, ed. Jane Anna Gordon, Lewis R. Gordon, Aaron Kamugisha, and Neil Roberts with Paget Henry (London: Rowman and Littlefield International, 2016), 27–58.

15. Mahmood Mamdani, *Citizen and Subject: Contemporary Africa and the Legacy of Late Colonialism* (Princeton: Princeton University Press, 1996).

16. For an exploration of these issues in the context of sign language and racism, see Derefe Kimarley Chevannes, "Creolizing Political Speech: Toward Black Existential Articulations," *Review of Education, Pedagogy, and Cultural Studies* 40, no. 1 (2018).

17. See Sigmund Freud, *Civilization and Its Discontents*, trans. James Strachey (New York: Norton, 1989).

18. Steve Bantu Biko, *I Write What I Like: Selected Writings* (Chicago: University of Chicago Press, 2002).

19. Lewis R. Gordon, *Bad Faith and Antiblack Racism* (Amherst, NY: Humanity Books, 1999). For more on *thinking*, see Michael Neocosmos, *Thinking Freedom in Africa: Toward a Theory of Emancipatory Politics* (Johannesburg: Wits University Press, 2016).

20. Richard Wright, *Native Son* (New York: Milestone Editions, 1940); Richard Wright, *The Outsider* (New York: Harper Perennial, 1993).

21. Floyd W. Hayes III offers a more detailed discussion in his chapter in this volume.

22. For more on this view of freedom, see Lewis R. Gordon, "Black Existence

in Philosophy of Culture," *Diogenes* 59, nos. 3–4 (2012): 104; and Allison Weir, *Identity and Freedom: Feminist Theory between Power and Connection* (Oxford: Oxford University Press, 2013), 95.

23. Wright, *Native Son*, 12.

24. Ibid., 13.

25. Ibid.

26. See Abdul R. JanMohamed's contribution to this volume and his book, *The Death-Bound-Subject: Richard Wright's Archaeology of Death* (Durham, NC: Duke University Press, 2005).

27. Jean Baudrillard, *Seduction*, trans. Brian Singer (New York: St. Martin's, 1979), 69.

28. See L. R. Gordon, *Bad Faith and Antiblack Racism*, 104–16.

29. Frantz Fanon, *Peau noire, masques blancs* (Black skins, white masks) (Paris: Éditions du Seuil, 1952). For elaboration, see Lewis R. Gordon, *What Fanon Said: A Philosophical Introduction to His Life and Thought* (New York: Fordham University Press, 2015).

30. Wright, *Native Son*, 17.

31. Ibid.

32. Ibid., 19.

33. For discussion, see Andrew Cross, *Kierkegaard* (New York: Routledge, 2004).

34. Jane Anna Gordon and Lewis R. Gordon, *Of Divine Warning: Reading Disaster in the Modern Age* (New York: Routledge, 2009), 113–14.

35. L. R. Gordon, *What Fanon Said*, 73–74, 166n56.

36. Fanon's critical discussion is in chapter 7 of *Peau noire, masques blancs* (see L. R. Gordon, *What Fanon Said*, 24–70). For Glen Sean Coulthard, see *Red Skin, White Masks: Rejecting the Colonial Politics of Recognition* (Minneapolis: University of Minnesota Press, 2014).

37. For more discussion, see J. A. Gordon and L. R. Gordon, *Of Divine Warning*, chap. 4.

38. Walter Lowrie, introduction to Søren Kierkegaard, *The Concept of Dread*, 2nd ed., trans. Lowrie (Princeton: Princeton University Press, 1968), xii.

39. J. A. Gordon and L. R. Gordon, *Of Divine Warning*, chaps. 2–4. See also Marilyn Nissim-Sabat's contribution to this volume, "Richard Wright's Mission: Initiating a Politics of the Human."

40. This phenomenon is also metaphysical (see J. Reid Miller, *Stain Removal: Ethics of Race* [New York: Oxford University Press, 2017], 40–41).

41. Wright, *The Outsider*, 586.

3

Richard Wright and the Critique of Class Theory

Cedric J. Robinson

In the midst of the black consciousness and nationalist movements of the 1960s, the seemingly irresistible dictates of the market compelled the republishing of *The Outsider* (1965), *Native Son* (1966), *Black Boy* (1966), *Eight Men* (1969), and later, *American Hunger* (1977).[1] They were works which spoke to a generation that Wright did not live to see but had anticipated. Significant, too, was the emergence of younger and equally militant Black writers and playwrights (among them John A. Williams, LeRoi Jones, Ed Bullins, Melvin Van Peebles, and Ishmael Reed). Much of their work would have fallen quite easily into what one American critic, Robert Bone, had called "the Wright School" ("For the Wright School, literature is an emotional catharsis—a means of dispelling the inner tensions of race. Their novels often amount to a prolonged cry of anguish and despair. Too close to their material, feeling it too intensely, these novelists lack a sense of form and of thematic line."),[2] except for the fact that Bone had already announced the death of that school twenty years earlier: "By the late 1940's the vein of literary material unearthed by Richard Wright had been all but worked out. The market for protest had become saturated."[3] It does appear that Bone was a bit premature.

More remarkable, however, than the sheer survival of Wright's work, is the theoretical and analytical power of his ideas. This achievement of Wright's, with the stimulus of historical materialism and psychoanalysis, fell much closer to an emergent European literature (Sartre, Merleau-Ponty, Koestler, Lukacs, Marcuse, Kolakowski) in the post–Second World War period than to any American fashion. Like many European Left intellectuals, Wright was moving beyond classical Marxism and the Marxism inspired by Lenin in order to come to terms with a world constituted of historically unique material and spiritual forces. Wright's reach, consequently, can be said to be much longer than that implied by the terms employed by many of his American critics. He was never merely a "racial novelist," a "protest writer," or a "literary rebel."[4] Indeed, much of his work was a direct confrontation with the leading ideas and ideational systems of contemporary Western political and social thought. His arena was the totality of Western civilization and its constitutive elements: industrialization, urbanization, alienation, class, racism, exploitation, and the hegemony of bourgeois ideology. His work thus constituted an inquiry.

Wright's persistence in his investigation of Western society was an important factor contributing to the achievement of a certain consistency in his work. As artist, as essayist, as critic, as political activist, it is clear that he arranged and rearranged many times the elements making up the phenomenological display of Western development. He knew the names of Western experience but was less certain of what he knew of their nature and their systemic and historical relationships. There were questions to which he still had to find answers: Was the working class a social reality? Could class consciousness supersede racism as an ideology? Was the party the vanguard of the proletariat? Was Marxism more than a critique of capitalism? These were some of the issues to which Wright had not found satisfactory answers in organized and organizational politics. Ultimately, it would be because of his particular skill for transforming theoretical abstractions and constructs into recognizably human experience that it became possible for him to make those distinctions between dogma and reality so important to his development.

Theoretically and ideologically, Wright came to terms with Western thought and life through Black nationalism. However, the basis for his critique of Western society was his experience of the historical formation of Black peoples in Africa and the diaspora, from the Gold Coast to the Mississippi Delta.[5] Psychically and intellectually he was drawn to attend those same forces which produced the critical inspections of W. E. B. Du Bois, George Padmore, and C. L. R. James. As Michel Fabre puts it:

> Wright's originality, then, is that he completely understood and often reiterated . . . that the situation of the Black in the twentieth century, and in particular during the crucial period from the Depression to the advent of Black Power, was exceptional. These years saw the awakening of the Third World and with it the enormous mutation of our civilisation. "The liberation of the colored peoples of the world is the most important event of our century," is a refrain that runs throughout Wright's work. The same message, delivered half a century before by W. E. B. Du Bois, did not have the same existentialist dimension.[6]

Wright had not created these forces which were transforming Western society, but it was his intention to give these events a meaning independent of those interpretations bounded by the interests of Western civilization as articulated by its intellectuals and ideologues.

When we consider Richard Wright's fictional and explicitly political work, three novels (*Native Son*, *The Outsider*, and *Island of Hallucination*, this latter eventually published under the title *American Hunger*) and one collection of short stories (*Uncle Tom's Children*) stand out. Together, these works both chronicle and interpret Wright's experiences with American communism and political action. They also constitute studies of Marxism as a theory of history and social revolution, of the social and psychological development of the American working class, and of the historical and ideological development of American Blacks. Serious attention to these works should not be deflected by the form through which Wright sought to articulate his ideas. Indeed, it must be recognized that his works are uniquely suited to their tasks. Using this form, Wright could reconstruct and weigh the extraordinary complexities and subtleties of radical politics as he and others had experienced it. His characters could live with and struggle through crises he had encountered. They could "test" the meanings and significances he had given to those experiences. His novels were consequently much more *authentic* documents than the conventional forms of history, biography, and political tract for they were constructed from lives with which he was intimate. In these novels, Wright could achieve his intention of weaving living consciousness into the impress of social theory and ideology.[7]

Wright had joined the American Communist movement in the early 1930s. This was a period which coincided with an intensification of the party's work among Blacks following the Sixth Congress of the Comintern's "Resolution on the Negro Question" in 1928 and the beginnings of the Scottsboro trials in 1931. Wright left the party a decade later. During those years he worked in the movement in the various capacities of organizer, member of a Black party cell in Chicago, officer in the John Reed Clubs, and writer for the Communist press. At first, his work for the party was to take place primarily in Chicago; later he was transferred to Harlem.[8] It was, of course, during this time that his writing was most directly influenced by the party. He proved to be very good at it. By 1937, the year he had published "Blueprint for Negro Writing" [which is reprinted in its entirety in this volume], he had become, in Daniel Aaron's words, "the Party's most illustrious proletarian author."[9]

Wright took this responsibility as a proletarian writer quite seriously. He was committed to the task of expressing working-class thought, consciousness, and experience. One recollection of this period is his first impression of the party: "The Communists, I felt, had oversimplified the experience of those whom they sought to lead . . . they had missed the meaning of the lives of the masses."[10] Wright meant to put this right; the proletariat had to be allowed its own voice. It was just as clear to him that he carried a particular, racial responsibility toward the Black working classes:

> The Negro writer who seeks to function within his race as a purposeful agent has a serious responsibility. . . . [A] deep, informed, and complex consciousness is necessary; a consciousness which draws for its strength upon the fluid lore of a great people, and moulds this lore with the concepts that move and direct the forces of history today.
>
> . . . [T]he Negro writer . . . is being called upon to do no less than create values by which his race is to struggle, live and die.
>
> . . . [B]ecause his writing possesses the potential cunning to steal into the inmost recesses of the human heart, because he can create myths and symbols that inspire a faith in life.[11]

As a Black writer, Wright was presuming that the intelligentsia had the obligation to construct the ideological and symbolic means through which an emerging Black movement would be formed. Still, the work of this intelligentsia had to be grounded in the culture of their people.

Working with these conceptions, Wright was clearly reflecting an earlier Marxian tradition, one in which Lenin had transformed a "renegade" petite bourgeoisie into a revolutionary vanguard.[12] (Wright appears to have always opposed the Stalinist anti-intellectualism that marked the Communist movement domestically and internationally in the 1930s.) But Wright was also mindful of a second and separate tradition that had emerged among Blacks in the United States during the late eighteenth and mid-nineteenth centuries. At these historical moments, from among the ranks of free Blacks, there had emerged an intellectually, economically, and politically elite class, which had assumed leadership on behalf of its largely enslaved Black masses. This nucleus later contributed significantly to the formation of the Black middle class. The ethos of this class and its sociohistorical traditions had been given its most enduring name by W. E. B. Du Bois: the talented tenth.[13] Wright was thus suffusing two distinct and opposing traditions. But more importantly, even here, while he was ostensibly addressing Black intellectuals, he was also going about the work of re-creating his world in its ideological terms.

Wright had entered the party naïve of its history, its factionalism, and its purgative vocabulary.[14] As we have seen, he had not been convinced earlier of the sincerity of American Communists. This is somewhat surprising given the enormous vitality of the party's "Negro work" at the time, work which included the defense of the Scottsboro boys; the confrontation with conservative Black organizations; the organizing of Unemployed Councils and Tenant Leagues; the development of the Black Belt Thesis on self-determination and the organizing of the League of Struggle for Negro Rights; and, on the international level, the International Trade Union Committee of Negro Workers.[15] Though he was then a hospital worker, he had identified himself as a writer, and as a writer, he was categorized by those in the party's ranks as an "intellectual." This meant that Wright was to be subjected to the diffidence shown to intellectuals but, more significantly among his Black comrades, that he was also to be held in suspicion for "petit-bourgeois tendencies"—i.e., selfish interests—and worse: Trotskyism. The result was inevitable: "Successive disillusionments had transformed his original enthusiastic and total dedication into wariness. His individualism was against him; he was at the mercy of leaders like Oliver Law and Harry Haywood, ostracized from unit 205 by certain black comrades and even denigrated."[16] Invited to the party trial of another Black party member (one upon whose early experience in the South Wright had based his short story "Big Boy Leaves Home"), Wright realized that the trial was also meant for someone else: "The blindness of their limited lives—lives truncated and impoverished by the oppression they had suffered long before they had ever heard of Communism—made them think that I was with their enemies. American life had so corrupted their consciousness that they were unable to recognize their friends when they saw them. I know that if they had held state power I should have been declared guilty of treason."[17]

He recognized among his Black coworkers an anger dammed up to the level of destruction of self. It was not an ideology which lay at the base of their need to physically violate errant comrades. Their dogmatism was an enveloping shield against ego-cide. Their conformity was a symptom of their desperate and collective need for each other. Wright would write later: "They're blind. . . . Their enemies have blinded them with too much oppression."[18]

This, then, is the crisis that informed the development of Bigger Thomas. *Native Son* was the result of Wright's resolve to have his say, his revision of American Marxism as it emerged from the lives and practices of American Communists: "I would hurl words into this darkness and wait for an echo; and if an echo sound, no matter how faintly, I would send other words to tell, to march, to fight, to create a sense of the hunger for life that gnaws in us all, to keep alive in our hearts a sense of the inexpressibly human."[19]

In *Native Son,* Wright sought to display a more authentic, more historical, more precise image of the proletariat to which the party had committed itself. He had begun this task in *Lawd Today,* and it came to fruition in the form of Bigger Thomas. Wright, hesitant at wrestling with Marxism on theoretical terms, pursued his critique of American Left ideology on his own terms: the novel. Bigger Thomas's lack of class consciousness—more precisely the odyssey of his development of consciousness—is deliberate and purposive. This was not simply a literary device but a means of coming to grips with the abstraction and romanticization of the proletariat that had infected Western Communist ideology.

At the time of Wright's sojourn in the party (1934–1942), the primary focus of the movement in western Europe and the United States was the defeat of fascism. It was a fundamental tenet of party work that fascism was an instrument of the ruling class designed to meet the crisis of world capitalism embodied in the Depression. As such, fascism as an ideology was presumed to be alien to the working class. Earl Browder, as general secretary of the American Communist Party, had made this position abundantly clear in reports, speeches, and articles during the late 1930s.[20] As the official voice of the American party, Browder had argued that the struggle of the movement was preeminently a political one: "What is the message that this powerful voice of the Communist Party is giving to America? First of all, it is the message of the need for the great mass of the people, the workers and farmers, to organize for their own protection."[21] Browder's strategy was a simple one: "The growth of the Communist Party is the greatest guarantee against reaction and fascism."[22]

Browder's leadership had positioned the party in support of the New Deal and Roosevelt's administration under the presumption that American workers were not ready to confront the issue of socialism.[23] In effect, the party pursued the contradictory aims of reform and revolution. This was in part a consequence, as Wilhelm Reich had pointed out with respect to the German Communist movement during the Weimar Republic, of failing to distinguish between the abstraction of class consciousness and its specific, historical form.[24] Just as critically, however, the party was committed by the instructions of the Comintern to a united front with its class enemies.

For Wright the question of the consciousness of workers and consequently that of political organization was more complex. It involved—as he was to write in defense of *Native Son*—"the dark and hidden places of the human personality."[25] In the essay, "How 'Bigger' Was Born," Wright was more explicit:

> The civilization which had given birth to Bigger contained no spiritual sustenance, had created no culture which could hold and claim his allegiance and faith, had sensitized him and had left him stranded, a free agent to roam the streets of our cities, a hot and whirling vortex of undisciplined and unchannelized impulses.
>
> . . . I was fascinated by the similarity of the emotional tensions of Bigger in America and Bigger in Nazi Germany and Bigger in Old Russia. All Bigger Thomases, white and black, felt tense, afraid, nervous, hysterical, and restless. . . . [C]ertain modern experiences were creating types of personalities whose existence ignored racial and national lines of demarcation.[26]

Wright was attempting to come to terms with the psychological consequence of a historical condition of which the leadership in the Communist movement was only vaguely aware. Wright was insisting on the necessity of understanding the working class in its own terms. He was concerned with the ability of proletarian masses to reproduce themselves spiritually and culturally. If they could no longer re-create the social ideologies that had sustained them, it would not be possible for them to fulfill the historical role that Marxian theory assigned them. Moreover, the fragmentation of personality, social relations, and ideology that Wright observed and re-created was so total that its political and historical implications seriously challenged the presumptions of the Communist movement:

> I felt that Bigger, an American product, a native son of this land, carried within him the potentialities of either Communism or Fascism . . .
> Whether he'll follow some gaudy, hysterical leader who'll promise rashly to fill the void in him, or whether he'll come to an understanding with the millions of his kindred fellow workers under trade-unions or revolutionary guidance depends upon the future drift of events in America. But . . . Bigger Thomas, conditioned as his organism is, will not become an ardent, or even a luke-warm, supporter of the *status quo.*[27]

He realized that no political movement which, for ideological reasons, presumed the progressive character of the working class would succeed.

Wright's novel, subsequently, was a refutation of radical dogma from the vantage point of Black experience. He sought first to re-create that experience, and in so doing to force a confrontation between it and socialist ideology. Bigger Thomas's character was specific to the historical experience of Blacks in the United States, but his nature was proletarian, that is world-historical. When Wright gave the consciousness of Bigger Thomas a nationalist character, he was addressing himself to both those aspects of his creation. He wrote that he was "confronted with that part of him that was dual in aspect . . . a part of *all* Negroes and *all whites.*"[28] If the American revolutionary movement could not come to terms with the *appeals* of fascism, then it could not begin to understand the immediate *nature* of the working class.[29] He agreed with Marx that capitalism as a form of organization led to the destruction of social consciousness founded on noncapitalist social orders. He did not accept, however, the notion that this process led to a new ideological synthesis. The truer result, the observed result, was "a world that existed on a plane of animal sensation alone."[30] The Nazi movement succeeded because it offered in the stead of an existential terror, a new, unambiguous social order, "the implicit, almost unconscious, or preconscious assumptions and ideals upon which whole nations and races act and live."[31]

Yet Wright's analysis did not end there. He had something more to say about the nature of revolutionary action. His analysis both underscored the absolute character of revolutionary commitment and spoke to Marxian class analysis: "I remember reading a passage in a book dealing with old Russia which said: 'We must be ready to make endless sacrifices if we are to be able to overthrow the Czar. . . .' Actions and feelings of men ten thousand miles from home helped me to understand the moods and impulses of those walking the streets of Chicago and Dixie."[32]

Wright recognized in his Bigger Thomases the desperation which was the precondition for the making of total and violent revolutionary commitments. He understood those commitments to be less ones of choice than of compulsion. The more total the degradation of the human being, the more total the reaction: "the *need* for a whole life and *acted* out of that need."[33]

He also refused to dismiss the Bigger Thomases as lumpenproletariat or to distinguish them from the proletariat. In *Native Son* he actually anticipated a thesis on violence and the lumpenproletariat that would become better known later through the work of Frantz Fanon. For Wright, the violence of the lumpenproletariat was not only an objective force of revolution; violence could not be separated out from the formation of consciousness. "I didn't want to kill," Bigger shouted. "But what I killed for, I *am*."[34] What, precisely, the Bigger Thomases would kill for, Wright could not answer. He had stated his thesis, and it was now left to the "future drift of events" to make that determination, i.e., the capacity of the American radical movement to develop a critical political theory. This, of course, was not to be the case.[35]

Wright had emerged from the Depression with a clear and powerful image of American society and world history. With the writing of *Uncle Tom's Children* and *Native Son* he had extracted from the misery of poverty and imminent social collapse an understanding of a systemic integration in which racism was a secondary, residual phenomenon. He had no reason to doubt that the disintegration of the capitalist world was really a promise of liberation—a promise that enveloped the whole of humanity. Yet he possessed few illusions about this process of disintegration. He knew, in social terms—even in human terms—that the immediate costs would be unparalleled violence, brutality, and vengeance. At first he hoped that this historical transformation would be surgical in its order. He believed in a conscious, deliberate, and magnanimous workers' movement. By the time he was writing *Native Son*, however, this ordered revolution had been replaced by a chaos consisting of the collective action of a brutalized human force. The destruction of capitalism would come at the hands of the brute social force it had itself created. Still, Wright saw this brutalized mass as the *promise* of the future. Unlike Marx, Wright anticipated barbarism *and* socialism.

Though immersed in the American radical movement with its Eurocentric ideology, it had not taken Wright very long to reach the conclusion that the historic development of Black people in the United States constituted the most total contradiction to Western capitalist society: "The workers of a minority people, chafing under exploitation, forge organizational forms of struggle. . . . Lacking the handicaps of false ambition and property, they have access to a wide social vision and deep social consciousness. . . . Their organizations show greater strength, adaptability, and efficiency than any other group or class in society."[36] Wright assumed that the alienation of Black workers from American society was more total than that experienced by the "white" working classes formed in Europe and America. This, indeed, was the more profound significance of Black nationalism, and one with which the Black intellectual had to come to terms:

> The emotional expression of group-feeling which puzzles so many whites and leads them to deplore what they call "black chauvinism" is not a morbidly inherent trait of the Negro, but rather the reflex expression of a life whose roots are imbedded deeply in Southern soil. Negro writers must accept the nationalist implications of their lives. . . . [T]hey must accept the concept of nationalism because, in order to transcend it, they must *possess* and *understand* it. And a nationalist spirit in Negro writing means a nationalism carrying the highest possible pitch of social consciousness. It means a nationalism that knows its origins, its limitations, that is aware of the dangers of its position, that knows its ultimate aims are unrealizable within the framework of capitalist

America: a nationalism whose reason for being lies in the simple fact of self-possession and in the consciousness of the interdependence of people in modern society.[37]

Wright's argument and its language strongly suggest the elements within the party with which he was in ideological conflict. In using the phrase "black chauvinism" (its second element being a term used most frequently within the party as a more objective interpretation of what was commonly referred to as nationalism), Wright designated his first target: white Marxian ideologues. His second target, deracinated Black intellectuals, were addressed as the recipients of a new history. They had to be made to realize that Black nationalism was an initial and historically logical stage of a more profoundly universal consciousness.

Wright was arguing that American Blacks had been re-created from their African origins by an oppressive system of capitalist exploitation which had at one and the same time integrated them into the emergent organization of industrial production while suspending them from the full impact of bourgeois ideology. Perhaps Wright put this most succinctly several years later in *The Outsider* when Ely Houston, one of Wright's two spokesmen in the novel, observed:

> The way Negroes were transported to this country and sold into slavery, then stripped of their tribal culture and held in bondage; and then allowed so teasingly and over so long a period, to be sucked into our way of life is something which resembles the rise of all men. . . .
> They are outsiders and. . . [t]hey are going to be self-conscious; they are going to be gifted with a double vision, for, being Negroes, they are going to be both *inside* and *outside* of our culture at the same time. . . . Negroes will develop unique and specially defined psychological types. They will become psychological men, like the Jews. . . . They will not only be Americans or Negroes; they will be centers of knowing, so to speak. . . . The political, social, and psychological consequences of this will be enormous.[38]

Wright believed that racism, the very character of the system by which Black workers had been exploited, had mediated their internalization of the ruling ideas of American society. He went on to assert that, unlike the dominant sectors of European and Euro-American proletariats, the Black proletariat—historically from the legal and political disciplines of slavery to its peculiar condition as free wage labor—had developed a psychic and cultural identity independent from bourgeois ideology. This construction of Wright's pushed the insights of Du Bois[39] and others far beyond the critique of Black–White labor solidarity. What Wright was suggesting went even beyond the most extreme position in the 1930s of American radicals that blacks were the vanguard of the American working class.[40]

In *The Outsider,* Wright sought to subvert the two ideological and philosophic traditions at the heart of modern Western culture. First, he ridiculed the Judeo-Christian tradition by creating a protagonist whose very name is contradiction: Cross Damon—the demon Christ. Cross Damon has escaped Judeo-Christian morality through the recognition of its operative psychic force: a destructive, debilitating dread—guilt. Just as Marx earlier had recognized that religion (that is Judaism) "is the sigh of the oppressed creature, the sentiment of a heartless world, and the soul of soulless conditions,"[41] Wright had perceived the truer historical significance of Christianity among Blacks as not an instrument of domination but as a philosophic adaptation to oppression.

Moreover, he understood the resignation of Black Christianity as only one element in the culture of Blacks. In Black music, another more strident voice existed opposing that guilt:

> This music was the rhythmic flauntings of guilty feelings, the syncopated outpourings of frightened joy existing in guises forbidden and despised by others. . . . Negroes had been made to live in but not of the land of their birth. . . . [T]he injunctions of an alien Christianity and the strictures of white laws had evoked in them the very longings and desires that religion and law had been designed to stifle. . . . [B]lue-jazz was a rebel art blooming seditiously under the condemnations of a Protestant ethic. . . . Blue-jazz was the scornful gesture of men turned ecstatic in their state of rejection . . . the recreations of the innocently criminal.[42]

The forces of science and technology and the processes of the proletarianization of Black workers were orchestrating the supercession of Black Christian resignation by this second, derisively angry, consciousness.

Yet Wright was also critical of Marxism, the second and more modern radical Western tradition. It, too, was profoundly limited theoretically, and subject to the abuses of narrow political interests. Marxism had ultimately failed to come to terms with nationalism, with consciousness, with racism, with Western civilization, with industrialization, and with the history of Blacks. Wright had already demonstrated some of its limitations in *Native Son*. Daniel Aaron, commenting on Bigger Thomas's Communist lawyer, has observed, "Even Boris Max never really understands Bigger, and is frightened by Bigger's vision of himself."[43] Wright made this same point even more tellingly in *The Outsider*. Wright maintained that the purposes of Marxism as employed in American Communism were less analytical than political. The result was neither theory nor praxis but the achievement of power. Ironically, in the second novel, it was the character of Hilton, also a party functionary, who spoke for Wright. Hilton, driven to candor by desperation, betrays the crude agreement upon which party support of Black liberation depended: manipulation. Wright (Cross) then reflects to himself: "Did the average white American suspect that men like Hilton existed, men who could easily rise above the racial hatred of the mob and cynically make use of the defensive attitudes instilled in Negroes as weapons in their own bitter struggle for power?"[44] But Wright would instruct us never to expect to hear such revelations as Hilton's. He had heard them as a part of his experience, an experience which he would subject to the Marxian critique that was now also a part of his way of grappling with reality.

Marxism as an ideology and theory of history, Wright argued, was a product of a petite bourgeoisie—in particular, the intellectuals:

> You must assume that I know what this is all about. Don't tell me about the nobility of labor, the glorious future. *You* don't believe in that. That's for others, and you damn well know it. . . . You Jealous Rebels are intellectuals who know your history and you are anxious not to make the mistakes of your predecessors in rebellious undertakings.[45]

He was no longer convinced that Marxism, as a theory of history or social revolution, was correct, but he did understand its seductiveness. He would write in 1960: "Marxist ideology in particular is but a transitory make-shift pending a more accurate diagnosis. . . . Communism may be but a painful compromise containing a definition of man by sheer default."[46] He suspected that Marxism, alike with Christianity as an ideology, masked the complexities of history and social experience. Its truer function was the social and intellectual cohesion of the petite bourgeoisie—a class very different from the proletariat:

> One minority section of the white society in or under which he lives will offer the educated elite of Asia and Africa or black America an interpretation of the world which impels to action, thereby assuaging his feelings of inferiority. Nine times out of ten it can be easily pointed out that the ideology offered has no relation to the plight of the educated black, brown, or yellow elite. . . . But that ideology does solve something. . . .
> . . . [I]t enabled the Negro or Asian or African to meet revolutionary fragments of the hostile race on a plane of equality.[47]

Still, in this, his most devastating criticisms of Communism, Wright was relying on a notion of class struggle: "These men who rise to challenge the rulers are jealous men. They feel that they are just as good as the men who rule; indeed, they suspect that they are better. They see the countless mistakes that are being made by the men who rule and they think that they could do a more honest, a much cleaner job, a more efficient job."[48] Such was Wright's thesis on the development of Marxism as a class-specific ideology. And in some ways, he was echoing Marx's own but more mystical explanation of Marxism: "Finally, in times when the class struggle nears the decisive hour, the process of dissolution going on within the ruling class, in fact within the whole range of society, assumes such a violent, glaring character, that a small section of the ruling class cuts itself adrift, and joins the revolutionary class, the class that holds the future in its hand. . . . [S]o now a portion of the bourgeoisie goes over the proletariat, and in particular, a portion of the bourgeois ideologists, who have raised themselves to the level of comprehending theoretically the historical movement as a whole."[49]

By the early 1950s, Wright had come to his similar conclusion—one which we have seen he retained for the rest of his life—but with a different meaning: Marxist theory was an expression of petite bourgeoisie consciousness, and its critique of bourgeois society and capitalism was most fundamentally addressed to that class's suffocation by the authority of the bourgeois ruling class.

Yet the opposition of Marxist theory to capitalist society was useful to Wright, *theoretically*. Indeed, the historical and revolutionary role which Wright assigned to Blacks had at its base a materialist dialectic. As previously indicated, Wright recognized Black nationalism as a product, in part, of both the objective necessities of capitalist development and accumulation, and its system of exploitation. As he turned toward the ideology of Black nationalism, he sought to comprehend its emergence in the contradictions of day-to-day experience: "Every day in this land some white man is cussing out some defenseless Negro. But that white bastard is too stupid to realise that his actions are being duplicated a million times in a million other spots by other whites who feel hatred for Negroes just like he does. He's too blind to see that this daily wave of a million tiny assaults builds up a vast reservoir of resentment in Negroes."[50] Thus Wright echoed another powerful contribution to the development of Marxism: Hegel's the Cunning of Reason.

But where Wright differed most with others who could employ a Marxist approach was in his characterization of the historical forces of ideology. Ideology was the special political instrument of the petite bourgeoisie. Wright was arguing that the renegades of this class, who had served historically to produce the dominant ideas of the bourgeoisie, had themselves become contemptuous of the ruling class. The Jealous Rebels had declared, as Marx himself had written: "the bourgeoisie is unfit any longer to be the ruling class in society, and to impose its conditions of existence upon society as an overriding law. It is unfit to rule because it is incompetent."[51]

In his criticisms of Marxism, then, Wright was not entirely rejecting it but attempting to locate it, to provide a sense of the boundaries of its authority. As a *theory* of society, he found it dissatisfying, indeed, reductionist. By itself it was insufficiently prescient of the several levels of collective consciousness. As an *ideology*, he recognized that it had never transcended its origins. It remained an ideology *for* the working classes rather than an ideology *of* the working classes. However, as a *method* of social analysis he found it compelling. He had not abandoned the conception of the relations of production as a basis for the critique of capitalist society nor the importance of the class relations of production. Still, the critique of capitalism was only the beginning of the struggle for liberation.

It is from this critical perspective that Wright joins with one of the few Black women he has sympathetically drawn, Sarah Hunter. When she cajoles her husband, Bob, the frightened and party-subservient Black organizer, she is speaking for Wright: "Everywhere I've looked... I've seen nothing but white folks kicking niggers who are kneeling down." "I want to be one of them who tells the *others* to obey, see? Read your Marx and organize."[52]

From his experience in the American Communist Party, and from *his* reading of Marx, Wright had come to the conclusion that no people's liberation is the result of their abject surrender of critical judgment. Certainly it was not the prerogative of Black intellectuals to surrender the cultural heritage of their people: the emergent revolutionary consciousness of Black nationalism.

Notes

From *Black Marxism: The Making of the Black Radical Tradition* by Cedric J. Robinson. Copyright © 1983 by Cedric Robinson. Preface and foreword © 2000 by the University of North Carolina Press. Reprinted in revised form by permission of the publisher. www.uncpress.unc.edu

1. *American Hunger* (New York: Harper and Row, 1977) is the title Wright originally suggested (among others) for his unpublished manuscript "Island of Hallucination" (Michel Fabre, *The Unfinished Quest of Richard Wright* [New York: William Morrow, 1973], 616n19). The material published under the former title is in large measure the parts of *Black Boy* (New York: Harper, 1945) that Harper expunged from its 1945 edition. Darryl Pinckney would appear to be wrong when he suggests in his review of *American Hunger* that Wright himself was responsible for the deletion (see Pinckney, "Richard Wright: The Unnatural History of a Native Son," *Village Voice*, 4 July 1977, 80), since Wright had published much of the material in the *Atlantic Monthly* (August and September 1944) under the title "I Tried to Be a Communist."

2. Robert Bone, *The Negro Novel in America* (New Haven: Yale University Press, 1965), 158.

3. Ibid., 160.

4. See ibid.; and Addison Gayle, *The Way of the New World* (Garden City, NY: Doubleday, 1976), for these characterizations of Wright's work. For good reasons Gayle does not cite his previous work in his biography of Wright.

5. For the Gold Coast (now Ghana), see Wright's report, *Black Power* (New York: Harper, 1954); and Cedric J. Robinson, "A Case for Mistaken Identity," paper presented to the African Studies Association Conference, Los Angeles, 1 November 1979.

6. Fabre, *Unfinished Quest*, xviii.

7. Quite early on in his party experience, Wright, while reflecting on his moth-

er's reaction of horror to Communist propaganda, had come to the conclusion that: "They had a program, an ideal, but they had not yet found a language" (Richard Crossman, ed., *The God That Failed* [New York: Harper, 1965], 107).

8. See Fabre, *Unfinished Quest*, 89–200; and Constance Webb, *Richard Wright: A Biography* (New York: G. P. Putnam's Sons, 1968), 114–66.

9. Daniel Aaron, "Richard Wright and the Communist Party," *New Letters* (Winter 1971): 178.

10. Crossman, *The God That Failed*, 107–8. For some other interesting attempts to deal with the development of American working-class thought, see Stanley Feldstein and Lawrence Costello, eds., *The Ordeal of Assimilation* (Garden City, NY: Doubleday, 1974); and "The Origins of Left Culture in the US: 1880–1940," special issue, *Cultural Correspondence/Green Mountain Irregulars* 6–7 (Spring 1978).

11. Wright, "Blueprint for Negro Writing" (1937), in this volume, 218.

12. See Alfred Meyer, *Leninism* (New York: Praeger, 1971), 40–41; and Leonard Shapiro, "Two Years That Shook the World," *New York Review of Books*, 31 March 1977, 3–4.

13. See Immanuel Geiss, *The Pan-African Movement* (London: Methuen, 1974), 163–75, 213.

14. See Benjamin Gitlow, *I Confess* (New York: Dutton, 1939), chaps. 15 and 16; and Joseph Starobin, *American Communism in Crisis*, 1943–1957 (Berkeley: University of California Press, 1972), 22.

15. See Wilson Record, *The Negro and the Communist Party* (New York: Atheneum, 1971); and Roger Kanet, "The Comintern and the 'Negro Question': Communist Policy in the United States and Africa, 1921–1941," *Survey* (Autumn 1973): 86–122.

16. Fabre, *Unfinished Quest*, 137.

17. Wright qtd. in Crossman, *The God That Failed*, 141–42.

18. Ibid., 146.

19. Ibid.

20. See Earl Browder, "Democracy and the Constitution," in *The People's Front* (New York: International, 1938), 235–48; and "Resolution on the Offensive of Fascism and the Tasks of the Communist International in the Fight for the Unity of Working Class against Fascism," *Communist International*, 20 September 1935, 951.

21. Earl Browder, "The 18th Anniversary of the Founding of the Communist Party," in *The People's Front*, 271.

22. Ibid., 275.

23. Browder, "Revolutionary Background of the United States Constitution," 266, and "Twenty Years of Soviet Power," 346, both in *The People's Front*.

24. See Wilhelm Reich's "What Is Class Consciousness?" in *Sex-Pol: Essays 1929–1934,* ed. Lee Baxandall (New York: Vintage, 1972).

25. Wright to Michael Gold, reported in Fabre, *Unfinished Quest,* 185.

26. Wright, "How 'Bigger' Was Born," introduction to *Native Son* (New York: Harper, 1966), xix.

27. Ibid., xx.

28. Ibid., xxiv.

29. In April 1940, Wright had written to Gold: "If I should follow Ben Davis's advice and write of Negroes through the lens of how the Party views them in terms of political theory, I'd abandon the Bigger Thomases. I'd be tacitly admitting that they are lost to us, that fascism will triumph because it alone can enlist the allegiance of those millions whom capitalism has crushed and maimed" (Fabre, *Unfinished Quest,* 185–86).

30. Wright, "How 'Bigger' Was Born," xix.

31. Ibid., xviii.

32. Ibid., xvii.

33. Ibid., xxiv.

34. Wright, *Native Son,* 391–92.

35. See Fabre, *Unfinished Quest,* 184–87, for a summary of the reactions of party leaders to *Native Son.*

36. Wright, "Blueprint for Negro Writing," in this volume, 214.

37. Ibid., 217.

38. Richard Wright, *The Outsider* (New York: Harper, 1953), 118–19.

39. See W. E. B. Du Bois, *Black Reconstruction in America, 1860–1880* (1935; New York: Free Press, 1962).

40. See Theodore Draper, *American Communism and Soviet Russia* (New York: Viking, 1960); Dan T. Carter, *Scottsboro: A Tragedy of the American South* (London: Oxford University Press, 1968); and Wilson Record, *The Negro and the Communist Party.*

41. Karl Marx, "Contribution to the Critique of Hegel's *Philosophy of Right:* Introduction," in *The Marx-Engels Reader,* ed. Robert Tucker (New York: Norton, 1972), 12.

42. Wright, *The Outsider,* 129.

43. Aaron, "Richard Wright and the Communist Party," 180.

44. Wright, *The Outsider,* 227.

45. Ibid., 334.

46. Richard Wright, "The Voiceless Ones," *Saturday Review,* 16 April 1960, 22. Raman K. Singh's analysis of Cross may be applied (as he suggested) to Wright: "In opposing Communism, Cross is not giving up Marxism; he is merely seeking to abolish the tyranny of the Party. And in adopting Existentialism, he is not

abandoning Marxism, but showing his awareness of both economic and cosmic consciousness" (Singh, "Marxism in Richard Wright's Fiction," *Indian Journal of American Studies* 4, no. 1/2 [June/December 1974]: 3–4). This is decidedly not the position taken by other writers who came out from the Communist movement as John Diggins sees them (Diggins, "Buckley's Comrades: The Ex-Communist as Conservative," *Dissent,* Fall 1975, 370–81).

47. Wright, *White Men Listen!* (Garden City, NY: Doubleday, 1957), 19–20.

48. Wright, *The Outsider,* 334.

49. Karl Marx and Friedrich Engels, *The Communist Manifesto,* in *The Marx-Engels Reader,* ed. Tucker, 343.

50. Wright, *The Outsider,* 221.

51. Marx and Engels, *The Communist Manifesto,* 345.

52. Wright, *The Outsider,* 176–77.

4

Alternative Readings of Bigger Thomas

Cyrus Ernesto Zirakzadeh

When Richard Wright's *Native Son* appeared in US bookstores in 1940, it was an overnight sensation. This was no mean feat, Ralph Ellison noted. Wright, who never finished high school, had shown remarkable courage in entering a field dominated by whites. But he had faith in himself: "Like a good Negro athlete, he believed in his ability to compete."[1]

In terms of literary innovations, the book was seminal for at least two reasons. First, never before in popular American fiction had there been a black character as psychologically complex, emotionally unstable, and behaviorally unpredictable as Bigger Thomas: browbeaten by his mother, excluded from ubiquitous economic opportunities simply because of his skin color, and overwhelmed by internal waves of fury and fear. Wright had invented a new literary archetype of black males in America (or, if one found Bigger's character traits offensive, a new negative stereotype).[2]

Second, the setting for much of the book was a segregated black inner-city neighborhood, an environment that seldom had been represented in US fiction prior to World War I. Unlike those novelists who during the 1930s were writing about white-ethnic working-class life, Wright depicted the South Side of Chicago in a distinctively "gothic" style, as the social historian Michael Denning has put it. There were pestilent rats, roaming gangs

Alternative Readings of Bigger Thomas

of hooligans, and bodily fluids on the floors of movie houses. Furthermore, there were no nurturing friendships or ad hoc systems of mutual aid, typical characteristics of what Denning has called the "urban pastoral" fiction of the 1930s.[3]

Both features stirred debate about the book's political message.[4] Were its fictional characters and setting inaccurate and potentially dangerous distortions? Or, were they reliable and true renderings of urban black life? Responding to the mounting questions and criticisms, Wright, a few months after the release of *Native Son,* delivered a lecture in Harlem on how the fictional character of Bigger was based on Wright's own life experiences and on his current historical observations. The talk, "How 'Bigger' Was Born," became a standard appendix to his novel.

As time has passed, readers have continued to debate the political meaning and value of Wright's novel.[5] To appreciate the range of the political lessons that one can extract and construct from Wright's text, this essay will contrast commentaries published by Irving Howe, Ralph Ellison, and James Baldwin during the 1950s and 1960s. Each of these writers decried white racism, but each saw its roots differently and proposed strikingly different methods for combating it. Approaching the novel from different political angles, they responded to Wright's art with varying amounts of enthusiasm, hope, and frustration.

Irving Howe's Defense of *Native Son*

Howe, who made his living as a professor teaching classes and writing books on Anglo-American literature, devoted his life to political debate and promoting social change. To that end, he cofounded *Dissent* in 1954. It was to be a space where artists, journalists, and academics sympathetic to socialist critiques of capitalism, to Trotskyist critiques of bureaucracy, and to liberal democratic values could exchange ideas. In 1959, Howe, having long found Wright's fiction and autobiographical writings fascinating, invited Wright to become one of the magazine's contributing editors.[6]

Howe's review of *Native Son* appeared in *Dissent* in 1963, almost a quarter century after the novel was originally released. By this time, Howe's aspirations for the United States were eclectic yet identifiably left-liberal. He vigorously defended civil liberties and rights of association and expression. He also wanted the federal government to play a larger role in checking the power of large corporations, in ensuring the rights of organized labor, and in providing a broad range of educational, medical, and housing services to the public (comparable to those already found in western European social democracies).[7] Howe thought these social changes could be achieved only through the patient building of an overwhelmingly large electoral alliance that would involve a wide range of nonwealthy Americans, including oppressed blacks, white trade unionists, the chronically unemployed, struggling small-business owners, indebted family farmers, and, of course, public intellectuals. Howe believed that to be effective, the coalition also would need to garner support from whites in southern states like Texas and Mississippi, and in seemingly staid organizations like churches and entrepreneurs' clubs: "If we are serious in our wish to affect American political life, we must learn to see the reality as it is. We have to seek out and prod the forces that exist. And I think it is a gross error—the kind of deep-seated conservatism that often alloys ultraradicalism—to say that everything in the major sectors of American society is static, sated, 'Establishment.'"[8]

The first task in building such a coalition, thought Howe, was to help potential coalition partners learn about each other's sufferings. Knowledge about real-world conditions, when combined with citizens' natural compassion and decency, would foster enlightened party politics. Herein lay the value of Wright's book, claimed Howe. "The day *Native Son* appeared, American culture was changed forever" because the novel "made impossible a repetition of the old lies" about racism being a phenomenon of the past, only surviving in backwaters of the South.[9] In Howe's opinion, Wright had described situations in the North "so oppressive that only violence can provide their victims with the hope of dignity."[10] The images of squalor and daily humiliation, when contrasted with images of white comfort and privilege, were so detailed and vivid that the book "forced" a typical white reader "to recognize himself as an oppressor."[11]

Howe found the fictitious conversations among the novel's black characters compelling. He thought the dialogue made it evident that real-life blacks in the United States blamed white Americans for the current maldistribution of material goods and economic opportunities. A white reader therefore could learn from the book that "Negroes, were far from patient or forgiving, that they were scarred by fear, that they hated every moment of their suppression even when seeming most acquiescent, and that often enough they hated *us*, the decent and cultivated white men who from complicity or neglect shared in the responsibility for their plight."[12]

Howe admitted that Bigger's behavior in the first part of the book matched a stereotype held by many white-skinned citizens, who believed that young black males were ultimately lustful rapists, petty criminals, or savage killers. In Howe's words, "Bigger was drawn—one would surmise, deliberately—from white fantasy and white contempt."[13] But instead of questioning the plausibility of Wright's artistic creation, Howe praised Wright's ability to use the conventions of naturalistic writing to make it clear that Bigger was not solely responsible for his behavior. He was reacting to a dehumanizing world. White society, by denying urban blacks opportunities for decent housing and steady work, had emotionally deformed Bigger and turned him into a moral cripple. Feeling shame over his social status and resentment over his limited prospects for advancement, he had no choice but to release his rage in ways that shocked polite society. In Howe's opinion, Wright had effectively laid bare "how wounding it is to wear the mask of a grinning nigger boy in order to keep a job."[14]

Howe therefore urged white readers to heed *Native Son*'s warning. Wright "brought out into the open, as no one ever had before, the hatred, fear, and violence that have crippled and may yet destroy our culture."[15] Only if whites welcomed blacks into currently all-white workplaces, neighborhoods, schools, churches, and hospitals (an interracial sharing of the American dream of personal wealth and autonomy that Howe called "integration"),[16] would racial peace occur. Until that time, brutes like Bigger would multiply, continually prowl, and wreak havoc.

Conversely, Howe denounced the growing popularity in the 1960s of black nationalist organizations and theories. He found nationalists' criticisms of US materialism nonsensical: "These intellectuals seem to me snobbish. For Negroes should have as much right to suburban pleasures as anyone else; they should be in a position just as much as the whites to choose the middle-class style of life."[17] Consequently, he wondered if self-declared black nationalists were in fact demagogues seeking unwitting followers. Or perhaps they were merely unsophisticated thinkers about matters of the human heart? "There is something a bit manipulative in the view that Negroes should be preserved from the temptations that, presumably, all the rest of us are entitled to. What's more, the Negroes themselves are far too experienced in the ways of the world to allow themselves to be cast in the role of sacrificial ascetic."[18]

In his criticisms of black nationalism, Howe revealed some limitations in his ability to think critically about the isolation, vulnerability, and betrayal (and the poisonous fear and envy) that characterize late liberal capitalist society. Instead of seeing white US society as composed of red-eyed careerists and hustlers who are constantly slipping and sliding down the pole of success and who, after falling, seek excuses for their "bad luck," Howe read *Native Son* in a peculiarly benign way. He disconnected the racial scapegoating by fictitious whites in the book from the economic treadmill that the fictitious whites ran daily. He treated the book as a melodramatic tale about the sufferings of oppressed individuals, not as a criticism of capitalism per se. Wright, as we shall see later in this chapter, saw American culture quite differently.

Neglecting the Importance of Community: Ellison's Critique of Bigger

Whereas Howe praised *Native Son* for its social awareness and psychological acuity, several other public intellectuals during the Cold War questioned the book's contribution to progressive politics. Ellison, for one, found the novel's depiction of misery in black urban neighborhoods one-sided, which resulted in both an overly mechanical psychological vision and a muddled political point. This does not mean that Ellison belittled the importance of Wright's novel. He appreciated that Wright offered young black authors an example of what is artistically achievable. Therefore, "I feel that *Native Son* is one of the major literary events in the history of American literature. I can say this even though at this point I have certain reservations about its view of reality."[19]

What troubled Ellison was that Wright's book minimized the local richness of black life in the United States.[20] The novel, instead, ruminated on the material hardships that black individuals endured, seemingly in total isolation from one another. There was no banding together, no collective adaptation, and no creativity. The South Side of Chicago resembled a Hobbesian state of war in which the black characters—including mothers and sons, girlfriends and boyfriends, brothers and sisters—instinctively viewed each other as potential threats, if not outright enemies. All of this, Ellison maintained, is wrongheaded. While Ellison agreed that life is incredibly hard in northern cities, "something else" occurs in places like Harlem that results "in strength, endurance, and promise. This is the proper subject for the Negro American writer."[21]

Ellison argued that to survive, blacks in the United States over the centuries have spontaneously constructed an array of local sanctuaries against systems of oppression. These alternative institutions included neighborhood churches, community stores, black colleges, and "music halls" and juke joints that were little more than additions to private homes. Here, away from the prying eyes of whites, black Americans have developed friendships, pooled resources, and launched collective projects. No less important, black Americans in these locales have developed the personal and collective dignity necessary for creativity. Thanks to their local countercultures, black Americans have acquired subtle and deft mannerisms, including "their resistance to provocation, their coolness under pressure, their sense of timing, and their tenacious hold on the ideal of their ultimate freedom" that, in Ellison's opinion, "are at least as characteristic of American Negroes as the hatred, fear and vindictiveness which Wright chose to emphasize."[22] Consequently, "I rejected Bigger Thomas as any *final* image of Negro personality."[23]

For Ellison, hardship and suffering prompt not loneliness and despair, but collective creativity. In other words, local enclaves should not be seen and treated as antiques and curious remnants of preindustrial folkways. They constantly evolve in response to ongoing experiences of domination, oppression, and exploitation. The bleaker the situation is for blacks, the more inventive have been their collective responses, regardless if they take place on the Delta plantations before the Civil War; in the segregated cattle towns of the Southwest after the Civil War;[24] or in urban neighborhoods like Harlem that white journalists, scholars, and other outsiders prematurely dismiss with phrases like "piss in the halls and blood on the stairs."[25] In all of these places, hardship and suffering take place, but they occur alongside refuges where blacks meet, commiserate, and create. "My point is that it isn't *only* hard," Ellison wrote, "but that there are many good things about it."[26]

Believing that there was a creative, collective side to blacks' experience of being downtrodden, Ellison responded angrily to what he considered to be Howe's, Howard Zinn's, and other white liberals' patronizing attitude toward impoverished blacks. White do-gooders, thought Ellison, too often viewed poor blacks as politically helpless, intellectually impaired, and morally primitive children. Ellison, turning the tables, argued that white liberals were morally and intellectually deficient because they had been raised in a competitive, cold, cash-first environment.[27] Black Americans, in contrast, had nurtured within their local enclaves ennobling habits, manners, and outlooks: "Today it is the black American who puts pressure upon the nation to live up to its ideals. It is he who gives creative tension to our struggle for justice and for the elimination of those factors, social and psychological, which make for slums and shaky suburban communities. . . . Without the black American, something irrepressibly hopeful and creative would go out of the American spirit, and the nation might well succumb to the moral snobbism that has always threatened its existence from within."[28]

Wright, thought Ellison, must have known from his own life experiences that local folkways are ubiquitous and provide oppressed people, regardless of skin color, with the mental toughness and nimbleness necessary not only to survive but to become creative agents, able to shape their existence. This is part of the reason Ellison found the character of Bigger so puzzling. His alleged modus operandi within South Chicago—brooding for hours and then exploding into fits of reckless rage—was implausible. Ellison surmised that Wright's ability to imagine such an incredibly impulsive and repulsive character must have been a by-product of Wright's early involvement in the Communist Party and his exposure to simplistic Marxist ideas that brutal social conditions fostered brutalized subhuman people.[29]

Wright should have known better, thought Ellison, because despite enduring taunts and threats throughout his own childhood and adolescence, Wright did not become brutalized. He "was able to free himself in Mississippi because he had the imagination and the will to do so." This, Ellison insisted, was not a matter of simple self-fashioning. Wright had acquired important character traits and personal resources from his environment—from family, neighborhood, school, and church rituals and the experiments with different techniques of avoiding subjugation and resisting submission: "He was as much a product of his reading as of his painful experiences, and he made himself a writer by subjecting himself to the writer's discipline."[30] Wright, however, portrayed Bigger as unable to escape the reckless, self-destructive impulses allegedly planted in his soul by a hard life. Wright, in other words, was proposing a one-sided form of social determinism that his own life contradicted.

Ellison and Howe repeatedly disagreed in public about the political value of Bigger's story.[31] In his review of *Native Son*, Howe chided Ellison and Baldwin for politically turning their backs on fellow blacks (because they had failed to follow Wright's footsteps and write protest novels about the horrors and mental sicknesses that characterized the modern black ghetto). Baldwin chose to ignore Howe's remarks. Ellison chose to challenge them, especially Howe's thesis that inner-city life transformed black people into thoughtless brutes.

Ellison, furthermore, cast aspersions on liberal proposals to end racism through state action. In his opinion, at least three generations of well-meaning black and white liberal leaders, from Booker T. Washington to Hubert Humphrey, had promised during election seasons to use the state to end discrimination and segregation. They then acted sheepishly when it came to proposing and implementing legislation enforcing social equality. This pattern had convinced Ellison that state-mandated racial equality was not on the country's legislative horizon.[32]

Ellison proposed an alternative political tack. He encouraged blacks to take advantage of the *associational opportunities* that America's liberal rhetoric and social habits currently afforded. The freedom for social experimentation, which both eighteenth-century and nineteenth-century settlers took advantage of, had made America a special country in the past, Ellison contended. Blacks should continue that pioneer tradition and refine the cultural experiments that their forebears had started in Chicago, Memphis, Oklahoma City, and Oxford, Mississippi.[33]

True, bottom-up social experimentation sometimes may result in some black-only organizations and traditions. But, Ellison thought, that is fine, at least for now. Parallel institutions, such as black music halls, black colleges, and black movie houses, provided black Americans with places where they could grow personally and develop a collective capacity.[34] This does not mean, of course, that Ellison endorsed racial segregation as some sort of final goal or that he viewed black nationalism as offering a satisfactory political dream. Rather, he viewed black enclaves as places where blacks could channel their energies into creative projects, such as the new musical form called "jazz." Ellison hoped that over time white Americans would come to appreciate what Ellison called the "humanity" of black Americans—in other words, their determination, inventiveness, cleverness, and intellectual dexterity. The long-term goal should be, in his words that predate today's parlance, the "inclusion" of diverse white and black ways of living, and not the "assimilation" into the white suburban lifestyle that Howe championed.[35] "So allow me to repeat it coldly," Ellison wrote: "I fear the implications of Howe's ideas concerning the Negro writer's role as activist more than I do the State of Mississippi. Which is not to deny the viciousness which exists there, but to recognize the degree of freedom which also exists there. . . . [L]et him learn more about the South and about Negro Americans if he would speak with authority."[36]

Baldwin and the Problem of White Innocence

Like Ellison, Baldwin considered the accounts of black American life in Wright's *Native Son* to be not only inaccurate, but politically dangerous.[37] The problem, in Baldwin's opinion, was that the novel reiterated rather than challenged the myths that are constitutive of US racism.

Baldwin claimed, for example, that Bigger's nearly irrepressible rage perpetuated a long-standing stereotype among white Americans: that persons with black skins are largely thoughtless beings unable to control base emotions. This can lead to crime or rampage at any moment. This blatantly false claim, Baldwin emphasized, was used at the founding of the United States to justify slavery, and it was used after the Civil War to deny social opportunities and political equality to blacks. In the middle of the twentieth century, it was being used to legitimate the exclusion of blacks from restaurants, bars, bowling alleys, hotels, jobs, schools, hospitals, and other public venues. Upon the stereotype of black madness, a racist nation had been founded and sustained.[38]

Baldwin conceded that Wright's picture of Bigger's intense fury revealed an important truth about being black in America. Like Bigger, Baldwin also "wanted to do something to crush these white faces, which were crushing me":[39]

> There is, I should think, no Negro living in America who has not felt, briefly or for long periods, with anguish sharp or dull, in varying degrees and to varying effect, simple, naked, and unanswerable hatred; who has not wanted to smash any white face he may encounter in a day, to violate, out of motives of the cruelest vengeance, their women, to break the bodies of all white people and bring them low, as low as that dust into which he himself has been and is being trampled.[40]

But, Baldwin insisted, blacks have additional social skills and character traits, including patience, forbearance, rationality, and love. As did other black Americans, Baldwin had learned over the course of his adolescence and childhood to corral his murderous impulses. He learned a "smile-and-the-world-smiles-with-you routine," even though he also "began to feel that there was another me trapped in my skull like a jack-in-the-box who might escape my control at any moment and fill the air with screaming."[41]

According to Baldwin, Bigger's lack of self-control was a blatant misrepresentation of the actual psychological development of the vast majority of black Americans. Bigger spent his endless days without work unable to control his temper and, therefore, constantly getting into scraps not only with whites but also with black friends and neighbors. Baldwin found the pattern of behavior implausible. Adult black Americans knew how to channel their rage over job discrimination, housing segregation, workplace harassment, and other types of offensive behavior. To survive, black Americans had learned how to resist domination, oppression, and exploitation through guile, humor, silence, and evasion. The idea expressed through the fictitious character of Bigger—that some humans are monsters driven primarily by bodily tensions and sudden surges of feeling—existed nowhere "except in the darkness of our minds."[42]

What made this obviously silly story dangerous was that white Americans tended to take the myth of subhuman blacks seriously. Therefore, as the political scientist Stephen Marshall has put it, Baldwin feared that "when white readers" of *Native Son* "encountered flesh-and-blood black people, they would either subsume blacks under the category of the monster or, as was more likely the case, perceive them as unintelligible and alien."[43]

The character called Bigger was only one point in Baldwin's overall critique of the novel. Baldwin said that Wright, in addition, had populated the novel with several impossibly noble white heroes.[44] The fictitious pair of idealistic Communist activists, Jan Erlone and Boris Max, were almost polar opposites of Bigger in terms of their eloquence, intelligence, and selfless commitment to the well-being of others. The contrast might be laughable were it not for the historical circumstances. White Americans, Baldwin wrote, always have had a deep emotional stake in hiding the truth of their racist attitudes and crimes from themselves. They cannot bear to admit that they repeatedly have violated the codes of equality and liberty that they champion before others, and they especially cannot bear to admit that they have routinely breached their moral code in order to enjoy the material and cultural benefits of institutionalized racism. So, they cling to narratives about their pure innocence.

However, Baldwin suspected that American whites at some level have always known the harsh truth. Unlike European slave traders, generations of white Americans have lived and worked alongside black Americans. Whites therefore must have become aware that they share a common humanity with those black Americans who were enslaved and are now mistreated. To salve their consciences, white Americans have constructed fantasies about being morally pure and lacking all untoward passions, desires, and ambitions. Meanwhile, they have conveniently projected the vile character traits they sense within themselves onto fellow citizens with darker skin, who are then deemed to be morally deformed, psychologically primitive, and intellectually childlike.

In Baldwin's opinion, Wright's cast of white and black characters was consistent with the Manichean worldview that has long defined white culture in the United States. Consequently, like *Uncle Tom's Cabin* and all popular protest books in the United States, *Native Son* offered white readers not a window onto reality but what Baldwin called a "medieval" ethical fantasy.[45] Race relations in America, Baldwin believed, would never improve until both black Americans and white Americans started to view themselves and each other in terms other than those used in the conventional protest-novel tradition.

White Americans, in particular, must recognize the complex motivations and contradictory interests bubbling within themselves, must discard their masks of innocence, and must acknowledge the pain that they inflict daily on others. However, whites probably will not be able to undertake this humbling and ultimately humiliating self-reckoning by themselves. They lack the maturity necessary to take stock of their lives and admit their faults and complicity in the suffering of others.[46] Hence, whites will need the constant goading as well as the constant support of black Americans.[47] Such help will not be welcomed, of course. So black Americans must be prepared for the derision, distrust, and hostility that their candor will generate from whites.

Baldwin conceded that among blacks, patience with the childishness of whites was starting to run dry. The temptation to say, "the hell with it" and destroy the status quo was growing. Violence, however, was an unrealistic option in his eyes because it surely would generate a backlash from the more powerful whites. The only way for blacks to end racism without risking self-destruction was through candid conversations marked by patience, compassion, and faith.[48]

Calling neither for the formation of a large progressive electoral coalition nor for the establishment of local black institutions, Baldwin championed small-scale efforts at mutual reconstruction that he labeled "love." The notion, in his writings, referred not to a naive, blind devotion that denies imperfections and shortcomings, but to a deep desire to help another person grow and to a faith that the beloved can become even more mature and attractive than she or he already is.[49]

Baldwin, like Ellison, insisted that such important cultural change cannot be accomplished through conventional politics, because elected politicians feed upon the inequalities, anger, and stereotypes that currently exist in society and have no interest in upending the cultural order.[50] Instead, black and white individuals, living and working alongside each other, must learn to discard their inherited melodramatic stereotypes. Baldwin therefore admonished his nephew to see beyond the contempt in which whites currently hold blacks and to help white Americans drop their false ideas of themselves: "And I mean that very seriously. You must accept them and accept them with love. For these innocent people have no other hope."[51]

Wright and the Insanity of Modern Capitalism

Howe, Ellison, and Baldwin published their reflections on the political value and limitations of Wright's novel around the height of the Cold War, when working-class Americans had enjoyed more than a decade of rapidly rising wages and ongoing prosperity, when highways and suburbs dotted the landscape for the first time, and when the civil rights movement was beginning to surge. Wright wrote *Native Son* at a much different time in terms of global tensions and the evolution of antiracist movements at home. He wrote the book prior to the United States' entrance into World War II, prior to the Supreme Court's *Brown v. Board of Education* decision, and prior to the Bracero worker-exchange program with Mexico and the subsequent "zoot-suit riots" in southern California. Moreover, Wright composed *Native Son* at a particular historical moment in the development of US capitalism: when the first generation of financial corporations and big businesses had finally become dominant voices in national politics; when enormous transportation hubs and centers for heavy industry were emerging on the prairies and along the Great Lakes; when memories of unprecedented booms and busts were fresh in workers' and business owners' memories; and when the commercial mass media—movies in particular—were reshaping the expectations and fears of Americans. In short, when Wright composed *Native Son*, the United States was finding its legs as a stable economic power of the first order, and this was part of his novel's message.

Wright reported in his addendum to standard editions of the novel that the idea of "Bigger" first entered his mind during his youth in Jim Crow Mississippi, where he observed young black men defying the region's laws and norms and refusing to accept their demeaning existence. They were fully aware of the potentially fatal costs of insubordination, yet they refused to cower. One day, Wright overheard whites on a train speak derogatorily about the need to discipline one recalcitrant black youth named "Bigger Thomas." Wright later decided to use that name to denote a reckless, almost foolhardy disposition among some blacks to ignore threats of punishment and to challenge white authorities in the name of individual freedom.[52]

Wright claimed that this initial insight developed in two unexpected directions after he moved to the North. First, Wright observed a large number of city-dwelling blacks whose behavior differed from what he had seen in the South. In the industrialized North, what Wright was beginning to call "Bigger characteristics" were more developed, more overt, more intense. This was not because of greater oppression in the North. Rather, America's industrial boom had teased residents with false promises of boundless wealth: "The urban environment of Chicago, affording a more stimulating life, made the Negro Bigger Thomases react more violently than even in the South. . . . It was not that Chicago segregated Negroes more than the South, but that Chicago had more to offer, that Chicago's physical aspect—noisy, crowded, filled with the sense of power and fulfillment—did so much more to dazzle the mind with a taunting sense of possible achievement that the segregation it did impose brought forth from Bigger a reaction more obstreperous than in the South."[53]

Second, Wright for the first time observed Bigger traits among the white workers he was meeting. They exhibited similar types of outrage, and likewise bristled at the thought of deferring to others and accepting their relatively low status and standards of living as permanent conditions: "I made the discovery that Bigger Thomas was not black all the time; he was white, too, and there were literally millions of him, everywhere. The extension of my sense of the personality of Bigger was the pivot of my life; it altered the complexion of my existence. . . . It was as though I had put on a pair of spectacles whose power was that of an x-ray enabling me to see deeper into the lives of men."[54]

Wright concluded that Bigger's thought processes, his desires, and his fears were "a part of *all* Negroes and *all* whites" who were struggling against the new "American scene."[55] Wrote Wright, "In both instances the deep sense of exclusion was identical."[56]

Wishing to delve into these insights, Wright decided to write a book about a huge theme: "the mental and emotional climate of our time."[57] The fictitious character known as "Bigger Thomas" was to embody a mentality that was spreading for the first time across North America, thanks to a new type of economy that Wright understood not abstractly as "affluent," "commercial," or "market organized," but as powered by dreams of unlimited upward mobility and unbridled consumption of glittering goods. The events of the story, Wright hoped, would clarify the institutional arrangements, such as the court procedures and the patterns of property ownership, that supported the "money-grubbing industrial civilization" in northern cities.[58]

While Wright gave Bigger a black skin to convey important truths about the nature of racism in America, there was also an "American part of Bigger which is the heritage of us all, that part of him which we get from our seeing and hearing, from school, from the hopes and dreams of our friends."[59] The "American part of Bigger" was a fantasy of boundless self-indulgence, which, Wright surmised, was fueled by the cultural apparatus of American capitalism—by movies and cheap magazines, by the glittering merchandise in stores, and by dazzling public displays of consumption by the super-rich. Spurred by this fantasy, all Americans—black and white, male and female, young and old—endlessly seek economic advancement, the private accumulation of wealth, and opportunities for conspicuous consumption.

Whereas bourgeois optimists might argue that the dream of endless accumulation helps society by encouraging initiative, focus, and diligence (in short, a good work ethic), Wright thought otherwise. He insisted that the seemingly inspiring dream of unlimited individual advancement often turned into a nightmare for at least three reasons. First, it promoted self-punishing, high-risk behavior, which sooner or later clashed with deeply seeded desires for physical protection and security that, Wright believed, was planted in all humans during their infancies.[60] Second, the narrow pursuit of material acquisition proved to be empty of joy—it provided no "spiritual sustenance," as Wright put it.[61] Last but certainly not least, the goal of living purely as one wished was unrealistic. It was, in reality, an unattainable goal for the vast majority of Americans.

All of these contradictions and trade-offs produced the frustration, anger, and self-loathing that Wright observed in urban Americans—both white and black. Underneath their daily cheerfulness, they were haunted by the awareness that the glittering dream they were pursuing was ultimately fool's gold. The United States, insisted Wright, had become a collection of superficially comfortable cities like Chicago, whose inhabitants suffered from their fantasies: "A world in which millions of men lived and behaved like drunkards, taking a stiff drink of hard life to lift them up for a thrilling moment, to give them a quivering sense of wild exultation and fulfillment that soon faded and let them down. Eagerly they took another drink, wanting to avoid the dull, flat look of things.... Speaking figuratively, they were soon chronic alcoholics, men who lived by violence, through extreme action and sensation, and through drowning daily in a perpetual nervous agitation."[62] The "pinch and pressures" of American capitalism had produced a continent without tranquility, filled with "silly fads and crazes," destabilized by "quicksilver changes in public taste," and infused with "hysteria and fears."[63]

The story of Bigger was intended to convey some of Wright's theses about the hysteria, fears, and perpetual nervous agitation that modern capitalism promoted. The story, in addition, referred at one point to Bigger's attraction to fascism: "He liked to hear of how Japan was conquering China; of how Hitler was running the Jews to the ground." According to the narrator in the novel, the ability to push others around and "blot out" weaklings (including weaklings who were black people) appealed to Bigger, who felt like a pawn and yearned to end his "fear and shame."[64]

Wright made it clear in his commentary that the novel's brief, almost casual reference to the attractiveness of Hitler for Bigger Thomas was intentional. In both Nazi Germany and Stalinist Russia, "white-skinned Biggers" had channeled their frustrations over the instability and insecurity of modern existence into support for authoritarian rulers. Wright perceived similar sentiments emerging among poorer black residents in the United States, who hoped to escape their cramped conditions and feelings of futility by uniting behind a single, determined leader:

> I've even heard Negroes say that maybe Hitler and Mussolini are all right; that maybe Stalin is all right. They did not say this out of any intellectual comprehension of the forces at work in the world, but because they felt that these men "did things." ... There was in the back of their minds, when they said this, a wild and intense longing (wild and intense because it was suppressed!) to belong, to be identified, to feel that they were alive as other people were, to be caught up forgetfully and exultingly in the wing of events, to feel the clean, deep, organic satisfaction of doing a job in common with others.[65]

Experiences with impotency in modern capitalist America, Wright feared, were contributing to a dangerous political aspiration among the majority in American cities. He hoped that nonwealthy people, both whites and blacks, might rally behind a democratic and socialist program. But, they also might back a cruel demagogue who oppresses others. Following this figure might be mistakenly perceived as the only way to act with freedom, agency, and power.

Whether Bigger will "follow some gaudy, hysterical leader who'll promise rashly to fill the void in him, or whether he'll come to an understanding with the millions of his kindred follow workers under trade-union or revolutionary guidance depends upon the future drift of events in America."[66] This was not a question of innate human tendencies, but of the social arrangements that Wright saw being established around him. Being the "product of a dislocated society" in the United States, Bigger Thomas "carried within him the potentialities of either Communism or Fascism."[67] Wright believed that this distinctively modern danger—what US citizens seventy-five years later would label "right-wing populism"—could be permanently cured only through radical reconstruction of America's economic culture. This daunting project would require collective action on a scale much larger than Ellison and Baldwin would later commend.[68]

Moving Forward

Within a quarter century of its publication, some readers found in *Native Son* a call for a liberal-left catchall party, a disturbing repetition of stereotypes that prop up US racism, an obtuseness toward the healing power of community, and a warning about the appeal of demagogy to modern nonwealthy classes. The variety of lessons that have been extracted from *Native Son* suggest that the book's political meaning is inconclusive. Different readers have seized upon and combined different elements of the novel. Presumably, future readers will do the same.

To some extent, the divergent responses to the novel reflect the historical situations of the readers. Raised in different times, places, and social circumstances, Howe, Ellison, Baldwin, and Wright were attuned to different palpable dangers and, consequently, dreamt of different sorts of justice and peace. Those orientations undoubtedly affected what they saw in the text.

But in reading the book, Howe, Ellison, and Baldwin were not unthinking puppets who passively discovered in the text details that aligned with their socially predetermined, preexisting prejudices. Each reader considered himself a historical actor and, therefore, wanted to use the book to advance a political project to which he was committed. Consequently, each seized upon different details in the text to think through and advance a preferred course of action: contemporary party politics (Howe), communitarian experiments (Ellison), interpersonal love (Baldwin), and fundamental economic reconstruction (Wright).

As the cultural theorist Stuart Hall has noted, works of popular culture acquire political meaning in this manner. Art that is produced for mass consumption, such as melodies in pop music, fictional characters in pulp fiction, and visual images on billboards, are never vehicles for single ideological positions. Because works of art are composites with different features, they do not have fixed and final political meanings. They are not in and of themselves "progressive" or "conservative;" "hegemonic" or "subversive"; "reformist" or "reactionary." The political meaning of any piece of art depends on how historical actors use its features. In other words, for what goals, interests, and causes does a political activist select aspects of a widely available artistic work and, conversely, against what goals, interests, and causes are aspects of the work used? The work's political meaning is a function of the struggle to which it is applied.[69]

The relevant question for today's readers of *Native Son*, thus, is not whether there is one "true" or "correct" meaning to the story of Bigger that has been identified in the past (or that a careful scholar will uncover in the future). The relevant question is: To what ends do we contemporary readers of *Native Son* wish to put Wright's literary creation?

Notes

1. Ralph Ellison, "A Very Stern Discipline" (1967), in *The Collected Essays of Ralph Ellison, Revised and Updated*, ed. John F. Callahan (New York: Modern Library, 2003), 737.

2. For a survey of the earliest interpretations of Bigger (typically either as a new archetype or as a negative stereotype) that appeared shortly after the release of the novel, see Hazel Rowley, *Richard Wright: The Life and Times* (Chicago: University of Chicago Press, 2001), esp. 191–98. For a convenient survey and creative synthesis of the contrary views on Bigger that appeared during and after the civil rights movement, see Robert Butler, *Native Son: The Emergence of a New Black Hero* (Boston: Twayne, 1991). Keneth Kinnamon, ed., *New Essays on "Native Son"* (Cambridge: Cambridge University Press, 1991) contains five examples of scholarly interpretations, informed by social history, in vogue toward the close of the twentieth century. For more contemporary interpretations of Bigger, see the chapters in this volume by Cedric J. Robinson and Lewis R. Gordon.

3. Michael Denning, *The Culture Front: The Laboring of American Culture in the Twentieth Century* (New York: Verso, 1997), 247–54. For further thoughts on Wright's urban vision, see the essays in this volume by Perry S. Moskowitz and James B. Haile III.

4. For a convenient survey of the earliest critical responses to the novel, see Rowley, *Richard Wright*, 191–94, 198–201.

5. Compare, for example, Cedric J. Robinson's extrapolation of the radical possibilities of Richard Wright's work (in chapter 3 of this volume) with Cornel West's insistence that possibilities for black collective insurgency were absent both in *Native Son* and in Wright's fiction more generally (Cornel West, "Black Radicalism," in *Prophetic Reflections: Notes on Race and Power in America*, ed. West [Monroe, ME: Common Courage Press, 1993], 174–75).

6. Gerald Sorin, *Irving Howe: A Life of Passionate Dissent* (New York: New York University Press, 2002), 190.

7. For Howe's own description of "democracy" as some sort of balance or fusion of individual freedom and economic equality, see Irving Howe, *Socialism and America* (New York: Harcourt Brace Jovanovich, 1985).

8. Irving Howe, "New Styles of 'Leftism'" (1965), in *Irving Howe: Selected Writings, 1950–1990* (San Diego: Harcourt Brace Jovanovich, 1990), 211.

9. Howe, "Black Boys and Native Sons" (1963), reprinted with postscripts in *Irving Howe: Selected Writings*, 121.

10. Ibid., 123.
11. Ibid., 121.
12. Ibid.
13. Ibid., 122.
14. Ibid., 124.
15. Ibid., 121.

16. For an example of Howe's stout defense of the integration (and, conversely, his opposition to the "social and cultural segregation" that he associated with "black nationalism"), see the 1969 postscript to his review of *Native Son* in *Irving Howe: Selected Writings*, 137–38. For thoughts on how Howe's seemingly inclusive vision of assimilation may have been linked to his sympathy for blackface as a form of cultural bridge-building, see Michael Rogin, *Blackface, White Noise: Jewish Immigrants in the Hollywood Melting Pot* (Berkeley: University of California Press, 1998), 99, 290.

17. Howe, "New Styles of 'Leftism,'" 208–9.

18. Ibid., 209. Although Howe denounced black nationalist politics throughout the 1960s and 1970s, he conceded toward the end of the century that he had underestimated the ability of black populations in the United States to create their own separate, vibrant cultures. See his January 1990 addendum to "Black Boys and Native Sons," 138.

19. Ellison, "Remembering Richard Wright," in *Collected Essays of Ralph Ellison*, 674.

20. Ellison published three extended discussions of Wright's work: "Richard Wright's Blues" (1945); "The World and the Jug" (1963); and "Remembering Richard Wright" (1971). All three pieces have been reprinted in *Collected Essays of Ralph Ellison*.

21. Ellison, "A Very Stern Discipline," 730.

22. Ellison, "The World and the Jug," 161.

23. Ibid., 165.

24. Ellison, who liked to quote Heraclitus's axiom that "geography is fate," had been raised in a segregated neighborhood of Oklahoma City, where slavery had never been established and where a local resident was mythologized for gunning down imperious Texas Rangers (Ellison, "Remembering Richard Wright," 663).

25. Ellison, "A Very Stern Discipline," 730.

26. Ibid., 750. See also "Harlem Is Nowhere," "If the Twain Shall Meet," and "The Charlie Christian Story," in *Collected Essays of Ralph Ellison*, 266–72, 320–27, 567–80. Ellison's celebration of the local communities sometimes feels paradoxical because he seems to have joined two very different political and social logics. For what might be called an ecological interpretation of his position that highlights its classically conservative features and claims, see Jerry Gafio Watts,

Heroism and the Black Intellectual: Ralph Ellison, Politics, and Afro-American Intellectual Life (Chapel Hill: University of North Carolina Press, 1994). For a much more individualist reading that stresses Ellison's contribution to modern liberal-democratic theory, see Jack Turner, *Awakening to Race: Individualism and Social Consciousness in America* (Chicago: University of Chicago Press, 2012), 65–87.

27. Ellison, "Richard Wright's Blues," 133–44; Ellison "The World and the Jug," 169–71; Ellison, "If the Twain Shall Meet," 566–80.

28. Ellison, "If the Twain Shall Meet," 587.

29. Ellison, "The World and the Jug," 162, 167. For Ellison's growing distrust not only of Communists but of Marxism as an intellectual outlook, see Barbara Foley, *Wrestling with the Left: The Making of Ralph Ellison's "Invisible Man"* (Durham, NC: Duke University Press, 2010).

30. Ellison, "The World and the Jug," 163. See also Ellison, "Richard Wright's Blues," 142–43.

31. For a point-by-point review of the charges and rebuttals by each writer, see Watts, *Heroism and the Black Intellectual*, 65–97.

32. For more on Ellison's doubts about ending racism through the liberal state, see Thomas Hill Schaub, *American Fiction in the Cold War* (Madison: University of Wisconsin Press, 1991), 94–99; and Danielle S. Allen, "Invisible Citizens: Political Exclusion and Domination in Arendt and Ellison," in *Nomos XLVI: Political Exclusion and Domination*, ed. Melissa S. Williams and Stephen Macedo (New York: New York University Press, 2005), 29–76. For Ellison's own thoughts about US liberal politics in the 1960s, see "If the Twain Shall Meet."

33. "What America Would Be Like without Blacks," in *Collected Essays of Ralph Ellison*, 582–86; Ellison, "Remembering Richard Wright," 663, 672–77.

34. Ellison, "The World and the Jug," 181–82; Ellison, "What America Would Be," 582–86; Ellison, "Remembering Richard Wright," 676–77.

35. Ellison, "What America Would Be," 586. See also Ellison, "Remembering Richard Wright," 677–78.

36. Ellison, "The World and the Jug," 181.

37. Most of Baldwin's criticisms of Wright's novel appeared in a short anthology, *Notes of a Native Son*, which contained two earlier written essays about *Native Son* ("Everybody's Protest Novel" and "Many Thousands Gone") as well as several autobiographical essays in which Wright's novel provided a thematic backdrop (James Baldwin, *Notes of a Native Son* [Boston: Beacon, 1955]).

38. See Baldwin, "Many Thousands Gone," 33–34; and Baldwin, "Notes of a Native Son," in *Notes of a Native Son*, 92–94.

39. Baldwin, "Notes of a Native Son," 96.

40. Baldwin, "Many Thousands Gone," 38.

41. Baldwin, "Stranger in the Village," in *Notes of a Native Son*, 161; Baldwin, "Many Thousands Gone," 102.

42. Baldwin, "Many Thousands Gone," 25.

43. Stephen H. Marshall, *City on the Hill from Below: The Crisis of Prophetic Black Politics* (Philadelphia: Temple University Press, 2011), 140.

44. This argument is developed most fully in Baldwin, "Everybody's Protest Novel," 13–23.

45. Ibid., 13.

46. On the psychological immaturity of white Americans, see Baldwin, "A Question of Identity," 128–31, 134–37, in *Notes of a Native Son;* and Baldwin, "Stranger in the Village," 166, 171–75.

47. For an exploration of the complexity of this process, see Jack Turner, "Baldwin's Individualism and Critique of Property," in *A Political Companion to James Baldwin*, ed. Susan J. McWilliams (Lexington: University Press of Kentucky, 2017), 301–33.

48. For Baldwin's criticism of rioting as a solution to the long history of strained race relations in the United States, see his essay "Notes of a Native Son," 85–86, 111–13. For Baldwin's warning to whites that some sort of civil war is an imminent possibility, see "Down at the Cross: Letter from a Region in My Mind," in *Fire Next Time* (New York: Random House, 1962), 14–106.

49. For expositions of Baldwin's theory of love as a difficult yet viable political strategy, see Marshall, *City on the Hill*, 128–68; George Shulman, *American Prophecy: Race and Redemption in American Political Culture* (Minneapolis: University of Minnesota Press, 2008), 131–73; Nick Bromell, *The Time Is Always Now: Black Thought and the Transformation of US Democracy* (Oxford: Oxford University Press, 2013), 29–31, 67–78; and Jack Turner, "Baldwin's Individualism and Critique of Property," in *A Political Companion to James Baldwin*, ed. Susan J. McWilliams (Lexington: University Press of Kentucky, 2017), 301–33. For some examples of Baldwin's writings on love and the struggle against racism, see "Notes of a Native Son," 85–114, and "My Dungeon Shook: Letter of My Nephew on the One Hundredth Anniversary of the Emancipation," in *Fire Next Time*, 1–10.

50. Baldwin, "Journey to Atlanta," in *Notes of a Native Son*, 73–84.

51. Baldwin, "My Dungeon Shook," 8.

52. "How 'Bigger' Was Born," in Richard Wright, *Native Son* (New York: HarperCollins, 1998), 434–37.

53. Ibid., 442.

54. Ibid., 441.

55. Ibid., 450–51.

56. Ibid., 443.

57. Ibid., 452.

58. Ibid., 462.
59. Ibid., 451.
60. Ibid., 452.
61. Ibid., 445.
62. Ibid., 446.
63. Ibid., 442.
64. Wright, *Native Son*, 115.
65. Wright, "How 'Bigger' Was Born," 440.
66. Ibid., 447.
67. Ibid., 446.
68. My interpretation of *Native Son* and "How 'Bigger' Was Born" differs in a couple of ways from the interpretations presented by Lewis R. Gordon and Cedric J. Robinson in chapters 2 and 3 of this volume. Robinson, for example, argues that Wright differentiates the reactionary potential of white working classes in the United States from the revolutionary potential of the black urban poor (or lumpenproletariat, to use Robinson's vocabulary), whereas I do not see that distinction in the text. Gordon offers an interesting dialectical account of the relationship among the various types of "Bigger Thomas" that Wright observed in the South and does not discuss Wright's ideas about "white Biggers" or about Chicago as a distinctive cultural milieu.
69. Stuart Hall, *Cultural Studies 1983: A Theoretical History* (Durham, NC: Duke University Press, 2016), 136–206.

5

Richard Wright's Mission

Initiating a Politics of the Human

Marilyn Nissim-Sabat

> Sartre is quite of my opinion regarding the possibility of human action today, that it is up to the individual to do what he can to uphold the concept of what it means to be human. The great danger, I told him, in the world today is the very feeling and conception of what is human might well be lost. He agreed. I feel very close to Sartre and De Beauvoir.
> —Richard Wright, journal entry, September 1947

I do not know the immediate context of this compelling journal entry by Richard Wright. Given that it was written just two years into the post–World War II period, it seems likely that the war loomed large in his mind, as well it might: it was a catastrophe that resulted in hecatombs of dead and maimed, genocidal decimation of the Jewish people, and a devastated continent. However, Wright's concern for "the very feeling and conception of what is human" predated this 1947 journal entry and is, moreover, one of the motifs that pervade his work. It is presaged in the final sentence of Wright's autobiographical epic, *Black Boy*,[1] wherein he declared his motive for becoming a writer: "I would hurl words into the darkness and wait for an echo, and if an echo sounded, no matter how faintly, I would send other words to tell, to march, to fight, to create a sense of the hunger for life that gnaws in us all, to keep alive in our hearts a sense of the inexpressibly human."[2] Just as in 1947, at the age of thirty-nine, Wright told Jean-Paul Sartre of his fear that "the very feeling and conception of what is human might well be lost," so, too, in 1936 (when *Black Boy* ends), at the age of twenty-eight, grappling with the dehumanizing forces beating down on him in catastrophically racist America, he expressed, in semantically equivalent terms, fear of losing "a sense of the inexpressibly human."

What did Wright mean by "a sense of the inexpressibly human" and the "feeling and conception of what is human"? The phrase "a sense of," taken together with Wright's stress on the "feeling" of being human, connotes several aspects of the experience in question: although the human as such is inexpressible, as something we "sense" it is felt, and further, as a feeling it enters consciousness with specificity—it is not an indeterminate feeling but is experienced as one's sense of oneself as human, and therefore not isolated from, but among other human beings. As a determinate feeling, humanness is not an abstraction; rather, it is a conception. It is a determinate meaning that is felt as such and is thus, though inexpressible, distinguishable from other felt meanings.

Wright implies, moreover, that the felt meaning or lived experience of humanness is a condition for the possibility of experiencing self-acceptance: "I had seen many Negroes solve the problem of being black by transferring their hatred of themselves to others with a black skin and fighting them. I would have to be cold to do that, and I was not cold and I could never be."[3] Implicit in Wright's realization that he "could never be" cold or unfeeling is this corollary: though acutely aware of the hatred of others for him, he was not afflicted with self-hatred. Absent self-hatred, Wright recognized that he would never suppress his feelings of empathy for others, for to do so meant suppressing his own humanity.

In this essay, I explore the significance of both the *absence* and *presence* of the feeling and conception of the human. Regarding absence, first-person accounts of the horrors perpetrated in Nazi Germany have played an irreplaceable role in our comprehension and combatting of oppression, as have slave narratives and other descriptions of the horrors of slavery and post–Civil War Jim Crow America, including depictions in great works of literature. One such work is Toni Morrison's *Beloved*,[4] which, like *Native*

Son, depicts both the absence and presence of the feeling and conception of the human.

In a remarkable passage toward the end of *Native Son*,[5] Wright created for his protagonist, Bigger Thomas, who was awaiting execution, an interior monologue that encapsulates the experience of both absence and presence of the feeling of humanness, of what was absent for and from Bigger, and what its presence could have been for him:

> If he reached out with his hands and touched other people . . . and felt other hands connected with other hearts—if he did that, would there be a reply, a shock? Not that he wanted these hearts to turn their warmth to him; he was not wanting that much. But just to know they were there and warm; just that and no more; and it would have been enough, more than enough. And in that touch, response of recognition, there would be union, identity; there would be supporting oneness, a wholeness which had been denied him all his life. Another impulse rose in him, born of desperate need, and his mind clothed it in an image of a strong blinding sun sending hot rays down and he was standing in the midst of a vast crowd of men, white men and black men and all men, and the sun's rays melted away the many differences, the colors, the clothes, and drew what was common and good upward toward the sun.[6]

Herein, the *presence* of the feeling and conception of the human—that is, of relations among human beings that engender that sense of "identity" and "wholeness" that "had been denied" to Bigger "all his life"—will be referred to as *connectedness*, understood as the antithesis of alienation from oneself and others. In light of the two contexts cited, the Nazi Holocaust[7] and the catastrophe of racism in America, the assumption here is that *absence* of connectedness potentiates behavior that evidences absence of empathic capacity in both individuals and groups.

Regarding presence of connectedness, Wright's rhapsodic soliloquizing of Bigger's inner state depicts Bigger's movement toward self-acceptance flowing as day from night into a sun-bathed sense, a presence, a givenness, beyond all differences, of the commonality of humanity. Wright shows that after this vision of connectedness, "of hands connected with hearts," Bigger's last words to Max, "Tell Jan hello,"[8] constituted the first attempt he had ever made to reach out toward a nurturant connectedness with another person. Bigger was able to do this because just then he felt equal to Jan and thus worthy of it. Undoing self-alienation, Wright shows us, is also the undoing of one's alienation from humanity as a whole.

In response to and in defense of the anxious concern for the human expressed by Wright, I will show that there are resources in his work that can provoke a politics directed explicitly toward reversing loss of the feeling and conception of humanness. Indeed, all liberatory work is or should be so directed. *Nevertheless, I think that a new level of clarity about and explicit analysis of the meaning of and political necessity for connectedness is needed.* Put slightly differently, what is needed is a philosophically grounded method for attaining this goal. I have dubbed this method "critical theory of transcendence."

Critical Theory of Transcendence

"Transcendence" is used here in the existential sense of Sartre: of human existence as freedom and as that which always and ever transcends itself through "projects" that impel us toward a future. Moreover, these projects are inseparable from the concrete situations of the acting persons.[9] Sartre understood his philosophical stance to be an instantiation of atheism, and Wright, raised, like Sartre, in a religious family, shared this attitude toward religion and therefore did not see it as a source of justification for moral judgment. For both Wright and Sartre, individuals are nevertheless responsible for their choices and for the outcome of their projects. In *Native Son*, Wright showed that Bigger's path to self-acceptance was also a path to grasping himself, for the first time, as an agent and thus as responsible for his choices.[10] Despite these similarities, however, it is not my intention to attribute to Wright any of Sartre's metaphysical views on, for example, ontological dualism or the notion that existence precedes essence.[11]

My intention is, rather, critically to appropriate transcendence as in itself the *trager*, or bearer, of the feeling and conception of the human. In what follows, I will develop the notion that the effective actuality of transcendence is a function of our connectedness to other human beings. This means that choices made in situations devoid of connectedness are not free. They are not acts of transcendence as the manifestation of human freedom; they are, rather, determined by the psychological consequences of psychosocial forces and conditions that, in damaging the individual's ability to form interpersonal, or, equivalently, intersubjective relations, severely compromise that individual's capacity to act freely, that is, to experience self-transcendence. Although, as freedom, transcendence, the projection of projects, is primordially and prereflectively ineliminable, it is in play, I aver, only to the extent that the subject simultaneously experiences connectedness with other human beings, only if the subject is a *relational* self. This concern with connectedness sets Wright apart from Sartre for, as Lewis R. Gordon, among others, has shown, in Sartre's existential perspective, intersubjectivity is not constituted.[12] A critical theory of transcendence is, I believe, implicit in Wright's work.

In *Native Son,* Wright's great naturalistic novel, Bigger's freedom, his transcendence, is restored to his consciousness when he realizes, as noted above, that connectedness with other human beings is what has been absent from his existence.[13] He also realizes that he is an agent, the author of his own deeds, and responsible for them and for their consequences. This realization inspires in Bigger not resoluteness in the face of death, as Heideggerians might predict, but rather a passionate wish to live: "I don't want to die."[14]

Theorizing Connectedness: Wright and Beauvoir

Vikki Bell is a feminist theorist who has written a fine essay, "Suffering: Thinking Politics with Simone de Beauvoir and Richard Wright," on the interrelation between the liberatory theories of Simone de Beauvoir and Richard Wright.[15] Bell shows that Wright's influence led Beauvoir to a perspective that enabled Beauvoir to transcend the potential of her feminist identity theory to decay into an expression of ressentiment that would then motivate a misguided impulse to politics.[16] Bell concludes that human *connectedness* (her term) is the antidote to such negative theoretical and actional potentialities, and can motivate the initiation of political action. In what follows, I will outline Bell's theoretical program, focusing on her analysis of the influence of Wright on Beauvoir. In the next section, I will critique what I see, and I believe Wright would have seen, to be crucial limitations of Bell's proposal, in contrast with Wright's, regarding the initiation of a liberatory politics.

Bell establishes two interpretive positions regarding Wright's influence on Beauvoir that correlate with two stances toward identity politics that she finds in *The Second Sex*. Bell's first interpretive position focuses on the way in which Bigger Thomas is present in *The Second Sex*.[17] She writes: "One might suggest that Beauvoir's purpose is to enhance her argument about sexual discrimination through the prism of the racial, that it is a form of rhetoric that is an argument by association. . . . Her rhetorical position moreover, . . . is one that does indeed proceed to a feminist politics that could be characterized by ressentiment."[18] Bell's first interpretive position, then, correlates with Beauvoir's first stance in *The Second Sex*: that aspects of Beauvoir's treatment of sex in relation to race leave Beauvoir open to a politics of ressentiment. Earlier, Bell pointed out that feminism has been attacked as being emotionally fueled by ressentiment, fueled by, that is, an oppressed group's hatred of the oppressor out of envy, out of desire for the benefits that the oppressor has over and against the oppressed.[19] Bell shows that identity politics can lead to a charge of ressentiment against feminism, a charge that implies that attaining social justice is not the primary motivator for feminist politics. The problem for Beauvoir's perspective is that the task she set for herself in *The Second Sex* was an instance of identity politics: to lay bare the actuality of gendered suffering, to show that women's oppression results in women's unique mode of suffering, suffering in their gender. Bell believes that this sense of unique oppression based on women's identity as women can easily fall into an expression of ressentiment, a claim that what women want is not equality and justice, but the prerogatives that men have.

Bell points out that Beauvoir's mode of incorporation of Bigger Thomas into *The Second Sex* can be read in this way in that Bigger, too, can be seen as a figure of ressentiment who hates whites because he wants, not "justice," but what they have. Beauvoir maintained further that the plight of women is worse than that of blacks in that sexist society demands not only that women subordinate themselves to males, but that they like it, that they embrace their condition of playacting.[20] Bell adds that "it seems as if de Beauvoir's use of the figure of Bigger Thomas . . . would characterize her feminist political aspiration as one in which and by which women realize their situation and their duplicity *in order to become* revolutionary in the same manner as the 'American Negro.'"[21] Bell implies here that this would be a fruitless way to initiate a liberatory politics.

In summary, Bell sees that, in her first stance, Beauvoir does not theorize any connectedness between the two oppressed groups, women and blacks. Beauvoir, Bell maintains, uses Wright to bolster a stance that borders on ressentiment. Bell avers, however, that this usage was prior to Beauvoir integrating into her thinking the full impact of Wright's influence on her. Thus, in her second interpretive position, correlative to what she sees as Beauvoir's second stance, Bell holds that within *The Second Sex* itself, under the influence of Wright, Beauvoir undergoes a transition to a stance much less amenable to ressentiment.

Bell's second interpretive position, correlated with Beauvoir's second stance in *The Second Sex*, emerges in Bell's last section, "Beyond Ressentiment: Modes of Connectivity." There, Bell discusses Wright's career and influences on him. After an extended discussion in which she shows that Wright did not essentialize black suffering, Bell goes on to provide quotations from *The Second Sex* that do indicate that, within the book itself, Beauvoir pivoted away from a conception of women's suffering that tended toward a ressentiment politics, her first stance, and toward a view, her second stance, that challenged the boundaries of sex and race as adequate to either understanding or struggling against oppression. In her initial remarks, Bell writes that Beauvoir's second line of argument is one that

> posits de Beauvoir's use of racialised figures as a blurring of the boundaries of feminism, a blurring which gives up the spirit of ressentiment precisely because the connection is made. . . . [I]n the moments in which suffering is posited as a shared condition, or that sympathy is allowed to pass across the lines of identity, there is less spirit of ressentiment and more the shared hunger that is weary, not of man . . . but of the categories that so bind us to declaring absolute specificities to our positionalities. . . . I want to explore the sense of connectivity that de Beauvoir suggests as a way to think of different modes of resisting imposed subjectivities and hence different modes of politics.[22]

Bell claims that Beauvoir, through the influence of Wright, finally arrives at this stance of "blurred boundaries" and a "sense of connectivity." Regarding Wright's influence on Beauvoir, Bell cites the passage in "How 'Bigger' Was Born" in which Wright expresses his own hard-won insight into the blurring of the boundaries of identity: "I made the discovery that Bigger Thomas was not black all the time; he was white too, and there were literally millions of him, everywhere."[23]

Bell goes on to show that in *The Second Sex* Beauvoir makes a series of comparisons between race and sex that transcend any presumed uniqueness of either identity category, and that she does so through arguments that closely echo Wright's formulations. Bell had previously pointed out that Beauvoir "seems to hold that women regard the order of things as fixed, and lack of physical power combines with this to produce her resignation to docility."[24] However, echoing Wright, Beauvoir also wrote in *The Second Sex* that "it is quite impossible for the Negro in the south to use violence against the whites; this rule is the key to the mysterious 'black soul'; the way the Negro feels in the white world, the behavior by which he adjusts himself to it, the compensations he seeks, his whole way of feeling and acting are to be explained on the basis of the passivity to which he is condemned."[25] Throughout *The Second Sex,* Beauvoir insisted that man wishes to condemn woman to passivity. In these passages, Bell shows that Beauvoir realized that black suffering is not different from the suffering of women. For Bell, this realization is essential to the project of initiating a liberatory politics.

Critique of Bell

Bell's critique of identity politics and its relation to ressentiment is an important contribution to the quest for a liberatory politics; so, too, is her recognition that overcoming the potential of ressentiment to derail the struggle requires experiencing connectivity across identity groups, thus rendering borders porous and establishing empathetic connections with people of other groups. However, in taking her argument further by expressing what *this sort of connectivity* means to her, Bell opens herself to a critique that I believe calls into question the relevance of important aspects of her philosophical stance.[26] Here is Bell's explanation of connectivity:

> The notion of connectivity does not refer to a mundane sense of connections between people, but it is about the modes, the different ways—not just in terms of experiencing suffering, powerlessness or economic hardship, but also those possible through music, or through sex[27]—that people's lives extend beyond the clarity often imposed by sociological models of power and subjectivity. Drawing on other routes of intertextuality therefore enables one to see models of politics that refuse the

easy presentation of a bounded group of the oppressed who, according to some very stark and reified division, demand to have the attributes and influences of the oppressor, as if their hope were to be remade in the very image of the oppressor.[28]

Neither here nor anywhere else does Bell elaborate on what *"a mundane sense of connections"* means to her, or in what sense she is using the term "mundane." Absent any explanation, I take her, provisionally, to hold that mundane connections mean connections that are ubiquitous in everyday life—the ordinary or usual connectivity between parents and children, friends, partners, students, and so on. Bell implies that this *mundane* mode of connectivity, or "sense of connections," insofar as it is mundane, cannot foster the cross-group connectivity that, as we have seen, is for Bell necessary to initiate a liberatory politics. Bell is correct, I think, but for a reason that she nowhere mentions, and that I will further discuss below: it is quite evident that mundane connectivity is entirely compatible with both individual and institutional racism, sexism, homophobia, and virtually all forms of oppression, of modes of erecting borders that radically separate groups and thereby stifle liberatory action. However, as I will discuss, this does not exhaust the limitations of mundane connectivity.

Bell believes, then, that the connectivity that Beauvoir found through her friendship with Wright and through her reading of his work ultimately fostered Beauvoir's realization that no oppressed group can claim to suffer uniquely. This realization, Bell believes, can be fostered by the kinds of connectivity that are "creative and open rather than fixed images that stem from models of power which attempt to reduce those connections."[29] However, Bell does not elaborate on how we are to understand the creativity and openness of this nonmundane connectivity.

It is important to note that the epigraph of this essay, in which Wright speaks of the fear that the "very feeling and conception of what is human might well be lost," is quoted by Bell in order to show that Wright's conversations with Sartre and Beauvoir impacted him greatly.[30] However, at no point in her essay does she allude to Wright's humanism, his belief that there is a "conception of what is human," or, in Bigger's fantasy, a vision of "what is common and good." Indeed, Bell is at pains to assert that she subscribes to no such concept. While both embedded in and critical of the work of poststructuralist and postmodern thinkers, Bell informs her readers that her notion of "community" or "being together with" is one that "retreats from the idea of common substance or identity that is constituted similarly for each and every existence that it purportedly 'represents,'" an approach also explored in Lori J. Marso's contribution to this volume.[31] This, it seems to me, rules out that which Wright held to be necessary to initiate liberatory action: our identity as human beings, as humanity. (Isn't this the reason why he feared its loss?) Furthermore, the notions and experiences of "creativity and openness" are not, and cannot be, I aver, limited in their relevance or context to experiences of cross-group connectivity. These notions and experiences are also relevant, as Wright shows in his depiction of Bigger, to our self-experience, our sense of self. Insofar as "self" or "subject" is an identity or the precondition for an identity, "openness and creativity" are relevant to our identities. It was just when Bigger experienced himself as a human being that he came into the felt experience of human freedom, into his identity as a free person.

The limitation of Bell's perspective is stated in the first sentence of her explication of connectivity: "The notion of connectivity does not refer to a mundane sense of connections between people." As noted above, I take it that Bell is not asserting that in our day-to-day lives human beings do not experience connectivity at all; I take her to mean, rather, that the kind of connectivity, "open and creative," that can break down barriers between identity groups—*this mode of connectivity* is not experienced in our mundane or everyday lives. Of course, our mundane lives are filled with connections to others and to our own projects or impulses to transcendence. So, it seems that, while Bell does, of course, acknowledge connectivity in our mundane or day-to-day lives, she apparently believes that the "creative and open" mode of connectivity that enables boundary crossing is not the type of connectivity that we mundanely experience.

This may indeed be the case for large numbers of people. However, the problem is this: Bell seems to locate actual and possible experiences of creative and open connectivity exclusively in the domain of cross-group interactions and relationships. If asked, Bell might aver that no, this mode of connectivity can occur in any human relationships. But doesn't the project of human liberation, if it is to be our project, our self-transcendence, require that we demand conditions for the possibility of openness and creativity in all of our relationships, in all of our experiences of connectivity, including intragroup relationships? Is this not what Wright intended when he spoke of "the feeling and conception of the human" that we are in danger of losing altogether?

As noted above, Bell does not mention or allude to Wright's humanism, which is certainly not incompatible with creativity and openness in relationships, despite that, or, rather, precisely because it posits a common humanity, a conception of humanness that as such is universal in that it is applicable to all persons. Moreover, as his autobiographical book *Black Boy* shows, Wright's conception of the human is inseparable from personal growth and creative and open self-transcendence.

It seems that Bell holds that mundane modes of connectivity between people are different from, even lesser than, connections that can transcend identity group boundaries and foster cross-group empathy and community. My point is that *there is no indication in her essay that Bell's stance is or implies a critique of mundane connectivity*. Yet, it seems to me that just such a critique is what is needed, and, what, for the sake of the clarity and meaningfulness of her work, is incumbent on Bell to provide. Absent indication of a critique of mundanity, Bell implies that such connections are fine as such, and that they reflect the nature and possibilities of mundanity. Bell, herself an academic sociologist, differentiates between mundane connections and those types of connectedness, "like music or sex," that enable "people's lives" to "extend beyond the modes of clarity often imposed by sociological models of power and subjectivity." Should we not seek to extend clarity regarding mundanity as such that is also beyond "sociological models of power and subjectivity," that is, beyond ideological distortion? That is to say, with respect to both feminism and antiracism and their actual or possible interrelation, Bell's formulations lack a critique of mundanity like, for example, that encapsulated in second wave feminism's slogan, "the personal is political." That is to say, all human relationships are degraded in an environment which is antagonistic to our humanity, an environment that eschews humanism, "the feeling and conception of the human."

In fact, mundane connections do, of course, include music and sex, yet these experiences can and do coexist with sexism and racism. Given this mundane coexistence of connectedness and sexism and racism, this question seems pertinent: in suggesting that in certain circumstances music and sex are nonmundane experiences that can open up borders between groups identified as gendered or racialized, isn't Bell assuming her conclusion? Isn't she in effect asserting a tautology: that, since not all experiences of music and sex enable border crossing, those that do are experiences of music and sex that enable border crossing? This tautological reasoning is transcended if we suggest what was likely: that the salutary impact of Wright on Beauvoir had much to do with the wholeness of Wright's personality, and perhaps even with his deep humanism, rather than having been simply a consequence of their sharing musical and other experiences. In other words, open and creative connections between people presuppose our common humanity as a condition for their possibility, whether or not people acknowledge this to be the case.[32] My point is that the everydayness and the mundanity of most forms and experiences of connection between people do not, by virtue of their ubiquity, rule out the possibility that they too can be experiences that affirm our humanity and that can lead to blurring the boundaries of identity groups. Grasping this does, however, lead us to think about the nature of oppression.

Is oppression—if we mean by this oppression of one group by another, for example, whites oppressing blacks, and all of its evils and horrors—categorically different *as suffering* from the horrors of intragroup oppression, cruelty, barbarism? If I interpret the passionate humanism (which Lewis R. Gordon also emphasizes in his chapter in this volume) of Wright correctly, he would understand all oppression, including those forms of it that he experienced and suffered directly himself (as recounted throughout *Black Boy*)—of children by parents, of women by men, of blacks by whites—as manifestations of the "problem of human unity that was more important than bread, more important than physical living itself." He felt and believed that "without a common bond uniting men, without a continuous current of shared thought and feeling circulating through the social system, like blood coursing through the body, there could be no living worthy of being called human."[33] Shortly after writing this and in the context of a challenge to his early ambition to become a writer, Wright posed the following question: "What was the danger of showing the kinship between the sufferings of the Negro and the sufferings of other people?"[34] Though it is the very same question that Bell poses to Beauvoir regarding women and African Americans, it must be understood in a context that Bell rejects—that of our common humanity. It is clear from the above that, for Wright, we need to create societies in which that common humanity is allowed to pervade our mundane existence. Creativity and joy can blossom only wherever and to the extent that they grow from the soil of our common bond, whether it is actual or only envisioned in the anguished fantasy of the oppressed. This, too, has been said in *Native Son* and *Black Boy*. This critique of mundanity, absent in Bell, is, and perhaps has always been, a powerful catalyst for political, even revolutionary, action.

In the passage quoted above in which Bell identified the types of experiences with the power to institute connectivity across boundaries, she included among these "experiencing suffering, powerlessness, or economic hardship." Did Bell mean to say here that a cross-group connectivity experience can arise through recognizing shared experiences of oppression (as Beauvoir did vis-à-vis race and gender), or through empathizing with, or even experiencing these forms of suffering, or both? Whether either or both, it appears that she excludes these experiences from the domain of the mundane sense of connection. Does Bell then, with this exclusion of the mundane, mean to say that by mundane forms of connection she means exclusively connections between individuals absent any group identity factor? But isn't the possibility of such connections just what "the personal is political" aimed to negate?

What Bell, with no explicit critique of mundanity, does *not* point out is that for people who, like Bigger's family, are overwhelmed by "experiencing suffering, powerlessness" and "economic hardship," these conditions *characterized* their mundanity. For them, mundane existence made any form of connectivity, mundane or otherwise, difficult or impossible, as depicted in the life and death of Bigger Thomas. My point here is that Bell fails to indicate awareness that there are those whose mundane existence prohibits any mode of connectivity, intra- or cross-group, or even those modes of connectivity that are compatible with cross-group divisiveness.

One might suggest that Bell was referring to experiences among people whose mundane, or everyday, lives, unlike Bigger's, do allow for "mundane forms of connectivity"—she simply wanted to say that those mundane forms of connectivity are not the types that can establish cross-group bonds. On the other hand, those mundane forms of connectivity are such that they are experienced as quite compatible, within the same consciousness, with racism, xenophobia, and many other forms of antihuman prejudice. They constitutively lack the feeling of common humanity that would foster not only more joyous mundane connectivity but also cross-border connectivity. Thus, while mundane forms of connection at the present time may not enable cross-group connectivity, on the other hand, they are not acceptable for any liberatory consciousness in that they are quite compatible with beliefs that powerfully militate against such bonds. Moreover, since mundane forms of connectivity are experienced in intragroup contexts, they are also, it seems, compatible with, for example, the unspeakable violence and oppression that is meted out to children and women intraculturally in many locales around the world.

Thus, I ask, are mundane connections between people so fulfilling that people's inhumanity to one another is on the way to being a thing of the past? It seems to me that attending to the quality of mundane connections between people is also a means—an essential means—of developing a politics of the human that seeks to end all oppression everywhere and is a project that decisively transcends ressentiment in *any* domain of human existence. Put another way, in failing to offer a critique of mundanity, Bell constricts the range of her conclusions to narrow concerns that are of limited value because they are structured through vital exclusions. She wishes to motivate a liberatory politics freed from the specter of ressentiment, but she fails to see or acknowledge that in her manner of doing so she presupposes that which she is loath to admit: the unity of humanity. But, even more, this exclusion would, it seems, be anathema to Wright's sense of his relationship to Beauvoir. In this sense, despite quotations, allusions to, and discussions of his work, *Wright's distinctive voice is elided in Bell's essay*.

However, the full foundation for a critique of mundanity has not yet come into view. To see this, we return to Bigger's vision of our common humanity: "Another impulse rose in him, born of desperate need, and his mind clothed it in an image of a strong blinding sun sending hot rays down and he was standing in the midst of a vast crowd of men, white men and black men and all men, and the sun's rays melted away the many differences, the colors, the clothes, and drew what was common and good upward toward the sun."

As Wright says, this vision was born in Bigger "out of desperate need." Need for what? Need to know: "He would not mind dying now if he could only find out what this meant, what he was in relation to all the others who lived, and the earth upon which he stood."[35] In his desperate need to know this, his relation to all others and to the earth, Bigger's mind conjures up a fantasy of universal harmony among people, transcending all differences. This is a fantasy, a dream of an ultimate satisfaction of some sort, a psychic undoing of his pain, suffering, alienation, and isolation. But is Bigger's vision only a fantasy, a desperate effort to escape from a terrible reality? Recall that Wright had a deep and abiding interest in "upholding the concept of what it is to be human." Bigger's fantasy is, too, an implicit recognition that upholding the concept of the human demands of us that we constitute a future in which we become more than we have been, and do so by creating societies that do not replicate the conditions that crushed Bigger Thomas but rather enable us to experience our common humanity in a way that would transform our everyday lives.

This is the critique of mundanity lacking in Bell's formulations. Stated explicitly, the forms of connectivity that Bell cites as occurring outside of mundane life should, in fact, characterize mundane life. Or, put another way, our expectations for fulfillment of our need for connectivity in our everyday lives are set too low; we are too often "satisfied" with far too little, and thus tolerate degrees of alienation that are dehumanizing and that desensitize us to the suffering of others. I believe that in his writings Wright hoped to inspire this abiding insight in us, and he believed that this insight would motivate us to political engagement. This is the basis on which I propose that what is needed today is a critical theory of transcendence as such: what counts is the qualitative feel of the lived experience of our being as transcendence, and the quality of that lived experience is profoundly affected by the quality of all of our connectedness, bar none, to ourselves and others. This then would constitute what I have referred to as Richard Wright's mission: to motivate a politics of the human.

Conclusion: Politics and Connectivity

Bell's exclusion of mundane connectivity from the domain of experiences that can motivate a liberatory politics is difficult to understand. Our mundane life comprises the greatest portion of our lives as a whole. Is it not the case that oppression affects the oppressed in the entirety of their existence and experiences, as depicted, for example, by Frantz Fanon in his writings about French colonialism in Algeria? It seems that in adopting this stance regarding mundane life Bell is involved in an act of elision. The elision is motivated, I suggest, by hesitance to reflect on the meaning of common humanity, of that sense of the "inexpressibly human" that so captured the imagination of Richard Wright. For, this notion of a common humanity raises the question of the *nature of commonality* itself: What is it? How can it be common to all persons? This of course trembles in the doorway of philosophical questioning of the nature of universals without presupposing their nonexistence. As noted above, Bell informs her readers that her notion of connectedness "retreats from the idea of common substance or identity that is constituted similarly for each and every existence that it purportedly 'represents.'"[36] This disclaimer is quite analogous to those of postmodern thinkers who generally do not only deny the existence of universals but, even more, claim that universals are the source of many of the evils extant in the world, for they are construed as absolutes and provide, it is claimed, a psychic rationale for absolutism of all kinds, including totalitarianism. It seems, however, that Bell wished to avoid confronting this problematic and so eschewed from her intellectual program consideration of the conditions for the possibility of human relationality, for our capacity for connectedness. For, openness to the possibility of a common humanity, including one manifested in human creativity and freedom, suggests reconsideration of the rejected notion of the universally human.

When Wright wrote of the "inexpressibly human" and of the "feeling and conception" of the human, did he have in mind a concept that was for him a universal in the sense of something that is prior to all experience and history, that in that sense inheres in all humans? Since Wright was deeply attuned to the relational dimension of human existence and to the profound ways in which we are formed and impacted by our social and historical environment, it is unlikely that he would entertain a concept of a universal that stands outside of the human world. A clue to his meaning can be found in his depiction of Bigger Thomas. When Bigger gained access to his agency and declared that he wanted to live, he gained access as well to at least a sense of his own creative possibilities. This sense of human free creativity comes very close, it seems to me, to our sense of human commonality, of the "inexpressibly human" of which Wright spoke and wrote.

In this respect, Wright had a great deal in common with Frantz Fanon. In his recent book *What Fanon Said*, engaging the problematic of human universality, Lewis Gordon expressed the meaning of Fanonian universality in terms that express equally well the meaning of human commonality for Wright.[37] In reference to Fanon's challenge to us, in the last lines of *The Damned of the Earth*, "to try to inaugurate a new humanity," Gordon writes: "Theorists taking up this challenge today are sometimes mistakenly placed under the rubric of 'theory from the Global South.' Fanon would find this unacceptable, since his argument is not one of reciprocal relativism. Such theorists are reaching for more *universalizing practices*. Although not *the* universal, because of the fundamental incompleteness at the heart of being human, the paradox of reaching beyond particularity is the simultaneous humility of understanding the expanse of possibility of reality and human potential."[38] Certainly, Wright was "reaching for more universalizing practices" that enable "the expanse and possibility of reality and human potential" to be liberated into free expressivity and that, Fanon believed, would be directed toward the creation of "a new humanity." Such practices would have to be relatable to all particulars without at the same time compromising their uniqueness. What concretely would such practices look like, and what are the conditions for their possibility? In view of the ideas developed here, they would be practices that generate or constitute in and for us our "very feeling and conception of what is human"; they would be practices of connectivity, practices that actualize the humanness that, Wright's creations cry out, is our birthright.

Notes

1. Richard Wright, *Black Boy* (1945), in *Richard Wright: Later Works* (New York: Library of America, 1991), 1–365.

2. Ibid., 365.

3. Ibid., 243.

4. Toni Morrison, *Beloved* (New York: Plume, 1988).

5. Richard Wright, *Native Son*, introduction by Arnold Rampersad (New York: Harper Perennial, 1998).

6. Ibid., 362.

7. The term *Shoah* is often used to refer to the specifically Jewish holocaust. "Holocaust" with the capitalized *H*, as in Holocaust Museum, is generally considered to be an acceptable alternative.

8. Wright, *Native Son*, 460.

9. Jean-Paul Sartre, *Being and Nothingness* (New York: Washington Square, 1968), 619–706.

10. For an interesting discussion of agency in *Native Son*, see Abdul R. JanMohamed, *The Death-Bound Subject: Richard Wright's Archeology of Death* (Durham, NC: Duke University Press, 2005), 126–28.

11. In this essay, I do not engage the issue of Wright's relation to existentialism. Already in 1949, Wright declared that he was not an existentialist (see M. Fabre,

The World of Richard Wright [Jackson: University of Mississippi Press, 1985], 137). Although he positions himself as a postmodern thinker, Jeffrey Atteberry, in his "Entering the Politics of the Outside: Richard Wright's Critique of Marxism and Existentialism," *MFS Modern Fiction Studies* 51, no. 4 (Winter 2005): 873–95, shows that Wright's *The Outsider* is actually a very trenchant critique of Heidegger's fundamental ontology. (Regrettably, Atteberry seems to equate Marxism with Stalinism.)

12. Lewis R. Gordon, "Sociality and Community in Black: A Phenomenological Essay," in *The Quest for Community and Identity: Critical Essays in Africana Social Philosophy*, ed. Robert E. Birt (Lanham, MD: Rowman, 2012), 110.

13. The determinative power of oppressive psychological and psychosocial forces had already been expressed by Theodor Dreiser and other writers who created American literary naturalism. Before he left the South, Wright had already discovered his great affinity for this style of writing and way of understanding human existence. It is important to note, however, that American literary naturalism was not as categorically pessimistic as was, for example, the naturalism of Émile Zola. As Donald Pizer, in *Realism and Naturalism in Nineteenth-Century American Literature* (Carbondale: Southern Illinois University, 1984), points out:

> The naturalist often describes his characters as though they are conditioned and controlled by environment, heredity, instinct, or chance. But he also suggests a compensating humanistic value in his characters or their fates which affirms the significance of the individual and of his life. The tension here is that between the naturalist's desire to represent in fiction the new, discomfiting truths which he has found in the ideas and life of his late nineteenth-century world, and also his desire to find some meaning in experience which reasserts the validity of the human enterprise. (10–11)

14. Wright, *Native Son*, 363.

15. Chapter 3 in Vikki Bell, *Feminist Imagination: Genealogies in Feminist Theory* (London: Sage, 1999), 40–61.

16. Though Bell prefers "de Beauvoir," I use the shortened version "Beauvoir."

17. Simone de Beauvoir, *The Second Sex* (1949; London: Everyman, 1993).

18. Bell, *Feminist Imagination*, 47.

19. Bell provides a citation to a text in which this charge is made against feminism (ibid., 40); however, she also avers that this charge is always a potential subtext in critiques of feminism, whether by supporters or detractors.

20. Beauvoir, *The Second Sex*, 313, qtd. in Bell, *Feminist Imagination*, 49.

21. Ibid., 51.

22. Ibid., 58.

23. Richard Wright, "Introduction: How 'Bigger' Was Born" in Richard Wright, *Native Son* (Harmondsworth: Penguin, 1987), qtd. in Bell, *Feminist Imagination*, 55.

24. Bell, *Feminist Imagination*, 58.

25. Beauvoir, *The Second Sex*, 348, qtd. in Bell, *Feminist Imagination*, 58.

26. Bell describes her philosophical stance as being "beyond both modernism and postmodernism" but as embracing a version of Foucault's genealogical method.

27. In singling out sex as an expression of that shared humanity, Bell is alluding to her earlier discussion of a Wright short story that involves a sexual relation between a black woman and a white man (Bell, *Feminist Imagination*, 61).

28. Ibid.

29. Ibid.

30. Ibid., 43.

31. Ibid., 149.

32. My argument here is analogous to the argument made by Lewis Gordon showing that Sartre, in denying intersubjectivity, actually presupposed it (see Lewis Gordon, *Existentia Africana: Understanding Africana Existential Thought* [New York: Routledge 2000], 72–80; see also Wright, *Native Son*, 363).

33. Wright, *Black Boy*, 302.

34. Ibid., 319.

35. Wright, *Native Son*, 363.

36. Bell, *Feminist Imagination*, 149.

37. Lewis R. Gordon, *What Fanon Said: A Philosophical Introduction to His Life and Thought* (New York: Fordham University Press, 2013).

38. Ibid., 129–30.

PART 2

Sexuality and Gender

Richard Wright and Black Women

Imagining the Feminine in The Outsider

Floyd W. Hayes III

Richard Wright is a towering figure in twentieth-century Africana literary, philosophical, and political thought. His attempts to extirpate the root motives that underlie Western civilization's violent antiblack racism and black people's struggle for meaning and liberation influenced subsequent generations of activists, writers, literary critics, philosophers, psychologists, sociologists, historians, and political scientists. Fearlessly, he exposed white people's "perpetual war against the human dignity of Black people—a war of which most white people had kept themselves blithely unaware."[1]

Responding to the oppressive character of Western and Anglo-American civilization, Wright created riveting images of black resentment, anger, outrage, nihilism, and violence. Prior to Wright, black writers constructed images of heroic blacks, mainly males, who were either polite or defensive in the face of white violence and terror. Wright boldly invented working-class and poor black characters who were angry and resentful about antiblack racism and capitalist exploitation, and who were willing to use violence to change those conditions.

Using a revisionist Marxist philosophy of history (that is explored in Cedric J. Robinson's chapter in this volume), Wright issued a blistering indictment of the West and the United States. He argued—for example, in his formidable novel of ideas, *The Outsider*, originally published in 1953—that it was imperialism, colonialism, and racism that set in motion the existential rebellion of non-European people against their white oppressors.[2]

But how did Wright construct the black feminine in his fiction? What did Wright imagine to be the role of black women in the struggle for black liberation? In general, he did not see black women as comrades. A notable exception is the figure of Aunt Sue in the short story "Bright and Morning Star." Confronting the Jim Crow South, Aunt Sue, a religiously devout black woman and mother, is transformed into a political radical who is willing to sacrifice her own life for her son and the radical political organization to which he belongs. Aside from this story, Wright marginalizes black women in his radical attacks on American racism and capitalism.[3]

Still, immediately after completing *Native Son*, Wright wrote that the societal position of black women required serious examination: "The writing of *Native Son* was to me an exciting, enthralling, and even romantic experience. With what I've learned in writing of this book . . . , I am launching out upon another novel, this time about the status of women in modern American society."[4] Unfortunately, that novel never was completed. Nonetheless, it is significant that Wright was interested in the question of the status of women, and it is worth considering how he might have approached the topic.

Some Conceptions of Womanist and Black Feminist Criticism

For decades, black female scholars, critics, and theorists have expressed consternation about the implicitly exclusionary practices of white feminists, who ignore writings by black and other nonwhite feminists. Deborah McDowell also urges black female scholars to analyze the work of black male writers from a black feminist perspective.[5] Black male scholars, meanwhile, have been less attentive to their sisters' concerns; those few black male scholars who have focused on black women's literature have not addressed the question of how black male authors depict black women.[6] Insightful *black male critics* are needed who employ black womanist or feminist perspectives in order to interrogate how black male writers construct images of the black feminine.

Building on the ideas of Alice Walker and Winston Napier about a distinction between womanism and feminism, this chapter will use the term "feminist" to punctuate antagonisms between women and men within a patriarchal system and will use "womanist" to refer to collective struggles by both black women *and* black men to overturn patriarchy and stereotypical, negative images of black women. bell hooks, for example, calls on black men to struggle alongside black women against patriarchy in the overall battle against racist oppression, economic exploitation, and male domination.[7]

Of course, black men, caught within the ideological clutches and gender privileges of a patriarchal society, often find themselves imitating or reenacting white male patriarchy. As Patricia Hill Collins notes, the institution of "masculine hegemony" is an integral dimension of the complex structures of racist domination and class privilege in Anglo-America and Western civilization.[8] Wright, like many black male thinkers, writers, and activists, was a victim of modern Western notions of patriarchy. Although black women have played major roles in the struggle for black liberation, Wright primarily employs female characters as props in order to illuminate the male protagonist's social and existential situation, rather than as actors in their own right.[9]

Richard Wright's Images of the Black Feminine

Why did Wright marginalize images of black women's active engagement in the centuries-long battle for collective black survival and development?

Part of the answer lies in history. The trauma of living in the Jim Crow US South both affected and infected every aspect of black people's lives—from the structures of domination to struggles for liberation.[10] Wright's family and his childhood experiences did not escape the atrocities of white supremacist patriarchy, segregation, and economic impoverishment. In his autobiography, *Black Boy,* Wright describes how racist and economic atrocities dehumanize and emasculate black men by rendering them unable to support their families or help rear their children. Significantly, he portrays his own family's dynamics as dominated by black women—his mother, grandmother, aunts, and other women—who are violent, fanatically religious, and anti-intellectual. In Wright's mind, black womanhood symbolized a situation of abjection: deep hunger, religious superstition, spiritual impotence, and manipulation. Because of Jim Crow apartheid, the black woman had become the domineering figure in the black family, in charge of young boys' stunted psychological, social, and spiritual development.[11]

Of course, Wright was well aware that black people were powerless in the face of white male domination, sadism, rape, lynching, and violence in the public sphere. As subjects of the dehumanizing system of quotidian white force and racism, blacks had no recourse to the justice system because, Wright wrote in *12 Million Black Voices*, "the law is white."[12] Within this white male–dominated world, Judith Butler shows, male perceptions, thinking, and actions tend to reflect the structure and dynamics of gender hierarchy in which men generally marginalize women's issues, consciousness, and concerns. Women's experiences and understandings scarcely matter in their own right because women have become the objects of male consciousness and desire.[13] As Simone de Beauvoir (whose relationship with Wright is explored in the chapters by Marilyn Nissim-Sabat and Lori J. Marso in this volume) asserts, the patriarchal regime constructs women as the "opposite sex," or the inferior "second sex," and as possessing no histories, agendas, or communities of their own.[14] Because women are silenced, the material conditions of their life become natural and normal. As political scientist Kathy Ferguson argues, "men and masculinity are the unnamed norm, and gender is silenced as an analytical category."[15]

Wright was a captive of this male-dominated system of being, thinking, and writing, which overshadowed his fictional and nonfictional work and exemplified a black male consciousness. Even when he constructed images of black females, they were presented primarily from the perspective of a male-ordered world. Even so, one is reluctant to call Wright a misogynist.[16] For all of his insight, he was a victim of the vocabulary that patriarchy in his era made available—one that did not empower him to think of gender as it is theorized today.[17] Significantly, the complex issue of gender still is being debated.

Examining Wright's portrayal of black women, some black female critics have argued that he was a misogynist. In "Papa Dick and Sister-Woman: Reflections on Women in the Fiction of Richard Wright," Sherley Anne Williams argued that Wright "fathered a bastard line, racist misogyny—the denigration of black women as justification for glorifying the symbolic white woman—and male narcissism—the assumption that racism is a crime against the black man's sexual expression rather than an economic, political, and psychological crime against black people—that was to flower in the fiction of black writers in the late sixties and early seventies."[18] Margaret Walker likewise wrote: "For Wright, a woman was an enemy, who failed to give him love and happiness by frustrating him in his search for meaning and success."[19] In another instance: "One feels that he hates black women; one senses early in his writing an unconscious hatred of black women."[20]

Again, for white feminism, women are oppressed by men in the system of societal patriarchy; therefore, men are the enemy. For black womanists, political, racist, and economic atrocities in the white male system of societal patriarchy target both black women and men. Hence, many black womanists invite black men to become comrades in the struggle to overturn what black feminist critic bell hooks terms "white supremacist capitalist patriarchy."[21]

Several male critics have examined Wright's discourse on sexual/racial politics and have concluded that his ordering of the world reflects male characters' experiences and understandings, and he then problematizes that vision by fitting women into that world. Generally absent is the use of feminist criticism by black males to interrogate black male writing. Aside from the literary critic Michael Awkward, black male critics have chosen not to build upon the arguments of feminist critics, black or white.[22]

Images of Women in *The Outsider*

The Outsider, a powerful and radical philosophical novel, illustrates how Wright was blinded by the patriarchal white-male language of his time and by his traumatic experiences as a child. Even though Wright's mother, grandmother, and aunts physically protected him, they also overwhelmed him and caused a great amount of pain, anguish, and anger.[23]

The Outsider encourages readers to think about the meaning of outsider consciousness—that is, what it means for a black man to experience severe alienation from the social order into which he was born. The novel is a protest against America's culture of pretense—no simple undertaking given the nation's multiple self-deceptions. Wright's protagonist, Cross Damon, asks himself: "Were there not somewhere in this world rebels with whom he could feel at home, men who were outsiders not because they had been born black and poor, but because they had thought their way through the many veils of illusion?"[24] Cross "sensed how Negroes had been made to live in but not of the land of their birth, how the injunctions of an alien Christianity and the strictures of white laws had evoked in them the very longings and desires that that religion and law had been designed to stifle."[25]

The Outsider (also discussed in Paul Gilroy's and Lewis R. Gordon's chapters in this volume) is usually read as a philosophical novel that examines a black man's effort to find meaning in his life and to become free of the concrete reality of racism in a world in which God is absent from the human condition. Believing in nothing and living in a godless world, Wright's working-class protagonist breaks the laws of civil society. Cross is a nihilist-rebel who tries to create his own meaning and rules by which he will live. Perhaps in god-like fashion, he tries to live beyond the ideological binaries of good and evil.[26]

The struggle for black liberation, however, cannot be an individual vocation. Liberation is a social phenomenon, which Wright affirms in his larger body of work and which is subtly shared here in view of Cross's ultimate fate. Freedom requires a collective struggle against the material conditions of oppression. Rereading *The Outsider* through the lens of black womanist and feminist theory and criticism, therefore, suggests that Wright's liberatory project is flawed because his vision precludes the active participation of black women. Rather, he sexually objectifies all women throughout the novel. Cross repeatedly refers to the female image in sexual terms as "woman as body of woman."[27] Moreover, throughout the story, all women—but black women in particular—are complicit in capitalist exploitation. The sole exception is Eva Blount, a white woman Cross embraces with a strange mixture of love and pity.

Black women, in contrast, appear as controlling figures who wish to constrain Cross in his struggle to be free. Consider the major black characters: There is Dot, Cross's underage and pregnant mistress, who wants to make him marry her. Then there is his moralistic mother, who constantly hassles him about his moral depravity. And there is Gladys, his vengeful wife. All the major black female characters in *The Outsider* bear striking resemblances to the historic stereotypes of black women in America: (1) sex object, (2) domineering matriarch, and (3) evil bitch. Because of the pressures these women bring to bear on him, Cross ponders his condition: "What a stupid situation for an intelligent man to find himself in! What greater shame was there for a man than to walk the streets cringing with fear of grasping women whose destructive strokes were draped in the guise of whimpers and accusations? Somehow, he would shake loose from this and never in all his life let himself be caught."²⁸ With good reason he views all these women as formidable foes who wield enough power to end his struggle for self-determination. With each woman, Cross is caught in the clutches of deception. Perhaps this is why manipulation—the predominant form of power manifested by the female characters and an exercise of power that often is considered womanly—so frustrates him. It is notable that manipulation is frequently the recourse of those without power, who employ deception as a means to reclaim agency and influence.

Cross's mother, for example, repeatedly yells: "God'll punish you! He will! You'll see before you die! You'll weep! God is a just God. And He's a hard and jealous God! If you mock Him, He'll show you His Power!"²⁹ Her screams are, in part, expressions of her troubled past. She was seduced by Cross's father, a soldier, during World War I. Because of his unfaithfulness, she turned to religion as a refuge and decided to give her son an ambiguous name and identity: Cross Damon, representing both good (the Christian cross) and evil (the Devil). Although Cross knows of his father's infidelities, he views his mother's religion as an illusion that she employs to dominate him.

Cross finds his wife a similarly conniving and thoroughly unappealing woman. Gladys's deception, not love, led to their marriage; hence, Cross falls into the same trap as his mother despite her efforts. When Cross plans to leave Gladys, their relationship degenerates into an open power struggle. He tries to frighten Gladys into leaving him by acting insane: Cross repeatedly comes home, slaps her, leaves, and then returns—feigning no recollection of having attacked her. Gladys, meanwhile, blackmails Cross into borrowing eight hundred dollars from the post office and signing the house and car over to her. Even though Cross feels manipulated by Gladys, he knows that he is implicated in this situation: "He was properly trapped. . . . This was a cold and vindictive Gladys created by him."³⁰ Although a victim of Cross's violence and apparently powerless, Gladys summons the agency to act it out in constrained and conditioned ways.

It is fitting that Dot's last name is Powers. Cross believes that Dot is a troublemaker who from time to time acts in cahoots with Gladys and his mother. He even thinks that Dot planned the pregnancy to force him to divorce Gladys, and fears that he could be charged with statutory rape. He soon sees her as another one of the "grasping women" who victimize him. He thinks to himself: "What an actress! How do they learn it? Is it instinct?"³¹

Feeling controlled by black women and despairing of a situation that he himself helped create, Cross decides to escape and launch his own quest for individual freedom. He abandons the three black women and expresses little remorse or concern about their welfare. Wright allows him to break all promises because, in Cross's mind, the bourgeois family and other relational attachments are mere veils of illusion, as are religion, law, race, ideology, and power. Cross becomes a rootless man, a wanderer. Here Wright employs a classic trope often found in white literature where the man who pursues his self-determination breaks with custom, community, and the women with whom he is associated. The difference in black literature is that black women play a more central role, as do Gladys, Cross's mother, and Dot in *The Outsider.*

A freak subway train accident allows Cross to escape his situation and develop his own philosophy of personal conduct. Thinking he is dead, Cross's family and friends mourn at his funeral. To maintain the ruse, Cross finds it necessary to kill a talkative, chatty friend who discovers that Cross is not dead and intends to tell others. Cross, then, almost immediately develops warm relationships with two white women: Jenny, a prostitute, and Eva, the naïve wife of a Communist Party leader called Blount.

Having escaped his obligations to family, friends, and employment (thanks to the subway train wreck), Cross checks into a local hotel that also houses female sex workers. There, Cross quickly becomes intimate with Jenny. As a poor, working-class woman, perhaps her only way of escaping oppressive community conditions and pursuing freedom in a capitalist society was to sell "affection," "love," and "intimacy." In contrast to the negative depictions of black women, Wright portrays Jenny in relatively positive terms. Feeling comfortable, Cross discloses some aspects of his recent past, but Jenny does not believe him. He leaves her in Chicago.

In New York, Cross rents an apartment from Blount and Eva. The party wishes to use Cross to draw public attention to problems and conflicts associated with the larger structures of capitalist and racist domination. Wright skillfully represents both a fascist apartment landlord, Herndon, and the Communists as exploiters of the black masses. In one of the most powerful scenes in the novel, Cross happens upon Blount and Herndon when they are engaged in a deadly fight. Cross decides to kill both men. In this fashion, he transcends the image of victimhood typical of fictional representations of black life in the United States.[32] Later, Cross kills another Communist Party leader who wishes to control him. Cross ultimately becomes the embodiment of a nihilist-radical.

Eva, meanwhile, agonizes about being duped by the Communist Party and suspects that the party exploits black people. Cross, having read her diary, knows that she hates the Communist Party and that she feels a naïve attachment to black people because of their suffering and desperation in the United States. While Cross pities Eva, he also loves her. As with the white prostitute Jenny earlier in the novel, Cross develops a similar, but even more intense, desire for Eva. However, when he tells her of his crimes and of his nihilist beliefs, Eva cannot handle these revelations. Feeling abandoned, adrift, and afraid, she commits suicide. This leaves Cross alone: a nihilist-rebel with neither men nor women as companions in his isolated struggle for freedom.

Wright's story thus offers strikingly different images of black women and white women. A captive of the dominant gender and racial attitudes of his time, he often fashions problematic or negative images of the black feminine. In this situation, he portrays white women—Jenny and Eva—positively; nevertheless, both are naïve and unable to comprehend the complexities of the black male experience. Moreover, black and white women seem to experience the intersection of racism and patriarchy quite differently. In essence, Wright knows the experiences and roles of black women more intimately than he does those of white women. However, Wright's relations with women of both races are problematic.

Wright clearly spoke through the patriarchal Western vocabulary of his time, for he did not possess the language to represent gender in more progressive terms. Perhaps he was also trying, in very challenging ways, to expose how alienation is expressed in and through misogyny and sexism. (For further exploration of the question of Wright and misogyny, see Paul Gilroy's chapter in this volume.) Since Cross is a lonely wanderer, believing himself to have no home, his existential situation surely could affect his relations with the women in his life. He might expect and want things to be effortlessly better with white women, only to discover different permutations of the same female archetypes. Consequently, Wright's male-centered narrative gives very little voice to the existential realities of the black women he constructs. To a large extent, they serve as objects or props in Cross's male-ordered world. Wright employs female characters mainly to explain the protagonist's social and existential situation. In *The Outsider*, Wright's refusal to give black women agency in the progressive antiracist and anticapitalist struggle limits collective black struggle. Cross follows a lonely path that leads ultimately to his death.

According to the Wright scholar Michel Fabre, Wright, in most of his literary constructions of the social relations between women and men, emphasizes "the male desire for superiority as well as the despair at still being imprisoned in a solitude which even sexual relations cannot destroy."[33] Wright's traumatic experiences with Jim Crow segregation produced intense personal pain and suffering that he could not relinquish. Rather, he constantly relived traumatic memories of the impact of Old South violence on black family dynamics.

Still, Wright was a creative intellectual whose fictional and nonfictional works could be described as a *literature of indictment* and whose ideas were consistent with the 1960s Black Power movement, which emerged shortly after his death. Absent in both visions of struggle was a role for black women.

Notes

1. Andrew Delbanco, *The Death of Satan: How Americans Have Lost the Sense of Evil* (New York: Farrar, Straus and Giroux, 1995), 93.

2. Wright's philosophical critique of Western society and thought necessarily called for the inclusion of a black nationalist consciousness. For him, capitalism, as practiced in the West, necessarily contained a racial character. Therefore, Wright's philosophy of history joined Marxist class analysis with black nationalist race analysis (see Cedric J. Robinson's chapter in this volume and his "The Emergent Marxism of Richard Wright's Ideology," *Class and Race* 19, no. 3 [1978]: 221–37; Richard Wright, *The Outsider* [New York: Harper Perennial, 1993]; and Richard Wright, "Blueprint for Negro Writing," included in this volume).

3. Abdul R. JanMohamed, *The Death-Bound-Subject: Richard Wright's Archaeology of Death* (Durham, NC: Duke University Press, 2005); Richard Wright, "Bright and Morning Star," in *Uncle Tom's Children* (New York: Harper Perennial, 1993), 221–63. In his novel *Pagan Spain,* Wright also offered an empathetic portrayal of heroic Spanish women who suffered religious, cultural, and economic oppression. On this topic, see William Dow's chapter in this volume.

4. Richard Wright, *Native Son* (New York: Harper Perennial, 1993), 461.

5. Deborah McDowell, "New Directions in Black Feminist Criticism," in

The New Feminist Criticism: Essays on Women, Literature, Theory, ed. Eleanor Showalter (New York: Pantheon, 1985), 186–99.

6. Michael Awkward, *Negotiating Difference: Race, Gender, and the Politics of Postcoloniality* (Chicago: University of Chicago Press, 1995).

7. See bell hooks, *Outlaw Culture: Resisting Representation* (New York: Routledge, 1994); Winston Napier, ed., *African American Literary Theory: A Reader* (New York: New York University Press, 2000); Alice Walker, *In Search of Our Mother's Garden* (New York: Harcourt, 1983); Sherley Anne Williams, "Some Implications of Womanist Theory," in *African American Literary Theory*, ed. Winston Napier, 218–23 (New York: New York University Press, 2000).

8. Patricia Hill Collins, *Black Feminist Thought: Knowledge, Consciousness, and the Politics of Empowerment* (Boston: Unwin Hyman, 2004).

9. For example, see Carole Boyce Davies, *Left of Marx: The Political Life of Black Communist Claudia Jones* (Durham, NC: Duke University Press, 2007); Angela Davis, *Women, Race & Class* (New York: Random House, 1981); Paula Giddings, *Ida: A Sword among Lions* (New York: Amistad/Harper Collins, 2008); Dayo F. Gore, *Radicalism at the Crossroads: African American Women Activists in the Cold War* (New York: New York University Press, 2011); John C. Gruesser, ed., *The Unruly Voice: Rediscovering Pauline Elizabeth Hopkins* (Urbana: University of Illinois Press, 1996); Gerald Horne, *Race Woman: The Lives of Shirley Graham Du Bois* (New York: New York University Press, 2000); Chana K. Lee, *For Freedom's Sake: The Life of Fannie Lou Hamer* (Urbana: University of Illinois Press, 1996); and Barbara Ransby, *Ella Baker & the Black Freedom Movement: A Radical Democratic Vision* (Chapel Hill: University of North Carolina Press, 2003).

10. Douglas A. Blackmon, *Slavery by Another Name: The Re-Enslavement of Black Americans from the Civil War to World War II* (New York: Doubleday, 2008); Philip Dray, *At the Hands of Persons Unknown: The Lynching of Black America* (New York: Random House, 2002); Ron Eyerman, *Cultural Trauma: Slavery and the Formation of African American Identity* (New York: Cambridge University Press, 2001); Steven Hahn, *A Nation under Our Feet: Black Political Struggles in the Rural South from Slavery to the Great Migration* (Cambridge: Harvard University Press, 2003); Danielle McGuire, *At the Dark End of the Street: Black Women, Rape, and Resistance—A New History of the Civil Rights Movement from Rosa Parks to the Rise of Black Power* (New York: Random House, 2010); Cameron McWhirter, *Red Summer: The Summer of 1919 and the Awakening of Black America* (New York: Henry Holt, 2011).

11. Wright, *Native Son*.

12. Richard Wright, *12 Million Black Voices* (New York: Thunder's Mouth, 1988), 44.

13. Judith Butler, *Gender Trouble: Feminism and the Subversion of Identity* (New York: Routledge, 1990).

14. Simone de Beauvoir, *The Second Sex* (New York: Knopf, 2010).

15. Kathy E. Ferguson, *The Man Question: Visions of Subjectivity in Feminist Theory* (Berkeley: University of California Press, 1993), 2.

16. Significantly, Wright and de Beauvoir maintained an intellectual friendship that resulted in an intellectual synergy. On Wright and womanhood, see Lori J. Marso's chapter in this volume. See also Vikki Bell, *Feminist Imagination* (Thousand Oaks: Sage, 1999), which is critically explored in Marilyn Nissim-Sabat's chapter in this volume.

17. "Several Re(a)d and the Black," in *Richard Wright: Critical Perspectives Past and Present*, ed. Henry L. Gates and K. A. Appiah (New York: Amistad, 1993), 149–55; Sylvia Keady, "Richard Wright's Women Characters and Inequality," *Black American Literature Forum* 10, no. 4 (1976): 124–28; Claudia C. Tate, "Rage, Race, and Desire: *Savage Holiday*, by Richard Wright," in *Psychoanalysis and Black Novels: Desire and the Protocol of Race*, 86–118 (New York: Oxford University Press, 1998); Alice Walker, *In Search of Our Mother's Garden* (New York: Harcourt, 1983). For black feminist critics who asserted that Wright was not a misogynist, see Barbara Christian, *Black Feminist Criticism* (New York: Pergamon, 1985); Jane Davis, "More Force Than Human: Richard Wright's Female Characters," *Obsidian* 1, no. 3 (1986): 68–83; and Sondra Guttman, "What Bigger Killed For: Rereading Violence against Women in *Native Son*," *Texas Studies in Literature and Language* 43, no. 2 (2001): 169–93.

18. Sherley Anne Williams, "Papa Dick and Sister-Woman: Reflections on Women in the Fiction of Richard Wright," in *Richard Wright: A Collection of Critical Essays*, ed. Arnold Rampersad (Englewood Cliffs: Prentice-Hall, 1995), 66.

19. Margaret Walker, *Richard Wright Daemonic Genius: A Portrait of the Man/A Critical Look at His Work* (New York: Amistad/Warner 1988), 107.

20. Ibid., 179.

21. hooks, *Outlaw Culture*, 5; Awkward, *Negotiating Difference*.

22. See Awkward, *Negotiating Difference*.

23. Richard Wright, *Black Boy: A Record of Childhood and Youth* (New York: Harper and Brothers, 1945).

24. Richard Wright, *The Outsider* (New York: Harper Perennial, 1993), 35.

25. Ibid., 178.

26. For additional discussion of *The Outsider*, see also Floyd W. Hayes III, "Richard Wright and the Dilemma of the Ethical Criminal: Can One Live beyond Good and Evil?," in *Richard Wright: Writing America at Home and Abroad*, ed. Virginia Whatley Smith (Jackson: University Press of Mississippi, 2016), 69–80.

27. Wright, *The Outsider*, 117, 176, 194.

28. Ibid., 48.
29. Ibid., 27.
30. Ibid., 88.
31. Ibid., 54.
32. On Wright and the Communist Party, see Cedric J. Robinson's chapter in this volume. See also Wright, *American Hunger* (New York: Harper and Row, 1977).
33. Michel Fabre, *The Unfinished Quest of Richard Wright* (New York: William Morrow, 1973), 62.

Masculinity, Misogyny, and the Limits of Racial Community

Paul Gilroy

Contemporary critical writing about the aesthetic and political traditions of African American literature has been dominated by a simplistic and overpolarized approach to fictional representations of the conflict between men and women. These discussions have raged with special ferocity around Richard Wright's literary legacy. This is because the very quality of racial authenticity prized in his early writings was thought to be inseparable from a hatred of women that some critics have found conveyed by the violence and contempt of Wright's male characters.[1] One of the ways in which *The Outsider* produces the effect of racial authenticity that Wright was so keen to deconstruct is through the bleak view of relationships between black women and men it presents, especially in the first book, "Dread." If Sarah Hunter, the wise wife of Bob the Pullman porter, provides something of an exception to these tendencies, Cross's dismal relationships with his wife, his mother, his girlfriend, and his children are all detailed representations of a black man's inability to form emotional attachments to those who are closest to him. These failures may or may not echo aspects of the author's own life, though it is probably significant that Cross is attracted to the white woman artist who becomes a vehicle for Wright's discussion of the problems of artistic form. In the "seemingly disassociated" shapes of her nonobjective painting, Cross finds a half-articulate response to the crises of modern living which is almost congruent with his own. The intimacy between them leads her to suicide.

It is important to appreciate that the violence of Wright's characters is not a simple product of their maleness. Violence articulates blackness to a distinct mode of lived masculinity, but it is also a factor in what distinguishes blacks from whites. It mediates racial differences and maintains the boundary between racially segregated, nonsynchronous communities. This enabled Wright to see a connection between life in the [US] South and conflictual colonial settings in which the social worlds of the colonizer and the colonized intersected only in the police station. For Wright, violence colored black social life as a whole. It was internalized and reproduced in the most intimate relationships. This meant that black women could also be violent and that other kinds of brutality were integral to Wright's view of the relationship between black parents and their children. Ralph Ellison is convincing when, in his reading of *Black Boy*, the first segment of Wright's life story, he argues that Wright connected the reproduction of this violence to culturally specific nurturing practices that could, in turn, be traced back to the impact of racial terror on the institution of the black family in the South: "One of the Southern Negro family's methods of protecting the child is the severe beating—a homeopathic dose of the violence generated by black white relationships. Such beatings as Wright's were administered for the child's own good; a good which the child resisted, thus giving family relationships an undercurrent of fear and hostility, which differs qualitatively from that found in patriarchal middle class families, because here the severe beating is administered by the mother, leaving the child no parental sanctuary. He must ever embrace violence along with maternal tenderness, or reject, in his helpless way, the mother."[2] This insight is valuable in making sense of Wright's work whether or not it contributes anything to understanding Wright himself or to building a materialist theory of the psychological birth and object choices of the black subject. It is cited here neither to excuse Wright's sexist attitude to women nor to legitimate the abusive patterns of nurturing to which black families—like families in general—regularly give rise. The key point is that Wright connected the violence found in the private, domestic sphere to the ritual, public brutality that was a means of political administration in the South. This public terror did more than help create conditions in which private violence could thrive. It was shadowed by the domestic authoritarianism and violence that it also required if the racially coercive social order was to function smoothly. Both varieties of brutality were shaped by the active residues of slave society in which lines between public and private became hard to draw. Wright treated so extensively upon the routine violence between blacks and whites as well as within the black community that James Baldwin used a discussion of his work to illustrate a more general observation about the place of violence in black literature: "In most novels written by Negroes . . . there is a great space where sex ought to be; and what usually fills this space is violence."[3] This became an orthodox critical line in discussions of Wright's fiction for many years.

Rather like his contradictory presentation of black music and vernacular culture, Wright's sense of the significance of violence in black social life was a site of irreducible ambivalence toward the idea of a closed racial community and the ideology of family that helped to reproduce it. This can be missed when the theme of violence is too swiftly monopolized by discussion of the complex and contradictory feelings that we can name as Wright's misogyny. The complicated term "misogyny" brings together a number of issues that should be clearly differentiated before we can comprehend their association. It has been used to illuminate the powerful critique of the family that emerges from both Wright's fiction and his autobiographical works, particularly *Black Boy*. It is required to interpret events like Bigger's horrible murder of his girlfriend Bessie in *Native Son*, which provides a notorious example of how Wright saw his female characters and their fates. It has also been used to connect these representations with accounts of Wright's own bad relations with the black women who were his collaborators and his kin.[4] While leaving the question of Wright's own views of women open, I want to suggest that attempts to make sense of the complex misogyny in his work should include less straightforward issues such as recognition of the important differences in his presentation of black and white women. They should also be able to connect that uneven misogyny to his pathbreaking inauguration of a critical discourse on the construction of black masculinity as well as to the few tantalizing feminist and protofeminist statements sprinkled around his work.[5] For example, Wright began his speech to the first *Présence Africaine* Congress by lamenting the absence of women from that event:

I don't know how many of you have noticed it [but] there have been no women functioning vitally and responsibly from this platform [and] helping to mold and mobilize our thoughts. This is not a criticism of the conference, it is not a criticism of anyone, it is a criticism that I heap on ourselves collectively. When and if we hold another conference— and I hope we will—I hope there shall be an effective utilization of Negro womanhood in the world to help us mobilize and pool our forces. Perhaps some hangover of influence from the past has colored our attitude, or perhaps this was an oversight. In our struggle for freedom, against great odds, we cannot afford to ignore one half of our manpower, that is the force of women and their active collaboration. Black men will not be free until their women are free.[6]

These words alone suggest that Wright may have been too simplistically denounced as a macho figure whose deep hatred of women also expressed his profound, though sometimes repressed, distaste for all other blacks. This crude and inadequate account of Wright's misogyny has a second aspect. This sees him dismissed repeatedly as the purveyor of a crude, protest-oriented fiction that not only refuses to validate the dynamic, vital qualities of black culture but denies artistic and political legitimacy to the affirmative literary enterprises that are today endowed with feminine qualities.[7] Wright is then positioned as one wing of the great family of African American letters while Zora Neale Hurston, the woman identified as his cultural and political opposite, is placed at the other. Her folksy and assertively feminine perspective is thought to indicate the direction of a more positive counterpart to the overpoliticized and rugged masculinity of Wright's more pessimistic and more self-consciously modernist work. Her conservatism answers his misguided bolshevism, her exaggerated respect for the authentic voice of rural black folk is interpreted as a welcome antidote to his contemptuous presentation of the bestial, desperate experiences involved in being black in some metropolitan hovel. Wright's celebrated 1937 review of Hurston's *Their Eyes Were Watching God* has become a key document in sustaining this conflict.[8] In it, Wright attacked what he saw as the unseriousness and emptiness of vapid fiction content to exist in the "safe and narrow orbit in which America likes to see the Negro live: between laughter and tears." His unfavorable verdict on Hurston has been frequently cited as the warrant for today's fashionable but unhelpful polarization, which inhibits adequate analysis of either writer. However, the intellectual justification for identifying Wright personally with the woman-slaying exploits of the protagonists of *Native Son* and *Savage Holiday* has simply not been provided.

The final story in *Eight Men*, "The Man Who Went to Chicago," is a small portion of Wright's autobiography. His publisher's rather arbitrary decision to end the narrative of *Black Boy* with the journey northward left a large amount of material unpublished. Wright used some of it in "I Tried to Be a Communist," his contribution to *The God That Failed*. The full text of the second part was eventually published separately as *American Hunger*. Wright's inclusion of an autobiographical statement at the end of an anthology of fiction is a strategy that needs to be explained. The continuity of fiction with autobiography and the articulation of personal history within imaginative writing are important cultural and aesthetic motifs in African American letters. But Wright's concluding story serves not simply to position the author in relation to the text as a whole but to accentuate his view of a racial community more marked by its internal conflicts and hostilities than by any ideas of mutuality or fellow feeling. The depressing account of exploitative and abusive relationships between the male agents of the Negro burial society and the impoverished women from whom they collect premiums provides a good example of Wright's unsentimental preparedness to air the race's dirty linen in public. The fact that he disclosed his own participation in this horrible system damns him in the eyes of those who crave pastoral representations of black social life. However, his own behavior is discussed in a tone of bewilderment and shame. The protofeminist undertones in this should not be misread as yet another outpouring of his racial self-hatred: "Some of the agents were vicious; if they had claims to pay to a sick black woman and if the woman was able to have sex relations with them, they would insist upon it, using the claims money as a bribe. If the woman refused, they would report to the office that the woman was a malingerer. The average black woman would submit because she needed the money badly."[9]

If the relationships between black women and black men were bad, the interaction between black men was scarcely better. The piece concludes with Wright's numbingly bleak account of his experiences working with three other black men as an orderly in a medical research institute, connected to one of the largest and wealthiest hospitals in Chicago. Two new themes relevant to Wright's commentary on modernity emerge from this episode. The first is the exclusion of blacks from the practices of this modern, scientific institution and its regime of knowledge. The second is Wright's growing sense that the black workers in this secular temple are in many respects closer to the animals experimented upon in the laboratory than to the white doctors who supervise the research:

> My interest in what was happening in the institute amused the three other Negroes with whom I worked. They had no curiosity about "White Folks' Things," while I wanted to know if the dogs being treated for diabetes were getting well; if the rats and mice in which cancer had been induced showed any signs of responding to treatment. I wanted to know the principle that lay behind the Ascheim-Zondek tests that were made with rabbits, the Wasserman tests that were made with the guinea pigs. But when I asked a timid question I found that even Jewish doctors had learned to imitate the sadistic method of humbling a Negro that the others had cultivated.
>
> "If you know too much, boy, your brains might explode," a doctor said one day.[10]

In this setting, Wright describes a feud between two of his coworkers, Brand and Cooke. He introduces the chronic conflict between these men as a moving symbol of the difficulties involved in maintaining genuine intimacy between blacks: "Perhaps Brand and Cooke, lacking interests that could absorb them, fuming like children over trifles, simply invented their hate of each other in order to have something to feel deeply about. Or perhaps there was in them a vague tension stemming from their chronically frustrating way of life, a pain whose cause they did not know; and, like those de-vocalised dogs they would whirl and snap at the air when their old pain struck them."[11] An explosive physical confrontation between these two puts this small racial community in jeopardy when it leads to the near destruction of the lab where they work. In another display of the sense of humor that Wright is not supposed to have had, he assesses the consequences for scientific knowledge brought about by the random redistribution of the animals the men had previously sorted into specific categories for the purposes of medical research. The half-conscious state on which the order of racial domination has come to rely is shown to have grave effects on the dominant as well as the subordinate participants when the doctors engaged in research fail to notice that the animals have been moved around.

Perhaps black artists experience community through a special paradox. It affords them certain protections and compensations, yet it is also a source of constraint. It provides them with an imaginative entitlement to elaborate the consciousness of racial adversity while limiting them as artists to the exploration of that adversity. The striking images of intraracial antagonism in "The Man Who Went to Chicago" present the inescapable conclusion that in the conditions of extreme privation and stress that define the limits of the modern world for blacks, racial identity guarantees nothing in terms of solidarity or fraternal association. That is still a message which must be given serious consideration.

Of all Wright's texts, it is *Pagan Spain* which is most directly concerned with questions of women's social subordination. But his most developed and sustained treatment of the issue of black masculinity appears in his last published novel,[12] *The Long Dream,* a book that has been overlooked and one that can be viewed as his most complete and successful attempt to write a philosophical novel in the black idiom.

Wright has been attacked for his seeming inability to present a living, functioning black community in his work. *Native Son, The Outsider,* and even *Lawd Today* all disappoint the illegitimate demand for positive images of black sociality, which he took pleasure in repudiating. Where community appears, it is usually conflict ridden, as in the hospital lab. People are bound to each other by virtue of the deep disagreements that constantly embarrass the claims of any common racial culture. However, *The Long Dream* presented Wright's portrait of a total, dynamic, black community. The price of this brief organic and systematic image was dearly bought by Wright's deep fascination with its economic, sexual, and cultural stratification. The book is a bildungsroman centered on the life of Rex "Fishbelly" Tucker. We see him growing into manhood through a variety of interactions with his parents, peers, and different adults and institutions, both black and white. Wright rendered Fishbelly's southern community without making any concessions to the pressures to produce a pastoral view. The homophobia, misogyny, and other antisocial attributes of black life were once again uncovered in a manner that must have won Wright few friends and brought forward the accusation of betrayal as well as the suggestion that he was out of touch with changing patterns of life in the South. Not all of these negative social traits were directly traceable to the effects of racism. There is nothing automatic about the choices that his characters make to reproduce social arrangements that work against their own interests. There is always scope for reflexivity and opportunities for black political agency. Several scenes in which Fishbelly and his teenage buddies torment Aggie West, an effeminate boy who is the church pianist and whom they believe to be homosexual, typify Wright's determination to undo the codes and conventions of positive writing, which suggests that feelings of racial community and identity are spontaneously produced:

> "Move on, queer Nigger!" Zeke screamed. "Shove off!"
> Aggie's lips parted, but he did not move or speak. Nervous hysteria made Sam advance and snatch the baseball bat out of Fishbelly's hand. Lifting the bat, Sam lashed Aggie across the chest. Tony, Zeke and Fishbelly kicked, slapped and punched Aggie. . . .
> "I tried to kill 'im," Tony spoke through clenched teeth. . . .
> "Hell, mebbe we oughtn't t've done that." Tony was regretful, . . .
> "We treat 'im like the white folks treat us," Zeke mumbled with a self-accusative laugh.
> "Never thought of that," Sam admitted frowning.[13]

Much of the book is occupied with an exploration of the relationship between Fishbelly and his undertaker father, Tyree. Tyree is one of two prominent black citizens who exercise control over the ghetto in formal collaboration with a body of corrupt local whites who share the profits from their illicit schemes and manipulate the local system of criminal justice to maintain this arrangement. The book's central philosophical and psychological dynamics are constituted via Wright's interest in the master/slave struggle. In Wright's perspective this relationship is widened and socialized. Its dialectic of dependency and recognition is shown to be the continuing basis of social and economic life in the segregated South. Tyree acts out the rituals of dependency that whites have been trained to expect from him and others like him, but he does this in order to manipulate them. The scope he enjoys to master them cannot match the power of the institutional order that they control, but it is certainly significant. He is an exceptional performer in the roles that subservience requires, so skilled indeed that his son initially misinterprets these performances of racial subalternity:

> Fishbelly understood now; his father was paying humble deference to the white man and his "acting" was so flawless, so seemingly effortless that Fishbelly was stupefied. This was a father whom he had never known, a father whom he loathed and did not want to know. Tyree entered the room and looked at him with the eyes of a stranger, then turned to watch the retreating white man. When the white man had turned a corner in the corridor, Fishbelly saw a change engulf his father's face and body: Tyree's knees lost their bent posture, his back straightened, his arms fell normally to his sides, and that distracted, foolish, noncommittal expression vanished and he reached out and crushed Fishbelly to him.[14]

The paternal relationship at the center of the book is reproduced at all other levels of the racial hierarchy that governs their town. Armed with a psychological theory derived from his reading of Mannoni as well as his Kojevian understanding of Hegel, Wright emphasizes the filial aspects of Tyree's relationship to the white authority figures who are his partners in the bar and brothel that he operates. This relationship is not just one in which the blacks are infantilized by those who dominate them but rather one in which they act out the role of infant as a means to draw certain useful responses from their white rulers. Tyree's performances work because he is able to manipulate the split self at the core of Wright's approach to modernity. The performed role of racial subservience becomes a weapon in Tyree's hands; "the harpoon of his emotional claims" sunk "into the white man's heart."[15] The capacity to draw this volatile compassion from the white is something that Wright traces explicitly back to the master/slave relationship, which lived on as a central structuring feature of social life in Mississippi:

> With all the strength of his being, the slave was fighting the master. Fishbelly saw that the terrible stare in the chief's eyes was so evenly divided between hate and pity that he did not know what the chief would do; the chief could just have easily drawn his gun and shot Tyree as he could have embraced him.... Tyree began timing his moves; he hung his head, his lowered eyes watching the emotionally wrought-up white man like a cat following the scurryings of a cornered mouse. The chief turned, not looking at anything or anybody. Fishbelly knew that Tyree was weighing whether to act further; then he sniffled and remained silent.[16]

These performances induce an ambivalence in the whites they are aimed at, which parallels the attraction and repulsion that the blacks feel for white and whiteness and culminates in a peculiar symbiosis. Wright was not suggesting that blacks were equally responsible with whites for this state of affairs, but he underscored the extent to which their fates, like their histories, were interlinked. This was further explored through one critical episode in Tyree's induction of his son into the distinctive rhythms of black male adulthood. Chris, a young black man whom Tyree has looked up to, is lynched as a result of his apparently consensual involvement with a white woman. Tyree, in his role as the town's undertaker, discusses the meaning of this ritual terror with his partner in corruption, the local doctor. Together the two older men try to propel the boy into emotional and psychological majority through a grisly confrontation with the mutilated corpse. This is the first of Fishbelly's several formative encounters with death:

> "The genitals are gone," the doctor informed.
> 	Fishbelly saw a dark coagulated blot in a gaping hole between the thighs and, with defensive reflex, he lowered his hands nervously to his groin. . . .
> 	"Killing him wasn't enough. They had to mutilate 'im. You'd think that disgust would've made them leave that part of the black boy alone. . . . No! To get the chance to mutilate 'im was part of why they killed 'im. And you can bet a lot of white women were watching eagerly when they did it.
> 	"You have to be terribly attracted to a person, almost in love with 'im to mangle 'im in this manner. They hate us, Tyree, but they love us too; in a perverted sort of way, they love us—"[17]

Analysis of Wright's legacy has been impoverished as a result of his being overidentified with the same narrow definitions of racialized cultural expression that he struggled to overturn. The part of his work that resists assimilation to the great ethnocentric canon of African American literature have been left unread, and much of it is now out of print. On either side of the Atlantic, historians of European literature and philosophy have shown little interest in his work or in its relationship to those European writers and schools of expression with whom he interacted. For example, Simone de Beauvoir may have acknowledged the impact of his understanding of race and racism on her capacity to conceive *The Second Sex*, but the implications of this connection for contemporary politics remain unexplored and undervalued.[18] Historians of ideas and movements have generally preferred to stay within the boundaries of nationality and ethnicity and have shown little enthusiasm for connecting the life of one movement with that of another. What would it mean to read Wright intertextually with Genet, Beauvoir, Sartre, and the other Parisians with whom he was in dialogue?

Examining his route from the particular to the general, from America to Europe and Africa, would certainly get us out of a position where we have to choose between the unsatisfactory alternatives of Eurocentrism and black nationalism. The first ignores Wright; the second says that everything that happened to him after he left America is worthless for the schemes of black liberation. Wright was neither an affiliate of Western metaphysics who just happened to be black nor an ethnic African American whose essential African identity asserted itself to animate his comprehensive critique of Western radicalism. Perhaps more than any other writer he showed how modernity was both the period and the region in which black politics grew. His work articulates simultaneously an affirmation and a negation of the Western civilization that formed him. It remains the most powerful expression of the insider outsider duality that we have traced down the years from slavery.

Notes

From *The Black Atlantic: Modernity and Double Consciousness*, published by Harvard University Press. Copyright © 1993. Reprinted in revised form by permission of the author, Paul Gilroy.

1. Miriam DeCosta-Willis, "Avenging Angels and Mute Mothers: Black Southern Women in Wright's Fictional World," *Callaloo* 9, no. 3 (Summer 1986): 540–51; Maria K. Mootry, "Bitches, Whores, and Women Haters: Archetypes and Topologies in the Art of Richard Wright," in *Richard Wright: A Collection of Critical Essays*, ed. R. Macksey and F. E. Moorer (Englewood Cliffs, NJ: Prentice Hall, 1984); Sylvia H. Keady, "Richard Wright's Women Characters and Inequality," *Black American Literature Forum* (Winter 1976): 124–28; Diane Long Hoeveler, "Oedipus Agonistes: Mothers and Sons in Richard Wright's Fiction," *Black American Literature Forum* (Summer 1978): 65–68.

2. Ralph Ellison, *Shadow and Act* (New York: Random House, 1964), 85–86.

3. James Baldwin, "Alas Poor Richard," in *Nobody Knows My Name* (London: Corgi, 1969), 151.

4. Margaret Walker, *Richard Wright: Daemonic Genius* (New York: Warner, 1988).

5. For example, *Pagan Spain*'s foregrounding of women's experiences under fascism would seem to be an anomaly in need of some explanation.

6. *Présence Africaine*, no. 8–9–10 (June–November 1956): 348.

7. Henry Louis Gates Jr., "A Negro Way of Saying," *New York Times Book Review*, April 21, 1985; Barbara Johnson, *A World of Difference* (Baltimore: Johns Hopkins University Press, 1987). June Jordan escapes this polarization in her classic essay "Towards a Black Balancing of Love and Hate," in *Civil Wars* (Boston: Beacon, 1981).

8. Richard Wright, "Between Laughter and Tears," *New Masses*, October 5, 1937.

9. Richard Wright, *Eight Men* (Cleveland: World, 1961), 189.

10. Ibid., 194.

11. Ibid., 198.

12. A final unpublished novel, "Island of Hallucination," is held in the Beinecke Library at Yale University.

13. Wright, *The Long Dream* (New York: Harper, 1987), 36; see also 204–5.

14. Ibid., 131.

15. Ibid., 264.

16. Ibid., 264–65.

17. Ibid., 78–79.

18. Deidre Bair, *Simone de Beauvoir* (London: Cape, 1990), 388–89; Axel Madsen, *Hearts and Minds: The Common Journey of Simone de Beauvoir and Jean-Paul Sartre* (New York: Morrow, 1977), 134.

He's a Rapist, Even When He's Not

Richard Wright's Account of Black Male Vulnerability in the Raping of Willie McGee

Tommy J. Curry

> I can hear Rosalee
> See the eyes of Willie McGee
> My mother told me about
> Lynchings
> My mother told me about
> The dark nights
> And dirt roads
> And torch lights
> And lynch robes
>
> The faces of men
> Laughing white
> Faces of men
> Dead in the night
> sorrow night
> and a sorrow night
>
> —Lorraine Hansberry, "Lynchpoem," 1951

Since the penning of Frederick Douglass's "Why Is the Negro Lynched?," black men in America have attempted to escape the caricature of white supremacy's sexual mythology of the black rapist, from the notion that to be black and male is not to be a man but to be some *thing*—a phallic *thing* animated by the libidinal phobias of whites and blacks alike. For many Americans, black men and boys embody sexual savagery. Because the black male is imagined as a rapist—and therefore invulnerable to violence, as not capable of suffering, and as only existing forever unchanged and bestial—writers who discuss the violence committed against black men have rarely referred to their subordinate *male* position.[1] As Douglass recognized in 1895, the myth of the black rapist is "an invention called into being by a well-defined motive, a motive sufficient to stamp it as a gross expedient to justify murderous assault upon a long enslaved and hated people."[2] This has blinded scholars and disciplines to the historical realities of black male vulnerability to rape and sexual violence. Black males have been characterized as incapable of being victims of rape or the objects of sexual coercion by white men and women. The heteronormative narrative of racism hides the homoerotic nature of slavery and Jim Crow and negates both black men's sexual vulnerability and their manhood. Instead, it is claimed that they are neither able to protect black women nor able to resist the allure of white women. Their rape by white women becomes unimaginable.

Black men, however, have long written about their sexual vulnerabilities to whites. Many have rightly emphasized lynching, most notably the image and telling of the story of Emmett Till. Yet several years before Till's murder, a civil rights case drew international attention to the brutality and murderous logic of the US South. The case involved the execution of Willie McGee, a black man in his mid-thirties who was falsely accused of raping a white woman, Wilmetta Hawkins. While the case of Willie McGee has been commented upon as an example of the violence the myth of the black rapist perpetuated under Jim Crow, its relevance to the political thinking of Richard Wright has received less attention.

Wright, an outspoken supporter of McGee, was frustrated by the inability of white Americans to comprehend the vulnerability of black men to white women. At the time, Wright resided in France, where he was a founding member and president of the Communist-inclined Franco-American Fellowship. This group of black Americans and French opponents to Jim Crow had petitioned the US Supreme Court to intervene in both the Martinsville Seven trial and the case of Willie McGee.[3] In May 1951, Wright published "Behind the McGee Case" in *Le Droit de Vivre*. That essay, announcing Wright's support of McGee and his condemnation of the racist Jim Crow courts of Mississippi, illuminates the political concerns informing Wright's 1961 short story "Man of All Work."

This chapter first offers a brief historical overview of black men's sexual vulnerability to whites from slavery to Jim Crow. It then describes the case of Willie McGee, citing commentaries by various historians, lawyers, and activists. Next, I analyze Wright's "Behind the McGee Case" to clarify his thinking about black male vulnerability to antiblack violence and sexual subjugation. The chapter closes with reflections on the short story "Man of All Work" as a fictional commentary on the sexual vulnerability of black males to white women and the sexual nature of antiblack racism.

Historicizing the Rape of Black Men by White Women

Despite historical evidence of black males being raped by white men and women, our present gender order resists the acknowledgment of black male sexual vulnerability in general, especially to white women.[4] Our present notions of rape as a form of female suffering and injustice have exerted a seemingly insurmountable moralization and revision of our past. If historian Danielle McGuire is correct when claiming that "Analyses of rape play little or no role in most histories of the civil rights movement . . . despite a growing body of literature that focuses on the roles of black and white women and the operation of gender in the movement," then the analysis of the rape of black men during Jim Crow borders on the impossibility of conceptualization for historians and theorists alike.[5] It has long been held that the exploitation, rape, and coercion of black females originated in slavery and persist to our present day. Black males, however, are not imagined as being victims of sexual violence or as being sexually objectified by white men and white women. There is no interpretive structure that connects the perceivable (individual) acts against black males to a larger historical pattern of rape and sexual abjection at the hands of whites—specifically white women.

The idea of white women as violent racists who lynched, murdered, and raped black bodies is unthinkable within most scholarly accounts and is denied by most disciplinary gender theory. This is suspicious given that

Ida B. Wells's *Southern Horrors,* an analysis of sexual violence and lynching, expresses concern for the "Afro-American Sampsons who suffer themselves to be betrayed by white Delilahs."[6] Throughout Wells's corpus on lynching, she documents cases of white women pursuing black men and the men's surrender to the advances for fear of being accused of rape. This fatalist paradox wherein black men under duress were forced to have sex with white women for fear of being accused of rape often resulted in the black male victims being lynched as a *rapist.* As Wells explains: "The miscegenation laws of the South only operate against the legitimate union of the races; they leave the white man free to seduce all the colored girls he can, but it is death to the colored man who yields to the force and advances of a similar attraction in white women. White men lynch the offending Afro-American, not because he is a despoiler of virtue, but because he succumbs to the smiles of white women."[7] This was a radical departure from Wells's earlier, self-acknowledged view of black men who were lynched. As she writes in *Crusade for Justice,* "Like many another person who had read of lynching in the South, I had accepted the idea meant to be conveyed—that although lynching was irregular and contrary to law and order, unreasoning anger over the terrible crime of rape led to the lynching; that perhaps the brute deserved death anyhow and the mob was justified in taking his life."[8] It took the death of her friends Thomas Moss, Calvin McDowell, and Lee Stewart to shift her thinking on the black male rapist.

The sexual vulnerability of black men has often been analyzed primarily through lynching and Wells's investigation into the alleged crime of rape. Black males, however, have not been silent about their sexual victimization. For example, Archibald H. Grimke's "The Sex Question and Race Segregation," published in 1915, accused white women of inheriting the lust of their white fathers toward black men and women. After describing the impunity with which white men of the dominant classes seduced and raped black women, Grimke adds: "But there is another aspect to this side of the subject which must not be entirely ignored, and that is the existence in a few instances of illicit relations between some white women and some colored men in the South. That such relations have existed in the past and do actually exist there at the present time, there is absolutely no doubt whatever."[9] Grimke boldly asks readers if they actually believe that black males simply consented to the advances of white women: "Has it ever been seriously considered that like father may occasionally produce like daughter in the South? And that such moral lapses by a few white women of that section may be accounted for in part at least by that mysterious law of atavism? The sons are like their fathers in respect to their fondness for colored women, why may not one daughter in, say, ten thousand, resemble those fathers in that same shameful, though not altogether unnatural respect?"[10] According to Grimke, white women, after observing their fathers, understood that whiteness gave them sexual power over the bodies of black men and women. White women learned that they could use black male bodies for their sexual pleasure while publicly invoking the myth of virtuous white womanhood to deny their desires. As Martha Hodes writes in *White Women, Black Men: Illicit Sex in the 19th Century South*: "To characterize all white women as pure had an important effect: it made sex between a black man and a white woman by definition rape, because a 'pure' white woman, no matter how poor, could not possibly (in white minds) desire sex with a black man."[11]

Akin to Glenda Gilmore's argument that Jim Crow was not only a racial caste system but also a deliberately constructed sexual order used to make the crimes of black men the crimes of the race,[12] Grimke contends that the southern social order was specifically tailored to condemn the sexuality of black males and their threat to white womanhood. Jim Crow utilized the myth of the black rapist not only to rationalize the homoerotic urge of white men whose desire for the death and dismemberment of black male bodies is described in great detail in James Baldwin's short story "Going to Meet the Man,"[13] but also to conceal white women's rape of black males through the overdetermination of the black male as rapist. The lynching of black men for the crime of rape was more than a manifestation of the mythology or stereotype of black men as rapists. The spectacle was designed to establish white rule through the sexual domination of the black male. The event masculinized the white man and white woman through the emasculation—the literal castration—of the black male body. Historian Grace Elizabeth Hale explains:

> White women often participated as announcers of the upcoming event, as spectators, and as gatherers of wood and other fuel. They directed the actions of large numbers of white men by alleging rape, attempted rape, or even an attempted stare, and by demanding tortures and egging mobs on. In one case, a woman even stood on a car and yelled

"roast the nigger" when it seemed the mob might show mercy. Not just the white man was empowered when the Black man was literally and symbolically deprived of his masculinity. The lynching narrative moved white women towards masculinity even as it subtly shifted white men away from maleness, embodied in the Black beast, that they were trying to capture through castration.[14]

The lynching of black males was not only an example of the most extreme violence of the US racial order but also a spectacle intended to unite white men and white women as the patriarchal rulers of America's sexual regime. Both a white woman's imagined vulnerability to the black rapist and the ability to castrate him empowered her to be an overseer of patriarchal violence against black men. This symbiosis of the white man and white woman against racialized men made patriarchy the dominant racial logic that simultaneously protected white womanhood and justified the violence of white manhood.

The Case of Willie McGee

The execution of Willie McGee is an important historical illustration of how the sexual power of white womanhood manifested itself toward black men during Jim Crow. On May 8, 1951, McGee was electrocuted in Laurel, Mississippi, on a much-disputed charge that he raped Wilmetta Hawkins. The trial garnered global attention, and both the NAACP and the now defunct Civil Rights Congress, an organization adamant in its Communist commitments, took up McGee's cause. The rape allegedly occurred on November 2, 1945, when a black man purportedly climbed through an open window, crawled toward Mrs. Hawkins on the floor, where she slept with her sick twenty-month-old daughter, raped her, threatened her life if she ever told, and ran out the front door. According to Alex Heard's *The Eyes of Willie McGee*, "Mrs. Hawkins said it was too dark to see the rapist's face but she knew he was Black by the texture of his hair."[15]

While Hawkins and other whites swore that McGee raped her, black testimony and historical records paint a vastly different story. In fact, contrary to Heard's work, many sources depict Mr. McGee as the victim of Wilmetta Hawkins's sexual advances. For example, Jessica Mitford, reflecting on her advocacy for McGee as part of the Civil Rights Congress, writes that there was "persuasive evidence" that Hawkins had long been McGee's mistress."[16] Some advocates for McGee have further suggested that he was a victim of coercion who had not willingly consented to Hawkins's advances. For example, McGee's lawyer, Bella Abzug, insisted that McGee was the victim of sexual coercion by Hawkins. Abzug cited the testimony of many local black residents and challenged the court to rid itself of the decadent mythology that every encounter between a white woman and a black man was in fact rape. The court, however, found her northern insinuation offensive. As Abzug recounts, the presiding judge declared: "If you believe or are implying that any white woman in the South who was not completely down and out, degenerate, degraded, and corrupted, could have anything to do with a Negro man, you not only do not know what you are talking about, but you are insulting us, the whole South. You do not know the South and do not realize that we could not entertain such a proposition; that we would not even consider it in court."[17]

The course of McGee's trial was all too predictable. Despite substantial evidence and testimony showing Hawkins to be the mistress of Mr. McGee, he was punished for sex with a white woman—an act that could only be understood as rape in the South. As noted author and civil rights activist Jessica Mitford explained:

> He [McGee] had been in prison, under sentence of death, for more than five years. The court transcript and eyewitness accounts of the three trials, together with stories from the local Mississippi press, made sickening reading; at the first trial, which lasted less than a day, the jury had taken two and a half minutes to reach a verdict. It was obvious that a ritual race murder was in the offing. At the heart of the case was the fact that no white had ever been condemned to death for rape in the Deep South, while in the past four decades fifty-one blacks had been executed for this offense.[18]

The logic of US antiblack racism holds that the black male is undesirable to the white woman because he is not a white man—her perfect (natural) mate. Racism constructs the black male as a brute. As such, the white woman can only despise and fear him because the only relation she can have with the melaninated beast is rape.[19] It is therefore the black male who craves the white woman. This justifies the killing of black males.

Unlike the narrative of Till's murder, where a white woman only took offense to the young boy's advances, in the case of McGee, a white woman actively participated in the violence against a black male. Hawkins imposed herself on McGee. As historian Danielle McGuire explains, "McGee entered into a long sexual relationship with his white employer, Mrs. Wilmetta Hawkins, after she threatened to cry rape if he refused her flirtatious advances."[20] Hawkins first propositioned Willie McGee in 1942. It is important to remember that he was a black male laborer in the Deep South during the 1940s, when jobs for black men were scarce. He therefore "was committed to taking odd jobs around her house" for his livelihood.[21] McGee recalled that "I was waxing the floors and she showed a willingness to get familiar."[22] Hawkins used work to mask her demands for illicit relations. McGee recounted that "she frequently sent for me to do work which gave opportunities for intercourse."[23]

McGee's wife learned of her husband's victimization firsthand, when Hawkins confronted both of them as they walked home from a movie theater and said to Willie: "I got my car over here. Come on into my car with me."[24] McGee told Hawkins to go away because he was with his wife, to which Hawkins replied, "Don't fool with any Negro whores."[25] McGee ultimately complied with Hawkins's demands, fearful of the violence Hawkins could bring to him and his family. His wife reportedly said to a friend, "People who don't know the South don't know what would happen if Willie told her no."[26]

This illicit relationship exhibits several of the sexual vulnerabilities black men endured at the hands of white women during Jim Crow. Sexual coercion was conditioned not only by the economic vulnerability of Willie McGee but by the sexual mythology of rape and the black male. McGee's material vulnerability placed him in proximity to a predatory white woman; McGee's mere contact with this white woman violated the segregationist code of the South; and McGee's maleness even today conveys to any white onlooker his culpability for rape and precludes the possibility that he was a sexual victim. Empowered by the supposed virtue and vulnerability of their womanhood, white women could make the accusation of rape synonymous with the black rapist and coerce black men through this threat of violence. In a white supremacist society, white men could not imagine that a white woman would ever desire, or lust for, being penetrated by a "nigger," so white women were allowed the freedom to sexually experiment with black men. Stated plainly, white women forced black men to penetrate them. If black men refused the advances of white women, they were accused of rape. If the black man was discovered, then the white woman who coerced, raped, and forced him to penetrate her appealed to the well-established idea of the *black man* as her rapist.

So far, few scholars have endeavored to document the violence suffered by black men who experience sexual victimization by whites. There is no single text comparable to Claudia Jones's 1949 study "An End to the Neglect of the Problems of the Negro Woman," which analyzes the economic and racial vulnerability of Negro women before white female managers of the white home. According to Jones, "The very economic relation of Negro women to white women which perpetuates the madam-maid relationships feeds chauvinism."[27] In contrast, the theoretical categories mapped upon black males make them mythological creatures, not historical persons whose complexity is worthy of study. Their designation—at best—as "men," which is little more than an extension of their alleged hypermasculinity and need to compensate for their lack of white manhood, replaces actual analysis of their consciousness of the world around them.

Political Theory in Richard Wright's "Behind the McGee Case"

Many Americans in the 1950s believed that the case involving McGee was simply political propaganda for black socialists and Russian Communists. The combination of anti-Communist fervor and antiblack racism created an insurmountable public perception that McGee was not only a rapist but an anti-American symbol promoted by sinister interests in the Soviet Union, France, and Communist China. Mainstream US publications like *Life* declared that McGee's death was the only appropriate outcome for the trial, even though no white man had ever been sentenced to death for rape.[28] Wright responded in *White Man Listen!* by arguing that white supremacy is a regime created for emotionally impoverished whites. They are driven by colonial greed, their supposed racial superiority, and illicit sexuality to "drain off the dammed up libido that European morality has condemned."[29] Unlike many theories today, which often link the concept of gender only to the bodies of women, Wright holds that white men and women eroticize the black male and female bodies they deem inferior in order to facilitate the fulfillment of their desires.[30] Fungible black beings become the experimental flesh of white cravings. This sexual and racist narcissism consumes black flesh in an effort to absolve whiteness of its repressed sexual excess.[31] Wright's view of southern racism as constituted by a libidinal economy that uses the black body as a hedonic object informs his support for and writing about Willie McGee.

Wright opens "Behind the McGee Case" with information from the Negro press. "McGee had known the white woman in question for four years, had known her intimately. The woman's husband, a traveling salesman, returned home unexpectedly and surprised them, hence the charge of rape."[32] At issue, says Wright, is far more than a case of adultery: behind "this simple, human incident stands a problem of vast import; the McGee case stands at the apex of an intricate social, political, pyramid whose base relies on the plantation economy of the Deep South."[33] Understanding the political economy, values, and entities at work in Mississippi's choice to kill McGee, Wright concludes that the execution is an attempt by whites to retain power despite their numerical disadvantages in southern states: "Outnumbered, the whites are determined to hold onto the reins of state power which consists of the police, the state national guard, the press, radio, church, banking, farming, industry, and the educational system. The entire social structure of Mississippi is so rigged as to allow expression to *whites only.*"[34] McGee was a casualty of the murderous attempt by whites to control black people.

Wright's account of Jim Crow violence does not differ greatly from his previous justification for the violence in *Black Boy* and *Native Son.* In his 1945 interview "This Too, Is America," Wright says that "the manner stems from the matter; the relationship of the American Negro to the American scene is essentially violent. He could not be kept in his present position unless there existed an apparatus of organized violence. Any attempt to deal with this situation must deal in terms of violence."[35] In "Behind the McGee Case," Wright writes that in the South, "a kind of daily race war rages on all levels of life."[36] Blacks engage whites daily in their homes, in factories, and so on, but "in things pertaining to the power structure of society, the whites are in undisputed control."[37] Racism is about whites maintaining the power to interact with blacks, but without being affected by the wills of black people: "This control is maintained only at a cost of nightmarish tension which suffuses the whole of daily life in Mississippi; this control is manifested formally in a code of rigid race laws which all Negroes must obey."[38] To retain power, whites in the South make the Negro into an object. For the political logic of the South to remain sound, the black male is made into a rapist and killed.

Because the laws alone cannot fully arrest the efforts of Negroes to gain state power, "it is necessary for each individual white man in the community to take it upon himself to act the role of a racial policeman."[39] Thus antiblack violence is the intermediary—the contouring force—between the white agent and historical structures. Through violence, individual whites advance their race's legacy of domination and preserve their society. Wright comments that, "The least infraction of the race code on the part of the Negro, such as drinking from the wrong water fountain, forgetting to say 'sir' to a white man, refusing to sit in the racially segregated section of a bus, street car or train, seeking to enter the front instead of the rear door of a white home—any of these acts merits instant reprisal."[40] This violence is multiplicative and evolves toward never-ending horrors: "When the Negro population became what the whites called 'intractable,' white mobs would form, drag a Negro from his home, charge him with rape, dip him in hot tar, roll him in feathers and then drench him in gasoline and burn him alive."[41] The inhumanity of the violence against the Negro male aims to achieve and then reflect his dehumanized state. Because he exists only as dangerous flesh, there is no limit to what his savageness allows.

According to Wright, this violence has generally been viewed in the South as extralegal. However, "Today, what used to happen *outside of the law* now takes place within the law. Ironically as it might sound, this switching from lawless to legal lynching represents a moral step forward in that it places the actions of Mississippi whites squarely and responsibly before the bar of world opinion."[42] Formerly, the officials of Mississippi could say that lawless mobs lynched Negroes; but "today they must try to defend legal actions that do not admit of moral or intellectual defense."[43] Whereas white supremacy in the South previously sought to maintain the illusion of integrity by suggesting that violence against the Negro was beyond the purview of the law, the murder of McGee shows that the law itself is a reflection of the antipathy that whites have for the Negro.[44]

Rather than being an exception to the white supremacist order of Jim Crowism, legal lynching lies at its foundation, alongside the sexual condemnation of the Negro. Wright's analysis foreshadows Calvin C. Hernton's argument in *Sex and Racism in America* that black men must be asexual to survive their encounters with white women in a white supremacist society. "Because he [the black male] must act like a eunuch when it comes to white women," Hernton writes, "there arises within the black man an undefined sense of dread and self-mutilation. Psychologically he experiences himself as castrated."[45] The notion of the self-castrated black male—the sexually censored and socially impotent black man—occupies Wright's later works in *Eight Men*, specifically his short story "Man of All Work."

Thinking through "Man of All Work"

"Man of All Work" is an attempt to correct our conceptualization of and blindness to black male vulnerability. In the story, Wright demonstrates that sexual violence against black men is rooted in the political order and amplified by black males' economic vulnerability due to unemployment. When he is without work, whites reduce the black male to a presumed base instinct and presocial disposition and will treat him as disposable. The plot revolves around the fate of Carl, an unemployed black man with a wife and two children. Despite his training as a professional cook, Carl cannot find work because only skilled industrial jobs are available. These occupations, as W. E. B. Du Bois reminds us, require apprenticeships and training largely denied to black male laborers.[46] Carl remarks: "No jobs for men in this paper.... But they're plenty of ads for domestic workers. It's always like that."[47] He then spots a job for a cook: "Cook and housekeeper wanted. Take care of one child and small modern household. . . . Colored cook preferred."[48] Lucy, Carl's wife, acknowledges that the fifty dollars a week could save their home. The problem is that the employers want a black woman. Desperate for work, Carl puts on his wife's dress. Lucy protests and threatens to disown him if he is discovered.

Wright's plot highlights two features of Carl's masculinity. First, the story illustrates that contrary to the asserted universalizing mythology of patriarchy, black men lack sustained or structural economic advantage over either black or white women. At least in northern cities, far more lucrative work was available to black women than black men. This is because most unskilled labor for black people was domestic work, and female workers were both expected and preferred. Because maleness in the United States is so deeply connected to work, black men have historically been targeted by the white-defined labor market because of their gender position. Because of their economic vulnerability to white employers, black men are dehumanized through the denial of work. As Huey P. Newton explained, "society responds to [the lower socioeconomic black man] as a thing, a beast, a nonentity, something to be ignored or stepped on."[49] Second, Wright's work demonstrates that the preferable political approach for black men facing white patriarchy is not imitation but resistance. For over a century, black men were thought to be feminine, child-like savages, or rapists.[50] There was no mention of black men as patriarchs in the twentieth century before the birth of black feminism, since even early formulations of the woman's oppression were modeled on the patriarchal subjugation of Negroes—especially Negro men—by white men.[51] It was not until the historiography introduced by Michelle Wallace's *The Black Macho and the Myth of the Superwoman* that black masculinity became understood as the outgrowth of black men's internalization of white society's view of them after integration.[52]

The dominant view of black men during Jim Crow was as an emasculated figure. Whereas E. Franklin Frazier's analysis in *The Negro Family in the United States* (1939) associated the lack of nuclear families to the trauma of slavery and working-class black men's wandering from their wives and homes to find work, white sociologists believed black men were ill-equipped for the demands of freedom and civil institutions like marriage well into the mid-twentieth century because of an inferiority complex. John Dollard's *Caste and Class in a Southern Town* was the definitive source of this idea. Dollard argued that the Jim Crow South was deliberately designed to destroy the will of black males. Any demonstration of independence by black men "[was] immediately recorded in threatening judgments of his behavior of the type we already know, he [was] said to be uppity or getting out of his place."[53] Dollard explains:

> Within the caste system situation Negro women can be somewhat more expressive of their resentment than can Negro men. . . . [T]hey can do and say things which would bring a severe penalty had they been men. It may be that white caste members do not fear the aggression of women, so much, especially since it cannot take the form of sexual attack, or the chivalry expected of men in our society toward women in general may come into play. There are, of course, distinct limits to what a Negro woman may do, but they are not so narrow as for men.[54]

Following Dollard, Abram Kardiner, a white sociologist famous for his Freudian inclinations, viewed lower-class black men as psychologically paralyzed by low self-esteem and self-contempt. Unable to find work because of racial discrimination, black men knew "that the female had better economic chances. His frantic effort to retain the dominant position in the family often ended in failure and despondency. If he left to take a job in another city, this step could be transformed into a permanent status of separation or informal divorce."[55] The sociology of the 1950s and 1960s described black males as irresponsible, deserters, sexually perverse, irreverent, and dangerous to women and children.[56] It maintained that the inability of black men to directly resist racism made them aggressive out of frustration.[57] These studies could not imagine a black male, as a father and husband, who would put on a dress to save his home and care for his family.

In "Man of All Work," Richard Wright is responding to the pathological account of black manhood solidified in the minds of theorists and social scientists alike in the 1950s. Wright's short story shows that it is the lack of work, the economic divestment of black men as human and laborer—able to produce through work—that marks the division between white patriarchy and the black male. Black males are victims of economic and sexual forces which lock them out of society. Wright's narrative insists that black men's oppression must be understood as an outgrowth of the white paternal order and that the racism that structures the *living out* of black maleness is about the sexual violence committed against black men and the dehumanization of being a black male, castrated by white racism, existing only as an emasculated (negation) of white masculinity: *rapist*. Baldwin, who had criticized the fatalism of Wright's *Native Son*, praised "Man of All Work." The short story "is a masterpiece," wrote Baldwin, who added "that I cannot avoid feeling that Wright, as he died, was acquiring a new tone, and a less uncertain esthetic distance, and a new depth."[58] In an interview, Baldwin described "Man of All Work" as a "beautiful, terrifying story. It really gets something which has been hidden for all these generations, which is the ways in which . . . it really suggests, more forcibly than anything I've ever read, the humiliation the Negro male endures. And it is this our country really doesn't want to know. And, therefore, when people talk about the Noble Savage and the greater sexuality of Negroes, and all that jazz . . . I could name six men who are on the needle just because . . . the demoralization is so complete."[59]

Carl introduces himself to his potential employer, Mr. Fairchild, as Lucy Owens and says that he is an excellent cook and very comfortable with children because he has two of his own. When Fairchild asks, "who looks after the young ones when you work?"[60] Carl replies, "My husband.... [H]e works at night in a lumbermill and is at home during the day."[61] This is a telling remark because, during the 1940s, black men's access to industrial jobs meant an end to their dependency on agriculture and white owners' leasing of property. Work in a lumber mill was a sign of upward mobility for black families. In addition, industry offered the prospect of wage work for black women.[62] Wright thus subtly marks the class position of Carl and suggests the class aspirations of the fictitious Lucy, who now appears as a viable worker rather than a poor Negro.

For Wright, the black domestic worker in a white household is a microcosm of larger societal sexual pathologies and obsessions with black flesh. Mr. Fairchild is a white man and a rapist. When he gets drunk, he wrestles with the colored women hired as domestic help. His wife, Anne, excuses it as an outcome of too much whiskey and, thereby, enables his ability to rape. Anne enjoys the luxuries of her white womanhood—being served, fed, and even bathed by the colored help—even though her comfortable home life rests on violence against and the rape of black men and women. In the minds of the two Fairchilds, white womanhood is to be protected from the black rapist. Meanwhile, the white man can be a rapist beyond reproach since his ideal mate is the pristine white woman.

Wright makes this relationship even more visible when Carl (dressed as Lucy) bathes Anne. Carl is terrified at the sight of Anne's naked body. He breaks out in a sweat when Anne asks him to wash her back. "Are you upset because I am sitting here naked in the bathtub?" she asks. Only after Carl washes Anne does she tell the domestic worker that she needed to get rid of her last maid because she was raped by her husband. Anne offers an explanation: "My husband Dave, likes to take a drink now and then—maybe a drop more than is good for him."[63] She then tells Carl, "As long as you don't drink, my husband won't bother you and you can very well defend yourself. Just push him away."[64]

When Mr. Fairchild returns home that night, he is drunk and attempts to rape Carl. They wrestle. Even though Anne had previously warned Lucy of Dave's predatory behavior, Anne does not hold her husband accountable for being a rapist and, instead, grabs a gun and threatens to kill both her husband and the maid. She screams: "Get out my way Dave. I'll be made a fool of no longer. For all I know, you might have sent this black bitch here to work. . . . [N]o wonder she came so early in the morning. Now I'm going to kill her."[65] Anne knows that Dave is a rapist, but when her womanhood is threatened, she chooses *to kill the nigger.* She feels deeply shamed by the very notion that her white man could desire a black woman (who is in reality an economically and politically castrated black man).

Enraged, Anne shoots Lucy. Believing that Lucy is dead, the Fairchilds contact a local doctor. When the doctor arrives to examine the body, the white world discovers that Lucy is really Carl. Anne panics, but Dave—the actual rapist—sees a solution: "I've got it solved. It's simple. This nigger put on a dress to worm his way into my house to rape my wife. . . . Then I detected im. I shot im in self-defense, shot im to protect my home. That's our answer! I was protecting white womanhood from a nigger rapist impersonating a woman! A rapist who wears a dress is the worst sort! Any jury'll free me on that."[66] The doctor asks Anne, "did this man molest you in any way in that bathroom?" Anne, understanding Carl's petrification and fear of her naked body, says, "He didn't touch me. If she is a man, she was scared to death, could barely move. Oh, I see it all now."[67]

The Fairchilds ask their doctor to negotiate with the nigger. The group agrees to give Carl the two hundred dollars necessary to save his home, if he, in turn, signs a contract promising to keep the incident quiet. Carl, as expected, agrees. When he returns home with the money, his wife asks him what happened. Carl simply assures her that he will never put a dress on again: "I was a woman for almost six hours and it almost killed me. Two hours after I put that dress on I thought I was going crazy."[68] She replies, "But, Carl, I warned you. It's not easy for a man to act like a woman."[69] Wright insists upon drawing the reader back to the emasculation, or what Abdul R. JanMohamed has remarked upon as a constant theme throughout Wright's work—the racial castration of the black male within the race-sex nexus of the United States. Because "racialized castration . . . is not really concerned with managing the principle of substitutive equivalence on the register or signification or the Symbolic as such, but rather on the register of political power and control,"[70] there is in Wright a demand to imagine Carl as a black, sexed as male, but devoid of masculinity. Current gender theory presumes, largely because of the phallic overdetermination of the black male body, that black maleness is synonymous with black masculinity, which, due to its *lack* of power, aspires to white masculinity. Wright argues that black maleness represents a completely different type of existence altogether.

Wright thus instructs the reader to attend to the impossibility—conceptually and materially—facing the castrated black man. Because he cannot act like a woman, a black man finds himself in a sexualized negation that denies the possibility of any realization. He is neither a (white) man nor a (black) woman. He is not recognizable because a castrated black man cannot be a black man. He cannot work; he cannot defend himself from white womanhood and the violence of white manhood. He is a nonexisting entity, simply undifferentiated flesh that cannot resist the social, economic, and political forces exerted upon him. His vulnerability allows him to become a convenient phobia of the white imagination, and his death is thereby rationalized as prophylactic—that is, as necessary to protect the purported code of honor that makes white racial life possible.

"Man of All Work" asks the reader to conceptualize the real as imaginary. Under the present gender order of America, the hypersexualization of black men is often described as a hypermasculinity. This ignores what Wright describes as the castrated state of black men. Unable to find work and deprived of education, black males find themselves dependent on whites to survive. Like McGee, Carl serves as a domestic worker in a white home. Whereas McGee was raped by a white woman, Carl is almost raped by a white man because he is a black man, which stands in relation to white men as feminine. Because Carl is an emasculated man—the only possible existence for black men in a white supremacist society—Wright correctly expresses the sexual violence that black maleness has historically been subjected to. In a white supremacist society, Carl personifies the racial dynamics of subjugated manhood made socially impotent through the denial of work, politically impotent through criminalization, and castrated through blackness. This is why he represents black maleness as a synonymity of rape, being the rapist, and being raped. Literal rape befalls both black men and black women because black men can only exist in a white supremacist society as lesser selves that are not *men*. Both the black male and the black female therefore can be and are raped.

But the black male suffers an additional burden because of his relation to white womanhood. He is also viewed as a rapist. Like McGee, Carl exists in Negrophilic and Negrophobic relations simultaneously—as both the victim of rape and the supposed perpetrator of rape. But, as in the case of McGee, Carl's vulnerability to rape is eclipsed by fear of his perpetration of it. Remember: McGee was forcibly raped for several years. His victimization was well known in the black community, but when the white world found out, he was constructed as a rapist. Like Carl, McGee is completely fungible. He becomes whatever the white world imposes upon him, whatever it desires him to be. This is the vision of black manhood that Wright pens, and that Baldwin suggests is the most accurate and insightful view of black males of the twentieth century.

Notes

1. Often characterized as racism, the sexual vulnerability of black men has been obscured under the categorical analyses of intersectional thought because maleness (even racial subordinate male positions) is theorized as sites of privilege. For a discussion of this problem in the study of male rape during slavery, see Thomas Foster, "The Sexual Abuse of Black Men under American Slavery," *Journal of the History of Sexuality* 20, no. 3 (2011): 445–64. If interested in how intersectionality theory fails to understand the sexual vulnerability of black men outside of patriarchy or male privilege, see Tommy J. Curry, *The Man-Not: Race, Class, Genre, and the Dilemmas of Black Manhood* (Philadelphia: Temple University Press, 2017).

2. Frederick Douglass, *Why Is the Negro Lynched?* (London: John Witby and Sons, 1895), 15.

3. Michel Fabre, *The World of Richard Wright* (Jackson: University Press of Mississippi, 1987), 181.

4. Foster, "The Sexual Abuse of Black Men under American Slavery"; and James Hoke Sweet, *Recreating Africa: Culture, Kinship and Religion in the African-Portuguese World, 1441–1770* (Chapel Hill: University of North Carolina Press, 2003), 74; Vincent Woodard, *The Delectable Negro: Human Consumption and Homoeroticism within U.S. Slave Culture* (New York: New York University Press, 2014).

5. Danielle McGuire, "It Was Like All of Us Had Been Raped: Sexual Violence, Community Mobilization, and the African American Freedom Struggle," *Journal of American History* 91, no. 3 (2004): 906–31, 907.

6. Ida B. Wells, *Southern Horrors and Other Writings: The Anti-Lynching Campaign of Ida B. Wells, 1892–1900*, ed. Jacqueline Jones Royster (Boston: Bedford, 1997), 53.

7. Ibid., 53–54.

8. Ida B. Wells, *Crusade for Justice: The Autobiography of Ida B. Wells*, ed. Alfreda M. Duster (Chicago: University of Chicago Press, 1970), 64.

9. Archibald Grimke, "The Sex Question and Segregation," in *The American Negro Academy Occasional Papers, 1–22* (New York: Arno, 1969), 1–37, 20–21.

10. Ibid., 21.

11. Martha Hodes, *White Women, Black Men: Illicit Sex in the 19th-Century South* (New Haven: Yale University Press, 1997) 202.

12. Glenda Gilmore, *Gender and Jim Crow: Women and the Politics of White Supremacy in North Carolina, 1896–1920* (Chapel Hill: University of North Carolina Press, 1996).

13. James Baldwin, "Going to Meet the Man," in *Baldwin: Early Novels and Stories* (New York: Library of America, 1998), 933–50.

14. Grace Elizabeth Hale, *Making [w]hiteness: The Culture of Segregation in the South, 1890–1940* (New York: Vintage, 1998), 74.

15. Alex Heard, *The Eyes of Willie McGee: The Tragedy of Race, Sex, and Secrets in Jim Crow South* (New York: HarperCollins, 2010), 3.

16. Jessica Mitford, *A Fine Old Conflict* (New York: Vintage, 1978), 161.

17. Harvey McGeehee quoted in *Bella Abzug: How One Tough Broad from the Bronx Fought Jim Crow and Joe McCarthy, Pissed Off Jimmy Carter, Battled for the Rights of Women and . . . Planet, and Shook up Politics along the Way*, ed. Suzanne B. Levine and Mary Thom (New York: Farrar, Straus and Giroux, 2007), 50.

18. Mitford, *A Fine Old Conflict*, 161.

19. E. Franklin Frazier, "The Pathology of Race Prejudice," *Forum* (1927): 856–61.

20. Danielle McGuire, *At the Dark End of the Street: Black Women, Rape, and Resistance—A New History of the Civil Rights Movement from Rosa Parks to the Rise of Black Power* (New York: Vintage, 2010), 58.

21. Ibid.

22. Ibid.

23. Ibid.

24. Ibid., 58–59.

25. Ibid., 59.

26. Ibid.

27. Claudia Jones, *Claudia Jones: Beyond Containment: Autobiographical Reflections, Essays, and Poems*, edited by Carole Boyce Davies (Banbury, UK: Ayebia Clarke, 2011), 74–86.

28. "Letter to the Editor," *Life*, June 11, 1951, 12.

29. Richard Wright, *White Man Listen!* (New York: Harper Perennial, 1957), 4.

30. In Angela Davis's *Women, Race, and Class*, she remarks, "As females, slave

women were inherently vulnerable to all forms of sexual coercion. If the most violent punishments of men consisted in floggings and mutilations, women were flogged and mutilated, as well as raped" (New York: Vintage, 1983), 7. Adrienne Davis, in "The Sexual Economy of American Slavery," in *Sister Circle: Black Women and Work*, ed. Sharon Harley (Piscataway, NJ: Rutgers University Press, 2002), 103–27, also excludes black males from gender vulnerability. The assumption in the aforementioned works and others suggest that rape (as a gendered form of violence) and sexual vulnerability are not part of maleness. This idea has of course been challenged by Oyèrónkẹ Oyèwùmí in *The Invention of Woman: Making African Sense of Western Gender Discourses* (Minneapolis: University of Minnesota Press, 1997); and Errol Miller's *Men at Risk* (Kingston: Jamaica Publishing House, 1991).

31. There have been previous works exploring the role of homoerotic sexual excess in southern racism (see, for example, Leslie A. Fielder, *Love and Death in the American Novel* [New York: Criterion, 1960]).

32. Richard Wright, "Behind the McGee Case," *Le Droit de Vivre*, May 1951, 1.

33. Ibid.

34. Ibid., 2.

35. Richard Wright, "This Too, Is America," in *Conversations with Richard Wright*, ed. Wright and Michel Fabre (Jackson: University of Mississippi Press, 1993), 67–71, 67–68.

36. Wright, "Behind the McGee Case," 2.

37. Ibid.

38. Ibid.

39. Ibid.

40. Ibid.

41. Ibid.

42. Ibid.

43. Ibid.

44. For more on the dilemma of death in Wright's work, see Abdul R. JanMohamed's "Notes toward a Political Economy of Life and Death: Reading Richard Wright with Frantz Fanon," in this volume.

45. Calvin C. Hernton, *Sex and Racism in America* (New York: Anchor, 1992), 60.

46. W. E. B. Du Bois, "Negro Nation within a Nation," *Current History* 42 (1935): 265–70.

47. Richard Wright, "Man of All Work," in *Eight Men* (New York: Harper Perennial, 2008), 113. It is important to note the contribution of James B. Haile III, who introduced me to this short story after discussing my theory of the *Man-Not*.

48. Ibid., 114.

49. Huey P. Newton, "Fear and Doubt," in *Essays from the Minister of Defense* (USA: Black Panther Party 1967), 15–17, 16.

50. See J. H. Van Evrie, introduction to *The Dred Scott Decision*, vol. 2 (New York: Van Evrie, Horton, 1859), iii–ix; and William Lee Howard, "The Negro as a Distinct Ethnic Factor in Civilization," *Medicine* 9 (1903): 423–26.

51. See Alva Myrdal, "A Parallel to the Negro Problem," in *An American Dilemma: The Negro Problem and Modern Democracy* (New York: Harper and Brothers, 1944), 1073–78; and Helen Mary Hacker, "Women as a Minority Group," *Social Forces* 30, no. 1 (1951): 60–69.

52. Michelle Wallace, *The Black Macho and the Myth of the Superwoman* (New York: Dial, 1979), 73–79.

53. John Dollard, *Caste and Class in a Southern Town* (New York: Doubleday/Anchor, 1937), 289.

54. Ibid., 290.

55. Abram Kardiner, "Explorations in Negro Personality," in *Culture and Mental Health: Cross Cultural Studies* (New York: Macmillan, 1959), 413–23, 421–22.

56. Lawrence E. Gary, ed., introduction to *Black Men* (Beverly Hills, CA: Sage, 1981), 1–17.

57. For a discussion of the frustration-aggression hypothesis in Wright's Bigger Thomas character, see Cyrus Ernesto Zirakzadeh's "Alternative Readings of Bigger Thomas" in this volume.

58. James Baldwin, "Alas, Poor Richard," in *Nobody Knows My Name: More Notes on a Native Son* (New York: Dial, 1961), 604–21, 605.

59. James Baldwin, "An Interview with James Baldwin" in *Conversations with James Baldwin*, ed. Fred L. Standley and Louis H. Pratt (Jackson: University Press of Mississippi, 1989), 3–23, 10–11.

60. Wright, "Man of All Work," 120.

61. Ibid.

62. See William Powell Jones, *The Tribe of Black Ulysses: African American Lumber Workers in the Jim Crow South* (Champaign: University of Illinois Press, 2006).

63. Wright, "Man of All Work," 128.

64. Ibid., 130.

65. Ibid., 140.

66. Ibid., 146–47.

67. Ibid., 147.

68. Ibid., 154.

69. Ibid.

70. Abdul R. JanMohamed, *The Death-Bound-Subject: Richard Wright's Archaeology of Death* (Durham, NC: Duke University Press, 2005), 249.

PART 3

Black Internationalism

Behind the McGee Case

Richard Wright

Since the state of Mississippi executed Willie McGee, many Europeans, burdened with a sense of acute distress, have asked me, "How could America, while preaching democracy, kill McGee and at the same time spare the lives of seven guilty Nazis?" Other Europeans questioned me in this fashion: "Why did not America spare the life of McGee and appease the sense of outraged justice in the world of democratic opinion?" And lastly, some asked, "Did our agitation here in Europe help or harm McGee?"

These questions seemed to me to be sincere and to indicate a genuine desire to know; Europe wonders with a sense of alarm at America's implacable determination to have her own way in administering "justice."

Let us at the outset settle the question of McGee's guilt. The Negro press in America states that McGee had known the white woman in question for four years, had known her intimately. The woman's husband, a traveling salesman, returned home unexpectedly and surprised them; hence the charge of rape . . .

But behind this simple, human incident stands a problem of vast import; the McGee Case stands at the apex of an intricate social, political, pyramid whose base rests upon the plantation economy of the Deep South. The McGee Case cannot be understood in isolation; its background must be taken into account.

The McGee Case occurred in the most backward of America's forty-eight states, the state of Mississippi whose health, educational, cultural, and social standards are lower perhaps than could be found in any part of Europe today. Illiteracy is widespread among both black and white. Since the Civil War little or no industrialization has occurred to relieve the sharp master-slave relations, and the domination of whites over blacks is complete and unmitigated. Also it must be recalled that the Negroes in Mississippi *outnumber* the whites, a fact which casts race relations at a pitch just short of daily violence.

Outnumbered, the whites are determined to hold onto the reins of state power which consists of the police, the state national guard, the press, radio, church, banking, farming, industry, and the educational system. The entire social structure of the state of Mississippi is so rigged as to allow expression to *whites only*.

How is this possible? Do the Negroes agree to this? They do not. Hence, a kind of daily race war rages on all levels of life among people who live *side by side as neighbors*. To understand the McGee Case one has to understand this proximity of the two races locked in daily combat. The two races pass each other on the streets each hour; black women nurse and cook in white homes; black men labor in the farms and in the factories of white bosses. In things essential to daily life, the races are mixed; in things pertaining to the power structure of society, the whites are in undisputed control. Yet this control is maintained only at a cost of nightmarish tension which suffuses the whole of daily life in Mississippi; this control is manifested formally in a code of rigid race laws which all Negroes must obey, laws which prescribe which schools Negroes can attend, which areas they must live in, what jobs they can perform, etc., etc.

Yet these laws are not enough to keep the numerically superior Negroes out of state power; it is necessary for each individual white man in the community to take it upon himself to act the role of a racial policeman. The least infraction of the race code on the part of a Negro, such as drinking from the wrong water fountain, forgetting to say "sir" to a white man, refusing to sit in the racially segregated section of a bus, street car or train, seeking to enter the front instead of the rear door of a white home—any of these acts merits instant reprisal, curses or blows, on the part of whites.

Naturally, such piece-meal methods of race repression on the part of whites do not work in the long run. More drastic measures are needed. Before World War II, these measures were simple and widespread. When the

Negro population became what the whites called "intractable," white mobs would form, drag a Negro from his home, charge him with rape, dip him in hot tar, roll him in feathers and then drench him in gasoline and burn him alive. This brutal act would take place in a public and dramatic manner, such as dragging the Negro's dead body through the streets of the Negro section of the city. The purpose of this was to throw fear into the hearts of the numerically superior Negroes. In short, the killing of one Negro was designed to serve as a lesson in terror to millions of other Negroes.

After World War II, America's position in world affairs and the protracted fight of progressive forces in America made it costly and difficult for even the backward state of Mississippi to continue this brutal and lawless practice. Hence, today, what used to happen *outside of the law* now takes place with the *sanction of the law*. Ironically as it may sound, this switching from lawless to legal lynching represents a moral step forward in that it places the actions of Mississippi whites squarely and responsibly before the bar of world opinion. Formerly, the officials of Mississippi could say, when a Negro was lynched, that lawless mobs did it; today they must try to defend legal actions that do not admit of moral or intellectual defense.

The killing of McGee in Mississippi was a symbolic act on the part of whites against Negroes. Yet the state of Mississippi did not anticipate that the killing of McGee would be so costly in terms of national and local prestige; they were stunned and worried when the global implications of their acts rolled back upon them, and embarrassed their government in the eyes of the world. The whites of Mississippi had two choices. They could spare the life of McGee or kill him. To have spared his life would have been tantamount to admitting that they were wrong; it would have involved a loss of "face" in front of the angry Negro masses. Yet, to kill McGee, they well knew, would make them look inhuman and barbarous in the eyes of the world. But since local pressures outweighed whatever prestige their national government would suffer, the Mississippi whites, exasperated, afraid, angry, carried out the sentence of death on Willie McGee.

Do not, for one moment think that the widespread agitation in defense of McGee did not have its beneficial effects. It most surely did. Today the whites of Mississippi will hesitate and think hard and long before staging another McGee legal lynching. They now realize that the tide of world opinion is definitely against them and their criminal race code. Of course, possessing the arms and the reins of state power, they can take another Willie McGee secretly from his home and shoot him and leave his body in some lonely swamp, but they will be less prone to boast about such a brutal and inhuman act.

Yes, the fight to save McGee was a moral victory. The men who killed him stand convicted before the world, and the cost to America on the international front has made many high American officials ponder the folly of race prejudice.

June 4, 1951

Note: Originally published as "Derrière l'affaire [McGee] (Behind the McGee case)," *Le Droit de Vivre,* June 4, 1951. The typescript carbon version of the English article is held in box 5, folder 82, of the Richard Wright Papers at the Beinecke Rare Book and Manuscript Library at Yale University. Reprinted courtesy of the Richard Wright Estate.

Seizing Freedom with Simone de Beauvoir

Lori J. Marso

Richard Wright's speech to the Paris Congress of 1956 ignited a firestorm of debate within black political and intellectual circles.[1] Describing freedom as the ability to break away from identities created through culture, religion, and tradition and thus create openings for new forms of collective political action, Wright's address challenged the idea of reclaiming "blackness" as a politically liberating identity. His speech, particularly when considered in dialogue with the writings of French existentialist and feminist Simone de Beauvoir, raises urgent questions about freedom, identity, and collective action, both for his time and ours.

Assembled as "blacks," the participants at the Paris Congress, hosted by the journal *Présence Africaine*,[2] included American, African, European, and Caribbean black intellectuals and artists. Richard Wright, arguably the most well-known black intellectual in the world at this juncture, was expected to speak in the voice he had made famous in *Black Boy* (1945) and *Native Son* (1940). Both books had been translated into several languages and were very popular in France. Many of his global contemporaries viewed Wright as an authentic black son, born and raised in Mississippi, and thus able to represent the "true" African American experience.

But Wright was no longer focusing on Bigger Thomas's individual, misogynist, and ultimately futile resistance to white supremacy.[3] By this time, he was considering the possibility of broader, worldly, collective political action and was determined to connect African American experience to that of oppressed peoples in Africa and beyond. Disheartened by racism in the United States, he had voluntarily exiled himself and his family to Paris in 1947. At the time of the Paris Congress, he had recently returned from sojourns in Argentina, Haiti, and Spain, as well as trips to Kwame Nkrumah's revolutionary Ghana, where he collected material for his book *Black Power*, and to Indonesia, where he reported on the 1955 Bandung Conference of Third World Nations.[4]

Although Wright was respected as the author of *Native Son*, when he stepped to the podium his audience wasn't quite sure what to expect. He was a committed leftist and an anti-imperialist, but Wright could not be counted on to adhere to any party or ideological line. His politics were very much his own, and unlike many of his peers at the Congress, he did not present himself as an ideological radical seeking to overthrow modernity. He also refused to don the role of an "authentic" black man.[5] He chose instead to identify as one who travels with others contesting racism, colonialism, and patriarchal oppression. Indeed, he lamented the absence of female voices at the Paris Congress and commented extensively on the role of women in revolutionary Ghana.[6]

By the time of the Paris Congress, he was articulating three main ideas: there is nothing essential to black identity; blacks can and should cross the color line and join in solidarity with other oppressed groups; and in order to be free, blacks must embrace modern ways of being in the world. Wright told those assembled in Paris that American blacks and Third World peoples needed to work with each other in solidarity, and that the path to freedom necessitates a reinterpretation, and ultimately the rejection, of cultural and religious identities. This message shocked the participants.

When we evaluate Wright's qualified embrace of modernity by putting his work in conversation with the writings of Simone de Beauvoir, we can see them together stimulating new ways of thinking about identity, solidarity, and freedom.[7] As we will see, Beauvoir's work traces a surprisingly similar path to Wright's. Rejecting forms of desire that are bound up with "femininity," she imagined alternative ways of being a woman in the world as she simultaneously envisioned new forms of solidarity. Because of mutual friends and similar philosophical and political interests, Wright and Beauvoir had met when he traveled to France in 1946. When Beauvoir came to the United States in 1947, she was hosted by Wright and his wife, Ellen. While many have noticed the friendship between Beauvoir and Wright, I will call attention to their intellectual synergy by putting Beauvoir's *The Second Sex* into conversation with Wright's 1941 essay and photo-documentary, *12 Million Black Voices*.[8] Learning from Wright's encounter with Beauvoir, my primary claim is that enacting freedom is only possible when we reach out to others not like ourselves. In these two works, each author treats traditional, religious, and normative identities as obstacles to a more expansive and creative form of political freedom that emphasizes collective action. Both acknowledged that the sediment of a collective cultural otherness (defined by political meanings attached to race, gender, and historically rooted habits of behavior and thinking) constructed and constrained the freedom for the individual that they prized. Although each saw oppression as built on pernicious meanings of bodies, they cautioned against political practices that mobilize political action based on alienated identities, and that limit politics to working with others like one's self. Moreover, they each argued that to promote blackness or femininity, for example, even when mobilized for resistance, ultimately holds us in thrall to victimization and suffering. When we read their work in conversation, we see that nurturing a liberatory political subjectivity entails rejecting all normative categories. For Wright and Beauvoir, freedom arises when we forge political bonds across different groups, are able with others to see and describe the world differently, and together take the risk of acting in concert to claim a new future.

The "Rot" of Tradition and Culture

In his speech to the Paris Congress, Wright boldly claimed that the "smashing" of the "irrational ties of religion and custom and tradition in Asia and Africa . . . [was] the central historic fact" that resulted from colonialism.[9] Surprisingly, he argued this "unconscious and unintentional" result of Western exploitation should be celebrated. Why should we celebrate what Europeans described as "the spread of civilization, missions of glory, of service, of destiny even,"[10] and rationalized as the "consecrated duty of converting or enslaving all infidels"?[11] Because today, according to Wright, "a *knowing* black, brown, or yellow man can say: 'Thank you, Mr. White Man, for freeing me from the rot of my irrational traditions and customs, though you are still the victim of your own irrational customs and traditions!'"[12]

It was audacious for Wright to call the traditions and customs of Africa "rot" given that the Paris Congress was organized partly to acknowledge the *dignity* of these same traditions and cultures, to celebrate the contributions of African civilization, and to reclaim and rebuild blackness as a distinct way of being in the world. Although Wright recognized, *insisted* even, that being black was a central category of modern politics and social history, he consistently rejected anything he regarded as approaching a "racialist" perspective. Wright's 1956 speech struck many attendees as discordant with the more romantic versions of Negritude, such as the one affirmed by Senegalese poet Léopold Sédar Senghor, who advanced "black values" as expressions of precolonial, communal Africa.[13]

Wright also embraced a qualified version of modernity. Drawing on his own experience as helping him move beyond fixed identity categories, Wright claimed a hybrid identity. Saying he was "black" *and* a "man of the West,"[14] Wright advanced his modern perspective as a "double-vision" rendering him "chronically skeptical," "restless," "eager, urgent," and "irredeemably critical."[15]

Pointedly, Wright admitted that he was "offended" by the "teeming religions gripping the minds and the consciousness of Asians and Africans,"[16] even though his sympathies were "unavoidably with, and unashamedly for, them."[17] At the same time, he condemned the religion, customs, and traditions of white people living in industrialized nations. In Wright's opinion, white history and its consequences were a "ghastly racial tragedy."[18] He argued that whites wallowed in their own "rot" by promoting slavery and colonialism and then taking refuge in a new religion of racism. The "Western environment is soaked in and stained with the most blatant racism the world knows." This racism resembled "another kind of religion,"[19] but "what a shabby, vile, and cheap home the white heart finds when it seeks shelter in racism."[20] To Wright's eyes, the continuing religious irrationalism of the masses in the Third World was confronting the modern irrational racism of the Western masses. As he saw it, irrationalism was meeting irrationalism.[21]

He nevertheless still saw the future as unfolding in Third World terms. Wright explicitly condemned colonial and imperialist ventures around the world, but he maintained that these ventures created possibilities for Third World peoples to seize freedom. He therefore urged his comrades to reevaluate their common plight *and* to reject "blackness" as a way to ground politics. As Manthia Diawara notes, Wright's dramatic opening phrase to his speech

("The hour is late and I am pressed for time") referred not only to the late hour and the exhaustion of the participants, but also to the need for the participants to become aware of their place in history and of the importance of seizing the moment.[22] In telling the "men of Europe" to "give that elite [leaders such as Nkrumah in Ghana] the tools and let it finish the job," Wright anticipated Frantz Fanon's argument in *The Wretched of the Earth* that aid to Africa is not charity but rather "reparation": the "final stage of a dual consciousness—the consciousness of the colonized that *it is their due* and the consciousness of the capitalist powers that effectively *they must pay up*."[23]

Since Wright died at the age of fifty-two in 1960, he couldn't know how hard the future would be for Africa. As early as 1964 "the bloom had come off the rose of Ghana's celebratory moment."[24] Nkrumah and the Conventional People's Party, arguably in response to Western hostility, had become increasingly authoritarian, bureaucratic, and divorced from the Ghanaian people who had supported his rise to power. Other new nations on the African continent were also struggling with internal problems and civil unrest, all the while trying to negotiate their relationships to the West and to the Soviet Union. The year Wright died, seventeen African nations had declared their independence from Britain, France, and Belgium. By 1968, there had been sixty-four coups or coup attempts in these new nations.[25] Each nationalist leader felt intense political pressure. The murder of Congo leader Patrice Lumumba in 1961, by Katangese secessionists who were allied with Belgians, intensified worries about Africa's future and enhanced African suspicion and distrust of Westerners.

The future path for Africa that Wright had hoped for and worked to achieve was the path not taken. Can this occluded African future offer us a critical purchase on forms of political action that we might advance today? To consider this question, it is necessary to make a short detour and recall Wright's trip to Nkrumah's revolutionary Ghana, where he deepened his philosophical commitment to existential freedom as well as to modern forms of political collective action.

Race Matters, but How? Wright's Trip to Ghana

Like many African Americans who traveled to Africa in the mid-twentieth century, Wright wanted not only to see the continent but also to take stock of his own identity as an African American. When his boat docked in Ghana, he immediately noticed how "black life was everywhere."[26] Fascinated by bare feet, by richly colored cloths, and by the fact that the "whole of life that met the eyes was black," Wright was startled to see a European family "threading its way through the black crowd."[27] His guide commented: "It's good *not* to be a minority for once, eh?,"[28] and Wright agreed. But then an African salesman in a shop recognized Wright as an American and asked from which part of Africa he came. Startled and upset by this question, one that he would confront again, Wright said: "Well, you know, you fellows who sold us and the white men who bought us didn't keep any records."[29]

Wright thus admitted from the outset that his perspective was that of a *Western* man of color, that he felt distant from his African heritage, and that he disassociated himself from African identity when seeing Africans wearing few clothes, dancing, singing, drumming, and taking part in funeral and other traditional ceremonies. Referencing his "Western" vision, Wright commented that African life was lived too publicly: women with babies strapped to their backs, nursing them as they are walking; people urinating and bathing in the open; the constant beat of drums in drum circles; the deformed beggars making heartrending appeals; and all this under the constant sun and its oppressive and cloying heat. In his words: "The intimacy of the African communal life can be witnessed in all of its innocence as it clusters about an outdoor hydrant."[30]

Wright was hyperaware of the fact that though he desired to understand what he saw, he could not: "faced with the absolute otherness and inaccessibility of this new world, I was prey to a vague sense of mild panic, an oppressive burden of alertness which I could not shake off."[31] Wright's "panic" and "alertness" arose from his efforts to figure out his heritage and his ties to a continent that confused him yet staked a claim on his identity. It also speaks to his awareness of the ways that what we see is conditioned by where we come from. His perspective as black and Western made him skeptical, alert, restless, and confused.

Maybe because Wright did not feel any natural tie to the continent, he also could not see any essential or special genius, ethics, or talent arising from having black blood. Wright admitted he was left cold when his Negro friends would boast: "We have a *special* gift for music, dancing, rhythm and movement. . . . We have a genius of our own. We were civilized in Africa when white men were still living in caves in Europe." As he explained to his readers, "talk of that sort had always seemed beside the point; I had always taken for granted the humanity of Africans as well as that of other people."[32] For Wright, race portended nothing about belonging to humanity; nor did it point toward privileged knowledge of how to change humanity for the better. Although Wright argued that racism played a primary role as one of the most important historical forces (if not *the* most) in the oppression of people worldwide, he also contended that race itself tells us nothing about identity, solidarity, or even the roots of oppression. Consequently, when he looked at history, he never used social or political beliefs about racial inferiority to explain the origins of slavery. He argued that "slavery was not put into practice because of racial theories; racial theories sprang up in the wake of slavery, to justify it."[33] In his opinion, the resiliency and resemblance of what seem to be black traditions in both Africa and North America pointed not to an essential quality in blackness but to how oppression manifested itself on the bodies and behaviors of all kinds of people.[34] During his trip, Wright was moving toward the position that modernity created the very concept and practices of what we call tradition, and that these behaviors and customs are part of the displaced core of modernity itself.

The intellectual and emotional distance that Wright, as a "man of the West," felt toward Africans enabled him to see Nkrumah's attempt to create a modern political movement out of a tribal culture and competing traditional religions sympathetically yet critically. Nkrumah's ability to mobilize tribal customs and religions impressed Wright. Defying the idea that Africans cannot rule themselves and must first slowly "learn" Western behaviors of citizenship, Nkrumah and the Convention People's Party demonstrated that self-rule can happen immediately. Wright believed that the people of Ghana understood the meaning of freedom even more deeply and urgently than did Westerners. After all, as Wright saw in Ghana, 4 million illiterate people from diverse tribes had organized themselves into a "we" who demanded freedom from an alien flag and sovereignty over their own land. In spite of their lack of formal education, Wright insisted that they were already acting as free citizens: "They had melted their tribal differences into an instrument to form a bridge between tribalism and twentieth-century forms of political mass organization; the women who danced and shouted were washerwomen, cooks, housewives, etc."[35] Nkrumah's Convention People's Party channeled people's "wild and liquid emotion" drawn from religious practices into a new outlet: "Mass nationalist movements were, indeed, a new kind of religion. They were politics *plus!*"[36] Upon meeting Nkrumah, Wright congratulated him: "You've done what the Western world has said is impossible."[37]

Not surprisingly, Wright urged Nkrumah to reject both the West *and* the Communists and to follow a distinctly African path, by forging a secular religion and building a social structure that could provide the "emotional sustenance" to escape from "the domination of foreigners."[38] As Manthia Diawara puts it, Wright advised Nkrumah to achieve independence by freeing West Africans "from themselves, from tribal religions which formed a psychological barrier between them and the modern world, and from the chiefs who had usurped a godlike position."[39]

Wright suspected, but did not know, that this path would not be open for new African nations. While in the 1956 address he urged the West to "give us the tools and we'll finish the job,"[40] Wright was well aware that Western nations would actively oppose freedom in the non-Western world. Nonetheless, his reflections on Ghana can help us think anew about freedom, solidarity, and collective political action across borders of identity.

Saying "We" with Simone de Beauvoir

Fifteen years prior to traveling to Ghana and prior to addressing the Paris Congress, Wright was thinking about these same questions in the United States. Wright's work had resonated deeply with the French existentialist Simone de Beauvoir, with whom Wright had become close friends. During her 1947 trip to the United States, Wright took her to Harlem, showed her his favorite places in New York City, and, in the meantime, helped her to think about women's situation as not so unique when studied in relationship to racial oppression.

Many scholars have judged this intellectual relationship one-sidedly. Wright's influence on Beauvoir is usually considered positive, as opening her eyes to racism (even though Beauvoir had already read extensively about the Jim Crow South in preparation for her travels). In contrast, Wright's interest in existentialism, particularly after his move to France, was seen by some as clouding, complicating, or even destroying Wright's authentic black voice.[41] Lamenting the tendency among academics to dismiss Wright's later thinking, Paul Gilroy (in his chapter in this volume) has urged scholars to study more carefully the intellectual ties between Wright and Beauvoir and their recognition that Western feminist and Third World antiracist liberation projects need not be seen as distinct, and certainly not as opposed, endeavors.[42]

The remainder of this essay takes up Gilroy's call. What we will see is that Beauvoir and Wright agree that oppressed individuals can forge bonds of solidarity, initiate change, and express their immanent freedom by reaching out to others. Attentive to varieties of experience *within* communities of blacks, and *within* communities of women, each author stressed that differences between groups (men/women, black/white) seem more pronounced when we fail to note the diversity of experiences inside these categories. Wright and Beauvoir thus foreswear identity to pluralize perspectives, even while constructing a political "we" that defines a concrete alternative to the false universalism of the American national story and the patriarchal norm. Wright produced a "we" out of 12 million individual black voices, even though he diligently detailed how oppression and violence affect blacks *perversely* as well as *differently,* depending upon situation—most notably location, generation, religion, and sex. Beauvoir did the same for women: she located a new common ground while challenging the myth of "Woman" by noticing women's divisions by class, age, religion, and nation.

In the preface to *12 Million Black Voices*, Wright expressed his wish to seize upon what is "qualitative and abiding in Negro experience."[43] Moving through slavery, Jim Crow, and the Great Migration, to urban poverty and discrimination, Wright's poignant text is accompanied by photos by Dorothea Lange, Walker Evans, Edwin Rosskam, Russell Lee, and Richard Wright himself. For this book Wright chose eighty-six pictures from thousands of photos that the government had commissioned to document suffering and its alleviation via New Deal agencies.[44] Wright was a skilled photographer at this point and gave a great deal of thought to the subjectivity of the photographer (himself or others), to the framing of the images (even where they should be placed on the page), and to the words that would complement the image. Wright had a complex relationship to photography and to the documentary image, one that fits with his complex relationship to modernity as expressed in his address to the Paris Congress and his writings on Ghana and Bandung. As Wright saw it, photography was a technology of modernity, one that might serve as a tool of oppression to confirm what whites thought they already knew about black lives, but it also might upend that same arrogance.[45] In other words, he was well aware of the contradictions at the heart of photography and its implicit promise to document "reality." In particular, Wright was attentive to what different viewers and readers might see in an image, and how they might interpret the photos through their "naturalized" identity as white or black. For example, the opening paragraph of the first chapter, titled "Our Strange Birth," was placed directly below a photo of an older black man looking straight into the camera, his face marked by deep lines.

Wright's words, openly acknowledging the deep divisions in the national "we," addressed white readers: "Each day when *you* see *us* black folk upon the dusty land of the farms or upon the hard pavement of the city streets, *you* usually take *us* for granted and think *you* know *us*, but *our* history is far stranger than *you* suspect, and *we* are not what *we* seem."[46] In this powerful opening passage, accompanied by the photo of the older black man, Wright addresses white readers as pupils, to argue that what "you" (white readers) assume about "us" (black people) is wrong. Wright demanded that white readers acknowledge blacks as a collectivity whose existence challenged any claim to a universal white nationality *and* whose diverse experiences as individuals defied caricatures of the presumed Negro character.[47] Doing so, Wright deconstructed any claim to national unity (or common interest) by addressing readers as black or white. He chastised whites and simultaneously drew attention to the population of all too visible, yet hidden, black Americans: a "we" of "millions of black folk who live in this land."[48] As Wright informs his readers, black Americans are part of "Western civilization" but were subjected to an especially "weird and paradoxical birth,"[49] because they were dragged to this nation on slave ships.

This "we" of black Americans, however, is itself not naturally unified, according to Wright. After dividing his audience into black and white readers, he then fractures the "we" of black Americans even further. He presents Americans blacks as *themselves* diverse: products of multiple forms of oppression, violence, and provincialism based on their own situations and experiences. Blacks therefore have to work to create a form of unity to oppose and change their collective situation. As Perry Moskowitz points out in his chapter in this volume, Wright's subversive curatorial aesthetic practice, witnessed in the way he edits the photos and the captions he writes, fractures as well as constructs the "we."[50] The structural history of slavery and the varied experiences of oppression might bring American blacks together, but this is merely a possibility, not a promise. A "we" of 12 million black voices must be *produced* rather than assumed: "Our outward guise

Seizing Freedom with Simone de Beauvoir

Sharecropper, Georgia. (Jack Delano, Farm Security Administration)

still carries the old familiar aspect which three hundred years of oppression in America have given us, but beneath the garb of the black laborer, the black cook, and the black elevator operator lies an uneasily tied knot of pain and hope whose snarled strands converge *from many points of time and space.*"[51]

Beauvoir used a similar strategy to destroy the illusion of the universal "we" among women. She showed that the identity of "Woman" was a male invention, developed from a male perspective. In contrast, she called for the production of a new and revolutionary "we" by positing a collective of women that previously did not exist. Just as Wright rejected the white world's expectation that all Africans or black Americans are essentially the same because of similar skin color, Beauvoir distanced herself from the idea of "Woman" as written in science, literature, and psychoanalysis. The introductory chapter to *The Second Sex* shows that women have been defined as "Other" to, and positioned as outside of, the universal. All of volume 2 of *The Second Sex* purports to "describe the world from [women's] point[s] of view,"[52] whereas volume 1 shows how "Woman" is invented as fixed, natural, essential, unchanging, and codified in science, psychoanalysis, literature, history, and myth. The idea of "Woman" wrongly assigns a stable meaning to sexual difference, and thus aids and abets women's second-class status. Throughout *The Second Sex*, Beauvoir shows that the meaning of sexual difference is always inherently *unstable* and women's experiences are diverse and contradictory. Within and from these diverse situations, each woman is expected to respond and react to the male position as the "One."

By recounting women's varied experiences, volume 2 of *The Second Sex* creates multiple conversations across women's lives (as well as between reader and text).[53] Beauvoir accomplishes this by compiling thousands of individual stories extracted and borrowed from her own life, the lives of acquaintances and friends, from autobiographies and biographies of famous women, from films, from literature. Beginning this project, Beauvoir says she noticed a disjuncture in her own life between what was expected of her as "Woman" and the diversity of human life and the meanings assigned to it. As she put it: "If I want to define myself, I first have to say, 'I am a woman'; all other assertions will arise from this basic truth. . . . There is an absolute human type that is masculine while women's ovaries and uterus are the particular conditions that lock her in her subjectivity."[54]

Putting it in the terms Wright uses, women have a "weird and paradoxical" relationship to the universal. Though women are human and experience themselves as free subjects, their road to freedom is blocked by their material conditions, by their own psychologically produced visions of what they can accomplish, and by their previous inability throughout history to adequately say "we" primarily due to the concrete material differences in their lives. Like Wright's black Americans, women are a "we" that must be produced rather than discovered.

In short, Wright and Beauvoir share the belief that though modernity *creates* oppressed subjects, it has failed to embrace them or enable their political subjectivity. The two thinkers track the enormous energy that goes into the creation of the subordinated status of the other for the sake of shoring up a whitened and masculinized self to whom history, transcendence, and sovereignty "rightly" belong. The whitened masculinized self, first of all, assigns immanence, ambiguity, mortality, and embodiment to the created "Other," and, secondly, insists that repetitive, alienated, flexible, and low-paid labor is naturally appropriate and ideally suited for the temperaments and talents of women and nonwhite (and lower-class white) men. As anticapitalists, both Beauvoir and Wright are also sensitive to the division of people by class as well as by race and by gender, and at least in Beauvoir's case, the way these categories not only intersect but also make each of us into oppressors and oppressed in different moments and situations. Beauvoir also is aware of discrimination based on age, on standards of beauty, and on ability.

The Second Sex thus attempts to counter the false subject of "Woman" and to produce a collective "we" from the lived experience of individual women constrained and enabled by their particular situations. Beauvoir demonstrates that while knowing little of women's lives, men make assumptions about women that perpetuate gendered myths. Like Wright, Beauvoir seeks to counter harmful myths by creating an alternative collective, one that neither assumes an identity prior to experience nor runs roughshod over the individual voices making up the potential collectivity. Beauvoir's text makes an appeal to an as yet unimagined political collectivity to forge solidarities across identities. These are solidarities knitted together from and across diverse lived experiences of oppression.

Through thousands of anecdotes from women about the experiences of girlhood, sexual initiation, menstruation, marriage, motherhood, prostitution, lesbian relationships, aging, and more, Beauvoir's almost eight-hundred-page tome links diverse women's experiences within and constituted by demands of femininity. For example, Beauvoir argues that the notion of motherhood as women's destiny and as the ultimate fulfillment of feminine desire is inherently oppressive. But she also noted that the oppressive norms of motherhood vary by culture, by ethnicity, and by class. Throughout history, women have experienced the demands of motherhood very differently: "Pregnancy and motherhood are experienced in very different ways depending on whether they take place in revolt, resignation, satisfaction, or enthusiasm," she says.[55] A woman who had desperately wanted a child might be surprised that she experiences motherhood as a burden, while other women might find in their child "the satisfaction of secretly harbored dreams."[56] Motherhood, therefore, should be a true choice rather than an obligation or a natural "destiny": "To have a child is to take on a commitment; if the mother shrinks from it, she commits an offense against human existence, against a freedom; but no one can impose it on her."[57] Although Beauvoir never discusses slave women's experiences in *The Second Sex*, her writing can be seen as a precursor to that of Hortense Spillers. The sensitivity to differing experiences of motherhood and consistent critique of the bourgeois ideal of the "mother" in Beauvoir's writing resonate with Spillers's exploration of how conventional gender categories were unavailable to black women under slavery and how their work of mothering fell outside the very category of motherhood.[58]

While Beauvoir recounted stories from individual lives to document the falseness of the idea of "Woman," in *12 Million Black Voices* Wright shows the invention of the Negro by collecting and presenting photos of individual blacks. Juxtaposing the delineation of the categories of black workers created by the "American attitude," the photos feature *individual* blacks performing specific tasks ("*The* black maid," "*The* black industrial worker," "*The* black stevedore," and so on). The individual faces expose the lie about the alleged kindness, geniality, and benevolence of white supremacy *as well as* the lie about the natural servility and cheerfulness of the black domestic worker and the natural inferiority of the Negro. Throughout the text, Wright exposes the lies whites tell about black people, documents the several and different ways racism is made material, and calls on blacks to build solidarity from the practice of reaching out toward others both like and unlike one's self to engage in collective action.

A good example of Wright's disruption of identity categories is his account of life in the "kitchenettes" in northern urban areas. As Wright explains, northern "Bosses of the Buildings" rented to blacks at vastly higher rates than those charged to white tenants.[59] Those crowded, filthy, one-room apartments, "havens from the plantations in the South,"[60] were also "our prison, our death sentence without a trial, the new form of mob violence that

Seizing Freedom with Simone de Beauvoir   173

assaults not only the lone individual, but all of us, in its ceaseless attacks."[61] Yet the kitchenette also affected individual blacks differently, in this case based on gender: "The kitchenette jams our farm girls, while still in their teens, into rooms with men who are restless and stimulated by the noise and lights of the city; and more of our girls have bastard babies than the girls in any other sections of the city."[62] One photo shows a young mother holding a baby, with two young children by her side. On the opposite page, a young black male, also pictured in a kitchenette, stares into the camera.

Interior kitchenette, Chicago. (Russell Lee, Farm Security Administration)

Interior, Washington, DC. (Arthur Rothstein, Farm Security Administration)

According to the text, "The kitchenette fills our black boys with longing and restlessness, urging them to run off from home, to join together with other restless black boys in gangs, that brutal form of city courage."[63]

In *12 Million Black Voices* and *The Second Sex*, Wright and Beauvoir thus begin from the concrete, particular, and diverse lived experience of oppressed subjects and then attempt to create solidarity by imagining collectivity built differently. The recounting of individual and collective lived experience reveals the deceit of a presumed universality and yields an alternative base for formulating a common life. Rather than call on the experience of oppressed subjects to show an ever widening and more inclusive universalism—for example, to include blacks in the American story, or women in philosophy and history—Wright and Beauvoir criticize exclusionary practices in order to produce a "we" that will lead somewhere else. According to Wright and Beauvoir, oppressed subjects cannot be folded back into the original and false universal through an ever-increasing circle of democratic inclusion. Instead, oppressed subjects need to produce a new vision of progress. Having deconstructed any "natural" basis for either "feminine" desire or "black" ways of being in the world, Beauvoir and Wright reject essentialism and refuse to look backward. They urge us to seize freedom by rejecting nature, tradition, and identity categories that situate the oppressed as outsiders to modernity, constricting and confining movement and possibility.

Wright in particular notices that what might potentially unify blacks and move them toward solidarity is sometimes the (unintended) consequences of oppressive intrusions. While blacks may have lost their claim to the land, subsequent generations have been able newly to see their potential ties to others. According to Wright, the children of the sharecroppers "have been influenced by the movies, magazines, and glimpses of town life, and they lack the patience to wait for the consummation of God's promise as we do."[64] Modern media, the auto industry, and steel factories, all have undermined folk life. "Thundering tractors and cotton-picking machines" are responsible for the Great Migration to the North, which changed not only the daily habits of black folk, but their consciousness too.[65] New, contingent practices introduce opportunities and alter situations in unexpected ways. As I showed earlier, Wright himself utilized the democratic potential of one of these new technologies (the camera) in the way he curated photographs of black experiences in *12 Million Black Voices* not simply to "represent" reality but to create new possibilities. Just as he does in his speech to the Paris Congress, here Wright claims that rather than reject modernity and its tools, we should claim them as a terrain of struggle.

Beauvoir similarly argues that promoting so-called "feminine" desires fails to address the ways the feminine itself is not only a construction but also a contested political site, wherein contingent practices open onto possibilities for new futures. In five chapters on "History" in volume 1 of *The*

Second Sex, Beauvoir demonstrates that while normative categories of sexual difference signify relations of power and are constitutive in social relationships, various material changes—such as introducing or eliminating private property, female suffrage, access to abortion, and even the rituals of courtly love—can substantively change women's situation. As both Beauvoir and Wright agree, promoting normative categories alleviates the psychic anxiety that sexual and racial difference always generates. But both of them believed that retrieving these same normative categories, even when coded positively, is the wrong way forward. For both Wright and Beauvoir, it was better to leave these categories open, unmoored, unsettled, because it opens up new ways of seizing freedom and constituting the "we" of solidarity. For each of them, destabilizing inherited ways of seeing and experiencing the world was one of the more promising interventions of modernity.

Notes

This is a shorter and revised version of my article "Solidarity *Sans* Identity: Richard Wright and Simone de Beauvoir Theorize Political Subjectivity," in *Contemporary Political Theory* (*CPT*) 13:3 (2014): 242–62. I thank *CPT* for permission to republish it in this collection in revised form.

    1. The speech is included in the collection titled *Black Power: Three Books from Exile* (2008) and is titled "Tradition and Industrialization." Manthia Diawara discusses Wright's address to the Paris Congress in *In Search of Africa* (Cambridge: Harvard University Press, 1998); see also Richard Iton's *In Search of the Black Fantastic: Politics and Popular Culture in the Post–Civil Rights Era* (Oxford: Oxford University Press, 2008).

    2. Wright was involved in founding the journal in 1947–1948, which was devoted to advancing the work of black writers on oppression, colonization, and the Black Diaspora.

    3. Bigger's individual acts of resistance included killing a white woman and a black woman.

    4. *Indonesian Notebook: A Sourcebook on Richard Wright and the Bandung Conference,* ed. Brian Russell Roberts and Keith Foulcher (Durham, NC: Duke University Press, 2016) collects the writings of Indonesian writers, journalists, and intellectuals, some of which challenge Wright's reporting on the conference. The editors challenge the myth of the "Bandung Spirit" that too quickly assumes the birth of the nonaligned movement of nations based on a global racial consciousness. Wright's work from Ghana, Indonesia, and related lectures are collected in *Black Power: Three Books from Exile: Black Power; The Color Curtain; and White*

Man Listen! (New York: Harper Perennial, 2008). The essay on Ghana titled *Black Power* will be referenced as *Black Power*, and all page numbers will refer to this collection.

5. In particular Alioune Diop of Senegal, founder of *Présence Africaine*, who made the opening remarks at the Congress, as well as Aimé Césaire of Martinique and Léopold Sédar Senghor of Senegal.

6. There are no comments on women recorded in the version of Wright's speech to the Congress printed in *Black Power*, but in the complete proceedings printed in a special issue of *Présence Africaine* (and also mentioned in Gilroy's chapter in this volume), it is recorded that Wright said the following: "I don't know how many of you have noticed it [but] there have been no women functioning vitally and responsibly upon this platform [and] helping to mold and mobilize our thoughts. . . . When and if we hold another conference—and I hope we will—I hope there shall be an effective utilization of Negro womanhood in the world to help us mobilize and pool our forces. . . . [W]e cannot afford to ignore one half of our manpower, that is, the force of women and their active collaboration. Black men will not be free until their women are free." These remarks are printed in *Richard Wright: A Documented Chronology, 1908–1960*, by Toru Kiuchi and Yoshinobu Hakutani (Jefferson, NC: McFarland, 2014), 339.

7. My *Politics with Beauvoir: Freedom in the Encounter* (Durham, NC: Duke University Press, 2017) shows how freedom is only realized within encounter and is a shared, relational, and collective practice.

8. Richard Wright, *12 Million Black Voices* (New York: Basic, 2008).

9. Wright, "Tradition and Industrialization," 718.

10. Ibid.

11. Ibid., 712.

12. Ibid., 719.

13. Robin D. G. Kelley reminds us that Negritude had many faces (see his "A Poetics of Anticolonialism." in *A. Césaire, Discourse on Colonialism* [New York: Monthly Review Press, 2000], 7–28). Aimé Césaire's version of Negritude did not rely on racial essentialism and was, as Kelley puts it, "future-oriented and modern" (23).

14. Wright, "Tradition and Industrialization," 704–5.

15. Ibid.

16. Ibid., 706.

17. Ibid.

18. Ibid., 721.

19. Ibid., 706–7.

20. Ibid.

21. Ibid., 717.

22. This is not in *White Man, Listen!* but is present in the original version. *In Search of Africa*, 22.

23. *Wretched of the Earth* (1963; New York: Grove, 2004), 59.

24. Manning Marable, *Malcolm X: A Life of Reinvention* (New York: Viking, 2011), 315.

25. Al Jazeera, "Africa: The First Fifty Years," 18 September 2010, posted online at www.aljazeera.com/indepth/2010/09/20109189268906591.html.

26. Wright, *Black Power*, 52.

27. Ibid., 53.

28. Ibid.

29. Ibid., 54.

30. Ibid., 71.

31. Ibid., 59.

32. Ibid., 20.

33. Ibid., 23–24.

34. Beauvoir also talks about what are considered to be distinctly feminine traits (being coy, demure, restrained) as forged in close relationship to the experience of the denial of freedom. These are formed in conditions of oppression but are also a way to create a shared world at the same time. When shared Beauvoir calls them the "female complaint." As Jane Gordon pointed out to me in conversation, elements that remain beyond oppression are often those that continue to have meaning under new circumstances. "Feminine" traits or cultural "blackness" sometimes characterize the distinct ways communities forge shared collective worlds. But since Wright was trying to understand what, if anything, black people shared from the African to other continents, he saw traditions that did not conform to modern ways solely as a product of marginalization. This was a blind spot on Wright's part as he most often failed to see anything positive or potentially transformative or sustaining in repetitive, spiritual, tribal, and "nativist" customs and traditions unless directed to serve modern goals and ends.

35. Wright, *Black Power*, 23–24. However, Dorothy Stringer correctly points out that Wright was not always able to see women as potential or actual political agents or as expressing political desire when they participated in tribal rituals, relying as he often does on sexist and primitivist tropes to describe what he sees in Ghana (see Stringer, "Psychology and Black Liberation in Richard Wright's *Black Power*," in this volume).

36. Ibid., 77–78.

37. Ibid., 85.

38. Ibid., 417.

39. Diawara, *In Search of Africa*, 68.

40. Wright, "Tradition and Industrialization," 728.

41. Paul Gilroy refers to these charges against Richard Wright in his chapter in this volume and originally in *The Black Atlantic* (Cambridge: Harvard University Press, 1993), 186. Several essays in Virginia Whatley Smith's edited collection titled *Richard Wright's Travel Writings* (Jackson: University Press of Mississippi, 2001) explore how Wright's deepening exposure to French existentialism after 1946 affected the way he saw African American identity and experience and its potential links to that of Asian and African peoples.

42. Paul Gilroy explores how Wright links the black vernacular to an "emergent, global, anti-imperialist and anti-racist" politics in *The Black Atlantic*, 148. Only a few scholars have taken up Gilroy's call. See, for example, Vicki Bell, "Owned Suffering: Thinking the Feminist Political Imagination with Simone de Beauvoir and Richard Wright," in *Thinking through Feminism*, ed. Sara Ahmed (London: Routledge, 2000), 61–76; and Margaret Simons, *Beauvoir and The Second Sex: Feminism, Race, and the Origins of Existentialism* (London: Rowman and Littlefield, 2001). Marilyn Nissim-Sabat discusses Bell's essay at length in "Richard Wright's Mission: Initiating a Politics of the Human," also in this volume.

43. Wright, *12 Million Black Voices*, xx.

44. Many of the photos that Wright took with Russell Lee, a photographer in Chicago, did not make it into *12 Million Black Voices* but are included in Maren Stange's *Bronzeville: Black Chicago in Pictures, 1941–1943* (New York: New Press, 2004).

45. Just as Western imperialism created the conditions for colonized, racialized others to claim freedom collectively.

46. Wright, *12 Million Black Voices*, 10, my emphasis.

47. See Jeff Allred in "From Eye to We: Richard Wright's *12 Million Black Voices*, Documentary, and Pedagogy," *American Literature* 78, no. 3 (2006): 549–83.

48. Wright, *12 Million Black Voices*, 12.

49. Ibid.

50. See Perry S. Moskowitz, "Many Dark Mirrors in Richard Wright's *12 Million Black Voices*," in this volume.

51. Wright, *12 Million Black Voices*, 11, my emphasis.

52. Simone de Beauvoir, *The Second Sex*, trans. Constance Borde and Sheila Malovany-Chevallier (New York: Vintage, 2011), 17.

53. See "(Re)Encountering *The Second Sex*," chap. 1 of *Politics with Beauvoir*, by Lori Jo Marso (Durham, NC: Duke University Press, 2017) on Beauvoir's literary practice. In volume 1, she creates conversations between enemies of women (authors of male myths about femininity), and in volume 2, she creates conversations between the women whose experiences she gathers and presents. Throughout, she creates encounters between readers and her text. Beauvoir's literary strategy of staging encounters within texts, and between texts and readers, shows

how feelings emerge within material conditions (via bodies encountering other bodies and things in situations) and move in and through ideologies, myths, and systems to produce, reproduce, or challenge inequality and oppression.

54. Beauvoir, *The Second Sex*, 5.
55. Ibid., 533.
56. Ibid.
57. Ibid., 566.
58. Spillers, "Mama's Baby, Papa's Maybe: An American Grammar Book," *Diacritics* 17, no. 2 (Summer 1987): 64–81.
59. Wright, *12 Million Black Voices*, 104.
60. Ibid., 105.
61. Ibid., 106.
62. Ibid., 110.
63. Ibid., 111.
64. Ibid., 75.
65. Ibid., 79.

Revisiting Richard Wright in Ghana

Black Radicalism and the Dialectics of Diaspora

Kevin Kelly Gaines

For students of black radicalism, Richard Wright's *Black Power* (1954), his report on the nationalist revolution in the Gold Coast colony (present-day Ghana), inevitably frustrates the expectations raised by its prophetic title.[1] Wright undermines his avowed anti-imperialism with numerous problematic assertions about African culture. Wright's evident disdain, in *Black Power*, for the folk cultures of peoples of African descent places him fundamentally at odds with major currents of black radical thought, which regard the cultural resistance of African peoples as imaginative responses to their subordination.[2] Wright's view of the backwardness of African peoples and culture, and his inability to question his teleology of modernization, have clouded his legacy and hindered recognition of *Black Power*'s importance in theorizing black radicalism and diaspora.[3]

In this essay, I argue that despite the considerable problems of *Black Power*, Wright demands our attention for his revisionist reading of the condition of blacks in the diaspora, which he understands dialectically as the product of slavery, dispersion, and oppression, and simultaneously, as the necessary condition for black modernity and the forging of an anti-imperialist critique of Western culture.⁴ However unfashionably idiosyncratic Wright may appear to us today, it is important to realize that he was not the lonely rebel he often made himself out to be. With fellow black radical intellectuals in exile, including George Padmore and C. L. R. James, Wright was engaged in theorizing about the revolutionary significance of black and African peoples' struggles against Western oppression. Moreover, like Wright, Padmore and James were vehement in their own rejections of Negritude, the politically charged assertion by some Francophone African nationalists of a transhistorical, transnational black cultural unity.⁵

Wright's revisionist reading of the African diaspora offers an explicit critique of the diaspora-homeland binary. This is of paramount importance, insofar as that binary powerfully underwrites nationalist and essentialist understandings of blackness and is frequently indicative of a black diaspora identity invested in an often diversionary quest for authenticity. Wright thus challenges both the black cultural commonplace of the African diaspora as the fallen condition whose resolution is obtained through reclamation of African roots as well as its converse: the equally irrelevant assertion that one cannot "go home" to Africa. Instead, Wright's discussion of anticolonialism recasts diaspora as the mobilization of black modernity toward a transnational, transracial community of struggle.

Wright's text, read in the context of his participation in transnational politics of decolonization and African liberation, suggests yet another sense of the dialectic of diaspora. Brent Edwards has given an account of the emergence of the term during the mid-1960s as a corrective to totalizing declarations of pan-Africanism that masked the waging of sharp political and ideological disputes within decolonization movements.⁶ This corrective sense of diaspora as the pragmatic recognition of a diverse black world fragmented by language, politics, and ideology is commonly displaced by those who invoke diaspora as the sign of incommensurability. Instead of perceiving internal tensions and differences as symptomatic of political struggle, defining diaspora as incommensurability simply acquiesces to the notion that national, geographical, or cultural differences pose insurmountable obstacles to transnational solidarity. This essentializing, reductive sense of diaspora as an unbridgeable gulf reinscribes the diaspora-homeland dyad and is routinely invoked in the wake of the destruction of pan-African and global black radical projects.

Wright's exemplary reflections on diaspora suggest a larger problem of the politics of location bearing on the transnational careers of black radical thinkers as varied as Wright, Padmore, Malcolm X, and others. If exile and expatriation have been vital and liberating for some black radical intellectuals, then what of the relationship of these intellectuals to communities of struggle, both within their countries of origin and elsewhere? What were the conditions either facilitating or mitigating the production and dissemination of knowledge between these intellectuals and audiences and vice versa? These questions move beyond issues of location framed by the diaspora "return" to the ancestral homeland as a gauge of authenticity. Their ultimate aim is an account of the interface of global black radical projects with the configurations of hegemonic power they confronted. Wright's reflections on black modernity are exemplary and necessary for our response to the enduring material and spiritual crises of underdevelopment in Africa and among New World blacks.

In *Black Power*, Wright developed an analysis of a pan-Africanism whose political solidarity is founded on a shared history of oppression and a critical, dialectical consciousness of the situation of blacks in the West. For Wright, this was infinitely preferable to facile assertions of racial or cultural unity. For all his criticism of the West's moral and religious hypocrisy in its conquest of Africans and native peoples, Wright would continue to identify himself as a man of the West, whose engagement with modern industrial society as a black man was both enabling and alienating. Even as he claimed what were widely considered to be the virtues of Western modernity—that is, secularism, scientific method, reason, individual rights, and artistic freedom—Wright was at pains to dissociate himself from the West's anticommunism. But Wright's views on communism as the obstacle to pan-Africanism yielded to his realization that the political consciousness of African peoples would be a decisive terrain upon which the success of the African revolution hinged. While he generally promoted neutralism as the preferred course for the development of fledgling African and Asian states, his and Padmore's appeals that the West support authentic independence lest the Third World be "lost" to communism showed that he remained beholden to the Cold War perspective that he labored to transcend. While the Cold War continued to exert a shadowy influence over his activities, toward the end of his life it became less salient in his analysis of the challenges facing Ghana. By then Wright believed that communism posed less of a threat to African independence than did the combined forces of the exploitation of tribal identities by the colonial powers, corruption, and the antagonism of Western and American powers to more dissident visions of African independence.

Although Wright had met numerous black anticolonial intellectuals in Paris and London, including Padmore, James, and Léopold Senghor, his trip to the Gold Coast allowed him to witness firsthand a democratic movement, and the experience sharpened his conception of the revolutionary potential of peoples of African descent. The narrative of *Black Power* is marked by Wright's uneasiness at those aspects of Ghanaian culture and society that he perceived as obstacles to the Ghanaian independence movement and African freedom. In other words, while Wright hoped to feel at home politically in the Gold Coast, as a self-described man of the West, he harbored a deep suspicion of traditional culture, viewing it as a barrier to the modern consciousness required for the struggle for independence. Wright identified the anthropological project of interpreting Akan culture so thoroughly with British imperialism that to him, any consideration of an autonomous realm of culture unmediated by colonialism was anathema.[7] Wright's criticism was not so much directed toward African culture per se as it was focused on the hybrid of Akan tradition and the missionaries' Christian imperialism. This hybrid culture represented to Wright a psychological adaptation to oppression among Gold Coast Africans.

Wright employed several thematic strategies to convey his stance of detached partisanship. First, he framed his narrative within a meditation on the memory of the slave trade and knowledge of the historical formation of the black diaspora. This historical knowledge of the origins of the African diaspora took precedence over Akan culture as an object of anthropological examination. Second, Wright expressed reservations about the nationalist movement's ambiguous embrace of modernity. In addition, Wright wrestled with the question of "African survivals," at times recognizing a similarity between African and African American cultural practices, but generally resisting the notion of a racial mystique binding Africa to its diaspora.[8] While he expressed dismay over the participation of Africans in the slave trade, Wright was unequivocal about the West's hypocrisy in orchestrating the slave trade, a critique that was intended to undermine the West's contemporary claims of moral authority as the "free world."

Wright, who had explicitly set forth his Marxist outlook in a preface (demanded by an editor anxious to shield the author—and more likely, Harper and Brothers—from McCarthy-inspired accusations of subversions), began his book with a historical overview of the slave trade and the European settlement of the Americas. Noting ironically that his account was drawn from non-Marxist historiography,[9] Wright stressed the economic origins of enslavement: "Slavery was not put into practice because of racial theories; racial theories sprang up in the wake of slavery, to justify it. It was impossible to milk the limited population of Europe of enough convicts and indentured white servants to cultivate, on a large and paying scale, colonial sugar, cotton, and tobacco plantations. Either they had to find a labor force or abandon the colonies, and Europe's eyes turned to Africa, where the supply of human beings seemed inexhaustible." From his brief visit to Liverpool and his reading of history, Wright concluded that "the foundations of the city were built of human flesh and blood."[10]

Wright noted the presence of many Africans in Western dress at Euston Station in London, where he caught a train to Liverpool, from which he sailed to Ghana. He was acutely aware that he, along with those other Africans, was retracing in reverse well-worn historical paths of forced migration: "This was the city that had been the center and focal point of the slave trade. Suffice it to say that the British did not originate this trading in human flesh whose enormous profits laid the foundations upon which had been reared modern industrial England." While that infamous distinction had fallen to the Portuguese, England had developed the slave trade into a system "whose functionings in some manner would touch more than half of the human race with its bloody but profitable agitations—the consequences of which would endure for more than four hundred years."[11]

Wright's descriptions of his arrival in Africa at the port of Takoradi and his trip by bus to the capital, Accra, invoke historical memory as the antidote to the shock he expressed at the profound difference and poverty of African life. Indeed, this theme of enslavement was framed by a Ghanaian's innocent query about Wright's untraceable African ancestors, and Wright's resentment at his inability to answer the question. Wright's narrative suggests an utter lack of preparation for the alienation he experienced: "The kaleidoscope of sea, jungle, nudity, mud huts, and crowded places induced me in a conflict deeper than I was aware of; a protest against what I saw seized me." Wright's protest was not against Africa or its people but against "the unsettled feeling engendered by the strangeness of a completely different order of life" (*BP*, 37). Stunned by the "absolute otherness and inaccessibility" of this new world, Wright could not be altogether innocent of racial preconceptions in his perception of such difference. This was, however, a visceral rebuttal to the idea of Negritude and other romantic visions of Africa. At such moments, Wright's narrative shifts to the familiar terrain of historical knowledge, which offered a more secure basis for human identification. As the bus passed Elmina, Cape Coast, and Anomabu on its seaside route, these "historic Gold Coast place names stirred me to a memory of dark and bloody events of long ago." These were the beaches across which "hundreds of thousands of black men, women and children had been marched, shackled and chained, down to the waiting ships to be carted across the ocean to be slaves in the New World" (*BP,* 37, 40).

Having begun with an account of the European origin of the slave trade, Wright concluded his narrative with his visit to the primal scenes of the genesis of the African diaspora and of Western industrialism and modernity. There, the American-born Wright confronted the physical monuments of the slave trade, the stark fortresses lining the western coast of Africa, over which Portugal, Sweden, Denmark, France, and England had battled for control of the lucrative trade. Wright wrote movingly of the castles where captive Africans were imprisoned before they were forced onto the ships that carried them to the Americas as human commodities: "I was told that the same iron bolts which secured the doors to keep the slaves imprisoned were the ones that my fingers now touched" (*BP,* 399). He invited his readers to contemplate along with him the tangible memory of the horror and suffering of the captives, a "memory" that dwells in the dungeons of the castles. With powerful and poetic imagery, Wright burnishes the memory of enslavement, subjecting the legend among Ghanaians of the existence of gold treasure within the walls of the castles to an inversion that recalls the human suffering that preceded and produced the vast wealth and industrial revolution of the West:

> If there is any treasure hidden in these vast walls, I'm sure that it has a sheen that outshines gold—a tiny, pear-shaped tear that formed on the cheek of some black woman torn away from her children, a tear that gleams here still, caught in the feeble rays of the dungeon's light—a shy tear that vanishes at the sound of approaching footsteps, but reappears when all is quiet, hanging there on that black cheek, unredeemed, unappeased—a tear that was hastily brushed off when her arm was

grabbed and she was led toward those narrow, dank steps that guided her to the tunnel that directed her feet to the waiting ship that would bear her across the heaving, mist-shrouded Atlantic.[12]

In a letter to the Padmores from Ghana, Wright related the difficulties he encountered in obtaining the political knowledge he had sought. He had hoped that the Convention People's Party (CPP) nationalists would serve as guides and translators and would take him into their confidence as a political ally. But he found the nationalist leaders uncommunicative and reserved. So instead of a report of the political situation, Wright was compelled to concentrate on the life of the people, despite his lack of their tribal languages. He described a trip with Nkrumah through Accra as "inspiring." Wright was impressed with the nationalists' "streamlined, modern political organization" and marveled at the enthusiastic response of crowds of Ghanaians as Nkrumah's motorcade passed: "They shouted a greeting to the Prime Minister in a tone of voice compounded of passion, exhortation, and contained joy: 'Free-dooom! Free-doooom!'" (*BP*, 53). Wright believed these Africans demonstrated a deeper comprehension of the meaning of freedom than did people in the West: "At a time when the Western world grew embarrassed at the sound of the word 'freedom,' these people knew that it meant the right to shape their own destiny as they wished" (*BP*, 53–54).

Later, at a women's political rally, Wright was astonished at the synthesis of Christian and Akan prayers and rituals that preceded pro-CPP speeches in both English and tribal languages. Wright was deeply impressed with Nkrumah's and his party's fusion of religion with modern politics. Nkrumah had understood the need for a religious basis for the mass political mobilization—necessary to fill the void in the people's lives created by the missionaries' assaults on indigenous culture. On further reflection, Wright claimed that only a native African like Nkrumah could have accomplished this blend of Christianity, native religion, nationalism, and socialism. Wright regarded Nkrumah's nationalism as the unintentional outcome of British colonial education. This dubious claim, possibly intended to foster Western audiences' identification with Gold Coast nationalism, glossed over the complexity of Nkrumah's formation, which owed as much to such paragons of black modernity as the Gold Coast educator and nationalist Kwegyir Aggrey, Garvey, Padmore, and Du Bois.[13] Wright was truer to the spirit of black modernity when he added that Nkrumah and the Gold Coast nationalists were the product of another synthesis that the British hardly anticipated: Marxism, along with a "racial and class solidarity derived from the American Negro's proud and defensive nationalism" (*BP*, 65). Wright admired Nkrumah's organizational acumen, which he claimed far outstripped the Soviet Union's attempts to gain influence in Africa with ideas that were "backward" compared to those of the CPP. But if Marxism had been a factor, its relevance to the Gold Coast situation was limited, as the CPP had sought to address the alienating effects of colonialism and modernity:

> Back of it all was something much deeper and more potent than the mere influence of Marxist thought. . . . [T]he twentieth century was throwing up these mass patterns of behavior out of the compulsive nakedness of men's disinherited lives. These men were not being so much guided as they were being provoked by elements deep in their own personalities, elements which they could not have ignored even if they had tried. The greed of British businessmen and the fumbling efforts of missionaries had made an unwitting contribution by shattering the traditional tribal culture that had once given meaning to these people's lives, and now there burned in these black hearts a hunger to regain control over their lives. White [colonizers] could never have realized how taunting were their efforts to save Africans when their racial codes forbade their sharing the lives of those Africans. (*BP*, 91)

Wright was impressed—but remained torn—about whether this synthesis of politics and religion ("politics *plus*," as he referred to it) could effectively produce industrial and technical mastery (*BP*, 64–66).

Wright's uneasiness at the tensions between tradition and modernity in Gold Coast nationalism emerged more clearly in the account of his reaction to Nkrumah's use of a quasi-religious oath through which women at the rally swore their allegiance to the CPP and its leader. An astonished Wright regarded this deployment of charismatic authority as radically out of step with the modern politics of the twentieth century, let alone an emancipatory project. Just as troubling as this monarchial lack of distinction between the state and its executive was Nkrumah's refusal to share with Wright the text of the oath. There was a sinister undercurrent to Wright's retelling, as Nkrumah, in response to his request for a copy, silently looked off into the distance and "slowly, seemingly absent-mindedly," pocketed the slip of paper containing the oath. Wright struggled to reconcile the contradictory presence of religious authoritarianism within a modernist political movement. In any case, Wright's uneasiness at Nkrumah's tendency toward self-glorification was prescient in light of the subsequent cult of personality the Ghanaian leader cultivated (*BP*, 60–61).

Wright's reservations about Nkrumah's appropriations of indigenous culture in the war of position with the petit bourgeois Ghanaian opposition were rooted in his view that the psychological consequences of colonialism on the people of the Gold Coast were far more serious than was their material exploitation.[14] What he described as the psychological distance between Africans and Westerners posed the most profound threat to the achievement of true independence. The "travesty" of colonial education and the missionaries' assault on the Ashanti's capacity for military resistance had wrought psychological damage to the African personality. Even Westernized elite men of the opposition reflected a sort of bad faith, cynically clinging to the trappings of an Ashanti culture in which they did not believe. Wright observed mutual self-deception between Western colonizers and Africans, as the British, pursuing their economic and religious aims, "cannot escape lending a degree of recognition" to African belief systems, thus reinforcing the African's distance from modernity (*BP*, 117). Wright remained skeptical of admonitions from Britons that juju, the magic of fetish priests, was not some mere superstition to be dismissed out of hand. But Wright wondered why the Africans had not used such supernatural power to defend themselves against the colonizers, and why it had taken a westernized African to lead the fight for freedom.[15]

Wright was keenly attuned to the magnitude of the problems facing Nkrumah: "From where would come the men to handle the work of administration when self-government came? Would Nkrumah have to impose a dictatorship until he could educate a new generation of young men who could work with him?" (*BP*, 66). Such trepidation suffused Wright's account of Nkrumah's speech before the legislative assembly petitioning for self-government—the landmark event he had come to witness. Ironically, because the country's best-trained men were members of the opposition, Nkrumah was compelled to rely on British administrators and civil servants: "In coming to power Nkrumah had to import more Britishers to serve in technical capacities than had ever been in the Gold Coast" (*BP*, 168). Wright believed that if not for the expatriates, not only the business of government but also Nkrumah's promises of social reforms in health, education, and housing for the masses would have been deferred.[16] Still, Wright was justified in his nagging concern that the British were quietly dictating the pace and terms of the transition to self-government. And he voiced the emerging analysis of neocolonialism in observing that "the mining, timber, and mercantile interests, all foreign," were unfazed by the petition, and "had their own ideas about what was happening" (*BP*, 169).

For Wright, colonialism had reduced the prospect of communication on a basis of equality between Africans and Westerners. Colonialism had also produced a deracinated Gold Coast petite bourgeoisie determined to resist the popular movement for freedom. But it was true as well that colonialism was also the source from which some hope might be salvaged. The coming of industries may have cheated Africans, but it brought them in contact with labor organization and, in a general sense, "the most progressive and dynamic aspects of the Western world." The future, Wright hoped, resided with these young nationalists who had been impressed by the techniques of Western industrial production (*BP*, 157).[17] Wright reasserted this notion of colonialism as a means of modernization in the paper "Tradition and Industrialization," presented at the Congress of Negro and African writers in Paris in 1956. This thesis, along with Wright's equally controversial claim that traditional culture was complicit in colonial subjugation and potentially an obstacle to freedom, had been reinforced during Wright's Gold Coast sojourn. That trip had been richly suggestive for Wright's analysis of the revolutionary implications of an emergent modern pan-African movement. In subsequent years, Wright was consistent in his advocacy of African liberation, which obliged him to pursue an unsentimental reckoning of the movement's internal contradictions and weaknesses.

The class, cultural, and political contradictions within Ghanaian society were no doubt what Nkrumah had in mind when he remarked to Wright that "the ideological development here is not very high" (*BP*, 63). With many of the best-educated men in the country, the Gold Coast elite, members of the opposition, Nkrumah's reliance on expatriates was of tremendous significance. In this connection, Wright's reflections on the psychological distance between Africans and Westerners were trenchant. He had discerned the most crucial challenge that Nkrumah's emancipatory project faced.

Had the ratio between foreigners and Africans within Nkrumah's movement and government been more equitable, then the notion of black diaspora and European "strangers" might have been less salient as an internal cleavage in the movement. As it was, despite their impassioned support for African independence, the foreign status of Wright, Padmore, and others, a notable example being Nkrumah's attorney general, Labour M.P. Geoffrey Bing, ensured that their experiences with Ghanaian politics were characterized by frustration. *Black Power* was far too candid in its criticisms of virtually every segment of Ghanaian society to be well received within leadership circles. Still, Wright was disappointed at not receiving an invitation to the festivities marking Ghana's independence in 1957. At the request of the Ghana government, George Padmore worked to establish Nkrumah's Bureau of African Affairs, which oversaw Ghana's attempts to forge political unity on the continent and to lend assistance to ongoing African liberation struggles. Wright followed developments in Ghana through correspondence with the Padmores. According to Dorothy Padmore, her husband had encountered petty obstructions from resentful Ghanaians, but by the time of his death in 1959, was beginning to gain recognition in Ghana and throughout Africa for his contributions to Africa, particularly in the critical area of international affairs.[18]

By the time of Wright's death, the accelerating US freedom movement was regarded by government authorities and opinion leaders as the preferable alternative to a disorderly radical black nationalism.[19] There were, however, enduring links between Wright and a later cohort of radical expatriates in Ghana. Indeed, Accra under Nkrumah became one of those historical beacons of radical hope for exiled African freedom fighters, African American and Caribbean intellectuals, writers and artists, and European leftists,[20] and in many respects constituted a realization of the political and intellectual promise of diaspora. Wright had been acquainted in Paris with the novelist William Gardner Smith, who later worked in Ghana's state television network. Wright's daughter Julia was a member of the black expatriate community in Ghana and an ardent supporter of Nkrumah's radical pan-Africanism. Generally, the expatriates were inspired by Nkrumah's invitation to members of the African diaspora (and sympathetic others) to contribute their talents and skills to nation building in Ghana and the African revolution. In this regard, Ghana had supplanted Paris as the preferred destination for some black radicals, as the pilgrimage to Africa fulfilled for many the yearning for community and revolutionary authenticity. Although for those who moved to Nkrumah's Ghana, the political stakes were perhaps higher than Wright's earlier project of publicizing the incipient revolution, the expatriates' quest for political community was similar to Wright's. They, like him, embraced Ghana and the African revolution as an independent black radical project, which, albeit complicated, represented to them a refuge from the Cold War constraints of US political culture and from the pitfalls learned from their experience with the white US Left and, by implication, European and Soviet communisms. For Wright and the expatriates, Ghana was appealing not solely because it was a black-led struggle; its appeal derived equally from the universalist aspirations of its liberation project, whose anti-imperialism would hasten the day of reckoning for capitalism in the West. (Of course, Wright knew from Dorothy Padmore's letters that the Western intelligence communities were firmly entrenched in Ghana, trying to destabilize the independent course charted by Nkrumah.)

Wright's and Padmore's difficulties in Ghana illustrated a divisive conception of diaspora deployed by some Ghanaian politicos as a symbolic displacement masking the complex internal and external obstacles to true political and economic independence. That divisive conception pitted a self-serving parochial view of diaspora as an essentializing mark of difference and incommensurability against a more expansive notion of diaspora predicated on pan-African solidarity. Public acceptance from Nkrumah of Wright's analysis would be tragically belated, coming not only after Wright's death but also after the overthrow of the Ghanaian leader's government. Nkrumah's endorsement of Wright was issued from exile in Guinea, where he had gained asylum after the coup. Amid the near-unanimous view in the Western press that Nkrumah's repressive regime had received its just comeuppance, Nkrumah invoked Wright's belief that Nkrumah could only implement his democratic revolution with dictatorial methods. Wright had called upon Nkrumah to ignore the West's hypocritical invocations of democracy: "As you launch your bold programmes, as you call on your people for sacrifices, you can be confident that there are free men beyond the continent of Africa who see deeply enough into life to know and understand what you *must* do, what you *must* impose."[21] In this light, Wright's open letter does not counsel Nkrumah as much as it defends him against the charges of antidemocratic tendencies Wright anticipated from Western critics.

Moreover, Wright's mention of "free men beyond the continent of Africa" proposed something akin to a broader, universalist Left united in solidarity with Nkrumah's project.

Taken together, even as postmortem assessments, Nkrumah's belated endorsement of Wright and the Ghanaian novelist Ayi Kwei Armah's post-Nkrumah reflections on the betrayal of the hopes unleashed by Ghanaian nationalism exemplify the very notion of diaspora as a transnational unity of purpose that Wright projected in *Black Power* and other writings. In *The Beautyful Ones Are Not Yet Born* (1968), Armah emphasizes the unliberated consciousness of Ghanaian elites as the signal failure of independence, as seen in the pervasiveness of corruption and neglect. So graphic is Armah's portrayal of moral and spiritual decay in Ghana, reflected in an urban landscape mired in ubiquitous and irreversible states of physical deterioration, putrefaction, and omnipresent filth, that Wright's narrative seems quite optimistic and restrained by comparison. There is a striking passage in Armah's novel that centers on the idea of diaspora as the explanation for the demise of the Ghanaian revolution. In that passage, one of Armah's characters, a rare member of the educated middle class morally unable to join the orgy of self-aggrandizing malfeasance, cynically cites the allegory of Plato's cave. Armah's retelling of the allegory is worth reproducing here. Out of the dark, cavernous hole filled with chained people unable to imagine anything other than their shadowy, confined existence,

> one unfortunate human being is able at last to break from the chains and to wander outward from the eternal circle of the lightless cave, and to see the blinding beauty of all the lights and colors of the world outside. . . . The wanderer returns into the cave [and] he shares what he has, the ideas and the words and the images of light and the colors of the world outside, knowing surely that those he had left behind would certainly want the snapping of ancient chains and the incredible first seeing of light and the colors of the world beyond the eternal cave. But to those inside the eternal cave he came as someone driven ill with the breaking of eternal boundaries, and the truth he sought to tell was nothing but the proof of his long delusion, and the words he had to give were the pitiful cries of a madman lost in the mazes of a mind being pushed too far out and away from the everlasting way of darkness and reassuring chains.[22]

Armah's diaspora allegory can be seen as a variant of Wright's reflections on diaspora as both barrier and precondition to emancipatory consciousness, a necessary pathway. While the disillusionment and cynicism of Armah's text may suggest otherwise, the allegory also suggests that the importance of diaspora sojourning and sensibility for a pragmatic black radicalism is undiminished by the likelihood of failure. Indeed, it is telling that for Armah, diaspora is the source of the knowledge necessary for freedom. As such, diaspora rejects the essentializing idea of a homeland in a way that resonates with Wright's understanding of the term. It is tempting, as well, to read Armah's use of Plato's allegory as a metaphor for Wright's relationship to the public culture of the "American Century," where his name often elicited the begrudging admiration or malicious dismissal reserved for prophetic dissenters dealing in unpopular truths.[23] In this instance there are limits to the cave analogy, for it does not require the disclosure of a conspiracy to note, as Wright did, that there were powerful opinion leaders who had a great interest in combating Wright's influence as an international radical public intellectual and depriving him of audiences. In any event, to regard *Black Power* as an idiosyncratic utterance neglects its inspiration by an anticolonial movement that constituted a momentous challenge to American and Western hegemony. Accordingly, Wright's international stature in promoting an oppositional political community was regarded with utmost seriousness by American officialdom. This is a most appropriate context for reading *Black Power*. Readers may disagree about the merits of *Black Power*, but on the liberation of Africa and its people, Wright's words are still relevant: "None but Africans can perform this for Africa" (*BP*, 350).

Notes

Kevin Gaines, "Revisiting Richard Wright in Ghana," in *Social Text*, Volume 19, no. 2, pp. 75–101. Copyright, 2001, Duke University Press. All rights reserved. Republished in revised form by permission of the copyright holder, Duke University Press. www.dukeupress.edu.

1. Richard Wright, *Black Power: A Record of Reactions in a Land of Pathos* (New York: Harper and Brothers, 1954); hereafter cited parenthetically in the chapter text as *BP*.

2. Examples include W. E. B. Du Bois, *Black Reconstruction* (New York: Harcourt, Brace, 1935); C. L. R. James, *Black Jacobins* (London: Secker and Warburg, 1938); C. L. R. James, *A History of Pan-African Revolt* (Chicago: Charles H. Kerr,

1995); Frantz Fanon, *The Wretched of the Earth* (New York: Grove, 1963); and Cedric J. Robinson, *Black Marxism: The Making of the Black Radical Tradition* (Chapel Hill: University of North Carolina Press, 2000).

3. Cornel West's review of *Black Marxism* exemplifies this impatience with Wright that precludes a more substantive engagement. West takes issue with Robinson's reading of Wright as an exemplary black nationalist critic of Marxist theory. For West, Wright's work is defined by "individualistic revolt" and sexism rather than any "sense of black collective insurgency." Without referring directly to *Black Power*, West claims that Wright "devalued and demystified" African nationalism and black power "as props for the petty bourgeoisie," which in his view placed Wright at odds with the radical black nationalism within which Robinson locates him (West, "Black Radicalism and the Marxist Tradition," *Monthly Review* 40 [September 1988]: 51–56).

4. Something akin to Wright's dialectical sense of diaspora is suggested by Cedric Robinson's account of the forging of black cultural resistance by "discrete societies [which] were slowly achieving the social organization which the attack on colonialism required." For Robinson, this process "was the dialectic of imperialism and liberation, the contradiction of which compelled the appearance of resistance and revolution out of the condition of oppression" (see Robinson, "Coming to Terms: The Third World and the Dialectic of Imperialism," *Race and Class* 22, no. 4 [1981]: 362–86).

5. It is interesting to note that Padmore and especially James have somehow escaped the scrutiny to which Wright is subjected, even though these intellectuals exhibit a similar complexity through their avowed allegiance to Western culture. I would argue that the legacy of the liberal orthodoxy dismissing Wright as "out of touch" with American and African American publics has influenced criticism of Wright by radicals and conservatives alike.

6. Brent Hayes Edwards, "The Uses of *Diaspora*," *Social Text* 66 (Spring 2001): 44–74.

7. Wright, *Black Power*, 118–19. Wright's position on anthropology in the service of colonialism is similar to that of Frantz Fanon (see Fanon, *Black Skin, White Masks* [New York: Grove, 1967]).

8. While riding with Prime Minister Nkrumah, Wright observed the celebratory dance of African women: "And then I remembered: I had seen those same snakelike, veering dances before. Where Oh God, yes; in America, in store front churches in Holy Roller Tabernacles, in God's Temples, in unpainted wooden prayer-meeting houses on the plantations of the Deep South. And here I was seeing it all again against a background of a surging nationalistic political movement! How could that be?" While Wright went on to claim that what he saw was an "exact duplicate" of what he'd seen among African Americans, he described the question

of how and why black people were able to retain, over time and distance, "such basic and fundamental patterns of behavior and response" as a "riddle" whose resolution he deferred (Wright, *Black Power*, 56–57).

9. In fact, he had not confined himself to non-Marxist interpretations of the history of the Gold Coast and the slave trade. Wright sailed from Liverpool on 4 June 1953, bringing stacks of books for research to occupy himself during the voyage to the Gold Coast and his stay there. He relied heavily on Eric Williams's *Capitalism and Slavery* for his account of the economic origins of the slave trade and Liverpool's colossal profits as a result of it. He had read George Padmore's *The Gold Coast Revolution* and had also brought along with him C. L. R. James's *Black Jacobins*, R. S. Rattray's study of Ashanti political culture, W. E. F. Ward's history of the Gold Coast, and Dr. J. B. Danquah's *The Akan Doctrine of God*. Wright had also previously read O. Mannoni's *La psychologie de colonialisme* (Constance Webb, *Richard Wright: A Biography* [New York: G. P. Putnam's Sons, 1968], 326).

10. Webb, *Richard Wright*, 9, 11.

11. Ibid., 7.

12. Ibid., 341–42.

13. The matter of Nkrumah's political development has received an impressively thorough treatment in Marika Sherwood, *Kwame Nkrumah: The Years Abroad, 1935–1947* (Legon, Ghana: Freedom Publications, 1996).

14. Ibid., 153.

15. With this assertion, Wright was disregarding the substantial record of African military resistance to colonialism at the turn of the century (*Black Power*, 247).

16. This scenario failed to consider that an Africanization program intended to reduce dependency on the British had already tripled the number of Ghanaians in the civil service since 1951 (see Manning Marable, *African and Caribbean Politics: From Kwame Nkrumah to Maurice Bishop* [London: Verso, 1987], 112).

17. Ibid., 157.

18. Dorothy Padmore to the Wrights ("Dear Richard and Ellen"), 14 March 1959, box 103, folder 1521, Richard Wright Papers, Beinecke Library, Yale University.

19. During the early Cold War, the vibrant black American anticolonialism that allied itself with wartime global anticolonialism was suppressed by the American government's anticommunist campaigns. Later this contest reasserted itself in the furor over Robert Williams's armed self-defense movement in North Carolina, resulting not only in a debate between Williams and Martin Luther King Jr. on the merits of nonviolence but also in Williams's suspension from the NAACP. Williams exiled himself to Cuba after becoming the object of a federal manhunt on trumped-up kidnapping charges. These moments of struggle for legitimacy between a quasi-official domestic movement for civil rights and internationalist black

radicalism or nationalism are detailed in Penny Von Eschen, *Race against Empire: Black Americans and Anticolonialism, 1937–1957* (Ithaca, NY.: Cornell University Press, 1997); and Tim Tyson, *Radio Free Dixie: Robert F. Williams and the Roots of Black Power* (Chapel Hill: University of North Carolina Press, 1999).

20. For this insight I am indebted to my colleague Mauricio Tenorio.

21. Qtd. in Kwame Nkrumah, *Dark Days in Ghana* (London: Panaf, 1968), 6.

22. Ayi Kwei Armah, *The Beautyful Ones Are Not Yet Born* (1968; repr., London: Heinemann, 1988), 79–80.

23. A fairly recent example of such damning by feigned praise is *New York Times* television critic Walter Goodman's review of a PBS documentary on Wright that reproduced what has become the liberal orthodoxy on Wright's career: that his greatest, albeit flawed, work occurred before he exiled himself to France. The result of this assessment is that the entire body of Wright's work after he left the United States can be summarily dismissed and forgotten. Here is Goodman's sketch of Wright, seen through a funhouse mirror of middlebrow liberalism: "Wright's last 20 years seem like a postscript. Lionized in France, he is pictured as enjoying Parisian café life. His writing fell off" (Walter Goodman, "Richard Wright's First Act Unmatched and Unforgettable," *Cleveland Plain Dealer*, 6 September 1995, E–9).

Psychology and Black Liberation in Richard Wright's *Black Power* (1954)

Dorothy Stringer

Richard Wright's 1954 *Black Power: A Record of Reactions in a Land of Pathos* describes his 1953 journey through the Gold Coast, the British colony that became Ghana (the first independent sub-Saharan African state) in 1957.[1] Despite its concern with the independence movement, however, *Black Power* is not straightforward reportage. Wright describes his demanding, uncomfortable, and sometimes dangerous physical travels in and around Accra, and then north into less populated areas, but that factual, progressive narrative is supplemented at every turn by an imaginative, temporally ambiguous, always-unfinished theoretical quest. Often, events fail Wright entirely, and speculative psychoanalytic thought takes over the writerly horizon. The result is an uncomfortable text, difficult to classify and severely demanding of its readers' attention and sympathy; perhaps consequently, *Black Power* has had relatively little academic readership to date.

Wright had been an avid reader of psychoanalytic texts for more than a decade prior to his trip. Psychoanalysis is not, however, the only psychological discourse he brings to bear on the Gold Coast. He also refers constantly to the account, deeply rooted in African American literatures, of the psychological legacy of black slavery. This literary tradition shares with psychoanalysis an interest in the socially transgressive character of desire, and it likewise investigates relationships between bodily facts, such as hunger and sexual arousal, and social values, especially women's roles, familial relationships, and conventions of modesty and decorum. But importantly, where the mainstream psychoanalytic theory of Wright's day avoided historical questions, passed over racial difference without comment, and evinced a strong Eurocentric, individualist, and bourgeois bias, African American perspectives on psychology emphasize the collective traumas of the slave regime, insist on the persistence of racial injustice, and explore present-day, psychic responses to historical disaster.

By combining these two theories, Wright was able to focus on experiences and desires conditioned by colonial and neocolonial Western economic control of African politics and African individuals' laboring bodies. *Black Power* maps a psychic topography shaped not only by the contingencies of the body, familial structure, and language but also by vast, impersonal, transhistorical, and transnational economic forces: neocolonialism, colonialism, and the slave trade. This travel narrative suggests that race—that is, not only racial difference as a historical given, but racial identity as a subjective experience—links individual psychic need to state and imperial geopolitical projects, such that feeling itself, and especially negative emotions like fear and confusion, serves established power.

For Wright at the beginning of his travels, past history and contemporary politics tended to converge in an intense, personal awareness of black identity. As he baldly states in conversation with Kwame Nkrumah: "I know from history and from my personal life what has happened to us—at least, I know some of it. I don't know Africa intimately. That's why I'm here. I'd like to understand all of this. I think my life has prepared me to do that."[2] Thus, resistance to slavery in the distant US past, resistance to Jim Crow in the recent US past, and the present African struggle for independence were all—regardless of the specific events of his own life—potentially Wright's own experiences, because they were also the experiences of "black people." Being a black citizen of the United States meant, for Wright as for many other African American authors both before and after him, to have a special relationship to the reality of racial oppression and the advent of freedom, one that need not respect borders between nations, or even distinctions between the past, the present, and the future. However, Nkrumah's only reply to this passionate expression of solidarity—"I'm a Marxist Socialist"[3]—pointedly refuses Wright's identification.

Despite this rebuff, Wright continues to hear the transatlantic past echoing into the African present. His estranging, phonetic rendering of a pervasive pro-Nkrumah political slogan, "'Free—doom! Free—dooooom!'"[4]—"free" separated from and canceled by "doom"—returns US readers to the scene of US racial slavery, and especially to the contradictory mix of Enlightenment ideals and deadly economic rationalism at the nation's foundation. The Gold Coast slogan seems to pose such philosophical problems anew, in contrast to the clichéd doubts about the possibility of human liberation habitually voiced by the Westerners of his Parisian intellectual milieu.[5] "Free-doom!" is thus at once more visceral and more theoretically demanding than any historical résumé, since it both draws on the enormous emotional charge that even indirect or misheard references to racial slavery produce in Wright and in many US readers and demonstrates the extent to which that affective experience, and the clichéd habits of mind it brings with it, delay his engagement with African politics.

A number of literary scholars have discussed *Black Power*'s generic features as a travel narrative, often focusing on Wright's oscillations between identification and culture shock. These scholars have reached widely divergent conclusions, some seeking to reveal Wright's capitulation to exclusionary, conservative, and Eurocentric discourses,[6] and others emphasizing Wright's struggle to find an adequate critical language for ambiguous and fleeting experiences.[7] Now, certainly Wright's account of the pro-Independence crowds' cry for "'Free—doom!,'" which "rang deafeningly in my ears,"[8] shows an ignorant, historically static US perspective asserting itself over and against contemporary Gold Coast perspectives. But it also extends the traveler's experience of "ignorance, disorientation, incomprehension, self-dissolution"[9] to his readers. Mistakes, misunderstandings, misheard words, words rendered meaningless through repetition: these are also to be read, and to be read specifically as the limit of reading.

Beyond or before Wright's Gold Coast encounter with "free—doom!," descriptions of shock and the associated, repetitive failure to understand a past disaster reflect his abiding interest in psychological trauma, and in psychoanalytic theories of trauma. As the comparatist Cathy Caruth explains: "Trauma seems to be much more than a pathology, or the simple illness of a wounded psyche: it is always the story of a wound that cries out, that addresses us in the attempt to tell us of a reality or truth that is not otherwise available. This truth, in its delayed appearance and its belated address, cannot be linked only to what is known, but also to what remains unknown in our very actions and our language."[10] In other words, traumatic repetitions—like the poetic ghost of black slavery in Wright's "free-doom!"—have as much to do with the present as the past, answering "what remains unknown"—an inexhaustible category, and one with deep resonance for the African American search for cultural origins—with the imperative to hear again and again the "attempt to tell us."[11]

In fact, while the geopolitical moment offered a context, the fearful desire to learn something about slavery's traumas, and about his own genealogical origins, was the major motivator of Wright's decision to visit the Gold Coast in the first place. As he relays the anecdote, on Easter Sunday, over coffee, Dorothy Pizer, "the wife of George Padmore, the West Indian author and journalist, turned to me and asked 'Now that your desk is clear, why don't you go to Africa?'"[12] Wright's wife, Ellen, chimes in, pressuring him with the declaration that he "must go"; Nkrumah is shortly to table a motion for independence, and the moment is historic. However, Wright's thoughts, in response to the suggestion, are interior and apparently apolitical:

> I heard them, but my mind and feelings were racing along another and hidden track. Africa! Being of African descent, would I be able to feel and know something about Africa on the basis of a common "racial" heritage? Africa was a vast continent full of "my people" . . . or had three hundred years imposed a psychological distance between me and the "racial stock" from which I had sprung? Perhaps some Englishman, Scotsman, Frenchman, Swede or Dutchman had chained my great-great-great-great-grandfather in the hold of a slave ship; and perhaps that remote grandfather had been sold on an auction block in New Orleans, Richmond, or Atlanta. . . . My emotions seemed to be touching a dark and dank wall. . . . But, am I African? Had some of my ancestors sold their relatives to white men?[13]

The mere name of "Africa" causes multiple wounds to cry out within him—what terrible things were done to us? What terrible things—selling members of the family, perhaps?—did "we" do? And will I have to participate in that trauma—as victim or as perpetrator—if I return? These unanswerable, yet undeniable, questions drive Wright's travels.

Wright, in planning his journey, carefully rejected any clear distinction between psyche and world, the personal and the historical, the Westerner and the African. Instead, he took a "roundabout" approach: "By going from spot to spot, talking to this person and that one, I had to gather this reality as it seeped into me from the personalities of others. There might be some merit in that kind of getting and giving a reality, but it might bore the reader. Conrad wrote all of his novels in that roundabout way. It involves going back to some extent over ground already covered, but each going back reveals more and more of the thing described."[14] Thus, the author actively hoped that the people and places of the Gold Coast would "[seep] into" himself; he sought to relinquish a measure of narrative and thematic control, even at the risk of losing readership, in the belief that "more of the thing" would thereby be revealed.

However, this ideal of cultural encounter as circulation or exchange across the boundaries of the self returns to the traumatic literality of its own guiding figure—chattel slavery. Every trade, every "getting and giving [of] a reality," in a place where reality includes a historical commerce in human beings, confronts certain radical indistinctions. Any trader could himself be reduced to an article of trade, or he could expropriate the lives of others to his own profit. Insofar as the system reduces everything to radically interchangeable units, to nothing but money, he could even do both—be sold and himself sell—as Wright's nightmare-genealogy of descent from someone sold by his own family attests. And in fact, much or most of the "going . . . over ground already covered" in *Black Power* reflects Wright's unrelenting, even obsessional, examination of his own role in specific economic transactions.

This vignette is one way Wright demonstrates this radical coincidence of imagined origins and present economics. As a wealthy foreigner, he is being served in a shop:

> "You wish to buy something, sar? [*sic*]"
> "No; I'm just looking."
> "You're American, aren't you, sar?"
> "Yes; how did you know?"
> "Oh, we know, sar," he said. Another salesman joined him. "What part of Africa did you come from, sar?"

I stared at him and then laughed. I felt uneasy.

"I don't know."

"Didn't your mother or grandmother ever tell you what part of Africa you came from, sar?"

I didn't answer. I stared vaguely about me. I had, in my childhood, asked my parents about it, but they had had no information, or else they hadn't wanted to speak of it. I remembered that many Africans had sold their people into slavery; it had been said that they had had no idea of the kind of slavery into which they had been selling their people, but they had sold them. . . . I suddenly didn't know what to say to the men confronting me.

"Haven't you tried to find out where in Africa you came from, sar?"

"Well," I said softly, "you know, you fellows who sold us and the white men who bought us didn't keep any records."[15]

These people know him to be foreign and wealthy. So they ask, do you wish to buy something, sir? He could not be there for any reason except to buy. But also, as a black "American," he could not be there for any reason except having been descended from slaves, having been sold.

The shop clerks' talk of ancestry indicates, not their literal ignorance of the Middle Passage, but rather their lack of familiarity with the radical social fracture that slavery enacted. As the historian of Madagascar Pier Larson notes: "If experiences and memories of enslavement and racial oppression are key to African identities in the Americas, similar trauma has been purposefully forgotten or differently remembered by many Africans in other parts of the diaspora. Although remembering and commemorating enslavement is characteristic of some Africans, countervailing forces of social amnesia are particularly robust in many parts of the continent, especially among the descendents of slaveowners. . . . [M]emorialization of trauma is not universal to the African diaspora."[16] Under question is not Wright's possible African family tree, but the ways in which his experience of ancestry, identity, and culture diverge from the clerks', despite their common awareness of the slave trade.

The clerks name "your mother or your grandmother" as the logical guarantor and guardian of ancestry, for example. But Wright is acutely aware that mothering was itself made to serve the purposes of mastery in the Americas. His maternal grandmother, born in slavery, was light enough to pass for white,[17] and demonstrated in her physical person the radical confusion of mothering and capital that slavery enacted, often by means of the sexual exploitation of black women by white men, and expressed in the rule that "the child shall follow the condition of the mother." Interestingly, by the time of Saidiya Hartman's mid-1990s travels in Ghana, slavery's translation of mothers into money and back had become familiar enough to Ghanaians to form the basis of a street hustle, in which young men seek to make contact with African American tourists by speaking sympathetically to them of how, "because of the slave trade, you lose your mother."[18] Yet this development, too, conforms to the logic of commerce; even mourning for those sold generations ago can become a commodity, a tourist trinket.

An experience of historical irony, no matter how intense, is of course neither morally nor analytically equivalent to that of the Middle Passage itself. Yet Wright's sense of connection to the past does not so much project a stable self into the place of the enslaved as index the degree to which a personal, psychic trauma is still current, still currency, within a specific West African historical and material situation. Wright's emphasis on historical and present-day practices that render persons equivalent to money is difficult to arrest or deny unless one gives up on memory and representation entirely.

One understands, now, Nkrumah's gesture of declaring himself a "Marxist Socialist" in order to deny Wright's identification, based in the Middle Passage, with the Independence-era Gold Coast: the prime minister was claiming to stand outside the unbroken circuit of money and trauma that such investments in the past describe. Moreover, this matter of the writer becoming currency, becoming a seller and the thing sold both at once, is also a pressing problem for ourselves, concerned as we are with our professional fortunes in a US academy that does not itself escape from capitalistic determinants. Imagining the enslaved as a kind of currency that circulates recasts psychoanalytically based trauma theory, away from the discrete, catastrophic, and mass-mediated events that sometimes dominate trauma studies, and toward an inquiry into dailyness, the repetitions we do not note as such, the constant, often invisible violences (such as racism; such as the neocolonial exploitation of underdeveloped countries) that characterize the quotidian. At the same time, though, we are faced with Wright's awareness that to enter such theorizations into the marketplace of ideas is not a way to stop selling people.

Wright thus shows his own, African American cultural politics, variously ignored, misunderstood, and implicated in the historical legacy of the slave trade. There exists, of course, another politics in the Gold Coast, that proper to "Africans" (Wright's habitual name for the black people he encounters in the Gold Coast). Wright's *Black Power* predates by more than a decade the "Black Power" concept[19] used by Kwame Ture (formerly Stokely Carmichael), Charles R. Hamilton, and others, but like the later activists, he names a massive reservoir of political energy whose very existence contests white and colonial control. However, unlike Ture and Hamilton, Wright imagines this energy as a radically ambivalent quantity, a pure potentiality whose very vitality generates troubling political contradictions. The properly "African" manifests as figures of uncanny return, psychically plangent and politically ambivalent.

The lifelong Marxist was "shocked,"[20] for example, by Convention People's Party (CCP) rallies that "fused tribalism with modern politics,"[21] using local celebrations and rituals, including oaths, libations, dancing, and (Christian) psalm-singing. Calling this a "new kind of religion . . . politics *plus!*,"[22] Wright eventually concluded that it reflected a worldview without contemporary Western parallel:

> The tribal mind is sensuous: loving images, not concepts; personalities, not abstractions; movement, not form; dreams, not reality. . . . From a strictly tribal point of view, they cannot really conceive of a political party except in the form of a glamorous leader. When they honor, adore, obey it's towards a person and it is absolute in its intensity. The tribal African does not really love, he worships; he does not hate, he curses; he does not rest, he sleeps; and when he works, his work becomes a kind of dance. . . . He transforms that which he touches into something else which is his, and his alone; he dreams naturally, spontaneously, without even being aware that he does so. To live, with the tribal African, is to create.[23]

Instrumentalism, abstraction, hierarchical distinctions between work and pleasure—the central features of Western, modern subjectivity, in short—are absolutely refused by "tribal Africans" in Wright's reading. Instead of projecting themselves into a future of dialectical struggle, they integrate parties and leaders, labor and aspiration, work and dreams, with their existing cosmogony.[24]

Wright's view of "the African" reflects the influence of *Présence Africaine,* a groundbreaking, Paris-based journal publishing African and African-diasporic writers, for which Wright was a contributor and founding editorial board member. The journal's 1947 inaugural editorial, by Alioune Diop, stated that "We [Africans] are *present in the concrete*—essentially in the concrete's natural and immediate succulence. . . . [T]he universe is, for us, unlimited and marvelous, an indefinite fecundity offered to our vigorous appetite. We care little to know or to dominate the world, preferring to enjoy the nourishment that fills the present moment."[25] Diop further asserted that colonial subjects (les hommes d'Outre-Mer) "constitute the substance to be impregnated by Europe."[26]

Both Wright and Diop wrote long before the constitution of postcolonial or feminist scholarly fields and academic vocabularies, and their license in attributing particular affects, states of consciousness, and forms of political agency (not to mention fecund female bodies) to "Africans" is grossly presumptuous in comparison to present-day conventions. And indeed, Wright's stance toward African cultures as they are practiced daily is often problematic. He repeatedly voices anger and disgust at local mores, including clothing, the social roles of women, non-European forms of governance along with the ritual practices that subtend them, and, in a memorable passage,[27] a form of lifelong servitude that he identifies directly with chattel slavery. At least one Gold Coast interviewee,[28] the Ghanaian statesman and anthropologist J. B. Danquah, wrote back to Wright. Danquah, who had reinvented "Ghana" (the name of an ancient kingdom) as a name for the new nation, challenged specific misrepresentations but also sought to educate Wright in the reality of West African cultures' dynamism and intelligent engagement with global histories.[29]

Despite its inherent limitations, both Diop and Wright used this clichéd schema of primitive and modern, concrete and abstract, female and male, in order to wrest acknowledgment of a traffic, a circulation of people, things, and power, between an underdeveloped Africa and the "the rational, urban, industrial (for whatever it's worth!) order of things."[30] The colonial "order" that subordinated, as a matter of principle, the non-Western, the preindustrial, the material, and the feminine also repressed its own knowledge of these things, and of their constitutive character for the West, for industrial capital, for the spiritual, and for the masculine. Diop and Wright seek to return this repressed content to the global politics of their day.

A return of the repressed also constitutes the only certain connection Wright witnesses between his own culture and West Africa. Watching a group of women dancing at a CPP rally, he "remembered: I'd seen these same snakelike, veering dances before.... Where? Oh, God, yes; in America, in storefront churches, in Holy Roller Tabernacles, in God's Temples, in unpainted wooden prayer-meeting houses on the plantations of the Deep South.... And here I was seeing it all again against a background of a surging nationalistic political movement! How could that be?"[31] Wright notes this dance, so startling that it makes the confirmed atheist invoke God, as continuous between African American and African cultures, yet that very continuity is something he experiences, not as belonging or recognition, but as uncanniness, confusion, and inability to speak: "This African dance was as astonishing and dumbfounding to me as it had been when I'd seen it in America.... [W]hat had bewildered me about Negro dance expression in the United States now bewildered me in the same way in Africa."[32]

In other words, manifestations of African spirituality for Wright were not only foreign and "primitive" compared to the cultural patterns of industrial modernity but also a traumatic return, intimate and shattering, intimate because shattering. His fear and confusion are not a rejection of the women's dance as foreign but quite the opposite—the unwilling acknowledgment of a feared, feminine part of his self. Not unlike Morrison's spectral Beloved (whose personality, as Yoshinobu Hakutani notes,[33] is very similar to that of Wright's "tribal African"), Wright's "Africans" and "Africa" do not arrive fully and cannot be fully told, precisely because they *are* familiar, intimately known, indeed a part of the self. To see one's own beginnings, sources, origins is by Wright's account to be traumatized.

As Caroline Rooney points out, for Africans, "Africa—traditional and modern—is not, obviously, a lost origin but, in its living reality, a source for vital and urgent attempts to try and forge an ethical and political vision."[34] Wright, transfixed by his own culture's traumas, rejected non-Western tradition as such,[35] later even endorsing the West's "moral right to interfere" in developing nations.[36] He did, however, examine his own false or partial reactions to what was before him in the Gold Coast: "One does not react to Africa as Africa is, and this is because so few can react to life as life is. ... Africa is a vast, dingy mirror, and what modern man sees in that mirror he hates and wants to destroy."[37] Referring to a well-known Pauline verse, 1 Corinthians 13:12 ("For now we see through a glass, darkly, but then [in the Kingdom of Heaven] face to face: now I know in part; but then shall I know even as also I am known"), Wright plays on "seeing darkly." But in making the obvious racial pun, he reveals the strange alliance between psychic needs and geopolitical imperatives that race creates. Seeing your soul reflected in Africa inspires loathing and violence; and, Wright implies, that loathing and violence has served the purposes of colonialism well.

Notes

1. Richard Wright, *Black Power: A Record of Reactions in a Land of Pathos* (New York: Harper and Brothers, 1954); henceforth cited as *Black Power*.
2. Ibid., 62.
3. Ibid.
4. Ibid., 53.
5. Ibid., 54.
6. See, in particular, Kwame Anthony Appiah, "A Long Way from Home: Wright in the Gold Coast," in *Richard Wright: A Collection of Critical Essays*, ed. Arnold Rampersad (Englewood Cliffs, NJ: Prentice Hall, 1995), 188–201; and Ngwarsungu Chiwengo, "Gazing through the Screen: Richard Wright's Africa," in *Richard Wright's Travel Writings: New Reflections*, ed. Virginia Whatley Smith (Jackson: University Press of Mississippi, 2001), 20–44.
7. Jack B. Moore, "The Art of *Black Power*: Novelistic or Documentary," *Revue Francaise d'Études Americaines* 31 (February 1987): 79–91; Mary Louise Pratt, *Imperial Eyes: Travel Writing and Transculturation* (New York: Routledge, 1992). See also Paul Gilroy, *The Black Atlantic: Modernity and Double Consciousness* (Cambridge: Harvard University Press, 1993), a selection from which is republished in this volume.
8. Wright, *Black Power*, 55.
9. Pratt, *Imperial Eyes*, 222.
10. Caruth, *Unclaimed Experience: Trauma, Narrative and History* (Baltimore: Johns Hopkins University Press, 1996), 4.
11. Jane Anna Gordon rightly points out in "Slavery Continued, Freedom Sought" in this volume that the persistence of slavery's institutions into Wright's lifetime was material and institutional, as well as psychological and cultural, as many specific forms of white manipulation and threat, particularly demands for obeisance and irrational accusations of fault or criminality, persisted in the Jim Crow South of his childhood.
12. Wright, *Black Power*, 3.
13. Ibid., 4, ellipses original.

14. Richard Wright to his agent, Paul Reynolds, qtd. in Michel Fabre, *The Unfinished Quest of Richard Wright*, 2nd ed. (Urbana: University of Illinois Press, 1993), 403.

15. Wright, *Black Power*, 35, ellipsis original.

16. Pier M. Larson, *History and Memory in the Age of Enslavement: Becoming Merina in Highland Madagascar, 1770–1822* (Portsmouth, NH: Heinemann, 2000), 278–79.

17. See Richard Wright, *Black Boy: A Record of Childhood and Youth* (New York: Harper & Brothers, 1945), 47–48.

18. Saidiya Hartman, *Lose Your Mother: A Journey along the Atlantic Slave Route* (New York: Farrar, Straus and Giroux, 2007), 85.

19. See Kwame Ture and Charles V. Hamilton, *Black Power: The Politics of Liberation in America* (1967; New York: Vintage, 1992), 187–200.

20. Wright, *Black Power*, 61.

21. Ibid., 59.

22. Ibid., 56, emphasis Wright's.

23. Ibid., 265, ellipsis original.

24. See James A. Snead, "On Repetition in Black Culture," *Black American Literature Forum* 15, no. 4 (Winter 1981): 146–54.

25. Alioune Diop, *"Niam n'goura* ou les raisons d'être de *Présence Africaine,"* *Présence Africaine* 1 (November–December 1947): 13.

26. Ibid., 14.

27. Wright, *Black Power*, 281–82.

28. Ibid., 219–22.

29. Qtd. in Smith, *Richard Wright's Travel Writings*, 186.

30. Wright, *Black Power*, 266.

31. Ibid., 56–57.

32. Ibid., 57.

33. Yoshinobu Hakutani, "Richard Wright, Toni Morrison, and the African 'Primal Outlook upon Life,'" *Southern Quarterly* 40, no. 1 (Fall 2001): 39–53.

34. Caroline Rooney, *African Literature, Animism and Politics* (New York: Routledge, 2000), 118.

35. For a broader discussion of Wright's antitraditionalism and rejection of what he took to be feminine and primitive aspects of non-Western cultures, see Lori J. Marso, "Seizing Freedom with Simone de Beauvoir," in this volume. For an acid contemporary takedown of Wright's idealized vision of decolonization through cultural revolution, see also James Baldwin's 1957 essay "Princes and Powers," in *Collected Essays* (New York: Library of America, 1998), 143–69.

36. Richard Wright, *The Color Curtain: A Report on the Bandung Conference* (1956; Jackson: University Press of Mississippi, 1994), 219.

37. Wright, *Black Power*, 158.

PART 4

Rhetorical Registers

Blueprint for Negro Writing

Richard Wright

I. The Role of Negro Writing: Two Definitions

Generally speaking, Negro writing in the past has been confined to humble novels, poems, and plays, prim and decorous ambassadors who go a-begging to white America. They entered the Court of American Public Opinion dressed in the knee-pants of servility, curtsying to show that the Negro was not inferior, that he was human, and that he had a life comparable to that of other people. For the most part these artistic ambassadors were received as though they were French poodles who do tricks.

White America never offered them any serious criticism. The mere fact that a Negro could write was astonishing. Nor was there any deep concern on the part of white America with what role Negro writing should play in American culture; and the role it did play grew out of accident rather than intent or design. Either it crept in through the kitchen in the form of jokes; or it was the fruits of that foul soil which was the result of a liaison between inferiority-complexed Negro "geniuses" and burnt-out white Bohemians with money.

On the other hand, these often technically brilliant performances by Negro writers were looked upon by the majority of literate Negroes as something to be proud of. At best, Negro writing has been something external to the lives of educated Negroes themselves. That the productions of their writers should have been something of a guide in their daily living is a matter which seems never to have been raised seriously.

Under these conditions Negro writing assumed two general aspects: (1) It became a sort of conspicuous ornamentation, the hallmark of "achievement." (2) It became the voice of the educated Negro pleading with white America for justice.

Rarely was the best of this writing addressed to the Negro himself, his needs, his sufferings, his aspirations. Through misdirection, Negro writers have been far better to others than they have been to themselves. And the mere recognition of this places the whole question of Negro writing in a new light and raises a doubt as to the validity of its present direction.

II. The Minority Outlook

Somewhere in his writings Lenin makes the observation that oppressed minorities often reflect the techniques of the bourgeoisie more brilliantly than some sections of the bourgeoisie themselves. The psychological importance of this becomes meaningful when it is recalled that oppressed minorities, and especially petty bourgeois sections of oppressed minorities, strive to assimilate the virtues of the bourgeoisie in the assumption that by doing so they can lift themselves into a higher social sphere. But not only among the oppressed petty bourgeoisie does this occur. The workers of a minority people, chafing under exploitation, forge organizational forms of struggle to better their lot. Lacking the handicaps of false ambition and property, they have access to a wide social vision and a deep social consciousness. They display a greater freedom and initiative in pushing their claims upon civilization than even do the petty bourgeoisie. Their organizations show greater strength, adaptability, and efficiency than any other group or class in society.

That Negro workers, propelled by the harsh conditions of their lives, have demonstrated this consciousness and mobility for political and economic action there can be no doubt. But has this consciousness been reflected in the work of Negro writers to the same degree as it has been in the Negro workers' struggle to free Herndon and the Scottsboro boys, in the drive toward unionism, and in the fight against lynching? Have they as creative writers taken advantage of their unique minority position?

The answer decidedly is *no*. Negro writers have lagged sadly, and as time passes, the gap widens between them and their people.

How can the hiatus be bridged? How can the enervating effects of this long-standing split be eliminated?

In presenting questions of this sort, an attitude of self-consciousness and self-criticism is far more likely to be a fruitful point of departure than a mere recounting of past achievements. An emphasis upon tendency and experiment, a view of society as something becoming rather than as something fixed and admired is the one which points the way for Negro writers to stand shoulder to shoulder with Negro workers in mood and outlook.

III. A Whole Culture

There is, however, a culture of the Negro which is his and has been addressed to him; a culture which has, for good or ill, helped to clarify his consciousness and create emotional attitudes which are conducive to action. This culture has stemmed mainly from two sources: (1) the Negro church; and (2) the folklore of the Negro people.

It was through the portals of the church that the American Negro first entered the shrine of Western culture. Living under slave conditions of life, bereft of his African heritage, the Negroes' struggle for religion on the plantations between 1820 and 1860 assumed the form of a struggle for human rights. It remained a relatively revolutionary struggle until religion began to serve as an antidote for suffering and denial. But even today there are millions of American Negroes whose only sense of a whole universe, whose only relation to society and man, and whose only guide to personal dignity comes through the archaic morphology of Christian salvation.

It was, however, in a folklore moulded out of rigorous and inhuman conditions of life that the Negro achieved his most indigenous and complete expression. Blues, spirituals, and folk tales recounted from mouth to mouth; the whispered words of a black mother to her black daughter on the ways of men; the confidential wisdom of a black father to his black son; the swapping of sex experiences on street corners from boy to boy in the deepest vernacular; work songs sung under blazing suns—all these formed the channels through which the racial wisdom flowed.

One would have thought that Negro writers, in their last century of striving at expression, would have continued and deepened this folk tradition, would have tried to create a more intimate and yet a more profoundly social system of artistic communication between them and their people.

But the illusion that they could escape through individual achievement the harsh lot of their race swung Negro writers away from any such path. Two separate cultures sprang up: one for the Negro masses, unwritten and unrecognized; and the other for the sons and daughters of a rising Negro bourgeoisie, parasitic and mannered.

Today the question is: Shall Negro writing be for the Negro masses, moulding those lives and consciousness of those masses toward new goals, or shall it continue begging the question of the Negroes' humanity?

IV. The Problem of Nationalism in Negro Writing

In stressing the difference between the role Negro writing failed to play in lives of the Negro people, and the role it should play in the future if it is to serve its historic function; in pointing out the fact that Negro writing has been addressed in the main to a small white audience rather than to a Negro one, it should be stated that no attempt is being made here to propagate a specious and blatant nationalism. Yet the nationalist character of the Negro people is unmistakable. Psychologically this nationalism is reflected in the whole of Negro culture, and especially in folklore.

In the absence of fixed and nourishing forms of culture, the Negro has a folklore which embodies the memories and hopes of his struggle for freedom. Not yet caught in paint or stone, and as yet but feebly depicted in the poem and novel, the Negroes' most powerful images of hope and despair still remain in the fluid state of daily speech. How many John Henrys have lived and died on the lips of these black people? How many mythical heroes in embryo have been allowed to perish for lack of husbanding by alert intelligence?

Negro folklore contains, in a measure that puts to shame more deliberate forms of Negro expression, the collective sense of Negro life in America. Let those who shy at the nationalist implications of Negro life look at the body of folklore, living and powerful, which rose out of a unified sense of a common life and a common fate. Here are those vital beginnings of a recognition of value in life as it is *lived*, a recognition that marks the emergence of a new culture in the shell of the old. And at the moment this process starts, at the moment when a people begin to realize a *meaning* in their suffering, the civilization that engenders that suffering is doomed.

The nationalist aspects of Negro life are as sharply manifest in the social institutions of the Negro people as in folklore. There is a Negro church, a Negro press, a Negro social world, a Negro sporting world, a Negro business world, a Negro school system, Negro professions; in short, a Negro way of life in America. The Negro people did not ask for this, and deep down, though they express themselves through their institutions and adhere to this special way of life, they do not want it now. This special existence was forced upon them from without by lynch rope, bayonet, and mob rule. They accepted these negative conditions with the inevitability of a tree which must live or perish in whatever soil it finds itself.

The few crumbs of American civilization which the Negro has got from the tables of capitalism have been through these segregated channels. Many Negro institutions are cowardly and incompetent. But they are all that the Negro has. And, in the main, any move, whether for progress or reaction, must come through these institutions for the simple reason that all other channels are closed. Negro writers who seek to mould or influence the consciousness of the Negro people must address their messages to them through the ideologies and attitudes fostered in this warping way of life.

V. The Basis and Meaning of Nationalism in Negro Writing

The social institutions of the Negro are imprisoned in the Jim Crow political system of the South, and this Jim Crow political system is in turn built upon a plantation-feudal economy. Hence, it can be seen that the emotional expression of group-feeling which puzzles so many whites and leads them to deplore what they call "black chauvinism" is not a morbidly inherent trait of the Negro, but rather the reflex expression of a life whose roots are imbedded deeply in Southern soil.

Negro writers must accept the nationalist implications of their lives, not in order to encourage them, but in order to change and transcend them. They must accept the concept of nationalism because, in order to transcend it, they must *possess* and *understand* it. And a nationalist spirit in Negro writing means a nationalism carrying the highest possible pitch of social consciousness. It means a nationalism that knows its origins, its limitations; that is aware of the dangers of its position; that knows its ultimate aims are unrealizable within the framework of capitalist America; a nationalism whose reason for being lies in the simple fact of self-possession and in the consciousness of the interdependence of people in modern society.

For purposes of creative expression it means that the Negro writer must realize within the area of his own personal experience those impulses which, when prefigured in terms of broad social movements, constitute the stuff of nationalism.

For Negro writers even more so than for Negro politicians, nationalism is a bewildering and vexing question, the full ramifications of which cannot be dealt with here. But among the Negro workers and the Negro middle class the spirit of nationalism is rife in a hundred devious forms; and a simple literary realism which seeks to depict the lives of these people devoid of wider social connotations, devoid of the revolutionary significance of these nationalist tendencies, must of necessity do a rank injustice to the Negro people and alienate their possible allies in the struggle for freedom.

VI. Social Consciousness and Responsibility

The Negro writer who seeks to function within his race as purposeful agent has a serious responsibility. In order to do justice to his subject matter, in order to depict Negro life in all of its manifold and intricate relationships, a deep, informed, and complex consciousness is necessary; a consciousness which draws for its strength upon the fluid lore of a great people, and moulds this lore with the concepts that move and direct the forces of history today.

With the gradual decline of the moral authority of the Negro church, and with the increasing irresolution which is paralyzing Negro middle-class leadership, a new role is devolving upon the Negro writer. He is being called upon to do no less than create values by which their race is to struggle, live and die.

By his ability to fuse and make articulate the experience of men, because his writing possesses the potential cunning to steal into the inmost recesses of the human heart, because he can create the myths and symbols that inspire a faith in life, he may expect either to be consigned to oblivion, or to be recognized for the valued agent that he is.

This raises the question of the personality of the writer. It means that in the lives of Negro writers must be found those materials and experiences which will create a meaningful picture of the world today. Many young writers have grown to believe that a Marxist analysis of society presents such a picture. It creates a picture which, when placed before the eyes of the writer, should unify his personality, organize his emotions, buttress him with a tense and obdurate will to change the world.

And, in turn, this changed world will dialectically change the writer. Hence, it is through a Marxist conception of reality and society that the maximum degree of freedom in thought and feeling can be gained for the Negro writer. Further, this dramatic Marxist vision, when consciously grasped, endows the writer with a sense of dignity which no other vision can give. Ultimately, it restores to the writer his lost heritage, that is, his role as a creator of the world in which he lives, and as a creator of himself.

Yet, for the Negro writer, Marxism is but the starting point. No theory of life can take the place of life. After Marxism has laid bare the skeleton of society, there remains the task of the writer to plant flesh upon those bones out of his will to live. He may, with disgust and revulsion, say *no* and depict the horrors of capitalism encroaching upon the human being. Or he may, with hope and passion, say *yes* and depict the faint stirrings of a new and emerging life. But in whatever social voice he chooses to speak, whether positive or negative, there should always be heard or *over*-heard his faith, his necessity, his judgment.

His vision need not be simple or rendered in primer-like terms; for the life of the Negro people is not simple. The presentation of their lives should be simple, yes; but all the complexity, the strangeness, the magic wonder of life that plays like a bright sheen over the most sordid existence, should be there. To borrow a phrase from the Russians, it should have a *complex simplicity*. Eliot, Stein, Joyce, Proust, Hemingway, and Anderson; Gorky, Barbusse, Nexo, and Jack London no less than the folklore of the Negro himself should form the heritage of the Negro writer. Every iota of gain in human thought and sensibility should be ready grist for his mill, no matter how farfetched they may seem in their immediate implications.

VII. The Problem of Perspective

What vision must Negro writers have before their eyes in order to feel the impelling necessity for an about-face? What angle of vision can show them all the forces of modern society in process, all the lines of economic development converging toward a distant point of hope? Must they believe in some "ism"?

They may feel that only dupes believe in "isms"; they feel with some measure of justification that another commitment means only another disillusionment. But anyone destitute of a theory about the meaning, structure, and direction of modern society is a lost victim in a world he cannot understand or control.

But even if Negro writers found themselves through some "ism," how would that influence their writing? Are they being called upon to "preach"? To be "salesmen"? To "prostitute" their writing? Must they "sully" themselves? Must they write "propaganda"?

No; it is a question of awareness, of consciousness; it is, above all, a question of perspective.

Perspective is that part of a poem, novel, or play which a writer never puts directly upon paper. It is that fixed point in intellectual space where a writer stands to view the struggles, hopes, and sufferings of his people. There are times when he may stand too close and the result is a blurred vision. Or he may stand too far away and the result is a neglect of important things.

Of all the problems faced by writers who as a whole have never allied themselves with world movements, perspective is the most difficult achievement. At its best, perspective is a pre-conscious assumption, something which a writer takes for granted, something which he wins through his living.

A Spanish writer recently spoke of living in the heights of one's time. Surely perspective means just that.

It means that a Negro writer must learn to view the life of a Negro living in New York's Harlem or Chicago's South Side with the consciousness that one-sixth of the earth's surface belongs to the working class. It means that a Negro writer must create in his readers' minds a relationship between a Negro woman hoeing cotton in the South and the men who loll in swivel chairs in Wall Street and take the fruits of her toil.

Perspective for Negro writers will come when they have looked and brooded so hard and so long upon the harsh lot of their race and compared it with the hopes and struggles of minority peoples everywhere that the cold facts have begun to tell them something.

VIII. The Problem of Theme

This does not mean that a Negro writer's sole concern must be with rendering the social scene; but if his conception of the life of his people is broad and deep enough, if the sense of the *whole* life he is seeking is vivid and strong in him, then his writing will embrace all these social, political, and economic forms under which the life of his people is manifest.

In speaking of theme one must necessarily be general and abstract; the temperament of each writer moulds and colors the world he sees. Negro life may be approached from a thousand angles, with no limit to technical and stylistic freedom.

Negro writers spring from a family, a clan, a class, and a nation; and the social units in which they are bound have a story, a record. Sense of theme will emerge in Negro writing when Negro writers try to fix this story about some pole of meaning, remembering as they do so that in the creative process meaning proceeds *equally* as much from the contemplation of the subject matter as from the hopes and apprehensions that rage in the heart of the writer.

Reduced to its simplest and most general terms, theme for Negro writers will rise from understanding the meaning of their being transplanted from a "savage" to a "civilized" culture in all of its social, political, economic, and emotional aspects. It means that Negro writers must have in their consciousness the foreshortened picture of the *whole,* nourishing culture from which they were torn in Africa, and of the long, complex (and for the most part unconscious) struggle to regain in some form and under alien conditions of life a *whole* culture again.

It is not only this picture they must have, but also a knowledge of the social and emotional milieu that gives it tone and solidity of detail. Theme for Negro writers will emerge when they have begun to feel the meaning of the history of their race as though they in one lifetime had lived it themselves throughout all the long centuries.

IX. Autonomy of Craft

For the Negro writer to depict this new reality requires a greater discipline and consciousness than was necessary for the so-called Harlem School of expression. Not only is the subject matter dealt with far more meaningful and complex, but the new role of the writer is qualitatively different. The Negro writers' new position demands a sharper definition of the status of his craft, and a sharper emphasis upon its functional autonomy.

Negro writers should seek through the medium of their craft to play as meaningful a role in the affairs of men as do other professionals. But if their writing is demanded to perform the social office of other professionals, then the autonomy of craft is lost and writing detrimentally fused with other interests. The limitations of the craft constitute some of its greatest virtues. If the sensory vehicle of imaginative writing is required to carry too great a load of didactic material, the artistic sense is submerged.

The relationship between reality and the artistic image is not always direct and simple. The imaginative conception of a historical period will not be a carbon copy of reality. Image and emotion possess a logic of their own. A vulgarized simplicity constitutes the greatest danger in tracing the reciprocal interplay between the writer and his environment.

Writing has its professional autonomy; it should complement other professions, but it should not supplant them or be swamped by them.

X. The Necessity for Collective Work

It goes without saying that these things cannot be gained by Negro writers if their present mode of isolated writing and living continues. This isolation exists *among* Negro writers as well as *between* Negro and white writers. The Negro writers' lack of thorough integration with the American scene, their lack of a clear realization among themselves of their possible role, have bred generation after generation of embittered and defeated literati.

Barred for decades from the theater and publishing houses, Negro writers have been *made* to feel a sense of difference. So deep has this white-hot iron of exclusion been burnt into their hearts that thousands have all but lost the desire to become identified with American civilization. The Negro writers' acceptance of this enforced isolation and their attempt to justify it is but a defense-reflex of the whole special way of life which has been rammed down their throats.

The problem, by its very nature, is one which must be approached contemporaneously from *two* points of view. The ideological unity of Negro writers and the alliance of that unity with all the progressive ideas of our day is the primary prerequisite for collective work. On the shoulders of white writers and Negro writers alike rest the responsibility of ending this mistrust and isolation.

By placing cultural health above narrow sectional prejudices, liberal writers of all races can help to break the stony soil of aggrandizement out of which the stunted plants of Negro nationalism grew. And simultaneously Negro writers can help to weed out these choking growths of reactionary nationalism and replace them with hardier and sturdier types.

These tasks are imperative in light of the fact that we live in a time when the majority of the most basic assumptions of life can no longer be taken for granted. Tradition is no longer a guide. The world has grown huge and cold. Surely this is the moment to ask questions, to theorize, to speculate, to wonder out of what materials can a human world be built.

Each step along this unknown path should be taken with thought, care, self-consciousness, and deliberation. When Negro writers think they have arrived at something which smacks of truth, humanity, they should want to test it with others, feel it with a degree of passion and strength that will enable them to communicate it to millions who are groping like themselves.

Writers faced with such tasks can have no possible time for malice or jealousy. The conditions for the growth of each writer depend too much upon the good work of other writers. Every first-rate novel, poem, or play lifts the level of consciousness higher.

Fall 1937

Note: Originally published as "Blueprint for Negro Writing," *New Challenge* (1937). Reprinted courtesy of the Richard Wright Estate.

Floating Facts on a Sea of Emotion

The Literary Journalism of Richard Wright

William Dow

Richard Wright's journalism, largely unexamined by scholars,[1] is infused with qualities that put him firmly in line with other African American novelists and poets who first established their reputations as writers of fiction but who nevertheless wrote literary journalism.[2] These include Langston Hughes, Alice Childress, Zora Neale Hurston, Melvin Tolson, W. E. B. Du Bois, Ralph Ellison, James Baldwin, Nella Larsen, and Jessie Fauset. While their primary objective was to change social policy, if not the entire social order, they also explored new expressive and stylistic forms. Wright's *12 Million Black Voices* (1940) and his exile writings *Black Power: A Record of Reactions in a Land of Pathos* (1954), *The Color Curtain: A Report on the Bandung Conference* (1956), and *Pagan Spain* (1957) illustrate how he, too, repurposed traditional journalism to promote a political solidarity with oppressed people around the world.[3]

Although Wright's major achievement as a writer was in fiction, his entire career was enlivened by his journalism and various forms of literary journalism. The journalistic forms that he learned as a writer and editor of the *Daily Worker*,⁴ the official newspaper of the Communist Party in the 1930s and 1940s, helped him develop the autobiographical prose for which he is most remembered. His research on lynchings, rent strikes, the Joe Louis–Max Schmeling fight, the Scottsboro case, peace parades, negro theater, and other contemporary events deepened his understanding of race relations and urban racial problems and prepared him for his later essayistic and politically infused fiction (*Native Son*, 1940; *Black Boy*, 1945) as well as his works of literary journalism (*12 Million Black Voices*, *Black Power*, and *Pagan Spain*). Meanwhile, his pieces of nonfiction for the *Partisan Review* ("Between the World and Me," 1934), *New Challenge* ("Blueprint for Negro Writing," 1937), *Atlantic Monthly* ("I Bite the Hand That Feeds Me," 1940; "I Tried to Be a Communist," 1944), *New Masses* ("Not My People's War, 1941), *Harper's Magazine* ("What You Know Won't Hurt You," 1942), *Présence Africaine* ("Bright and Morning Star," 1946), and *Ebony* ("The Shame of Chicago," 1951) gave him opportunities to develop his hybrid combinations of literary, nonfictional, and autobiographical writing, which would later reappear in his longer works. As such, Wright's fiction and journalism, engaging in a dynamic dialogue within and among communities (e.g., Memphis, Chicago, New York, Paris, Jakarta, Spain), debated the major racial, philosophical, and social issues of the early and mid-twentieth century while questioning conventionally accepted definitions of modernism and modernity.

12 Million Black Voices

The photo-essay *12 Million Black Voices* was Wright's first long work that used literary-journalistic techniques. Wright's prose was accompanied by photographs that the photographer Edwin Rosskam had selected from the files of the Farm Security Administration (FSA) during the Depression. The work presents itself as a "true-life" story and draws on the techniques that Horace J. Cayton and the Chicago school of sociology had used when chronicling urbanization, juvenile delinquency, and ethnic groups during the 1930s and 1940s.⁵ Wright adopts the posture of a "sociological informant,"⁶ treats the individual as representative of a group (as he did in *Native Son* and *Black Boy*), and thus shows his comfort with "the deterministic slant" of the Chicago school of urban sociology.⁷

This style of sociological reasoning led Wright to innovative narrative devices and experiments that were more conducive to his experiences and thoughts than were straightforward fictional and nonfictional narratives. He was one of the 1930s writers whom Michael Thurston has characterized as "writ[ing] not only out of a sense of political mission but also out of an aesthetic sense independent of political orthodoxies."[8] Although "documentary fiction" is the standard term for classifying *Black Voices,* I prefer the term "literary journalism." A documentary, according to William Stott, is "the presentation or representation of actual fact that makes it credible and vivid to people at the time. Since all emphasis is on the fact, its validity must be as unquestionable as possible."[9] Literary journalism, in contrast, makes no such claim to pure nonfictiveness and "fact." It openly flaunts its fictionality and figuralizations, and, in *Black Voices,* presents itself as a textuality of modernity—literary, poetic, visual—to more effectively expose the oppression experienced by African Americans and the "paternalistic code"[10] employed by whites toward them. The goal of this literary-journalistic text is to put the reader in the position of struggling African American migrants and other urban populations, and to use narrative techniques that depend on both factual knowledge and symbolic awareness.

Black Voices offered Wright freedom from causality and from his well-known naturalistic trajectory. As Wright explained in a 1941 interview about *Black Voices:* "The main thing [is] to show the movement from folk life to urbanization. . . . I want to show the inner complexities and scars that take place when a people are torn away from one culture and are forced to adjust themselves to another."[11] He was concerned less with historically verifiable fact than with the emotional patterns and spiritual developments of African Americans migrating from rural areas to cities, which Wright, being himself a participant in the Great Migration (1910–1930), knew intimately.

Wright's Literary-Journalistic Inflections: "We" and "You" in *12 Million Black Voices*

Simultaneously expanding and contravening the attitudes and positions of the FSA-rooted documentary, Wright's self-consciously modernist experiment[12] both cross-examines documentary conventions and, in its modernist guises, compels attention to the world beyond representation.[13]

For example, drawing upon his literary and journalistic training, Wright uses "we" to infuse "ordinary people with divine speech"[14] and to create the text's "literary voice." He also relies on sociological data to build a collective story, but as Jeff Allred notes, Wright takes such data and transposes them into "the classical epic's encompassing range of space and time and its ambition to speak to a wide audience about an unprecedented emergence."[15] He infuses the epic form with photographs from the files of the Farm Security Administration, with veiled references to his own participation in the Great Migration, with published statistics from public records, and with his own accounts of black intellectual history. These infusions not only make the processes *12 Million Black Voices* exposes progressive and ongoing, as opposed to closed and final, but elicit the reader's involvement with the characters in the work and the historical forces they face. Wright's "we" prompts readers to criticize, rather than accept, the social and racial conditions *Black Voices* enumerates. At the same time, Wright's use of "we" reflects many of the strategies found in the high modernist arsenal[16] ("fragmentation, the primacy of form, the integration of non-poetic material, and the sense of a culture in crisis")[17] but with a crucial difference: Wright foregrounds the social realities of class and race in his history of African Americans.

Through the use of "we," Wright initiates a conversation with the reader, who, according to the opening pages of *Black Voices*, does not know "us" for "we are not what we seem."[18] The collective narrator imagines the reader—much as Rebecca Harding Davis imagines her readers in *Life in the Iron Mills* (1861)—to be white, bourgeois, and misinformed about the rural "folk" and immigrant laborers. Because there are no verbally and semantically autonomous characters whose speech discloses a belief system, there is, in M. M. Bakhtin's sense, no "second language."[19] The narrator becomes the "situation monitor" for each observation and the controlling authority of African American subjectivity.[20] The narrator's principal task is to reveal the "uneasily tied knot of pain and hope whose snarled strands converge from many points of time and space."[21]

Wright employs the "we" narration in a nonrealistic antimimetic way and transgresses fundamental cognitive and rhetorical categories. In a standard literary-journalistic mode of the American and French 1930s and 1940s (employed, for example, by Joseph Kessel, Blaise Cendrars, Dorothy Day, Meridel le Sueur, Jessie Fauset, James Agee), the narrator becomes a persona in his/her own story.

> Each day when *you* see us black folk upon the dusty land of the farms or upon the hard pavement of the city streets, *you* usually take us for

granted and think *you* know us, but our history is far stranger than *you* suspect.... We had our own civilization in Africa before we were captured and carried off to this land. *You* may smile when we call the way of life we live in Africa's "civilization," but in numerous respects the culture of many of our tribes was equal to that of the lands from which they come.[22] (my emphasis)

Directly addressing the reader, Wright places her/him on the same plane of reality as those in the book.[23] The narrator acknowledges that his vision is both subjective and grounded in actual historical fact. By placing his reader in a variety of positions of receptions (through his use of "we" and "you"), the narrator bends his story and complicates the dichotomy that Carla Cappetti argues for in her discussion of the relationship between literature and sociology: "[The sociological theory] articulate[s] and evolve[s] the [literary text] into a set of concepts and categories, the [literary text] dramatizes [the sociological theory] and demonstrat[es] its functioning in the concrete details of a life-story."[24] Wright has it both ways because *12 Million Black Voices*, as a literary-journalistic and modernist text, serves *several* functions at the same time: it is self-reflective and objective, literary and reportorial, detached and engaged.

Wright's Literary-Journalistic Use of Analogy

In *12 Million Black Voices*, Wright redescribes the dominant white plantation and landowners in the American South as the "Lords of the Land"[25] and the white industrial elite of the North as the "Bosses of Buildings."[26] For Wright, these two analogic forces are the "operatives" of "the New World."[27] Mimicking such sociological definitions as St. Clair Drake and Horace C. Cayton's "Native White," "Foreign Born-White and Other Races," "older Immigrant groups,"[28] Wright creates his own definitions and categories. Then he places on the grid of abstract and objective 1930s sociological postulations and theories *individuated* examples of the black maid,[29] the black industrial worker,[30] the black stevedore, the black dancer,[31] and the black sharecropper[32] as narrative markers for the photographs that represent these professions. He speaks for and to his subjects, but with enough objective distance to discern, for example, in reference to the plantation system, "patterns of psychological reaction, welding us together into a separate unity with common characteristics of our own."³³ In deploying such analogical devices, the narrator individuates but doesn't dwell on any one close-up (in photographic or narrative descriptive form) for too long because he doesn't want to take the reader away from the implications of individual lives in broader social contexts.

Similar to his mixings of the "we" narrative and direct address, Wright mixes archival research and fieldwork data with the conventions of fictional narrative. When combined with historical statistics, his symbolic literary and analogic appellations ("Bosses of the Buildings," "Lords of the Land") harken back to Drake and St. Clair's use of charts, facts, and numbers in *Black Metropolis:* "The Bosses of the Buildings feed upon the Lords of the Land, and the Lords of the Land feed upon the 5,000,000 landless poor whites and upon us, throwing to the poor whites the scant solace of filching from us 4,000,000 landless blacks what the poor whites themselves are cheated of in this elaborate game."³⁴ This analytic shape-shifting contributes to the impressionistic and modernistic structure of the text and allows Wright to reconstruct his own role as a black writer as he exposes the complicity of racial segregation and capitalism. *Black Voices* thus focuses not on the "so-called talented tenth"³⁵ but on "that vast and tragic school [of Negroes] that swims below in the depths, against the current, silently and heavily, struggling against the waves of vicissitudes that spell a common fate."³⁶ The book's emphasis on the relationship of poverty to race and class challenges the era's Rooseveltian claims about a single national identity.³⁷

Literary Journalistic Techniques in *Black Power*

Black Power, The Color Curtain, and *Pagan Spain,* all written during the 1950s and concerned with diasporic and global revolutionary movements, expand the form as well as the content of Anglo-American modernism by disrupting expected continuities, resorting to narrative discontinuities and deferrals, and moving toward a pluralism or fusion of narrative forms.

Many scholars have considered *Black Power, The Color Curtain,* and *Pagan Spain* examples of travel writing. But this classification is more problematic than it may first seem.³⁸ Judith Hamera and Alfred Bendixen offer a typical definition of travel writing in their introduction to the *Cambridge Companion to American Travel Writing*: "Travel writing [is] a non-fiction genre based, at least in theory, on the real experiences of actual travelers rooted in the specific details of both history and geography. . . . American travel writing also exposes cultural and genre fault lines. It exists betwixt and between the factual report and the fictional account, personal memoir and ethnography, science and romance."[39] Hamera and Bendixen emphasize that the "boundary between travel writing and fiction can be especially murky and that travel writing is much like autobiography" in that "fact and fiction . . . intermingle in individual works as well."[40]

Although *Black Power, The Color Curtain,* and *Pagan Spain* incorporate some of the traits that Hamera and Bendixen highlight, Wright's writings fit more comfortably with constructs and theories of literary journalism, which offer more comprehensive and convincing explanations about the relations between "fact" and "fiction" than is presently found in American travel-writing criticism. Moreover, these three texts ask hard questions about race, class, gender, national belonging, and the international struggle for human rights that go beyond most definitions of travel literature. In addition, the texts have a sociologically discursive dimension (reminiscent of *12 Million Black Voices*) that allows Wright to enter the ongoing debates during the twentieth century about the reinvention of the United States amid colonial legacies and new geopolitical arrangements. These topics stray from the preoccupations of most travel literature (nor does Wright in any of these works define himself as a "traveler"). Finally, Wright's use of a modern narrative art form departs from the conventions of realistic travel accounts. It is no surprise, then, that "[Wright's] publishers, agents, and critics in the 1950s and through the 1980s did not consider [these exile writings] travel books."[41] They simply didn't know what to call them because Wright had produced works years ahead of their time.

Black Power was Wright's first extended examination of an African country, Ghana—called the Gold Coast in 1953. Through the intervention of George Padmore, the Trinidadian author of *Pan-Africanism or Communism?* (1956), Wright was invited by the Gold Coast prime minister, Kwame Nkrumah, "to do some research into the social and historical aspects of the country."[42] "This volume," Wright explains, "is a first-person, subjective narrative on the life and conditions of the Colony and Ashanti areas of the Gold Coast, an area comprising perhaps the most highly socially evolved native life of present-day Africa."[43] Later, Wright toured Ghana, Sierra Leone, and other African countries; and from these experiences he composed *Black Power*. During most of the summer of 1953, Wright attended a session of the legislative council in which Nkrumah proposed constitutional changes that would lead to the Gold Coast's eventual independence and self-government. Wright believed that the measures that were debated, while adequate for an eventual independence from Britain, weren't enough. (On Wright's question of whether African political experiments are liberating, see the essays on *Black Power* by Dorothy Stringer and Kevin Gaines in this volume.)

He therefore ends *Black Power* with a ten-page open letter to Nkrumah and a plea for the Gold Coast to "militarize" itself:

AFRICAN LIFE MUST BE MILITARIZED! . . .

I'm speaking simply of a militarization of the daily, social lives of the people; I'm speaking of giving form, organization, direction, meaning, and a sense of justification to those lives. . . . I'm speaking of a temporary discipline that will unite the nation, sweep out the tribal cobwebs, and place the feet of the masses upon a basis of reality.[44]

Wright called for "a military form of African society" that, through a compulsory draft, "will atomize the fetish-ridden past, abolish the mystical and nonsensical family relations that freeze the African in his static degradation."[45] Furthermore, in Wright's opinion the inhabitants of the Gold Coast must enter the modern industrialized world, but they cannot do so by ignoring world capitalism and Soviet communism: "Above all, Africans must be regimentalized for the 'long pull,' for what will happen in Africa will spread itself out over decades of time and a continent of space. . . . You know as well as I that what has happened in the Gold Coast is just the beginning; and there will be much marching to and fro; there will be many sunderings and amalgamations of people; there will be many shiftings and changes of aims, perspectives, and ideologies—there will be much confusion before the final redemption of Africa is accomplished."[46] Wright buttressed his letter with the same kind of sociological discourse that he relied on in *12 Million Black Voices*. Countering what Eric Schocket has called "the assimilative dictates of literary discourse,"[47] Wright makes his didactic points about the relationship of race to exploitation and about suffering under global capitalism in a rather traditional way.

But *Black Power* is not straightforward journalistic narrative. Wright felt alienated and estranged from the Africa he was discovering, and he responded through highly subjective descriptions of anxiety and fear. For example, upon seeing the mud huts outside of Takoradi, he writes: "I was gazing upon a world whose laws I did not know, upon faces whose reactions were riddles to me. There was nothing here that I could predict, anticipate, or rely upon and, in spite of myself, a mild sense of anxiety began to fill me. . . . I was prey to a vague sense of mild panic, an oppressed burden of alertness which I could not shake off."[48] Wright drops the collective "we" that he had used in *12 Million Black Voices* as he "explores Africa's alterity and his own lack of feeling of racial connection,"[49] and uncertainty about his identity and place. He decides to remain "rational" and "areligious," and to cling to his "Western sensibilities."[50] By his own appraisal, he was *not* a spiritual descendant of Africa.

Although *Black Power* is a factual narrative, it is constantly infiltrated by the narrative techniques that Wright had mastered in his fiction. The book makes use of a clarifying narrator, a persona of Wright, who explains or justifies himself to others, be they readers, other characters, or some imagined or real community. "If I become polemic," Wright stated in a 1960 interview, "it is because I am trying to tell the reader something and I am afraid he does not understand."[51] In both *Black Power* and *12 Million Black Voices*, the assumption is that the reader will not understand without the narrator's explanation—or, one of Wright's favorite terms, a "revelation": "I have always taken the writing of literature very seriously and I've looked upon fiction and writing in general as a means of revealing the truth of life and experience rather than purely as a means of entertaining people. . . . [L]iterature ought to be a sharp instrument to reveal something important about mankind, about living, about life whether among whites or blacks."[52] By creating a voice to elucidate a collective sense of black life in Africa, the United States, and elsewhere, Wright departs from most previous forms of African American writing. He not only portrays "his liberal-radicalness, his blackness, his maleness, his Americanness,"[53] but he offers a new global perspective and humanitarian vision, which invariably included a look backward at the injustices, hunger, and despair of his earlier life. (On the question of solidarity, see Lori J. Marso's essay "Seizing Freedom with Simone de Beauvoir," in this volume.)

Black Power is thus more of a novel than a travel narrative, and more a literary-journalistic account than a novel.[54] An early critic, baffled by its form, called it "a curious mixture of history, biographical sketches, exposition of social customs and political chicanery."[55] Wright's black archetypes,[56] his profuse dialogue,[57] his use of a first-person persona who explores unknown territory and is bewildered by it, and his extensive turns to symbolism[58] and imagery[59] render *Black Power* more "literary" than nonfictional and reveal Wright to be an experimental fictionalist.

But perhaps even more importantly, *Black Power* makes evident his struggle to find an effective critical language to express his impressions, fears, and disappointments on the Gold Coast. Despite his problematic stance toward African culture, his anger and distrust over African customs and mores, and his schematizing of such concepts as "non-Western" or "pre-industrial," he attempts to locate black modernity through a transnational lens. *Black Power* is thus "a subjective narrative" in which Wright offers his own experiences as a template for contemporary history and offers his own "political and psychological rebellion"[60] as a method for resisting the chaos and repression of his US experience.

The Color Curtain

Wright had envisioned *The Color Curtain* as a companion piece to *Black Power*.[61] Wright's hybrid prose and quest to understand the relationship between racism in the United States and the global realities of colonialism and capitalism in Africa and Asia dominate both works.[62] In the spring of 1955, Wright attended the Bandung Asian-African Conference in Indonesia. The conference attracted participants from twenty-nine independent and "non-aligned" nations—including China, Indonesia, Burma, Turkey, Egypt, the Philippines, and Ethiopia. The gathering focused on problems of special interest to Asian and African peoples (for example, "national sovereignty . . . racialism and colonialism,"[63] "the promotion of world peace and co-operation,"[64] and the development of social and economic solidarity between these countries' impoverished populations).

The Bandung Conference provided Wright with yet another lens with which to view the dehumanization of modernity. Near the beginning of the book, he criticizes the Western media's account of the conference: "These men . . . representing some of the world's biggest and most powerful news gathering agencies, knew less, perhaps, than even I about what was going on. . . . I soon realized that American newsmen had at least two grave disabilities in trying to grasp what was happening: one they had no philosophy of history with which to understand Bandung; two, they were trying to understand actions initiated by someone else and they could not quite grasp the nature of the terms in which those actions were being projected."[65] He then analyzes excerpted samples from the mainstream newspaper, magazine, and radio-television reports that covered the event, including *Newsweek*, the *Christian Science Monitor*, Paris *Herald Tribune*, *New York Times*, and Manchester *Guardian*. He glosses an excerpt from a speech about the conference by the US secretary of state, John Foster Dulles:

> The words that cut short and hurt the Asian-African delegates most came from no less than the American Secretary of State, John Foster Dulles. In a radio-television address in Washington on the 8th of March, 1955, he referred to the conference as follows:
>
> Three of the Asian parties to the Pacific Charter, Pakistan, the Philippines and Thailand, may shortly be meeting with other Asian countries at a so-called Afro-Asian conference.
>
> (The single phrase, "so-called Afro-Asian conference," echoed and re-echoed at Bandung as proof of American contempt; and the people who called attention to it were not Communists . . .)[66]

Wright observed that conventional media outlets were variously condescending, supportive, critical, guardedly optimistic, and patronizing. This set "the atmosphere, brooding, bitter, apprehensive, which greeted the conference."[67] Wright found these press accounts inconclusive and partial because they ignored the deeper issues of psychology, emotion, and spirituality that are needed "to penetrate the color curtain,"[68] by which Wright meant a Western-created "buffer between [the Occidental countries] and the illiterate yellow and brown and black masses."[69] To offer a psychological and sociological critique on the relationship between race and geopolitical space, he conjoined his literary journalism to his transnational modernism.

Although Wright interviewed Mohammed Natsir and Sutan Sjahrir, transcribed the speeches of Jawaharlal Nehru, Gamal Abdel Nasser, and Sir John Kotelawala, and described the conference's principal themes, including anticolonialism,[70] his real interest was literary. He was creating characters, psychological portrayals (including of himself), and dramatic constructions of "race consciousness."⁷¹ Before departing for Jakarta, he explains to his wife why he is going:

> My life has given me some keys to what they would say or do. I'm an American Negro; as such, I've had a burden of race consciousness. So have these people. I worked in my youth as a common laborer, and I've a class consciousness. So have these people. I grew up in a Methodist and Seventh Day Adventist churches and I saw and observed religion in my childhood; and these people are religious. I was a member of the Communist Party for twelve years and I know something of the politics and psychology of rebellion. These people have had as their daily existence such politics. These emotions are my instruments. They are emotions, but I'm conscious of them as emotions. I want to use these emotions to try to find out what these people think and feel and why.⁷²

As in *12 Million Black Voices* and *Black Power*, Wright combines emotional expressiveness with social fact. "I try to float these facts," Wright contends, "on a sea of emotion, to drive them home with some degree of artistic power, as much as humanly possible, to the level of seriousness which characterizes science."⁷³

In *The Color Curtain*, Wright places documented evidence alongside his assembled dramatic dialogues, personal meditations, and descriptions of everyday Indonesian life. As in *12 Million Black Voices* and *Black Power*, his voice is the central consciousness of the text. It selects and describes the on-site conference speeches and re-creates dialogue. Interviewees are denoted by their representativeness (for example, the Indonesian-born European;⁷⁴ the Roman Catholic Singaporean journalist;⁷⁵ the Eurasian;⁷⁶ and the imperialistic Dutch)⁷⁷ and are described without any kind of "unique voice,"⁷⁸ distinctive tone, or inflection. This resembles Wright's technique in *12 Million Black Voices*, in which the narrator prohibits the existence of a verbally and semantically autonomous character and does not allow a character's speech to dominate the formulation of a belief system.

For example, Wright's interview with the anonymous "Eurasian," Mr. X, is dominated by the narrator's response to the Eurasian's "psychological reaction[s]," his personal history, and his positions on Asian culture and politics: "He is married, fifty years of age, has six children. . . . He feels that the state should not have anything actively to do with religion. . . . He feels that the overrunning of the continents of Asia and Africa by the white

Western nations was a mixture of good and bad. . . . He attends many international conferences but feels that the Asian-African Conference is but a political gesture to bolster the local political regime in Indonesia."[79] These observations often seem to precede Mr. X's stated positions, as opposed to following them. As a result, the narrator's interpretive prose buries the reported speech. Meanwhile, the narrator seems self-absorbed and introspective: "There was no doubt, in my mind, that my Indonesian educator was correct on the plane of abstract logic, but logic cannot solve problems whose solutions come not by thinking but by living. His approach implied a denial of collective thought processes, of mass organic experiences embedded in the very lives and social conditions about him. . . . Regrettably, one could safely assume that his influence upon Asian reality would be nil."[80] Wright could be accused of trying to have it both ways: concentrating on social fact yet using subjective interpretations, which foreground his emotional and spiritual experiences. His presentation of the narrator as "a super intellectual and visionary acutely perceptive of world affairs and Western threats more than anyone else"[81] echoes his own attempts between his exile period (1946) and his death (1960) to become a global public intellectual and activist who uses ethnographic and scholarly research polemically to change existing social beliefs and perceptions.[82]

These purposes go hand in hand with evolving techniques of his transnational modernism. In *The Color Curtain,* Wright adds the psychological (a traditional high modernist mainstay) to his earlier modes of assessment and focuses on various psychological pressures: "[Asian and African] countries feel that if they do not become quickly modern, if they do not measure up to the West almost overnight, they will be swallowed up again in what they feel to be slavery."[83] Asian and African populations had been subjugated on the assumption that they were in some way biologically inferior and unfit to govern themselves, and the white Western world that had shackled them had either given them a Christian religion or else had made them agonizingly conscious of their old, traditional religions to which they had had to cling under conditions of imperial rule.[84]

Wright wants his narratives to matter; he always *presumes* a cultural and racial relevance. He therefore seeks new rhetorical ground and is attracted to the power and effect of a modernist fictionality. At the same time, Wright's literary journalism is always concerned with a communicative alignment and coherence between fictional and nonfictional discourses.

For Wright, fictionality (especially in its modernistic forms) is a rhetorical source integral to the direct and pragmatic use of language within a real-world (the Depression-era United States, independence-era Africa, a financially repressed Indonesia), urgent context.[85]

During the mid- and late 1950s, Wright's literary journalism flowed naturally from his increasing status as a humanist "citizen of the world" and from his goals as a writer: "to create new life by intensifying the sensibilities and to work toward world understanding by improving living conditions."[86] His response to dominant (classical, high) modernist modes was founded on personal perception—a crucial feature of literary journalism. In his words, "the artist must bow to the monitor of his own imagination: must be led by the sovereignty of his own impressions and perceptions; must be guided by the tyranny of what troubles and concerns him personally."[87]

Pagan Spain

Pagan Spain is Wright's only literary-journalistic book about a European country and is one of his few works (fiction or otherwise) not outwardly about race. The book is based on trips that Wright took to Spain in 1954 and 1955 and chronicles the unconscious irrationality that he believes had "feudalized" the country. Wright's primary theses are that Spain was actually more pagan than Christian, that Spaniards were trapped under the cruel dictates of censorship and dictatorship, and that Spain, sexually repressed, was an isolationist culture fixated on the past.

Like Wright's other exile works, *Pagan Spain* is difficult to categorize. Wright simultaneously uses the methods of an anthropologist, an ethnographer, a historian, a writer, and a tourist—though a tourist quite different from that of his African travels. He thereby contravenes the genre of travel literature by making the work "a highly poetic social and political dialectic."[88] Herbert Matthews, in a 1957 review for the *New York Times,* called *Pagan Spain* "a provocative, disturbing, and, at times, sensational book."[89] The reviewer Richard Strout similarly argued, "There are so many ways of misunderstanding this vivid book of travel-journalism that it is likely to kick up a controversy—a Negro writing about whites, a man of Protestant background appalled by the degradation of a quasi-Church-state, an expatriate drawing upon his native land for occasional comparisons, an ex-radical describing Franco's Falange."[90] The back-cover blurb of a later Harper Perennial edition (1995) perhaps comes closest to the mark by baldly asserting that Wright "brilliantly expanded his literary horizons with *Pagan Spain*."[91]

At the beginning of *Pagan Spain*, Wright recalls his response to the Spanish Civil War when he was a reporter: "During the Spanish Civil War I had published, in no less than the New York *Daily Worker*, some harsh judgments concerning Franco; and the dive bombers and tanks of Hitler and Mussolini had brutally justified those judgments. The fate of Spain had hurt me, had haunted me; I had never been able to stifle a hunger to understand what had happened there and why."[92] Wright offers a justification for going to Spain that echoes his earlier reasons for going to the Gold Coast and to Indonesia. This helps establish his narrative authority: "God knows, totalitarian governments and ways of life were no mysteries to me. I had been born under an absolutistic racist regime in Mississippi; I had lived and worked for twelve years under the political dictatorship of the communist party of the United States; and I had spent a year of my life under the police terror of Peron in Buenos Aires."[93] Wright then comments on his philosophy of religion: "I have no religion in the formal sense of the word. . . . I have no race except that which is forced upon me. I have no country except that to which I'm obliged to belong. I have no traditions. I'm free. I have only the future."[94] *Pagan Spain* thus can be seen to be more about Wright than about Spain. It is a personal report with a description of a country still suffering from the Spanish Civil War and the fascist Falangist party.

Pagan Spain is arguably the most novelistic of Wright's literary-journalistic books. It is a compendium of first-person narration, participant-observer witnessing, character sketches, eyewitness reporting, and dramatic monologues and dialogues. It was reminiscent of his then recently published novel *The Outsider* (1953), in that Wright incorporates aspects of pulp fiction and the crime novel into several descriptions. For example, when recounting his first confrontation with the Spanish Civil Guard, he fearfully comments: "I blinked, understanding nothing; I was in a police state and I thought: This is it."[95] In a later description of another encounter with the Civil Guard, Wright writes: "I drove over the bridge and rolled on, uncertain, feeling a naked vulnerability creeping down the skin of my back. I was not accustomed to armed strangers of unknown motives standing in my rear and I waited to hear a *raatatatatat* and feel hot slugs of steel crashing into my car and into my flesh."[96] Wright also detects and interprets the thoughts of others (a conventional fictional device) when describing two young men who are helping him find a "pensión": "It was beginning to make sense; I was a heathen and these devout boys were graciously coming to my rescue. In their spontaneous embrace of me they were acting out a role that had been implanted in them since childhood. I was not only a stranger, but a 'lost' one in dire need of being saved. Yet there was no condescension in their manner; they acted with the quiet assurance of men who knew that they had the truth in existence and they were offering it to me."[97] Wright, working toward what he conceived of as a cosmopolitan "genre,"[98] simultaneously uses exposition, ethnography, and literary journalistic methods to interpret Spanish sexual mores[99] and the plight of Protestants[100] and to debunk Catholic rituals.[101] Thus *Pagan Spain*, in its style of representation, is a panoply of subjects, discourse, and disciplines.

This influences Wright's depiction of women. Although his fiction is often criticized for its problematic portrayals of members of the female sex,[102] Wright focuses on the suffering and fortitude of Spanish women in *Pagan Spain:*

> The daily striving and suffering of Spanish women make what little structure there is to Spanish society, knitting together in a web of care and love what would otherwise be a landscape of senseless anarchy.[103]
>
> The mighty maternal instinct of the Spanish woman is the anchor of responsibility that holds the ship of Spanish life steady while the Spanish man babbles abstract nonsense in the countless smoky coffee houses.[104]

As Dennis F. Evans has noted, Wright's treatment of Spanish women "is uncharacteristically empathetic and gives a view of Wright that is unavailable in any of his other works, both travel and fictional."[105] But I would add that Wright's literary journalism can result in a different way of thinking about how he works with themes of gender. (For additional discussions of Wright on the question of women and gender, see the essays in this volume by Floyd W. Hayes III, Paul Gilroy, and Tommy C. Curry.) That is to say, as opposed to the portrayals of women in his fiction, in his literary journalism he generally makes his views about women more positive and multidimensional.

According to the narrator, "*All was religion in Spain,*"[106] and women are the first to suffer from this fact: "Given the conditions, the moral attitude of the Church toward sex, the poverty, the ignorance, this was bound to be. It was all socially determined."[107] When describing Spanish women and their plight, Wright abandons his usual sociological and ethnographic discourse and rarely relied on social statistics. Instead, he focuses on the rigid Catholic expectation that a Spanish woman must be a virgin before she marries, and contrasts that cultural fact with the massive problem of female prostitution in Spain.[108] Victims of "the Spanish religion and its effects,"[109] women powerfully represent the present condition of Spain: "women who plow the fields; who wash clothes in country streams; who drive the oxen-drawn carts; who satisfy their men and nurse their babies; and who, at the beginning and the end of the day, creep forward and kneel humbly before the weeping and jeweled Virgins in the dim and drafty cathedrals."[110]

Wright also adopts a symbolic stance in his examination of poverty in Spain. He sees Seville as "the city whose cathedral held the body of Christopher Columbus. Though rich in oranges, sugar beets, olives, wheat, rice, the impression of poverty was so all-pervading, touching so many levels of life that, after an hour, poverty seemed to be the normal lot of man; I had to make an effort to remember that people lived better lives elsewhere."[111]

Wright similarly depicts Señora Flamenco's apartment in the city of Granada as "proclaiming pride and poverty" in its every detail,[112] and applies that descriptor, more generally, to all "the people of Spain [who] are suffering."[113] For Wright, poverty degrades human relationships, subverts norms, and fuels class divisions. It also drives its victims within Spain in a delusional, misguided direction: toward the Catholic Church. In Wright's view: "Spanish Catholicism was one of the odd fatalities of the world":[114] Back of the indigenous poverty and supporting it is a naively pagan attitude toward life that "is the opposite of the practical: a love of ritual and ceremony; a delight in color and movement and sound and harmony; an extolling of sheer emotion as the veritable end of human striving; a deification of tradition that lifts them out of the world that is shared by most of Western mankind . . . all of which finds its ultimate sanction and justification in the practices and canons of Spanish Catholicism."[115]

Poverty induces a distinct mind-set in *Pagan Spain*, explaining Spain's ruined (and anachronistic) spiritual world and its "paganism" and "feudalism."

Hazel Rowley, a biographer of Wright, argues that "*Pagan Spain* contains absorbing stories, interesting characters, first-rate dialogue. More than simply a travel essay, it is personal, subjective, and controversial." She additionally asserts, "Wright's narrative voice—personal, honest, wry, humorous, and occasionally self-mocking—in many ways resembles the voice of 'New Journalism' in the mid-1960s."[116] Although *Pagan Spain* does carry 1960s New Journalistic features and is a kind of "fact reporting,"[117] the book is too literary, too socially polemical, and too hybrid to fit well into that category. *Pagan Spain* mourns the damage inflicted by modern capitalism in conjunction with traditional religion. The narrator "had not been prepared for what he encountered."[118] The result is a discontinuous, multidisciplinary, and appropriately modernist writing. As such, Wright's techniques take the reader far beyond New Journalism, documentary writing, or travel literature.

In his longer literary journalism—beginning with *12 Million Black Voices* and continuing with *Black Power, The Color Curtain,* and *Pagan Spain*—Wright transposed conventional narrative forms and converted journalism into a vehicle for a perception of contemporary reality. He incorporated sermonizing traditions, jeremiads, personifications, documentary film, photojournalistic techniques, and fiction to create a certain alternate racial history, vision, and humanism. His literary journalism introduced a disruption or disequilibrium into a storyteller's and interpreter's mental model of the world. This narrative form should be seen not only as a crucial part of his intellectual and artistic growth but also as his distinct claim to a transnational modernism.

Notes

1. Although offering a helpful overview of the nineteenth- and twentieth-century black press, *The Black Press: New Literary and Historical Essays*, ed. Todd Vogel (New Brunswick, NJ: Rutgers University Press, 2001) is representative of the scant coverage given to Wright's journalism. Vogel devotes only four pages to Wright, focusing on his 1951 piece for *Ebony*, "The Shame of Chicago." Surprisingly, there have been no individual or collective studies on the substantial journalism/literary journalism that Wright wrote for the *Daily Worker, New Masses, Harper's Magazine,* and other important journals and magazines of the American 1930s and 1940s. Earle Bryant's *Byline Richard Wright: Articles from the* Daily Worker *and* New Masses (Columbia: University of Missouri Press, 2015) is an exception to this critical neglect.

2. Much work remains to be done on defining "literary journalism" as a multifarious, multigeneric, and multimedia field of study that is best addressed within international coordinates. I prefer the term "literary journalism" over "nonfiction" and other narrative classifications because these works by Wright are not merely

editorials, essays, autobiographies, memoirs, or travel narratives, as conventionally defined. The artistic practices that he uses to investigate social, racial, cultural, or political circumstances resemble those of other writers who first established themselves as fictionalists (or have highly developed literary sensibilities) and then composed powerful polemical forms of literary journalism.

    3. Some of my ideas on Wright's "modernism" and exile writings are based on the arguments that I previously presented in Alice Mikal Craven and William Dow. eds., *Richard Wright: New Readings in the 21st Century* (New York: Palgrave Macmillan, 2011); and "Richard Wright," in *The Cambridge Companion to the American Novel*, ed. Timothy Parrish (Cambridge: Cambridge University Press, 2013), 156–67.

    4. In 1938 the *Daily Worker* was the only white-owned newspaper in the United States to employ black writers on its staff and to give regular space in its pages to black social issues.

    5. Brian Dolinar, "The Illinois Writer's Project: Introduction," *Southern Quarterly* 46, no. 2 (Winter 2009): 85.

    6. Carla Cappetti, *Writing Chicago: Modernism, Ethnography, and the Novel* (New York: Columbia University Press, 1993), 182.

    7. Henry Louis Gates and Nellie Y. McKay, eds., *The Norton Anthology of African American Literature*, 2nd ed. (New York: Norton, 2004), 1401.

    8. Michael Thurston, *Making Something Happen* (Chapel Hill: University of North Carolina Press, 2001), 8.

    9. William Stott, *Documentary Expression and Thirties America* (Chicago: University of Chicago Press, 1973), 14.

    10. Richard Wright, *12 Million Black Voices*, introd. David Bradley (New York: Basic, 1941), 18.

    11. Keneth Kinnamon and Michel Fabre, eds., *Conversations with Richard Wright* (Jackson: University Press of Mississippi, 1993), 45.

    12. See Sara Blair, *Harlem Crossroads: Black Writers and the Photograph in the Twentieth Century* (Princeton: Princeton University Press, 2007), 76.

    13. Wright was not alone in doing so. See, for example, James Agee's *Let Us Now Praise Famous Men* (1941), Agnes Smedley's *Daughter of Earth* (1929), and Meridel LeSueur's *Salute to Spring* (1940).

    14. Jeff Allred, *American Modernism and Depression Documentary* (Oxford: Oxford University Press, 2009), 138.

    15. Ibid.

    16. The literary influences inherent in *12 Million Black Voices* reflect Wright's consideration that "Eliot, Stein, Joyce, Proust, Hemingway, and Anderson; Gorky, Barbusse, Nexo, and Jack London no less than the folklore of the Negro himself should form the heritage of the Negro writer" (Richard Wright, "Blueprint for Negro Writing," in this volume, 219).

17. Michael Coyle, ed., *Ezra Pound and African American Modernism* (Orono, ME: American Poetry Foundation, 2001), 86.

18. Wright, *12 Million Black Voices*, 10.

19. Terence Patrick Murphy, "The Uncertainties of Conversational Exchange: Dialogue Monitoring as a Function of the Narrative Voice," *Style* 39, no. 4 (Winter 2005): 398.

20. Ibid., 399.

21. Wright, *12 Million Black Voices*, 11.

22. Ibid., 10, 13.

23. Wright's use of the "we" and direct address in *12 Million Black Voices* is certainly part of a narrative tradition beginning with the authors of slave narratives (Harriet Jacobs, Frederick Douglass), abolitionist writing (George W. Clark), antislavery publications (William Wells Brown) and extending to such fictional and nonfictional writers as Du Bois, Jean Toomer, Nella Larsen, Jessie Fauset, and James Baldwin. Toomer's *Cane* (1923) is an especially interesting case of how a narrator wishes to inspire actual readers through the "you" in the text. *Cane*'s narrator, by directly addressing a witnessing community, prepares a participation that not only intensifies his voice within the community but also allows him to become the community's spokesperson and storyteller.

24. Carla Cappetti, "Sociology of an Existence: Richard Wright and the Chicago School," *MELUS* 12, no. 2 (Summer 1985): 28.

25. Wright, *12 Million Black Voices*, 26.

26. Ibid.

27. Ibid.

28. St. Clair Drake and Horace R. Cayton, *Black Metropolis: A Study of Negro Life in a Northern City* (Chicago: University of Chicago Press, 1970), 8, 17.

29. Ibid., 18.

30. Ibid., 19.

31. Ibid., 21.

32. Ibid., 17.

33. Ibid., 41.

34. Ibid., 35.

35. Ibid., xx.

36. Ibid.

37. See Jeff Allred, "From Eye to We: Richard Wright's *12 Million Black Voices*, Documentary, and Pedagogy," *American Literature* 78, no. 2 (September 2006): 550.

38. Virginia Whatley Smith, ed., *Richard Wright's Travel Writings: New Reflections* (Jackson: University Press of Mississippi, 2001), i–xv.

39. Judith Hamera and Alfred Bendixen, eds., *The Cambridge Companion to American Travel Writing* (Cambridge: Cambridge University Press, 2009), 3, 2.

40. Ibid., 3.

41. Smith, *Richard Wright's Travel Writings*, xii.

42. Richard Wright, *Black Power* (1954), in *Black Power, Three Books from Exile: Black Power; The Color Curtain; and White Man, Listen!*, introd. Cornel West (New York: Harper Perennial, 2008), 13.

43. Ibid., 13.

44. Ibid., 415.

45. Ibid.

46. Ibid., 415–16.

47. Eric Schocket, *Vanishing Moments: Class and American Literature* (Ann Arbor: University of Michigan Press, 2006), 255.

48. Wright, *Black Power*, 56, 59.

49. Sara Blair, *Harlem Crossroads: Black Writers and the Photograph in the Twentieth Century* (Princeton: Princeton University Press, 2007), 104.

50. Wright, *Black Power*, 72.

51. Kinnamon and Fabre, eds., *Conversations*, 240.

52. Yoshinobu Hakutani, *Richard Wright and Racial Discourse* (Columbia: University of Missouri Press, 1996), 117.

53. Jack B. Moore, "A Personal Appreciation of Richard Wright's Universality," *Mississippi Quarterly* 50, no. 2 (Spring 1997). Web.

54. For an examination of *Black Power* as a "novel," see Jack B. Moore, "The Art of *Black Power:* Novelistic or Documentary," *Revue Française d'Etudes Américaines* 31 (February 1987): 79–91.

55. Fred R. Conkling, "Wright Sees West Africa in Turmoil," *Fort Wayne News Sentinel*, 9 October 1954.

56. Wright, *Black Power*, 79.

57. Ibid., 67.

58. Ibid., 399.

59. Ibid., 75.

60. Richard Wright, *The Color Curtain* (1956), in *Black Power, Three Books from Exile*, 441.

61. See Amritjit Singh, afterword to *Black Power, Three Books from Exile*, 615.

62. For various discussions of this relationship, see the introduction and chapter prefaces of Craven and Dow, eds., *Richard Wright: New Readings*.

63. Wright, *Color Curtain*, 439.

64. Ibid.

65. Ibid., 493.

66. Ibid., 498.

67. Ibid., 503.

68. Ibid., 586.

69. Ibid.
70. Ibid., 548.
71. Ibid., 440.
72. Ibid., 440–41.
73. Horace Cayton, "Discriminations—America: Frightened Children of Frightened Parents," *Twice-a-Year* 12–13 (1945): 263.
74. Wright, *Color Curtain*, 454.
75. Ibid., 455.
76. Ibid., 464.
77. Ibid., 577.
78. Cayton, "Discriminations—America," 263.
79. Wright, *Color Curtain*, 464–65.
80. Ibid., 471.
81. Smith, "Richard Wright's Passage to Indonesia," in *Richard Wright's Travel Writings*, 99.
82. About this role, see John Lowe, "Richard Wright and the CircumCaribbean," in *Richard Wright: New Readings*, ed. Craven and Dow, 249–66.
83. Wright, *Color Curtain*, 568.
84. Ibid., 542.
85. I am indebted here to Richard Walsh, "The Pragmatics of Narrative Fiction," in *A Companion to Narrative Theory*, ed. James Phelan and Peter J. Rabinowitz (Madison, MA: Blackwell, 2008), 150–64.
86. Michel Fabre, *The Unfinished Quest of Richard Wright* (New York: William Morrow, 1973), 203.
87. Michel Fabre, *The World of Richard Wright* (Jackson: University Press of Mississippi, 1985), 67.
88. Dennis F. Evans, "The Good Women, Bad Women, Prostitutes and Slaves of *Pagan Spain*," in *Richard Wright's Travel Writings*, 166.
89. Ellen Ann Fentress, "Journalism: *Pagan Spain* by Richard Wright," *Oxford American: The Southern Magazine of Good Writing*, August 27, 2012. Web.
90. Richard Strout, "Richard Wright's Spanish Excursion," *New Republic* 136 (February 18, 1957): 18.
91. Richard Wright, *Pagan Spain,* introd. Faith Berry (New York: Harper Perennial, 1995), back-cover blurb.
92. Ibid., 4.
93. Ibid.
94. Ibid., 21.
95. Ibid., 5.
96. Ibid., 8.
97. Ibid., 12.

98. After the publication of *The Outsider* (1953), Wright experimented with various nonfiction genres. He stated in 1954: "I'm inclined to feel that I ought not to work right now on a novel. This does not mean that I'm giving up writing fiction, but, really, there are so many more exciting and interesting things happening now in the world that I feel sort of like I am dodging them if I don't say something about them" (qtd. in John Lowe, "Richard Wright as Traveler/Ethnographer," in *Richard Wright's Travel Writings,* 119).

99. Wright, *Pagan Spain,* 177–81.

100. Ibid., 162.

101. Ibid., 280–83.

102. See, for example, Mary K. Moore, "Bitches, Whores, and Women Haters: Archetypes and Typologies in the Art of Richard Wright," in *Richard Wright: A Collection of Critical Essays,* ed. Richard Macksey and Frank E. Moorer (Englewood Cliffs, NJ: Prentice Hall, 1984), 117–27; and Nagueyalti Warren, "Black Girls and Native Sons: Female Images in Selected Works by Richard Wright," in *Richard Wright: Myths and Realities,* ed. C. James Trotman (New York: Garland, 1988), 59–77.

103. Wright, *Pagan Spain,* 103.

104. Ibid., 220–21.

105. Evans, "Good Women, Bad Women," 167. Wright has sympathetically portrayed black women in *12 Million Black Voices, The Long Dream* (1958) and "Long Black Song" (1938). For a reassessment of Wright's views on gender, see Barbara Foley's "'A Dramatic Picture . . . of Women from Feudalism to Fascism': Richard Wright's *Black Hope,*" in *Richard Wright in a Post-Racial Imaginary,* ed. Alice Mikal Craven and William E. Dow (New York: Bloomsbury, 2014), 113–26.

106. Wright, *Pagan Spain,* 229.

107. Ibid., 107.

108. Ibid., 177.

109. Ibid., 231.

110. Ibid., 221.

111. Ibid., 209.

112. Ibid., 199.

113. Ibid., 200.

114. Ibid., 274.

115. Ibid., 178.

116. Hazel Rowley, *Richard Wright: The Life and Times* (Chicago: University of Chicago Press, 2001), 476.

117. Gay Talese et al., "The New Journalism," *Writer's Digest,* January 1970, 34.

118. Wright, *Pagan Spain,* 227.

15

Many Dark Mirrors in Richard Wright's *12 Million Black Voices*

Perry S. Moskowitz

According to James Baldwin, Richard Wright's *Native Son* continues the American literary tradition of "Everybody's Protest Novel"—a mawkish representation that sentimentalizes oppression and decontextualizes experience,[1] failing to incorporate the complexity, interiority, ambiguity, and skepticism of lived experience.[2] The book's failure "lies in its rejection of life, the human being, the denial of his beauty, dread, power, in its insistence that it is [the author's] categorization alone which is real and which cannot be transcended."[3] One could say that Wright substitutes symbolic phantoms for lived experience and thus creates what Walter Benjamin calls phantasmagoria.[4] In Baldwin's opinion, the novel's protagonist, Bigger Thomas, is a "phantom," a "shadow," and a "living image."[5] Wright reduces Bigger's character to that of a monster, symbolizing the ills created by American racism, and he functions as a general symbol for reality, as an "image of the Negro."[6] As a result, what Baldwin calls Wright's *representative* politics can only "redeem a symbolic monster."[7] Because Wright's main character lacks "flesh and blood" complexity, white supremacist political systems and institutions can cite the symbolic phantom to legitimize their existence.[8]

Baldwin's searing critique of *Native Son* continues the long-standing political debate among African American authors about how to navigate the politics of racialized representation under conditions of antiblack racism and white supremacy.[9] At the heart of this debate are questions about the political consequences of aesthetic formulations of race in African American literature and about how racialized representations both reflect and produce lived experience. In his famous novel, Wright seems tethered to the position of literary realism, or the belief that literature should portray experience accurately or truthfully.[10]

This essay questions Baldwin's claim that Wright's preoccupation with racial representation prevented him from creating a nuanced account of "some thirteen million people."[11] Looking at Wright's *12 Million Black Voices*, the chapter contends that Baldwin may have failed to grasp how Wright's textual practices informed a more subversive representative politics.[12] Indeed, Wright appears to be aware of how racial realism problematically aestheticizes and simplifies the conditions of black experience. When Viking Press offered Wright an opportunity to compose an essay that would accompany the Farm Security Administration's (FSA) collection of photographs documenting black poverty during the Great Depression, Wright in all likelihood knew that the press viewed him as a "representative" of millions of American blacks, or at least as someone who could identity their common denominator.[13] Wright admits as much in the preface: "I select the conditions of their lives as examples of normality . . . to place within full and constant view the collective humanity whose triumphs and defeats are shared by the majority."[14] But even though asking the racialist question "what does the Negro want?" might seem progressive, given the perverse logic of literary realism, Wright seems to have been subversively engaged with the orthodox politics of representation advertised in the text's presumptuous title.[15] After all, when writing the text, he composed a series of montages—"montage" being a term from Walter Benjamin's political glossary that describes the intentional juxtaposition of two or more different textual elements. Montage resists the reductive aestheticizing of racial realism by interrupting the assumption that social realities of race can be comprehensively represented.

Wright's textual practices deserve our consideration because of his awareness of the political consequences of compositional choices.[16] In *12 Million Black Voices* he meticulously curated the images, the prose, and the architecture of the text.[17] His self-conscious aesthetic practice resisted the white supremacist use of documentary logics. He was, in other words, deeply invested in resisting the racialized realism so often attributed to his work.

Through his montages Wright invited other voices to interpose their own distinct and often inconsistent content into the narrative's first-person plural "we." He was undermining his own authorship, was refusing to become a single voice that represented *12 Million Black Voices*, and was indicting the power structures that attempted to invest representative authority in him and thereby legitimize this racial project.[18]

Wright and Benjamin on Montage

Wright and Benjamin share more than a similar opposition to phantasmagoria. Benjamin viewed montage as one way of resisting phantasmagoria. Wright likewise used montage to subvert racialized phantasmagoria.

According to Benjamin, montage occurs when two things are placed against one another in order to interrupt, fracture, and reconstruct the terms of discourse otherwise under way. Textual montages can use stylistic contrasts (fiction/nonfiction), perspective shifts (first-person singular/first-person plural), or two counterpoised mediums (photographs/text). Compared to traditional forms of textual explication that assign an a priori meaning to a representation, montage challenges the phantasmagoria of representations by allowing the text's diverse materials to constellate across collaged juxtapositions. Benjamin characterizes his *Arcades Project*, which he calls literary montage, thusly: "I needn't say anything. Merely show. I shall purloin no valuables, appropriate no ingenious formulations."[19] For Benjamin, montage has a dual function: as a form of resistance to the pretenses of phantasmagoric representation, and as an alternative practice of representation.

By juxtaposing two or more representations, montage interrupts the spectator's attempt to comprehend a representation as fixed reality.[20] By foregrounding inconsistencies, montages disturb the alleged stability of representations; and by amplifying the numerous representations that all representations disclose, montages constellate across unfixed points. A montage thereby dismantles linear thinking and concomitantly decentralizes the distribution of representative authority. Benjamin tells us, "the truly important thing is . . . the discovery (or defamiliarization) of situations." This leads to radically creative "discovery."[21]

Montage is an illuminating conceptual framework to think about *12 Million Black Voices* as a nontraditional compilation of photographs, poetry, historical data, fiction, and captions. Concentrating on technical practices notably recalibrates the relationship among various textual elements, whose operational capacity and agency frequently exceed the meanings Wright prescribed to them. As James Martel notes, montage dramatizes "the way that language is as much an interruption as it is a means of conveying messages."[22] The interruptions resituate the relationship between the spectator (a reader in the case of Wright's text) and what is being represented. They induce a sort of ataxia between reader, content, and author.[23] To borrow Benjamin's formulation, the reader must follow "the movements of his mind" as the constellative mediums juxtaposed "[call] forth distances, belvederes, clearings, prospects at each of its turns like a commander deploying soldiers at a front."[24]

Wright's use of montage shows how a black author might speak from a situated experience and speak with a collectivity, while at the same time resisting a white supremacist logic of representation.[25] He uses the first-person plural pronoun "we" to indicate that he has a distinct and united group in mind. Yet, his concurrent use of montage advances a radically different story. Wright represents 12 million black experiences as a collective set of voices, as a "we." He, furthermore, discloses his own implicit critique of representation as fallible especially when it is predicated on a unified, or boundaried group. Wright's montage thus draws attention to the ways that entrusting a single author to pen an exhaustive representation of black experience is a phantasmic production of white supremacy. This brings us to the question: Who, then, is the "we" in *12 Million Black Voices*?

Interrupting, obfuscating, and shattering the presumed unity of the "we" (that is, the phantasmic notion of a cohesive black experience), Wright demonstrates that "we" is a diverse, precarious, and in no way united group. His montages thereby call into question the ability of a single author to represent the group.[26] He also discloses that white supremacy relies on phantasmal modes of representation, or what Benjamin Balthaser calls the "documentary regime of knowledge."[27]

Far from affirming the uniformity of black experience, Wright decomposes the "we" that he simultaneously constructs.[28] He allows multiple groups to claim the same "we" simultaneously. He thereby emphasizes the fragility of any representation of "we" and disallows the reader from participating in the phantasmagoric notion that a black "we" is a unified concept with consistent and identifiable features. Through montage, the constructed "we" represents voices assembled across inconsistent identities, spaces, perspectives, and temporalities. Moreover, Wright uses montage to represent a "we" that encompasses past, present, and future generations of black Americans. "We" ranges from experiences of slaves on southern plantations, through sharecroppers embarking on the Great Migration at the turn of the twentieth century, and to their assumed progeny. Through the mix of photographs and Wright's provocative prose, this "we" also spans numerous intersectional positions (gender, age, class). As Lori J. Marso notes, "this 'we' of black Americans . . . is also fractured and in no way naturally unified . . . blacks may potentially constitute a 'we' of *12 Black Million Voices*, but it has to be produced rather than assumed."[29]

Wright has words, readers, photographs, authors, symbols, photographers, and subjects of photographs serve as coauthors, creating thought-provoking ambiguity about who constitutes the "we." In one example, he composes the caption "we, who had barely managed to live in family groups" to accompany Edwin Rosskam's photo "Alley dwelling,"[30] a photograph of a Washington, DC, family living in a small alley apartment. In the photograph, a man and woman (presumed to be the father and mother) flank each side of the frame. In the center is a doorway with children receding into a confined space. Our inability to discern with certainty who constitutes this family, what roles they occupy, or what their relation is to one another buttresses the claim made by Wright's caption. At the same time, because the family conveys a singular material experience, it is impossible to discern who is saying "we." Although the "we" of Wright's overarching narrative seems to represent a large-scale collective experience, the "we" in the caption has several potential representatives: Wright, the family in the image, or a larger demographic group. Wright's employment of the first-person plural thus begs the questions: To whom and for whom is he speaking? While Wright's prose decentralizes the representative function of his authorship, a more convincing form of authorial subversion thereby manifests in his curatorial practices.[31] Even though Wright curates particular photographs to complement the themes in his narrative, the photographs exhibit an autonomous authorial agency that disrupts Wright's representative authority (while also cooperating with it). Wright invites the photograph's authority to supersede his own and proffer an autonomous account of black experience. The camera, the photographer, and the subjects of the photograph suggest that Wright's representative capacity can be supplanted, or at the very least refashioned to include multiple agents.

But the subversive role of the photographs in *12 Million Black Voices* does not stop there. They interrupt all singular authorial claims (not only Wright's) by interposing their own authority. Of course, each photograph is perpetually tied to the goals of the FSA photography project.[32] Anna Pochmara explains that the official purpose of these images was to serve as "a justification of government support for the underprivileged by depicting their difficult predicament in a way that highlighted their human dignity, industriousness, and respectable family relationships."[33] The visual representations therefore not only represent their own specular truth but are infused with a particular political orientation.[34] Two white photographers, Edwin Rosskam and Russell Lee, are coauthors of the book. Their involvement in the representation of black experience severely compromises Wright's authorship of a united black "we," gestures to the collective political construction of the first-person plural (a black "we"), and dispels the phantasmic notion that the construction emanates from a single author.

An illustration of the constellated authorship of *12 Million Black Voices* occurs in the "Inheritors of Slavery" chapter, in which Wright sets out to chronicle the importance of Sunday church services to rural southern communities. He emphasizes that churches provide spaces in which blacks can communicate personal experience, oppression, and desire outside of the "presence of the Lords of the Land."[35] Wright turns to poetics: "What we have not dared feel in the presence of the Lords of the Land, we now feel in Church. Our hearts and bodies, reciprocally acting upon each other, seeking out into the meaning of the story the preacher is unfolding. Our eyes become absorbed in a vision . . ."[36] He concludes his sentence with ellipses that transform it into an italicized sermon, accompanied by images of four unspecified church services in Georgia and Illinois.[37] The juxtaposition of Wright's texts and the photographs (and their array of agents) dislocates, but does not dispose of, Wright as a narrator. Wright's voice as an author is interrupted and obscured by images of impassioned worshipers receiving the words of a sermon. The preacher's words, which logically emanate from Wright, appear to be emanating from within the photograph. Working against the documentary form of knowledge, Wright's text allows the photographs and the reader to constellate their own relationship with the prose.

By convening a space wherein multiple authors put forth contradictory messages, montages refuse centralized authority necessary for Wright to engage in a form of delegate representation. Whatever representation of black experience emerges, it does not consolidate over an "outward guise" carrying an "old familiar" narrative of oppression, although Wright's readers may have expected as much.[38] By contrast, montaged representation attests to the "uneasily tied knot of pain and hope whose snarled strands converge from many points of space and time."[39] Although some interpreters of Wright contend that his use of nondescript and repetitively similar images give credence to a nameless folk that "remain anonymous . . . devoid of any intersectional identity signifiers," Wright's montaged approach rejects such an interpretation.[40] The subjects of the photographs and the characters in the text lack immediately recognizable visual and literary representations of subjective experience. As a result, they can advance new experiences by showing rather than saying.

Black Mirrors: Montage as Constellatory Method

Wright is aware that even radical approaches to representation, such as montage, can never dispel phantasmagoria. In addition, Wright acknowledges that there are unique sets of political forces that make the erasure of phantasmagoria particularly unattainable when one is trafficking in race images in a racialized space. But montage can dramatize the incompleteness and obscurity of all representations. For Wright, montage is not just a means toward a more complex explanation of black experience. Such an approach would still concede that phantasmagoria can be dispelled and that, as author, Wright could serve as an informative delegate to his white readers. Contrarily, montage is a way of placing the reader at that center of the phantasmagoria that accompanies racial representation. To that end, montage is used by Wright to reframe the politics of representation. Rather than explain, montage calls on the reader to wade through the many dubiously constructed racial logics that besiege representations of blackness in phantasmagoria.

Stressing that each visual portrayal of black experience is mired in phantasmagoria, Wright begins *12 Million Black Voices* addressing his presumably white reader, "Each day when you see us black folk upon the dusty land of the farms or upon the hard pavement of the city streets, you usually take us for granted, you think you know us, but our history is far stranger than you suspect, and we are not what we seem."[41] From the outset, Wright challenges the central conceit of the book: that particular images can ever fully illuminate any truth. In so doing, Wright provocatively poses questions about the validity of the two images of black men that flank his prose. Montage allows each picture the opportunity to constellate its own relationship among the "many points of time and space" where representations collide. Wright's prose, also, exposes whiteness as a potential coauthor of experience by drawing attention to the white photographers and readers who are also implicitly voices in the photomontage portending to speak for the "uneasily tied knot of black experience."[42]

In telling a history "far stranger than you suspect," Wright uses a constellative approach that recalls Benjamin's idea of a history "based on a constructivist principle."[43] The method speaks to what Wright calls the strange birth of black Americans. What is strange is not only being literally "torn from native soil" and experiencing enslavement as a form of birth, but becoming a particular "we" that is encountered in each and every representation of blackness.[44] Speaking about "our strange birth," Wright does not seek to admonish a collective identity but to challenge the phantasmagoric elements within which blacks are entangled. For Benjamin, a constellatory approach to history means to stop "telling the sequence of events like the beads of a rosary."[45] Wright similarly affixes temporal connection through the surreal suggestion that the millions of black folk who currently abide in Western civilization were also those who endured the transatlantic slave trade and chattel slavery. In the following fictive scene, Wright employs the first-person plural to communicate a common experience endured by those "who live in this land": "Bound by heavy chains, we gazed impassively upon the lecherous crew members as they vented the pent-up bestiality of their starved sex lives upon our sisters and wives. This was a peculiar practice which, as the years flowed past, grew into a clandestine but well-established institution which the owners of cotton and tobacco plantations upheld, and which today in large measure accounts for the widespread mulatto population in the United States."[46] Wright's use of the first-person plural makes "history" (in Benjamin's terms) "the subject of a structure whose site is not homogeneous, empty time, but time filled by the presence of the now [Jetztzeit]."[47] The fictional "we" of the distant past is not old or even past: the semantic opposition to "our guises still carries the old familiar aspect which three hundred years of oppression in America have given us."[48] Wright prompts consideration of a more constellative historical arrangement between past and present. Because the montages make the identity of "we" opaque, the spectator can partake in the "we" alongside Wright, alongside the subjects of the photographs, alongside the photographers, and alongside the novelized versions of those individuals directly and indirectly involved in the transatlantic slave trade.

Because of the contradictory temporalities, logics, spaces, and experiences, the spectator finds the present to be as unfamiliar as the future and the past.[49] The objectivity and the spatial/temporal distance needed to produce a racially realist representation are destroyed. While the reader may be either interpolated or misinterpolated into the "we," those using the text as a racially comprehensive object find their own subjective experience in tension with the narrative. Wright uses the phrase "the sphere of conscious history" against an image of an elderly black sharecropper and younger black trash collector.[50] These two images of present-day black experience become attached to the past; a link is drawn between these two men and "three hundred years of oppression in America."[51] The juxtaposition evinces Benjamin's thesis that "to articulate the past historically does not mean to 'recognize the way it really was' (Ranke). It means to seize hold of a memory as it flashes up at a moment of danger."[52]

Additionally, Wright's positioning of the two images intercept and interrupt one another. The straightforward gaze of the elderly sharecropper's face clashes with the pose of the young trash collector, whose face and body are turned away from the camera lens. Their bodies and countenance manifest Wright's claim that the guises of American oppression emerge diversely and discretely across time and space. At the same time, their dissimilar posture presents them as orthogonal, thereby unmaking Wright's conjuration of collectively recognizable pain. Moreover, their opposing posture interrupts the rapport established between the reader and Wright. Interrupting the coherence of Wright's claim, the images demand that the particularities and contingencies of their account must be attended to, in spite of whatever complications this may pose to any sweeping idea of blackness. Montage recalibrates the authorial equation allowing multiple presentations of black experience to constellate across a set of contradictory particularities.

The conclusion of Wright's "Strange Birth" chapter further illustrates the constellative paradoxes of representing a collective history. Wright tells us that "we" (black American slaves) were freed because of a host of structural, ethical, and political conditions. But the following sentence uses "we" for a different set of people: "we black men and women in America today, as we look back upon the scenes of rapine, sacrifices, and death, seem to be children of a devilish aberration, descendants of an interval of nightmare in history, fledglings of a period of amnesia."[53] The text operates as discordant montaged fragments that disclose the very interconnectedness of these two seemingly disparate temporalities. Only through a dramatized and somewhat paradoxical claim that both sets of blacks are "we" can Wright elucidate their historical entwinement. Underneath his prose about two different, but deeply entangled, sets of "we," Wright places a photograph of a thirteen-year-old sharecropper in Georgia against a vast and empty background of a cotton field.[54] The image suggests a radical singularity to lived experience, and thus interrupts Wright's verbalizing of a collective pain.

Disagreeable, Dark Mirrors

Baldwin criticized Wright for failing to disclose the contingencies and paradoxes of the relationship between representation and reality. Although Wright's prose in *12 Million Black Voices* might lend itself to Baldwin's criticism, Wright's application of montage serves as counterevidence to Baldwin's critique. However, if Wright was not attempting to expose and curate an authentic black experience, then what is Wright advancing?

Baldwin in "The White Man's Guilt" suggests that blackness operates as "a most disagreeable mirror," so much so that a person with black skin, "must spend a great deal of . . . energy . . . reassuring white Americans that they do not see what they see."[55] Lacking the "energy to change the condition," white Americans hope that black Americans will disavow the history of systemic antiblack racism that is shown in the reflection of the disagreeable mirror.[56] Baldwin suggests that when asking to be absolved of the guilt that they feel when looking into a disagreeable mirror, white Americans are making a futile request to blacks to change the mirror's countenance. How could black Americans change a record that is so plainly written in the color of Baldwin's skin; it is "there for all to read. It resounds all over the world. It might as well be written in the sky."[57]

Ultimately, Baldwin calls upon white readers to examine how their sight is constructed by their own racial experiences—to peer into what is difficult so that they may "face their history to change their lives."[58] Baldwin hopes that white Americans "would read, for their own sakes, this record and stop defending themselves against it."[59] To that end, Baldwin suggests that the record or mirror can be used restoratively. Although one cannot look into a mirror without "great pain and terror," looking into the mirror promises the opportunity to "enter into battle with that historical creation, Oneself, and attempts to recreate oneself according to a principle more humane and more liberating; one begins the attempt to achieve a level of personal maturity and freedom which robs history of its tyrannical power, and also changes history."[60]

At the end of *12 Million Black Voices*, Wright offers his own version of Baldwin's disagreeable mirror. The final section begins with what Wright terms the "dark mirror of our lives."[61] Like Baldwin, Wright calls on his reader to engage with the mirror and discourages political disavowal: "We black folk, our history and our present being are a mirror of all the manifold experiences of America. What we want, what we represent, what we endure is what America is."[62] At the same time, Wright does not call on his readers to use the mirror reflexively. At first glance, Wright's invocation of "our" seems to exclude his white readers from what is reflected.

Herein lies an instructive point of difference between the representative politics offered by Wright's and Baldwin's respective mirrors. By contrast to Baldwin, Wright presents the contradictions inherent to any reflexive project as a more critical component of racial politics. Wright's "dark mirror" challenges the directness and almost avoidable clarity of Baldwin's mirror.

Calling on the United States to "[look] into the mirror of our consciousness," Wright claims that a dark mirror only further confuses the spectator and spectated:[63] "Look at us and you will know yourselves, for we are you, looking back at you from the dark mirror of our lives!"[64] Wright's dark mirror fundamentally challenges that the relationship between the United States and black folk can be disentangled by claiming to be indivisible representative of the "you" (America) and "we" (black folk). For white Americans to know themselves requires that they admit that a dark mirror cannot disclose any truth, and that coming to a more nuanced historical account of America requires them to navigate through the complexity of black experience.

Just as Wright's dark mirror functions poorly as a mirror, Wright's politics of representation function poorly as a centrally ordered representative politics. Wright and the other agents of *12 Million Black Voices* do not reject representation. Rather, they mobilize highly representative practices (photography) and collective narrative to untangle the relationship between representation and claims of offering a comprehensive capture of all black experience. In doing so, Wright recharacterizes the role that the representative ought to perform. *12 Million Black Voices* instantiates a shift in the concept of representation. It refers no longer to someone who portends to clarify the relationship between representation and reality but to someone who disrupts the emulous and prevailing relationship between representation and the reality it claims to serve.

Notes

1. I would like to thank Jane Gordon, Ernie Zirakzadeh, P. J. Brendese, Quinn Lester, Lori Marso, Samuel Chambers, Stephanie Erev, Jishnu Guha-Majumdar, Lester Spence, and Brianna Thompson for their helpful feedback and commentary on this essay.

2. Baldwin accuses Wright of creating an ahistorical character. Hence, what makes Bigger monstrous is not only his socially monstrous actions but his timeless and placeless experience.

3. James Baldwin, "Everybody's Protest Novel," in *Notes of a Native Son* (Boston: Beacon, 1984), 23.

4. Ibid. Phantasmagoria is Benjamin's concept for any representation that substitutes itself for reality (see Margaret Cohen, "Walter Benjamin's Phantasmagoria," *New German Critique* 48 [Autumn 1989]: 87–107).

5. Cohen, "Walter Benjamin's Phantasmagoria," 37, 44.

6. James Baldwin, "Many Thousands Gone," in *Notes of a Native Son* (Boston: Beacon, 1984), 37, 38.

7. Ibid., 34, 42.

8. Ibid., 42.

9. For more on the relationship between Wright and Baldwin and on the character of Bigger Thomas, see "Alternative Readings of Bigger Thomas," by Cyrus Ernesto Zirakzadeh, in this volume.

10. Andrew Gene Jarrett, *Representing the Race: A Political History of African American Literature* (New York: New York University Press, 2011), 7; Andrew Gene Jarrett, *Deans and Truants: Race and Realism in African American Literature* (Philadelphia: University of Pennsylvania Press, 2007), 1. According to Jarrett, Wright was among the writers who entered the debates over literary realism in the 1930s and 1940s.

11. Although there is no evidence that Baldwin's phrase "some thirteen million people" was an intentional reference to Wright's *12 Million Black Voices,* the number could have been Baldwin's attempt to update Wright's title for 1955. This

is especially plausible given that by 1955 the text had become a relic of Wright's previously strong association with the Communist Party USA.

12. It is worth noting that Baldwin's position on Wright evolved over the course of Baldwin's life. In a piece written in response to Wright's death, Baldwin offers a reading of Wright's novels as subversive to white supremacist logics of representation (see Baldwin, "Alas, Poor Richard," in *Nobody Knows My Name* [New York: Vintage, 1993]). For other discussions of the subversive and radical politics of *12 Million Black Voices,* see the essays by Jane Anna Gordon, Laura Grattan, and Lori J. Marso in this volume.

13. Viking Press's decision to solicit Wright as the credible and authoritative voice of the text reflects his celebrity as one of the foremost black authors during the Great Depression. For information on Wright's involvement in the Federal Writers' Project, which employed him to conduct journalistic work on the status of black Americans, see New Deal Programs: Selected Library of Congress Resources, "Federal Writers' Project," Library of Congress, Online: www.loc.gov/rr/program/bib/newdeal/fwp.html.

14. Richard Wright, *12 Million Black Voices* (New York: Basic, 2008), xx.

15. The turn of phrase is from James Baldwin's "A Talk to Teachers," in *The Price of the Ticket: Collected Non-Fiction, 1948–1985* (New York: Saint Martin's, 1985), where Baldwin famously deconstructs the antiblack racism that informs the question, "What does the negro want?"

16. Several of Wright's essays make evident his understanding of compositional choices as a form of politics (see, for example, "How 'Bigger' Was Born," in *Early Writings* (New York: Library of America, 1940), 853. I use "curate" rather than "author" or "disclose" because it attends to the multiple sovereign and nonsovereign authors and powers that are involved in the presentation of black experiences through aesthetic mediums in the text.

17. For further discussion of the literary techniques used by Wright, see William Dow's "Floating Facts on a Sea of Emotion: The Literary Journalism of Richard Wright," in this volume.

18. What I later will call Wright's "constellative method" of representation corresponds to the radical possibilities that Paula Rabinowitz sees in documentaries that "invoke the authenticity of experience through the first person—the talking head—turn the lens slightly, and divert the narrative—a subject with whom the spectator can identify as the source of truth, as the authority, as the author. The documentary text, then, is deeply invested in narrative forms of difference. Who looks at whom?" (Rabinowitz, *They Must Be Represented: The Politics of Documentary* [London: Verso, 1994], 12).

19. Walter Benjamin, *The Arcades Project* (Cambridge: Harvard University Press, 1999), 460.

20. An example would be a family scene in a play by Brecht that is suddenly interrupted in the presence of a stranger (Benjamin, "What is Epic Theatre? [III]," in *Walter Benjamin: Selected Writings*, vol. 2, pt. 1, *1927–1930*, ed. Michael W. Jennings, Howard Eiland, and Gary Smith [Cambridge: Harvard University Press, 1999], 305). This anticipates Wright's use of the reader's agency to introduce a stranger into the familial scene of "we," which will be discussed later in this essay.

21. Benjamin, *Arcades Project*, 463.

22. James Martel, "Walter Benjamin's Black Flashlight," *Political Theory* 53, no. 5 (2015): 575–99, 10.

23. Susan Buck-Morss refers to the "friction that generates cognitive sparks, illuminating the reader's own life-world." Montage thus "places unusual demands on the reader" to discover a new situation by reassembling the matter and meaning of a representation (Buck-Morss, *The Dialectics of Seeing* [Cambridge: MIT Press, 1997], 17).

24. See *Walter Benjamin: Selected Writings*, vol. 1, *1913–1926*, ed. Michael W. Jennings, Howard Eiland, and Gary Smith (Cambridge: Harvard University Press, 1999), 31.

25. For more reading on how Wright's *12 Million Black Voices* challenges and surpasses Baldwin's critique of the figure of Bigger Thomas, see Laura Grattan's "Reading Richard Wright beyond the Carceral State: The Politics of Refusal in Black Radical Imagination," in this volume.

26. For discussions of additional ways that Wright obfuscates the "we" in *12 Million Black Voices*, see William Dow's contribution to this volume.

27. According to Benjamin Balthaser, a "documentary regime of knowledge" uses documentarian aesthetics to locate power in the "self-evident specular truth" that a piece of documentation conveys to the spectator (Balthaser, "Killing the Documentarian: Richard Wright and Documentary Modernity," *Criticism* 55, no. 3 [2013]: 355–90).

28. For more on Wright's challenge to subjectivity and solidarity, see Lori J. Marso's essay in this volume, "Seizing Freedom with Simone de Beauvoir."

29. Lori J. Marso, "Solidarity sans Identity: Richard Wright and Simone de Beauvoir Theorize Political Subjectivity," in *Contemporary Political Theory* 13 (2014): 242–62. My analysis complements Marso's reading of the politics in Wright's authorial choices, which lead him to produce a political representation that is not "naturally unified."

30. Here, Wright's sardonic use of the word "barely" illustrates how the rhetoric of responsibility can be used subversively alongside the ambiguous "we." Using a "we" that interpolates the reader into the collective, Wright offers a send-up to the white supremacist stereotype of black family structures as broken because of a lack of black capacity to maintain them. In doing so, Wright draws attention to the ways

that the inability to maintain heteronormative white family structures is inextricably linked with the circumstances of enslavement and the refusal to recognize that slaves had kin. I thank Jane Gordon for her assistance on this point.

31. Recent scholarship has considered how Wright subverts the white supremacist aura of documentary regimes of knowledge by showing that photographs are not empirical representations of experience but rather material that is always interpreted and explained (see William Dow, "Unreading Modernism: Richard Wright's Literary Journalism," *Literary Journalism Studies* 5, no. 2 [Fall 2013]; Balthaser, "Killing the Documentarian: Richard Wright and Documentary Modernity"; and Anna Pochmara, "Richard Wright Narrates FSA Photography," in *Projecting Words, Writing Images: Intersections of the Textual and the Visual*, ed. John R. Leo and Paryz Marek [Newcastle upon Tyne: Cambridge Scholars Publishing, 2011], 251–75). Yet, there has been little scholarship on how Wright reciprocally subverts his interpretation by inviting the photographs to challenge his narrative.

32. My reading of photography builds off of Ariella Azoulay's challenge to a photograph as solely a form of documentation and the product of an event. Azoulay's text modifies this conception by politicizing photography to include a variety of spaces, perspectives, and agents that move beyond a Western liberal conception of sovereignty (see Azoulay, *Civil Imagination: A Political Ontology of Photography* [New York: Verso, 2012]).

33. Pochmara, "Richard Wright Narrates FSA Photography," 253.

34. As we will see, Wright's clashes of image against text allow the photographs to disclose the world to us and to subvert the white documentarian logics, in which the photographs are simply a referent for the success of the FSA's policies or merely evidentiary material.

35. Wright, *12 Million Black Voices*, 68. It is worth noting that Wright's exploration of the church recalls his montaged surrealist approach to representing the black church service as a third reality (see Wright, "Lawd Today," in *Black, Brown, and Beige: Surrealist Writings from Africa and the Diaspora*, ed. Franklin Rosemont and Robin D. G. Kelley [Austin: University of Texas Press, 2009], 215).

36. Wright, *12 Million Black Voices*, 68.

37. Ibid., 69–72.

38. Ibid., 11.

39. Ibid.

40. Pochmara, "Richard Wright Narrates FSA Photography," 259.

41. Wright, *12 Million Black Voices*, 10.

42. Ibid., 11.

43. Benjamin, "On the Concept of History," in *Illuminations*, by Benjamin (New York: Schocken, 1968), 264.

44. Wright, *12 Million Black Voices*, 12.
45. Benjamin, "On the Concept of History," 263.
46. Wright, *12 Million Black Voices*, 12.
47. Benjamin, "On the Concept of History," 261.
48. Wright, *12 Million Black Voices*, 10.
49. I would like to thank P. J. Brendese for his assistance with this point.
50. Wright, *12 Million Black Voices*, 147.
51. Ibid., 11.
52. Benjamin, "On the Concept of History," 255.
53. Wright, *12 Million Black Voices*, 27.
54. Ibid.
55. James Baldwin, "The White Man's Guilt," in *Price of the Ticket*, by Baldwin (New York: St. Martin's, 1985), 409. Baldwin writes, "What they see is an appalling oppressive and bloody history known all over the world."
56. Ibid.
57. Ibid.
58. For a more thorough treatment of this dynamic, see Lawrie Balfour, "A Most Disagreeable Mirror," *Political Theory* 26, no. 2 (1998): 346–69.
59. Baldwin, "The White Man's Guilt," 410.
60. Ibid.
61. Wright, *12 Million Black Voices*, 146.
62. Ibid.
63. Ibid.
64. Ibid.

Richard Wright

The "Nature" of Politics, The "Politics" of Nature

James B. Haile III

> It seems as though we are now living inside of a machine . . . [N]o longer do our lives depend upon the soil, the sun, the rain, or the wind; we live by the grace of jobs and the brutal logic of jobs. We do not know this world, or what makes it move. In the South life was different. . . . [T]he world moved by signs we knew. But here in the North cold forces hit you and push you. It is a world of *things*.
> —Richard Wright, *12 Million Black Voices*

Richard Wright tells a political story in his novels, short stories, and visual history that foregrounds nature and its relation to the human world. Through an examination of Wright's oeuvre, this chapter identifies three principal ways that "nature" functions within Wright's work: (1) as a politics of natural disaster and witnessing; (2) as a way of distinguishing southern rurality and northern urbanity; and (3) as a way of exploring political possibility. In this chapter, I will examine each of these ways.

While many interpreters of Wright have viewed his oeuvre through a realist political lens, a growing number of scholars are drawn to his nature writing and nature thinking through his haiku.[1] This chapter brings together both elements—Wright's political realism, and his nature writing and thinking in his haiku—to rethink "politics" as both an engagement with how social and material goods are organized and distributed *and* a reflection on how we think and feel about this organization and distribution. In placing Wright's political realism together with his nature writing and thinking, this chapter, additionally, seeks to locate Wright within the history of African American nature writing and thinking.[2]

The "Nature" of Politics

According to African American literary scholar Houston Baker: "Displacement and denial of the African personality is compensated—within the very spaces of the holes of ownership and commodification—by a new operational law of personality. That law is a law of placeless place, and it transforms a commercial dispossession into a mirroring alternative to Western economic arrangements. What emerges from the confined, imprisoning hole is an instability that gives rise to a distinctive folk culture."[3] Analyzing psychic and material dispossession (or, dispossession of land and political power), Baker concludes that African Americans exist within "placeless places." They are alienated from the possibility of defining the world concretely for themselves and, thus, unable to constitute the sort of identity necessary to construct from the bare material expanse of "space," the specifics of "place": "The appearance of the plane in both *Invisible Man* [Ralph Ellison] and *Native Son* [Richard Wright] signifies what might be called a traditional dynamics of Afro-American place. The transport and the skywriter suggest the narrow confinement of black life; they point to a dreadful dichotomy between black and white experience in the New World. Airplanes and their soaring capabilities are, in one reading of the scenes, signifiers of American industrial/technological arrangements that make traditional Afro-American geographies into a placeless place."[4]

Baker then adds: "Defining space as the possibility of motion . . . place is a pause invested with value. From the limitless and uncertainty of unexplored space, we win pauses that familiarize space because we invest them with value. . . . For place to be recognized as actually PLACE, as a personally valued locale, one must set and maintain the boundaries. If one is constituted and maintained, however, by and within boundaries set by another, then one is not a setter of place but a prisoner of another's desire. . . . Such confinement is always a function of interlocking institutional arrangements."[5] For Baker, African Americans, in the bowels of the transatlantic slave ship and upon the shores of the New World, experienced a dual "birth" of "placeless place," which is tied both to land alienation—experienced both as natal alienation from mother country and the alienation of unrecognized and unremunerated labor in the fields of the New World—and the institutional arrangement of chattel slavery.

Baker's view of "place" is complex. On the one hand, it is tied to the material world—to the boundaries one sets up within the material world; on the other hand, it is an interrelated psychological reality—place, here, is directly related to how one views the world given the material fact(s) of one's existence. For Baker, the usage of the airplane in *Invisible Man* and *Native Son* exemplifies each aspect of this complexity—for Baker, being barred from actually flying a plane due to society's racial hierarchy, yet having to witness planes in flight, helped to shape the consciousness of each character in the novels as to the material possibilities for their future. Baker's example, though, may be interpreted differently—one may offer another reading of the relationship of consciousness to the material world. Rather than shaping consciousness negatively—in terms of a *lack*—from the formation of "boundaries" and "confinement," one could read this example as the possibility of the creation of an alternate "place," one that is neither material nor psychological (or the intersection of the two), but somewhere else.

Elizabeth Alexander has skillfully shown that, despite land alienation and the boundaries of white supremacy, African Americans have made for themselves a "home," but it is not the "home" that can be easily recognized. For Alexander, African American "place" as "home" is what she terms the "black interior." In her view, the "black interior" is both literal and metaphorical: it includes how black people cultivate physical, interior "home" spaces and interior psychic/existential spaces to reflect the interior for and of the self. She asks, "When we are not 'public,' with all the word connotes for black people, then how do we live and who are we?"[6] Alexander believes this is ultimately a question of choice: what African Americans decide to show the outside world and what they keep for themselves. For Alexander, this is a third way of understanding "place" to be added to Baker's alternatives of "placeless" place. In her view, the "black interior" *is* within African

American control; it is the construction of one's own boundaries—and, as such, it is not "placeless," but place-full. Alexander explains her view of the black interior through an analysis of the work of twentieth-century African American artist Romare Bearden: "Romare Bearden's totemic series, 'The Block,' is a key work for thinking about the public display of African American private life.... Bearden has painted the illusions of 'cuts' into buildings not solely in the regular spaces where windows would be but rather at random spots, as though cutting through the brick itself. In this way the viewer feels less like a Peeping Tom and more like a *privileged observer* placed squarely in the middle of life lived. The irregularity of the cuts adds to the element of spontaneity and therefore 'authenticity.'"[7] Alexander's emphasis on Bearden's aesthetic technique reveals a choice he has made in constructing his own boundaries, of what to disclose and what to conceal. In other words, Bearden's aesthetic technique is intentional and agential, showing the viewing audience certain aspects of the inner life—that is, the interior home space—of African Americans, linking the idea of consciousness, the organization of one's home-space—no matter how impoverished, no matter if one has been redlined into that space—and the act of revealing and concealing, aspects missing from Baker's assessment of "placeless place." In stressing alienation, even while acknowledging "a mirroring alternative to Western economic arrangements" and the emergence of a distinctive folk culture, Baker does not highlight interior home-space as a viable foundation for thinking of African American place.

Folding Alexander's theory of the "black interior" into Baker's notion of "placeless" place allows us another reading of Wright's work. Wright's short story "The Man Who Saw a Flood" is about one family's devastation after the Mississippi flood of 1927. The family returns to the farm they are sharecropping to discover the house knocked off its foundation, farming tools and other rations destroyed, the interior of their house disheveled, and their fields turned to mud. The title of the short story alerts the reader that Wright, like Bearden, is giving them a "cut" into the interiority of the family's life and that they are in the position of a "privileged observer," witnessing the destruction. This short story, then, is not just one man's perspective, but his family's "black interior." Like Bearden, Wright is also implicating the viewer in the scene—the viewer cannot passively watch the destruction from afar, as one could do with Baker's example of the airplane and material and existential detachment but, as a privileged observer, is involved in the scene, in the destruction itself. The viewing audience is witnessing what the man is witnessing—the destruction of his house and his fields, his farming tools and his rations; but the reader is also forced to bear witness to the historical moment of the historic flood and also the historical fact of sharecropping. Placing the reader into the scene as privileged observer, Wright gives the reader insight into the politics of natural disaster and witnessing. Here is what the reader witnesses through Tom:

> When they attempted to open the front door, it would not budge. It was not until Tom placed his shoulder against it and gave it a stout shove that it scraped back jerkily. The front room was dark and silent. The damp smell of flood silt came fresh and sharp to their nostrils. Only one-half of the upper window was clear, and through it fell a rectangle of dingy light. The floors swam with ooze. Like a mute warning, a wavering flood mark went high around the walls of the room. A dresser sat cater-cornered, its drawers and sides bulging like a bloated corpse. The bed, with the mattress still on it, was like a giant casket forged of mud. Two smashed chairs lay in the corner, as though huddled together for protection. . . .
> "Waa, Ahma git a bucket n start cleanin," said May. "Ain no use in waitin, cause we's gotta sleep on them floors tonight."[8]

This scene plays on multiple fronts. On the one hand, it displays Baker's notion of alienation and "placeless place" in the sense that it is clear that the space the family occupies is not their own but one in which they have been placed by external institutional forces. On the other hand, Wright gives us a glimpse, or a "cut," into the interior space of the family *through* a view into their house. It must be mentioned that though destroyed, the family does not view themselves as destroyed, and, thus, they begin rebuilding the interior of their space. Significantly, although the space reflects death—the dresser drawers like a "bloated corpse," and the mattress like a "giant casket"—the family represents life in the reorganization of space through the action of "cleanin." Though it could be interpreted as making the best of a bad circumstance, it could also be interpreted as the endurance of conscious life, and that Wright gives the reader this "cut" to represent this enduring quality.

The pause between the destruction (Tom and his family standing in the doorway, staring into the dark and silent room), and the *counterstatement* of value (getting the bucket to begin cleaning) can be seen as the "black interior," what is hidden within Baker's "pause invested with value." In the face of the devastation, there is a deliberate "re-constitution" of the meaning of space through its cleaning and arrangement.

Wright, though, offers additional "cuts" or glimpses into the interior of life of Tom and his family. They now face, in addition to the cleaning up their home, cleaning their fields, repairing tools, and replacing rations, the dilemma that they still owe the white landlord for the tools unfixable and the supplies destroyed, *and* the costs of new tools and rations. Tom states: "Lawd, but Ah sho hate t start over wid tha white man. Ah'd leave here ef Ah could. Ah owes im nigh eight hundred dollahs. N we needs a hoss, grub, seed, n a lot mo other things. Ef we keeps on like this tha white man'll own us body n soul."[9] At the end of the story, Tom nevertheless must accept the terms of the white landlord, Burgess, the terms that will have him owned "body n soul," given the circumstance in which he finds himself. Wright, here, is instructing the reader of the limits of interior life—it is not a solution to the dilemma of black social and political life but a glimpse into conscious life within it, as in this exchange between the white landlord and Tom:

> "Get in the buggy and come with me. I'll stake you with grub. We can talk over how you can pay it back." Tom *said nothing*. He rested his back against the post and looked at the mud-filled fields.
>
> "Well," asked Burgess. "You coming?" Tom *said nothing*. He got slowly to the ground and pulled himself into the buggy. May watched them drive off.
>
> "Hurry back, Tom!"
>
> "Awright."
>
> "Ma, tell Pa t bring me some 'lasses," begged Sally.
>
> "Oh, Tom!"
>
> Tom's head came out of the side of the buggy.
>
> "Hunh?"
>
> "Bring some 'lasses!"
>
> "*Hunh?*"
>
> "Bring some 'lasses for Sal!"
>
> "Awright!"[10]

The reader is given another "cut" or glimpse into Tom's interior family life. Tom is not merely an exploited laborer; he is also a father and a husband. Situating Tom as both exploited laborer *and* husband and father, Wright offers complexity to Tom's interior life. The reader is witnessing natural disaster and the way it can be made to serve the interests of a racist institutional order; but the reader is also witnessing the ways in which Tom is willing to be exploited—to not run off—for the sake of his family.

Tom is not merely "black" in an exploitative and historical sense. He *knows* he must leave with Burgess, not only due to his blackness but because he is a husband to his wife and a father to his daughter. The last "cut" or glimpse Wright offers is that the historical circumstances themselves do not constitute the consciousness of all of the family members. May does not necessarily see her father as exploited or situate him or her family historically within sharecropping; rather, she sees him as her father, the one who will bring her some "'lasses." Here, Wright balances the politics of economic labor exploitation with the politics of inner family dynamics.

The "Landscape" of Politics

In *12 Million Black Voices,* Wright similarly describes the interior space of a typical African American kitchenette (a one-room apartment with a small stove shared by four or five, sometimes six people) in the Black Belt of Chicago. Wright, though, does not describe these kitchenettes as the "home-space" as in "The Man Who Saw a Flood." Instead, the kitchenettes represent the physical expression of the aimlessness—what Baker refers to as "placeless places"—of black lives during the transition from southern rurality to northern urbanity. In contrast to the assertion of "place" described in "The Man Who Saw a Flood"—the reconstitution of order with "cleanin'"—we see a kind of home*less*ness, the inability to create order within chaos. Wright writes: "Sometimes five or six of us live in a one-room kitchenette, a place where simple folk such as we should never be *held captive.* A war sets up in our emotions: one part of our feelings tells us that it is good to be in the city, that we have a chance at life here. . . . [A]nother part of our feelings tells us that, in terms of worry and strain, the cost of living in the kitchenettes is too high, that the city heaps too much responsibility upon us and gives us too little security in return."[11] Wright expands:

> The kitchenette throws desperate and unhappy people into an unbearable closeness of association, thereby increasing latent friction, giving birth to never-ending quarrels of recrimination, accusation, and vindictiveness, producing *warped personalities*. . . .
>
> . . . [T]he kitchenette is the funnel through which our pulverized lives flow to ruin and death on the city pavements, at a profit.[12]

Similar to Tom's house, the kitchenette is impoverished. Nevertheless, the two spaces are inherently different. Although Tom's house is destroyed, his family was able to reconstitute it as a home-space reflecting the strength of their "black interior" lives. On the other hand, for Wright, the kitchenette of the Chicago Black Belt revealed the interior life of a "desperate and unhappy people." The distinction of the two places discloses Wright's subtle argument about regionalism and human consciousness. It is this distinction that Baker leaves out of his reading of the "placeless place" of black living.[13]

In the South, black people—even if oppressed—can construct place, in Alexander's sense of the "black interior." The North, even though reputed to be a beacon of possibility, turns out to be a space of alienation. As a result, southern rurality and northern urbanity differ in their effects on human personalities and the consciousness emergent within each. This contributes to a second distinctive feature of Wright's political theory: southern rurality versus northern urbanity.

Consider the following excerpts: the last scene from the autobiographical novel *Black Boy*, the first scene from *American Hunger*, and a passage from the opening of part 3 from *12 Million Black Voices*. From *Black Boy*: "With ever watchful eyes and bearing scars, visible and invisible, I headed North, full of a hazy notion that life could be lived with dignity, that the personalities of others should not be violated, that men should be able to confront other men without fear or shame, and that if men were lucky in their living on earth they might win some redeeming meaning for their having struggled and suffered here beneath the stars."[14] From *American Hunger*: "My first glimpse of the flat black stretches of Chicago depressed and dismayed me, mocked all my fantasies. Chicago seemed an unreal city whose mythical houses were built of slabs of black coal wreathed in palls of gray smoke, houses whose foundations were sinking slowly into the dank prairie. Flashes of steam showed intermittently on the wise horizon, gleaming translucently in the winter sun. The din of the city entered my consciousness, entered to remain for years to come."[15] Finally, from *12 Million Black Voices:*

> We look up at the high southern sky and remember all the sunshine and the rain and we feel a sense of loss, but we are leaving. We look out at the wide green fields which our eyes saw when we first came into the world and we feel full of regret, but we are leaving. We scan the kind black faces we have looked upon since we first saw the light of day, and, though pain is in our hearts, we are leaving. We take one last furtive look over our shoulders to the Big House—high upon a hill beyond the railroad tracks—where the Lord of the Land lives, and we feel glad, for we are leaving.[16]

In the third passage, Wright establishes the relationship among political action, human consciousness, and nature as home-space. With the repetition of the phrase, "but we are leaving," Wright signals both a sense of loss and sense of gain set within the natural world. In doing so, Wright alerts the reader to the existential element of the Great Migration—what was left behind were not only loved ones and the Big House but also the land itself; what was gained was the possibility of happiness in the future. Wright's phrase, then, can be read as loaded with both the emotional reality of the "black interior," the political oppression of external boundaries, and the possibilities of an alternative political future.

In all three passages, the sky is a key metaphor. In *Black Boy*, the sky represents infinite expanse and is juxtaposed with the concrete political reality of limitation. While one's social and political life may be constricted by racial boundaries, the sky offers the possibility of answering the unanswerable questions. Somewhere, though not in the South, men would be able to "confront other men without fear or shame"; the sky offered the possibility that somewhere else, beneath these same stars, under this same sky, men may "win some redeeming meaning for their having suffered here beneath the stars." For Wright, the North represented this possibility opened up to him by the stars, by the sky itself. It is this same southern sky and its possibilities for human meaning that help to generate the courage in the phrase, "but we are leaving," and the hope of the Great Migration discussed in *12 Million Black Voices*. In this way, the sky as an endless expanse allows Wright to imagine other possibilities of the present and future and enables him to imagine the North as a place of political and existential possibility.

Yet, in *American Hunger*, the sky no longer represents infinite possibility, for Wright has arrived in Chicago. The sky in *American Hunger* is no longer the southern sky of "sunshine and rain" but the "flat black stretches" of "mythical houses . . . built of slabs of black coal" of the northern sky of Chicago. It is this sky that confronts Wright's consciousness with the reality of northern life, no longer hope but the warning "palls of black smoke" signaling that the sky has changed, that his social and political life and consciousness are also about to change. It is this sky that shocked and dismayed Wright; it was also this sky that entered into his consciousness to remain.[17]

One can see in these passages a parallel between the "black interior," the natural world of the sky, and political imagination of southern versus northern life. Tom's southern sky promised the possibility of an unknown future, which parallels Tom's interior life—his family's capacity to rebuild their life after devastation. On the other hand, the threatening sky of Chicago and the collapse of hope parallel the collapse of the "black interior" and the "placeless place" of the kitchenettes.

Without understanding the tension between southern rurality and northern urbanity and without understanding the role of natural and social environments in shaping the human personality, it is difficult to understand the political thought inherent in Wright's *Black Boy* and *12 Million Black Voices*, in contrast to *American Hunger*. If we use only Baker's definitions of space and place as a metaphor for the limitation of black lives and, thus, for black imagination, then we may have difficulty understanding the ways Wright is using "cuts" or glimpses of the interiority of black lives to reveal the connection between spaces and consciousness—the natural landscape of the South with the urban blight of the North.[18] It is also difficult to understand remigration. That is, why, if the South is the place of boundary and confinement, African Americans would and did desire to return and did duplicate aspects of it elsewhere. As Wright observes in *12 Million Black Voices*, African Americans, while in the North, replicate the cultural and material structures created in the South—the "ardent religious emotionalism," the storefront church in which they "perform their religious rituals on the fervid levels of the plantation revival," and "even elderly women, hungry for the South but afraid to return, will cultivate tiny vegetable gardens in the narrow squares of ground in front of their hovels."[19] Place, for Wright, is not merely a conceptual reality reflecting social and political facts; place is the intersection of the physical environment and the interior life of people in relation to their external world.[20]

The "Politics" of Nature

In Wright's novels, short stories, and his visual history, nature is a force that at once envelops, nourishes, and invades the human world. It extends, reflects, and magnifies the "facts" of the social world in which the poor and the black are vulnerable—or made vulnerable—due to political and economic exploitation. Some natural events therefore become natural disasters. Because Tom was poor and black, he and his family were exposed to the flooding of the river. Likewise, those poor blacks living in the Chicago Black Belt kitchenettes were exposed to avoidable maladies like "scarlet fever, dysentery, typhoid, tuberculosis . . . and malnutrition."[21]

The tension inherent in Wright's work, between the natural world and the political world, between human consciousness and the natural disaster, reveals a complex and seemingly contradictory relationship between African Americans and the southern and northern regions of the United States. This relationship is not always straightforwardly clear. In *12 Million Black Voices*, for instance, Wright describes how African Americans left the plantation and the Big House *with regret* and replicated many of the cultural and structural elements of southern living in the North. This signals that it was the social and political worlds African Americans fled, not the land. It also establishes the idea that the land itself, or nature itself, was not the source of African American alienation—why else replicate the social and cultural structures of southern religious life, and the material culture of land cultivation in northern gardens?

In part 3 of *12 Million Black Voices*, "Death on City Pavements," Wright shows how the lack of the natural world in the industrial North spelled the death of folk culture: "We encountered for the first time in our lives the full effect of those forces that tended to reshape our folk consciousness, and a few of us stepped forth and accepted within the confines of our personalities the death of our folk lives."[22] It is not merely that the Chicago tenements he first encountered entering the city appeared to him to be "vertical slave ships"—southern blacks had, after all, lived and worked on plantations. It was that these vast buildings made it difficult to reproduce the folk cultures that allowed for black southern culture to thrive; and, in their place, arose a different consciousness. "The sands of our simple folk lives run out on the cold city pavements," Wright observes. "Winter winds blow, and we feel that our time is nearing its end. Our final days are full of apprehension."[23]

This tension explores the conditions in which folk culture emerges—within the natural world that both nourishes and destroys. This tension also reveals that, for Wright, the North was a place of material deprivation *and* social death, where folkways were difficult to reproduce, whereas the South was the place in which folkways could exist alongside the destruction of the natural world. For example, the cycle of the river flooding as a natural event can be understood in the human world by the *meaning* of that cycle—why do certain people fall prey to these natural cycles while others are materially improved by them?[24] Wright portrays the resulting effects the meaning of these cycles have for human consciousness. Yet, as Wright notes in the contrast between *Black Boy* and *12 Million Black Voices*, it is folk culture itself that bridges human consciousness and the natural world and allows for "black interior" life to emerge out of difficult natural/social conditions. Without folk culture, there would be nothing but death.

In *Black Boy*, Wright writes extensively about the natural world and the folk interpretation of it:

> Each event spoke with a cryptic tongue. And the moments of living slowly revealed their coded meanings. There was the wonder I felt when I first saw a brace of mountainlike, spotted, black-and-white horses clopping down a dusty road through clouds of powdered clay. . . .
>
> There was a vague sense of the infinite as I looked down upon the yellow, dreaming waters of the Mississippi River from the verdant bluffs of Natchez. . . .
>
> There was the experience of feeling death without dying that came from watching a chicken leap about blindly after its neck had been snapped by a quick twist of my father's wrist.
>
> There was the great joke that I felt God had played on cats and dogs by making them lap their milk and water with their tongues. . . . And there was the quiet terror that suffused my senses when vast hazes of gold washed earthward from star-heavy skies on silent nights.[25]

There are two important elements in Wright's writing about nature in the above quotation. First, Wright is interpreting natural phenomena through the experiences and consciousness of his own southern identity. The Mississippi River continues to have both a metaphorical and material meaning in southern culture, from the song "Old Man River" to Mark Twain's *Huckleberry Finn*. Wright's mentioning of it alludes to both aspects. The killing of chickens with one's bare hands implies farming and rural living and the imposition of a theological reading of dogs and cats drinking water implies a larger normative context of southern folklore reminiscent of the *Uncle Remus Stories*.

Second, Wright's two-page rumination on nature immediately follows a scene in which Wright sets his living room curtains on fire and is beaten unconscious, "almost killed," by his mother. Nature, here, represents a specific way Wright responds emotionally to social and material conditions, especially those of violence and tragedy. Nature can be seen, in this way, as critical for reconstructing Wright's own consciousness.[26]

In contrasting Wright's *Black Boy, 12 Million Black Voices,* and *American Hunger,* what is revealed is the idea that (1) nature and the natural landscape can be both nourishing and threatening—what can flood and destroy property and take lives can also be the foundation for folk culture and heritage; and (2) the natural world is fundamental to the constitution of consciousness. Both of these elements in Wright's work help to situate him within the history of black nature writing.

Camille T. Dungy opens her curated collection *Black Nature: Four Centuries of African American Nature Poetry* with the following poem from Lucille Clifton:[27]

> surely i am able to write poems
> celebrating grass and how the blue
> in the sky can flow green or red
> and the waters lean against the
> chesapeake shore like a familiar
> poem about nature and landscape
> surely   but whenever i begin
> "the trees wave their knotted branches
> and . . ."   why
> is there under that poem always
> another poem?[28]

Clifton's haunting statement sounds more like a question—"surely i am able to write poems/celebrating grass and how the blue/in the sky can flow green . . ."—and leaves the reader wondering why she would pose such a question as an assertion that seems unsure of itself. Given the fact that Dungy opens her anthology of black nature writing with this poem of unsure certainty, the reader is left to draw the connection: is it Clifton's blackness that makes her unsure if she can write a poem celebrating the grass and the sky? Why would her blackness have any influence on her ability to write poems, or to determine their thematic content as relating to the natural world? Dungy's choice of this poem as the epigraph for her collection on African American nature poetry suggests that the reader is not too far astray in postulating the importance of Clifton's blackness to her nature thinking and nature writing.

Dungy later explains her choice of Clifton's poem:

> As much as the trees of the American South reminded me of a history steeped in often arbitrarily brutal and always dehumanizing racism, they also helped teach me how to make myself at home . . .
>
> . . . For years, poets and critics have called for a broader inclusiveness in conversations about ecocriticism and ecopoetics, one that acknowledges other voices and a wider range of cultural and ethnic concerns. African Americans, specifically, are fundamental to the natural fabric of this nation but have been noticeably absent from tables of contents. To bring more voices into the conversation about human interactions with the natural world, we must change the parameters of the conversation.[29]

Dungy then specifies what changing the parameters would look like:

> Many black writers simply do not look at their environment from the same perspective as Anglo-American writers who discourse with the natural world. . . . Rather, in a great deal of African American poetry we see poems written from the perspective of the workers of the field. Though these poems defy the pastoral conventions of Western poetry, are they not pastoral? The poems describe moss, rivers, trees, dirt, caves, dogs, fields: elements of an environment steeped in a legacy of violence, forced labor, torture, and death.
>
> Are these not meditations on nature? We find poems set in urban

streets. Can these not be landscape poems? The natural world, aligned with or in opposition to the human world, mediates the poems of this anthology. The poems reveal histories stored in various natural bodies. They document natural and human-provoked disasters and their effects on individuals and communities. They explore sources of connection to, but also alienation from, the land.[30]

Recalling Wright's "The Man Who Saw a Flood," and his concluding remarks in *Black Boy*, we see both connection to and alienation from the land. It is a complex relationship that cannot be reduced either to an idyllic understanding of the natural world or to a neat juxtaposition of the modern industrial postnatural world and quaint preindustrial worlds. Rather, as Wright notes in *12 Million Black Voices*, African Americans remember the preindustrial world rife with similar struggles they faced in the urban industrialized North—economic and labor exploitation.

Instead of idealism or dichotomy, a reader finds in Wright a human ecological approach to natural and humanistic studies. One can think of how Wright describes the skyline in Chicago, the buildings, and the steam from the industrial factories on the horizon altering the brightness of the sun and entering his consciousness. Here, Wright situates the natural as an influential part of the human world and as altering his consciousness—these are the elements of an ecologically informed natural and humanistic study.

Wright offers an even more direct example of this approach in *Black Boy*, where he famously writes, "in leaving [the South], I was taking part of the South to transplant in alien soil, to see if it could grow differently, if it could drink of new and cool rains, bend in strange winds, respond to the warmth of other suns, and perhaps, to bloom."[31] Here, we can see Wright writing about the Great Migration, himself, and human society as part of the natural world. Wright describes taking southern consciousness and transplanting it into foreign northern soil, to see how the new winds, rain, and sky of the North will affect it, and to see what new consciousness will grow and develop. African American nature writing beyond Wright has also existed at the intersection of history, geography, sociology, and ecology to help us understand both the ways in which race has always constituted the natural world and its relationship to the human world and human conflict, and also the ways in which human society has affected the natural world and natural disaster.

In one of his earliest poems (published with Langston Hughes in 1939), "Red Clay Blues," Richard Wright speaks to each of these complex aspects of African American nature:

> I miss that red clay, Lawd, I
> Need to feel it on my shoes.
> Says miss that red clay, Lawd, I
> Need to feel it on my shoes.
> I want to see Georgia cause I
> Got them red clay blues.
>
> Pavement's hard on my feet, I'm
> Tired o' this concrete street.
> Pavement's hard on my feet, I'm
> Tired o' this city street.
> Goin' back to Georgia where
> That red clay can't be beat.
>
> I want to tramp in the red mud, Lawd, and
> Feel the red clay round my toes.
> I want to wade in that red mud.
> Feel that red clay suckin' at my toes.
> I want my little farm back and I
> Don't care where that landlord goes.
>
> I want to be in Georgia, when the
> Big storm starts to blow.
> Yes, I want to be in Georgia when that
>
> Big storm starts to blow.
> I want to see the landlords runnin' cause I
> Wonder where they gonna go!
>
> I got them red clay blues.[32]

The poem repeats several themes in *Black Boy* and *American Hunger* as well as *12 Million Black Voices:* longing for the southern earth, the deprivation and alienation of the northern urban landscape, and leaving the South to escape racial oppression and the white landowner. The reader can see in this poem the intersection of history, geography, sociology, and ecology.

But Wright adds to these intersecting themes an additional element in the inversion of power dynamics. In "The Man Who Saw a Flood" and in *12 Million Black Voices,* we see African Americans as victims of natural disasters, vulnerable to flooding in the South and disease-infested living quarters in the North, due to their relatively impoverished social and political positions. Yet, in this poem, it is the white landowner who is victim to the "Big storm" and the strong wind of Georgia. Here, the white landowner's privileged social position does not prevent him from experiencing the same vulnerability within the natural world. This, for Wright, opens up an interesting question. The white landowner's inability to adjust to destruction, like the African American southern worker, is due to the fact that the white landowner's consciousness or "interior" life is not constituted in relationship to the land but constituted in exploitation of the land and the black laborer. If we recall Wright's "The Man Who Saw a Flood," the white landowner's relationship to Tom and to the land was one of exploitation in the form of debt. Tom, and other African Americans, owed him money, and the land was his way of creating the debt and control over the lives of the African American farmers.

While Wright's analysis/critique of the white landowner suggests that the white landowner will have no "place" to go if his land is destroyed, his analysis of the "interior" life of African Americans does suggest the possibility of return, or remigration.[33] In *12 Million Black Voices*, Wright refers to African American northern migration as full of regret rather than the hope expressed in *Black Boy.* In *12 Million Black Voices*, African Americans had already experienced the disillusion hinted at in the beginning of *American Hunger.* This disillusion, for Wright, caused African Americans to cling tighter to southern folk culture and to attempt to replicate some of it in the North. For Wright, this continued connection signals a kind of belonging, and a returning "home," that had little to do with material ownership of the land itself but was, instead, a reclamation of a spiritual relationship fostered through cultivation.

In "Red Clay Blues," he notes:

I want to wade in that red mud.
Feel that red clay suckin' at my toes.

> I want my little farm back and I
> Don't care where that landlord goes.

Wright is making an existential claim to land rights, one that is political, but not legal. I want "my little farm *back*" suggests that, in the context of the poem, land has been taken by the white landlord.

It is important to keep in mind that "Red Clay Blues" was published in 1939, and *12 Million Black Voices* was published in 1941. The ideas here intersect with the historical reality of the aftermath and failure of Reconstruction, which aimed to redistribute land throughout the southern states. In short, the desire for reclamation of land and the claiming of land rights for African Americans arose at the end of slavery and is rooted in the 1865 US Bureau of Refugees, Freedmen and Abandoned Lands, commonly known as the Freedmen's Bureau. The Bureau's constitution promised, among other things, to redistribute lands confiscated from or abandoned by the Confederacy. The government was to transfer such lands to ex-slaves *and* destitute whites in the war-ravaged South. The Bureau was short lived, however. Andrew Johnson revoked the Bureau's declaration, issued a presidential pardon that restored original ownership, and evicted African Americans. Land ownership was directly transformed into the serfdom of sharecropping. According to Thomas W. Mitchell, "The story of the federal government's failure to deliver 'forty acres and a mule' to freed slaves after the Civil War has long been a part of African American folklore."[34]

Mitchell's insights are significant for interpreting Wright and locating him within the African American nature-writing tradition. Wright's work both fictionalized historical events and interpreted current events in light of this history, telling a narrative of race through natural disaster and a narrative of natural disaster through race. Not only were African Americans denied land rights after slavery, they were reenslaved vis-à-vis the land itself.

In *12 Million Black Voices* Wright argues:

> Our way of life is simple and our unit of living is formed by the willingness of two or more of us to organize ourselves voluntarily to make a crop, to pool our labor power to wrest subsistence from the stubborn soil. We live just as man lived when he first struggled against this earth. After having been pulverized by slavery and purged of our cultural heritage, we have been kept so far from the sentiments and ide-

als of the Lords of the Land that we do not feel their way of life deeply enough to act upon their assumptions and motives. So, living by folk tradition, possessing but a few rights which others respect, we are unable to establish our family groups upon a basis of property ownership. For the most part our delicate families are held together by love, sympathy, pity, and the goading knowledge that we must work together to make a crop.[35]

African American folk life, or "black interior" life, for Wright, is constituted not by legal ownership but by a spiritual relationship to land nurtured through its cultivation or what emerges when people work together, "to make a crop, to pool our labor power to wrest subsistence from the stubborn soil." In fact, Wright argues that African American life is so far removed from legal ownership that they cannot act on the "sentiments and ideals of the Lords of the Land." Rather, they organize their living around "love, sympathy, pity." Taken together with "Red Clay Blues," one sees in Wright a developing theme: African American cultural tools of love, sympathy, pity, and cooperation allow for a cultural response of rebuilding and community and family reliance to land dispossession or natural disaster, while the cultural life of oppression and exploitation by the Lords of the Lands, or the white landowner, provides little to no cultural response to natural disaster. In other words, the white landowner has legal land rights but lacks the spiritual or cultivated connection to land, for they do not or, perhaps, cannot work the land to "make a crop."

Nobody: The "Politics" of Wright's Haiku Moment

Wright's distinction between legal ownership of and spiritual/cultivated relationship to land necessitates a closer look into some of his last publications before his death: his haiku. Thomas L. Morgan argues that "Wright's inversion of the logic of the 'haiku moment' offers him a new generic form with which to explore the themes of alienation, dehumanization, and inequality appearing in his earlier works. Wright's reformulation of the haiku moment allows him to reengage the same cultural and social mores seen in his earlier works in a different generic context, one stripped of the pre-inscribed notions of identity that influence the critical reception of his prior works."[36] Morgan defines the "haiku moment" as "an instant in which man becomes unified to an object, virtually becomes that object and realizes the eternal, universal truth contained in being."[37] Morgan's "haiku moment" reads very similarly to what Camille T. Dungy writes of the Anglo-American or Transcendental moment in nature writing. "The traditional context of the nature poem in the Western intellectual canon," Dungy argues, as "solidified by the Romantics and Transcendentalists, informs the prevailing views of the natural world as a place of positive collaboration, refuge, idyllic rural life, or wilderness."[38] What Morgan shares with Dungy is not the Anglo or Transcendentalist merging of the subject with the natural world but the moving away from the "subject" altogether.

Wright, however, places history and the historical "subject" at the center of what should be a "subjectless" fusion of man and nature. He refuses to abandon the social and historical "subject," *and* he refuses to abandon the natural world. Wright keeps both together in creative tension. In "'I Am Nobody': The Haiku of Richard Wright," Richard A. Iadonisi argues that "Wright radically reinvents the haiku form, making of it revolutionary poetry that offers and then savagely undercuts the possibility of Zen oneness; in the process, the haiku serve as a vehicle that articulates the author's anticolonial position."[39] The opening piece in Wright's *Haiku: This Other World* illustrates this point.

> I am nobody:
> A red sinking autumn sun
> Took away my name.[40]

Morgan sees in the poem "a loss of subjectivity" that results not from a failure of man and nature to come together; rather, "the 'red sinking sun' . . . actively removes the writer's 'name' to make the speaker into a 'nobody.'" In other words, the haiku does not merge the "subject" with nature, dissolving both into a "unified object." Rather, Wright's haiku highlights the ways in which the "subject" is removed, his name *taken* from him—like the land taken away from African Americans and indigenous Americans, the natural world (the sinking autumn sun), rather than offering him a moment of unification, obliterates his own subjective position by taking away his name.

What is the reader to make of the subject of Wright's haiku? This is, perhaps, the central question of *12 Million Black Voices* and *American Hunger:* What becomes of the African Americans in Chicago's Black Belt, having migrated from the South with the expectation of a new sky, new rain and wind, and new soil, and having been met, instead, with "City Pavements"? What becomes of those people of a "Strange Birth" who are "Inheritors of Slavery"? Is it just "Death on City Pavements"? Wright gives us something of an answer in the book's final section, "Men in the Making." It is one expounded by Dungy, engaging explicitly with Wright's haiku: "These [African American] poems implicate the natural world in a personal or collective history of trauma. The plants, animals, water, and weather seem to be complicit within society, creating various taunts and tragedies even while flaunting potential beauty and possibility."[41] It is between these two realities of black life—potential beauty and possibility and the "taunts" and the "tragedies"—that one can begin to understand black life and the politics of black living within the flux of history and the natural world. Between one of Wright's earliest poems, "Red Clay Blues," and one of his final haiku, we see the recurrent theme of nature as both nourishing and threatening, but nevertheless constitutive of human consciousness and the human personality.

Notes

1. For more on Richard Wright's haiku, see John Zheng, ed., *The Other World of Richard Wright: Perspectives on His Haiku* (Oxford: University of Mississippi Press, 2011); Richard Wright, *Haiku: The Last Poems of an American Icon* (New York: Arcade, 2012); Yoshinobu Hakutani, *Richard Wright and Haiku* (Columbia: University of Missouri Press, 2014); and Richard Wright, *Richard Wright and Haiku* (Columbia: University of Missouri Press, 2014).

2. For more on the history of African American nature writing, see Kimberly K. Smith, *African American Environmental Thought: Foundations* (Lawrence: University Press of Kansas, 2007); Camille T. Dungy, *Black Nature: Four Centuries of African American Nature Poetry* (Athens: University of Georgia Press, 2009); and Dianne D. Glave, *Rooted in the Earth: Reclaiming the African American Environmental Heritage* (Chicago: Chicago Review Press, 2010).

3. Houston A. Baker, "Richard Wright and the Dynamics of Place in Afro-American Literature," in *New Essays on Native Son*, ed. Keneth Kinnamon (Cambridge: Cambridge University Press, 1990), 93.

4. Ibid., 86.

5. Ibid., 86–87.

6. Elizabeth Alexander, *The Black Interior* (St. Paul, MN: Graywolf, 2004), 11.

7. Ibid., 12.

8. Richard Wright, "The Man Who Saw a Flood," in *Eight Men* (New York: Harper Perennial, 1940), 104–5.

9. Ibid., 105–6.

10. Ibid., 108, emphasis added.

11. Richard Wright, *12 Million Black Voices* (New York: Basic, 1941), 103–4, emphasis added.

12. Ibid., 108–11, emphasis added.

13. For more on the relationship between phenomenological embodiment and the interior life of existential freedom in Richard Wright, see Laura Grattan's chapter in this volume.

14. Richard Wright, *Black Boy* (New York: Harper and Brothers, 1945), 284–85.

15. Richard Wright, *American Hunger* (New York: Harper and Row, 1977), 1.

16. Wright, *12 Million Black Voices*, 92.

17. For more on Wright and regionalism, see Thadious M. Davis, "Race and Region," in *The Columbia History of the American Novel*, ed. Emory Elliott (New York: Columbia University Press, 1991); and Mary Hricko, *The Genesis of the Chicago Renaissance: Theodore Dreiser, Langston Hughes, Richard Wright, and James T. Farrell* (New York: Routledge, 2009).

18. For more on Richard Wright's *12 Million Black Voices* as counterstatement to racialized realism, see Perry S. Moskowitz's chapter in this volume.

19. Wright, *12 Million Black Voices*, 135.

20. For more on Richard Wright's human ecological theory, see Susan Scott Parrish, "Richard Wright's Environments: Mediating Personhood through the South's Second Nature," in *Reading African American Autobiography: Twenty-First Century Contexts and Criticism*, ed. Eric D. Lamore (Madison: University of Wisconsin Press, 2017).

21. Wright, *12 Million Black Voices*, 107.

22. Ibid., 144.

23. Ibid., 136.

24. Another critical short story exploring this theme is Richard Wright's "Down by the Riverside," in *Uncle Tom's Children* (New York: Harper and Brothers, 1940).

25. Wright, *Black Boy*, 14–15.

26. For more on Richard Wright's southern thinking, see Thadious M. Davis, *Southscapes: Geographies of Race, Region, and Literature* (Chapel Hill: University of North Carolina Press, 2011).

27. Camille T. Dungy's *Black Nature* is the first edited collection dedicated to African American poets and writers' thoughts on the natural world. The collection curates more than 180 works from more than ninety poets and writers. Richard Wright's haiku as well as *12 Million Black Voices* are included. For more on black

nature writing, see Glave, *Rooted in the Earth*; and Kimberly N. Ruffin, *Black on Earth: African American Ecoliterary Traditions* (Athens: University of Georgia Press, 2010).

28. Dungy, *Black Nature*, xix.

29. Ibid., xx–xi.

30. Ibid., xxi–xxii.

31. Wright, *Black Boy*, 284.

32. Richard Wright and Langston Hughes, "Red Clay Blues," *New Masses*, August 1, 1939, www.unz.org/Pub/NewMasses-1939aug01-00014.

33. The theme of remigration is the subject of Carol Stack's *Call to Home: African Americans Reclaim the Rural South*, in which she writes: "Return migration was a surprise to scholars. We had been led to believe that the great migrations that formed the modern states were one-way, permanent movements. People's footsteps, it seemed, were facing one way, as if they had stopped cold in their tracks somewhere out here in the urban diaspora. We had assumed that people in the modern world, once torn from their roots, never look back" (xiv). According to Stack (and also Dungy), most scholars are overlooking place-making and the psychic hold of place. Wright's work belongs in the conversations about reverse migration because of his analysis of the conditions and psychic relationship people had *before* they ever left, which is an important element of the migration/remigration narrative.

34. Thomas W. Mitchell, "From Reconstruction to Deconstruction: Undermining Black Ownership, Political Independence, and Community through Partition Sales of Tenancy in Common Property," *Northwestern University Law Review* 95 (2001): 505–82.

35. Wright, *12 Million Black Voices*, 60.

36. Thomas L. Morgan, "Inverting the Haiku Moment: Alienation, Objectification, and Mobility in Richard Wright's *Haiku: "This Other World,"*" in *The Other World of Richard Wright: Perspectives on His Haiku*, ed. Jianqing Zheng (Jackson: University of Mississippi Press, 2011), 92.

37. Ibid., 92–93.

38. Dungy, *Black Nature*, xxi.

39. Morgan, "Inverting the Haiku Moment," 93.

40. Wright, *Haiku: This Other World*, 99.

41. Dungy, *Black Nature*, xxxi.

PART 5

Uncle Tom's Great-Grandchildren

Joe Louis Uncovers Dynamite

Richard Wright

"*Wun-tuh-threee-fooo-fiiive-seex-seven-eight-niine-thuun!*"
 Then "JOE LOUIS—THE WINNAH!"
 On Chicago's South Side five minutes after these words were yelled, and Joe Louis' hand was hoisted as victor in his four-round go with Max Baer, Negroes poured out of beer taverns, pool rooms, barber shops, rooming houses, and dingy flats and flooded the streets.
 "LOUIS! LOUIS! LOUIS!" they yelled and threw their hats away. They snatched newspapers from the stands of astonished Greeks and tore them up, flinging the bits into the air. They wagged their heads. Lawd, they'd never seen or heard the like of it before. They shook the hands of strangers. They clapped one another on the back. It was like a revival. Really, there was a religious feeling in the air. Well, it wasn't exactly a religious feeling, but it was *something*, and you could feel it. It was a feeling of unity, of oneness.
 Two hours after the fight the area between South Parkway and Prairie Avenue on 47th Street was jammed with no less than twenty-five thousand Negroes, joy-mad and moving to they didn't know where. Clasping hands, they formed long writhing snake-lines and wove in and out of traffic. They seeped out of doorways, oozed from alleys, trickled out of tenements, and flowed down the street; a fluid mass of joy. White storekeepers hastily

closed their doors against the tidal wave and stood peeping through plate glass with blanched faces.

Something had happened, all right. And it had happened so confoundingly sudden that whites in the neighborhood were dumb with fear. They felt—you could see it in their faces—that *something* had ripped loose, exploded. Something which they had long feared and thought was dead. Or if not dead, at least so safely buried under the pretense of goodwill that they no longer had need to fear it. Where in the world did it come from? And what was worst of all, how far would it go? Say, what's got into these Negroes?

And the whites and the blacks began to *feel* themselves. The blacks began to remember all the little slights, and discriminations and insults they had suffered: and their hunger too and their misery. And the whites began to search their souls to see if they had been guilty of something, some time, somewhere, against which this wave of feeling was rising.

As the celebration wore on, the younger Negroes began to grow bold. They jumped on the running boards of automobiles going east or west on 47th Street and demanded of the occupants:

"Who yuh fer—Baer or Louis?"

In the stress of the moment it seemed that the answer to the question marked out friend and foe.

A hesitating reply brought waves of scornful laughter. Baer. Huh? That was funny. Now, hadn't Joe Louis just whipped Max Baer? Didn't think we had it in us, did you? Thought Joe Louis was scared, didn't you? Scared because Max talked loud and made boasts. We ain't scared either. We'll fight too when the time comes. We'll win too.

A taxicab driver had his cab wrecked when he tried to put up a show of bravado.

Then they began stopping streetcars. Like a cyclone sweeping through a forest, they went through them, shouting, stamping. Conductors gave up and backed away like children. Everybody had to join in this celebration. Some of the people ran out of the cars and stood, pale and trembling, in the crowd. They felt it, too.

In the crush a pocketbook snapped open and money spilled on the street for eager black fingers.

"They stole it from us, anyhow," they said as they picked it up.

When an elderly Negro admonished them, a fist was shaken in his face. Uncle Tomming, huh?

"Whut in hell youh gotta do wid it?" they wanted to know.

Something had popped loose, all right. And it had come from deep down. Out of the darkness it had leaped from its coil. And nobody could have said just what it was, and nobody wanted to say. Blacks and whites were afraid. But it was a sweet fear, at least for the blacks. It was a mingling of fear and fulfillment. Something dreaded and yet wanted. A something had popped out of a dark hole, something with a hydra-like head, and it was darting forth its tongue.

You stand on the borderline, wondering what's beyond. Then you take one step and you feel a strange, sweet tingling. You take two steps and the feeling becomes keener. You want to feel some more. You break into a run. You know it's dangerous, but you're impelled in spite of yourself.

Four centuries of oppression, of frustrated hopes, of black bitterness, felt even in the bones of the bewildered young, were rising to the surface. Yes, unconsciously they had imputed to the brawny image of Joe Louis all the balked dreams of revenge, all the secretly visualized moments of retaliation, AND HE HAD WON! Good Gawd Almighty! Yes, by Jesus, it could be done! Didn't Joe do it? You see, Joe was the consciously felt symbol. Joe was the concentrated essence of black triumph over white. And it comes so seldom, so seldom. And what could be sweeter than long nourished hate vicariously gratified? From the symbol of Joe's strength they took strength, and in that moment all fear, all obstacles were wiped out, drowned. They stepped out of the mire of hesitation and irresolution and were free! Invincible! A merciless victor over a fallen foe! Yes, they had felt all that—for a moment . . .

And then the cops came.

Not the carefully picked white cops who were used to batter the skulls of white workers and intellectuals who came to the South Side to march with the black workers to show their solidarity in the struggle against Mussolini's impending invasion of Ethiopia; oh, no, black cops, but trusted black cops and plenty tough. Cops who knew their business, how to handle delicate situations. They piled out of patrols, swinging clubs.

"Git back! Gawdammit, git back!"

But they were very careful, very careful. They didn't hit anybody. They, too, sensed *something*. And they didn't want to trifle with it. And there's no doubt but that they had been instructed not to. Better go easy here. No telling what might happen. They swung clubs, but pushed the crowd back with their hands.

Finally the streetcars moved again. The taxis and automobiles could go ahead. The whites breathed easier. The blood came back to their cheeks.

The Negroes stood on the sidewalks, talking, wondering, looking, breathing hard. They had felt something, and it had been sweet—that feeling. They wanted some more of it, but they were afraid now. The spell was broken.

And about midnight down the street that feeling ebbed, seeping home—flowing back to the beer tavern, the pool room, the café, the barber shop, the dingy flat. Like a sullen river it ran back to its muddy channel, carrying a confused and sentimental memory on its surface, like water-soaked driftwood.

Say, Comrade, here's the wild river that's got to be harnessed and directed. Here's that *something*, that pent-up folk consciousness. Here's a fleeting glimpse of the heart of the Negro, the heart that beats and suffers and hopes—for freedom. Here's that fluid something that's like iron. Here's the real dynamite that Joe Louis uncovered!

October 8, 1935

Note: Originally published as "Joe Louis Uncovers Dynamite," *Daily Worker* (1935). Reprinted courtesy of the Richard Wright Estate.

Notes toward a Political Economy of Life and Death

Reading Richard Wright with Frantz Fanon

Abdul R. JanMohamed

In the final chapter of *The Death-Bound-Subject*, I began to explore what I call a "political economy of life and death" in the context of "slavery" as excavated in Richard Wright's fiction. I investigated, for example, the diverse modes of exchange implicit within the "unconscious death contract" between the master and the slave. My theorizing, which occurred at the intersection of Marxism and psychoanalysis, failed to include an analysis of "primitive accumulation," which I now believe can further illuminate the political economy that underwrites the unconscious death contract between the master and the slave.[1]

The following discussion builds upon my previous analysis of the short stories in Wright's anthology *Uncle Tom's Children* and traces Wright's gradual discovery of the "dialectics of death"—that is, a structure of relations between social death, actual death, and symbolic death. Those stories promote an understanding of "primitive accumulation" that can be applied not only to material "dispossession" of the slave's world but also to the appropriation of his or her subjectivity. I will argue that the slave's subjectivity is profoundly disarticulated or disaggregated and that aspects of that subjectivity are (dis)possessed and rearticulated by the master. Complex struggles for psycho-political control inevitably follow the expropriation of oppressed subjectivities, although often the struggles occur unconsciously. However, before reexamining Wright's stories, I first will explore the sociopolitical role of the threat of death in the processes that collectively constitute "primitive accumulation"; the theoretical implications for a political economy of life and death contained in foundational concepts, such as "homo sacer" or "bare life," as well as in the almost universal disavowal of death; and offer a phenomenological description of how the slave subject experiences death in Wright's poem "Between the World and Me" and in Frantz Fanon's fifth chapter of *Black Skin, White Mask*, "The Lived Experience of the Black Man."[2]

Following in the footsteps of Rosa Luxemburg, David Harvey has recently revived our interest in the Marxian notion of "primitive accumulation," which he views as a process of "accumulation by dispossession" that does not rely on the basic structures of exchange proper to a capitalist economy and, instead, depends on the use of "extra economic means," namely violence. Samir Amin, among others, has argued that centuries of European colonization of the Global South, including the entire process of enslavement, consisted essentially of primitive accumulation. Marx himself writes that the "so-called primitive accumulation . . . is nothing else than the historical process of divorcing the producer from the means of production" and "in actual history, it is a notorious fact that conquest, enslavement, robbery, murder, *in short force,* play the greatest part [in primitive accumulation]."[3]

Massimo De Angelis, in his very thorough interpretation of Marx's discussion of dispossession, points out that at every turn Marx identifies "separation" between the worker and his means of production as the operative mechanism of primitive accumulation. But neither De Angelis nor Marx specifies the means used in this separation. They point simply toward violence or "force." They do not, however, examine which modes of violence are most effective in separating the worker from his means of production. While we do not have the space here to examine various modalities of violence, I would argue that the threat of death, accompanied by actual killing or lynching, is the fundamental form of violence that subtends all others forms. Among a nexus of different forms of violence that together constitute "force" or "violence" in general, I would argue that the threat of death functions as what Louis Althusser calls the "structure in dominance." All other forms of violence, I would argue, are metonymies of the threat of death and of actual execution. And if the threat of death is fundamental to separation, enslavement, and primitive accumulation, then it may prove useful to examine its role not only in the separation of the material, sociopolitical relations between the worker and his or her means of production but also in the "separation" of the psycho-political structures that compel the slave to permit the forceful separation of his or her labor (as a commodity) from his or her body and, more importantly, from his or her life as a project and process, to which his or her labor is integral: in short, the role of the threat of death in the disaggregation of the subject.[4]

To map the dispossession of the slave via the threat of death, it is necessary to distinguish three "moments" of this process: first, the separation between the slave subject and his or her material property (land, cattle, and so forth); second, the separation of the slave subject from her or his "labor"; and finally the disaggregation of the slave subjectivity itself—that is, the systematic destruction of the quasi-coherence or unity of that subjectivity and the subsequent possession or control of various components of that disaggregated psyche. The first moment is, of course, clearly illustrated by the entire history of Euro-American colonization, and it needs no elaboration here. The second moment is implicit in the establishment of slavery and the use of force to induce various subjects to "allow" the master to control their labor. For example, E. A. Brett and Richard D. Wolff document how the British occupiers in Kenya used various military and economic devices to force the Gikuyus to offer their "labor" on the agricultural or plantation market when previously labor had never been a commodity that could be exchanged for a wage. Violence, punitive taxation, and other forms of coercion were used by the British to separate the "labor" of the Gikuyus from its integral and integrated place in the ongoing life processes of an individual or community. Finally, the threat of death is used to shatter the putative unity of a subject—that is, the continuity and relative coherence of his or her life—and forces the slave to exchange the postponement of his or her death for his labor as well as his or her pride, dignity, and so forth. As slave narratives and novels such as *Incidents in the Life of a Slave Girl* and *Beloved* testify, the threat of death permeates and disaggregates even maternal love and insinuates itself in the intimate relations between mother and child. Unlike the first two moments, the dispossession of the slave's subjectivity needs further theoretical elaboration.[5]

To appreciate this form of dispossession, it is useful to turn to Giorgio Agamben's well-known definition of homo sacer or "bare life" as life that can be killed by anyone at any time without that death being seen either as sacrilege or a homicide.[6] Certain individuals are placed beyond the border of the human and the sacred, which leaves them vulnerable to infinite exploitation. This legal-political understanding masquerades as an ontological distinction and thus becomes foundational to all subsequent modes of dispossession. The designation of "killability" implies that the killer is not culpable on either sociopolitical or ethical-religious registers. The effective possession of the "life" of a person deemed killable—including all the contents (property) and the processes (all the practices that constitute the sociality) of that life—is transferred to those in control of defining him or her as "bare life." Thus, the very definition of someone as bare life establishes an implicit structure of exchange, in which a potential killer not only takes possession of all the property of another person but also offers to spare his or her life and, in exchange for an agreement to become a slave, conditionally commute the death sentence. The master-to-be allows the slave-to-be to have "possession" of his or her life from one day to the next in exchange for his or her implicit promise to turn over almost all the fruits of his or her labor and subjectivity to the master. The designation of someone as killable thus constitutes the cornerstone of primitive accumulation on the material as well as the symbolic registers.[7]

The notion of "homo sacer" draws attention to attempts to institute an implicit system of exchange through the intersection of epistemological and ontological registers. A similar political economy of life and death is grounded existentially by an almost universal tendency to disavow death. The disavowal covers the entire spectrum of human life, from somatic experience to exalted symbolic structures such as religion. To use Fanon's important distinction, the disavowal permeates ontogenesis as well as sociogenesis.

Martin Heidegger characterizes the human tendency to ignore or deny the facticity of death, as well as its penetration into every aspect of our daily lives, as an "inauthentic" attitude to death. But this tendency to deny death is grounded not in some "inauthentic" ontic attitude. I would argue that it is grounded in the somatic imperative to do everything possible to avoid death and to stay alive no matter how terrible the privation, no matter how relentless the oppression, and no matter how inhospitable the conditions of existence. As Roberto Esposito has noted, all organisms avoid death whenever possible and seek to survive as long as possible.[8]

I would add that at the psychic level, this somatic avoidance transforms itself into a disavowal that allows us to acknowledge consciously, when forced to, that we are mortal, and that also permits us to deny unconsciously the fact of mortality. The somatic imperative to negate death translates itself affectively into an abject fear of death, as an eventuality to be avoided at all cost. This imperative to deny death and fear permits us to tolerate the most horrendous forms of oppression and exploitation so long as we can continue to live. Most people, including slaves and wage-slaves, will adamantly live on despite abject misery and severe deprivation, and will seek to remain alive in the worst of all possible conditions rather than face, let alone accept, death. They will give up anything and everything for the "privilege" of being allowed to live a bare, minimal existence.[9]

Death's ability to infiltrate and control life from the inside, so to speak, and thereby determine the quantity, quality, and direction of all erotic energy, is evident in monotheistic religions. All three great monotheistic religions attempt to guarantee the continuity of "life" after death. They either rearticulate death as a nondeath or as a pseudodeath, or depict earthly existence as a transition from a less-than-perfect life to a perfect "after-life" from which death has been abolished. Achieving the mythic alternative to death is contingent upon behaving according to the religious precepts of what constitutes a "good" life—that is, a life subservient to the prevailing religious ideology or theology. The true believer is in fact asked to relinquish control of his or her life, including vast quantities of erotic energies (which are sources of various products, "commodities," and sociopolitical structures), in exchange for the abolition of death and the radical denial of death. Put differently, these religions appropriate, rearticulate, and redirect the vast quantity of erotic energies in exchange for the denial of death. Monotheism thereby establishes a complex political economy centered on the use value and the exchange value of life and death.

The wondrous beauty of cathedrals, mosques, and temples, the complex theological edifices and doctrines, the prolonged management of vast populations, and indeed the construction of entire civilizations are all indices of the erotic energies that can be accumulated and channeled in exchange for the denial of death. But we must not forget that equally powerful quota of thanatos that is also channeled by this exchange mechanism. The believer is licensed—indeed, often required—to "justifiably" kill the countless enemies of his or her God. These killings are then articulated as part of the glorious, erotic struggle necessary to protect the status of one's God, who in turn protects one from death. Existential anxiety about and the disavowal of "natural death" brought about by old age, disease, or accident (or, death that is not brought about by human agency) clarifies how that anxiety and disavowal are subsequently appropriated and deployed in the fabrication of "political death" brought about by human agency (as in the above practice of designating certain individuals and communities as "bare life").[10]

These theories of bare life and the somatic resistance to and social disavowal of death contribute to a fuller understanding of the political economy instituted around the opposition of life and death. This opposition that, like Marx's dialectical opposition between use value and exchange value, must be understood as simultaneously mutually constitutive and mutually exclusive. The explosiveness of the confrontation with political death is conveyed by Wright's poem "Between the World and Me" and by Fanon's brief chapter "The Lived Experience of the Black Man."

Fanon's chapter, after opening with the fact of the racializing gaze ("'Dirty nigger!' or simply 'Look! A Negro!'"), continues as follows: "I came into this *world* anxious to uncover the meaning of things, my soul desirous to be *at the origin of the world*, and here *I am an object* among other objects." Fanon firmly locates the gaze as intervening *between the world and the subject* that is being racialized. Fanon's subject enters the world desiring to be at its center. The subject's project is a "worlding of the world." But, the gaze intervenes between the subject and the world and thus turns the former from a putative subject into an object. The results are that "*I explode. Here are the fragments put together by another me.*" The chapter then maps the diverse ways the subject experiences that explosion and finds itself dispersed across the social, psychological, and political landscape. The racializing gaze thus destroys the dialectical relationship between the subject and the world and leaves in its wake a "body-in-pieces," scattered across a vast sociopolitical landscape. Fanon's body-in-pieces is clearly a version of Jacques Lacan's "corps morcelé," which is a powerful manifestation of the facticity of and anxiety about death. In short, the racializing gaze *kills* the subject by subverting the centripetal synthesizing, worlding activity that ontologically motivates the subject and hence forms it. Fanon is mapping the fundamental "disaggregation" or dismemberment of the racialized subject that is the logical and political precursor of a process that will then proceed to "possess" different parts of that dismembered subject. And that process of (dis)possession is, in turn, a crucial component of the "primitive accumulation" of the enslaved subjectivity.[11]

Fanon ends his chapter with a reference to Wright's character Bigger Thomas, and to Bigger's overwhelming fear, which is the title of the first of the three parts of *Native Son*. Fanon says that Bigger fulfills his destiny (he "answers the world's expectations") by exploding and imploding and, in the process, killing others and himself. With Bigger becoming a corps morcelé, Fanon ends the chapter where he began.

Wright traces a similar scenario in his early poem. The persona of "Between the World and Me" is implicitly a black man, who wanders into a clearing in the woods and onto the site of a recent lynching. The first half of the poem describes, in an "objective" mode, the scene of the lynching and the remnants of body parts of the man who was torn apart before being lynched (the corps morcelé). The second half of the poem expresses the subjective mode of that experience. The persona suddenly becomes the individual who is being tortured, castrated, and lynched while being burned at the stake.[12]

The threat and actuality of lynching in Wright's poem resemble the racializing gaze in Fanon's essay. In both cases, death intervenes between the subject and the world. In both cases, the possibility of political death prevents the subject from forming itself coherently and with purpose. In addition, both the poem and the chapter map a tripartite development of the structure of the subject. Each text begins with what we may call a "naïve" subject, who has not yet been exposed to the reality of political death and who hopes to weave a beautiful world around him or herself. Then, the subject experiences the brutal reality of being exploded and disaggregated. Finally, both texts end with a subject who has somehow survived the disaggregation and is able to reconstitute himself. Fanon writes, "Here are the *fragments* put together by *another me*," while Wright's poem is implicitly written by someone who has survived a lynching. Both the poem and the chapter trace a journey through three positions that I have elsewhere analyzed as the components of the dialectics of death: social death, actual death, and symbolic death. Fanon's essay and Wright's poem both begin with a subject already formed by social death, both then elaborate the experience of actual death (albeit metaphorically in Fanon's essay), and then, from the grounds occupied by symbolic death, both authors reaggregate the subject that has been disaggregated by colonialism and racism.[13]

Wright's and Fanon's disaggregation and reaggregation of the death-bound subject lead to a series of questions about how various psycho-political and sociopolitical components of any given subjectivity are dispossessed by the master and can be repossessed by the slave. Put differently, what psycho-political struggles traverse the subjectivity that has experienced radical disaggregation and that is attempting to reaggregate itself? Fanon explores various aspects of this struggle in *Black Skin, White Masks* and in *The Wretched of the Earth*. In composing the anthology *Uncle Tom's Children*, Wright was motivated by one overarching question: "What quality of 'will' must a Negro possess to live and die with dignity in a country that denied his humanity?" Does "will" mean for Wright a fortitude of desire for specific goals that together constitute a project? If so, then the book's overarching question is about strength of desire as well as about the power of cathexis that is required to fight against the master's negation of the slave's desire and attempts to break his or her will. Wright is focusing on the political economy between eros (the processes of binding necessary for the assertion of desire and will) and thanatos (the deployment of the threat of death in order to "dispossess" the slave's erotic capacities and destroy the bonds between his will and desire, bonds without which no project can be completed).[14]

The first story in Wright's compilation is about the education of Big Boy. His education consists of witnessing the fundamental principle that constitutes "bare life" in Jim Crow society: that, to use Toni Morrison's phrase, "anybody white could take your whole self for anything that came to mind." Big Boy is not a particularly reflexive, thoughtful character, but by watching the lynching of his friend, Bobo, Big Boy becomes aware that his life can be dispossessed at will and without any legal or moral restraint. The story, in addition, implies that a more complex economy of dispossession exists, which includes an inverted equivalence between the supposed "rape" and the lynching of Bobo and the potential killability of Big Boy. Just as rape is a violation of the privacy, the integrity, and the explicit or implicit boundaries of a subject, so is lynching a violation of similar boundaries. While there are many important differences between these two forms of violation, what I wish to stress here is that Bobo is lynched for the supposed crime of rape. Allegedly, the projected sexual desires of the black boys, which violate the boundaries between the inner and outer, are equivalent to an actual lynching, which also violates Bobo's subjective boundaries. Again, Bobo is lynched not for an actual crime of rape but for an *imputed desire* to rape. It is assumed that the life of a "black boy" can be dispossessed in exchange for the very possibility of his sexual desire. Desire, and particularly sexual desire that involves the potential crossing of the racial boundaries, is itself prohibited and severely policed, and hence is subject to potential dispossession.[15]

Having been forced to witness the lynching of his friend, Big Boy can no longer "disavow" the possibility of his own death. In this coming-of-age story, Big Boy's maturation entails the dispossession of the normal and normative disavowal of death. For a black "boy" to become a man in Jim Crow society, he must accept his politico-ontological status as a death-bound subject and acknowledge that he is a killable subject and that his "bare life" is a site in which life and death can be exchanged instantaneously.

The next story, "Down by the Riverside," moves beyond the theoretical avowal of death and portrays the active embrace of death as a political gesture of resistance. In the process, the story reveals some of the finer details about "subjective dispossession" and the psycho-political processes involved in the unconscious "acceptance" and the more conscious resistance to the coercive possession of one's subjectivity. Wright bifurcates the life of his primary character, Mann. On the one hand, Mann is fully dedicated to saving other people's lives. His labor allows them to "possess" their lives. On the other hand, Mann lacks the capacity to control or possess his own life. In the story, he skillfully rows his expectant wife and unborn child to the hospital and adroitly saves the lives of the Heartfield family. Both events demonstrate that he is fully in command of his labor and "possesses" his labor as a process. Yet, the story shows that his "self-possessed" labor is in turn totally controlled and possessed by his white masters. He is never able to master his labor or his subjectivity in the service of his own life. Because he knows that his rescue of the Heartfield family may well lead to his own death, his passivity about his fate demonstrates a radical split between knowledge and the will to act. Apparently, an unconscious "slave contract" permits the slave to possess labor-power but prohibits the slave from owning that power. Mann never contemplates deploying his power for his own welfare or to preserve his life. He paradoxically controls his life only at the end of the story, when he no longer adopts a passive attitude toward his death and decides actively to possess his death. As he "runs" and knows that he will be shot momentarily, he conjoins his labor-power with the *telos* of his life. His active embrace of his death is, in effect, a momentary repossession of his life.

The somatic (ontogenic) and the consequent psychic (sociogenic) disavowal of death seem to be prerequisite for Mann's formation of, as well as his acceptance of, social death. The unconscious psychosomatic injunction against death (or, put conversely, the unconscious imperative to stay alive at all costs) determines both the slave's acceptance of and the social institutionalization of social death or slavery. This injunction/imperative is crucial for inaugurating slavery because only the adamant nature of the unconscious, unexamined imperative to live (to *not* die) explains why anyone would "accept" slavery. Arguably, just as attachment to one's life precedes the formation of social death, so a clear avowal of death must precede the eventual embrace of death that frees the slave.[16]

Wright encapsulates the entire movement from external to internal control of death in five short sentences: "They were going to kill him. Yes, now, he would die! He would die before he would let them kill him. Ahll die fo they kill me! Ahll *die*."[17] In this passage, Mann recognizes that "they" are the agents who control death. He then acknowledges the facticity of death, "he would die," which radically brackets the question of agential control of death. Finally, Mann himself become the agent of his death—"Ahll die fo they kill me! Ahll *die*." The syntactic structure stresses the matter of ownership or possession of death. Mann decides to embrace death before *they* actually shoot him. The emphasis on "*die*" is unqualified by issues of temporality or agency. It is simply an illocutionary utterance that transforms him from someone who is not in control of his death, and therefore of his life, to someone who is finally asserting control over his death and thereby repossessing, in principle, his life; his decision to die becomes the moment in which he repossesses control of his life. Wright compresses this process of the avowal of one's own death into an infinitesimal moment. An examination of similar decisions by people like Frederick Douglass, Harriet Jacobs, Steve Biko, and Nelson Mandela, who have faced analogous circumstances through this process of avowals of death, would reveal a similar temporal and cathectic decision in the acknowledgment of death that precedes the embrace of actual death. As we will see, Wright also explores the temporal and psycho-political space between the moment of avowal and the moment of actual death.

In contrast to the tightly compressed temporality of Mann's embrace of death, that of Silas in "Long Black Song" is far more measured and deliberate. Silas successfully resists Jim Crow society's attempts to dispossess him economically and materially. However, he interprets Sarah's rape or seduction (the story is deliberately ambiguous about this) as a personal and subjective form of dispossession. In Silas's view, Jim Crow society has appropriated his land, his freedom, his woman, and then his "life" traces—in other words, there is a movement from the material register to the discursive and affective elements that constitute his subjectivity. "Long Black Song" thus opens up a glimpse of the struggle regarding the details of (dis)possession within the interiority of the subject who attempts to resist overall socioeconomic dispossession. In the story, Wright's assignment of affect and eros to Silas's wife and "hardness," rationality, and materiality to Silas revolves around the function of "fear," which operates as a metonymy of affect in general. To the extent that the oppressive mechanisms of slave and Jim Crow societies operate predominantly via the inculcation of widespread and generalized fear (and fear of death in particular), the subject who attempts to resist his or her oppression must first "dispossess" himself or herself of his fear. Silas's courageous decision to fight the posse that comes to arrest him and to stay in the house and be burned to death without uttering a sound of pain clearly implies an overcoming of the fear of death.

This raises a question about an economy of the relations between (dis)possession of fear and courage: does the subject have to distance or decathect himself or herself from the former in order to cathect sufficiently with the latter? Moreover, how does an oppressed subject who has been possessed by fear dispossess himself or herself of it, and to what extent is successful resistance dependent on the outcome of the psycho-political play of (dis)possession within his or her psychic structures? Wright explores these questions in the anthology's next two stories. They make clear that the Marxian theory of the notion of "'primitive' accumulation by dispossession" cannot be confined to the realm of *material* accumulation and dispossession; to map that theory more thoroughly, one must also explore the processes of cultural, symbolic, and psychic (dis)possession.

In "Long Black Song," Wright also considers questions about the relative value of the freedom to possess material resources, which the protagonist, Silas, clearly has mastered, and the value of psychic "possessions" such as dignity, honor, and integrity, for which Silas is willing to die. Indeed, his willingness to die for these possessions suggests that in the slave's struggle to regain significant mastery over life, repossession of subjective attributes like honor and dignity take phenomenological precedence over the repossession of material resources. Moreover, Wright's deliberate separation of eros (by associating it with Sarah and then banishing her from the house and having her witness the fight to the death from a distant hill) from Silas's adamant willingness to kill and be killed implies that erotic binds can be distractions and hindrances when a slave is fighting for his or her freedom. Nonetheless, the banishment of eros in some sense parallels the master's appropriation of the slave's erotic energies. And Silas's "hardness," instantiated most forcefully by his refusal to cry out while being burned to death, further suggests that the slave must not be distracted by a desire to regain freedom and must not attempt to repossess the erotic energies that the master has already appropriated. Wright further explores this dichotomy between "hardness" as a political necessity and distracting emotions as apolitical luxuries in *Native Son*. In *Native Son,* Wright returns to these issues by creating another "hard" character, Bigger Thomas. Bigger's eventual meditation on the relation between his external hardness and an internal "softness" and his very different suturing of murderous and erotic energies shed new light on the dialectic of eros and thanatos in the slave's struggle for freedom.

In the remaining two short stories in this anthology, however, Wright returns to the political economies that attend the shifting of (dis)possessions from one sociopolitical register to another. Both stories begin with the protagonists' adamant bondage to Christianity: both Reverend Taylor, the protagonist of "Fire and Cloud," and Sue, the protagonist of "Bright and Morning Star," find refuge from oppression in their strong belief in the protection supposedly proffered by their charitable God. Taylor, however, is forced to abandon that spiritual investment when he is whipped in the cemetery and his God does not intervene to protect him; he then turns to a deep investment in the political movement as many of his congregants, including his son, have been urging. Sue, by contrast, willingly abandons religion because of her love for her sons, who have invested their energies and faith in the political efficacy of the Communist Party.

In examining the shift of energies from the religious to the political register, Wright reveals other ancillary mechanisms of the political economy of symbolic and psychic (dis)possession. "Fire and Cloud" discloses two formulations. The first is revealed by the way in which Taylor is forced to abandon the Christian God of love and mercy: the whipping, the repeated spasms of pain, and the failure of God to materialize despite Taylor's pleas for His assistance, together imply that one's investments in and possessions of sustaining ideologies and beliefs can change only under the pressure of severe and systematic destruction of everyday habits and practices, within which powerful ideologies are deeply buried. The shifting of registers and ideological commitments, Wright implies, is not simply a matter of epistemological rearticulations or understandings but, instead, requires something close to a dramatic somatic restructuring. Ideological investments are deeply affective and function most effectively by "possessing" individual and collective subjects. Taylor's transference from religious to political commitment implies that such conversions can be efficacious only when accompanied by change in the modality of identifications that bind the individual to the collective. Taylor's identification with his God, and with the religious structures entailed therein, has been sutured primarily on the "imaginary" register (in the Lacanian sense). However, his identification with his political community begins first with him talking to himself in a mirror. He then reidentifies himself by using his community as a mirror, and finally he sutures himself with that community via clear and forceful *verbal* articulation of the collective predicament. In other words, this transformation entails a move from the imaginary to the symbolic register. This story, like the next one, thus implies a dispossession of imaginary identification so that politically more productive identification can take place on the symbolic register. This entails a shift from relatively unconscious structures of identification to more conscious and deliberate ones.

The same modification is rearticulated and emphasized in "Bright and Morning Star." Sue's transference of her commitment from her sons' spiritual salvation to their political salvation marks a shift from group formations that are more biologically and ontologically structured to ones that are sociopolitically structured. In Fanonian terms, she overcomes her ontogenetically structured identification with one that is sociogenetically determined to the extent that the "biological" family is much more an extension of the natural processes of reproduction than is the "political" family. The former involves far fewer choices than does the latter; the former is more of an unconscious (often a pro forma) formation than the latter.

This shift is stressed at the end of the story, when Sue is forced to witness her son being tortured. She struggles against her "natural" maternal instincts to alleviate her son's pain by shooting him and, instead, waits for the man to whom she has betrayed the party membership. If she killed her son, it would be a mercy killing because it would spare him the pain of torture; but it is more politically important for her to kill the traitor than to alleviate her son's pain. Thus she subordinates the attachments and obligations of a "natural," biological, and affective family in favor of a socially, politically, and rationally conceived family. She sacrifices both her maternal love and her son to protect the political community. At this point, the "life" of the political community determines the efficacy and the nature of death for both her son and herself. "Normally" the slave's desire to stay alive (rather than face his or her death) means that fear of death determines and controls the mode of living practices. Thanatos determines eros. However, as in Toni Morrison's *Beloved*, in this story eros determines thanatos. Sue's "love" of her political community motivates her to watch her son being tortured and then to kill him (after she has killed the traitor). Like Sethe, Sue sacrifices her child for the sake of a free political life of the community. Her broader commitment can be formulated via the notion of "dialectical overcoming," which refers to a mode of overcoming that preserves experiences that are historically and sociopolitically local and specific while at the same time rearticulating them on a more general, universal, and theoretical level. Sue's love entails the transformation of the personal into the political, the biological into social life, and the ontogenic into the sociogenic, all the while subordinating thanatos to eros—rather than, as in "normal" slave life, allowing the fear and desire to avoid death to determine the courses and valences of one's life and, thereby, reducing life to "social death."[18]

Uncle Tom's Children can be seen, in light of the preceding analysis, as a condensed, metonymic response to the question that motivated Wright: "What quality of 'will' must a Negro possess to live and die with dignity in a country that denied his humanity?" In addition, Wright's stories raise a larger set of questions regarding the forms of psycho-political possession and dispossession that are entailed within or that accompany the processes of material (dis)possession central to primitive accumulation. These questions preoccupied Wright throughout his career. *Native Son*, in particular, traces in great, labyrinthine detail the dispossession of the psyche of a "black boy" and the kind of struggle that is required for the repossession and reintegration of that psyche; a reintegration that culminates, like Mann's illocutionary statement, with Bigger's embrace of his impending death.

In spite of the poststructuralist doxa about the decentered subject and the need to abolish "identity politics," individual subjects are strongly driven to center themselves and to make their lives as coherent and unified as possible. Most important of all, they are constantly preoccupied by the attempt to "possess" their lives as a complex, ongoing (and often contradictory) process. Colonization, racialization, genderization, enslavement, and similar forms of oppression rely profoundly on disrupting the attempts by oppressed people to possess control of their daily living practices. These struggles over possession of living practices, which include beliefs, ideologies, and values, constitute a central if not primary battlefield on which primitive accumulation takes place. What is at stake is not only the master's attempt to possess our property and our labor but also the innermost recesses of our subjectivities. Our subjectivities are therefore the sites of ongoing battles for (dis)possession and primitive accumulation.

Notes

1. Abdul R. JanMohamed, *The Death-Bound-Subject: Richard Wright's Archeology of Death* (Durham, NC: Duke University Press, 2005), 266–300.

2. For a definition of the dialectic of death, see the final chapter of JanMohamed, *Death-Bound-Subject*.

3. On Luxemburg's insistence that primitive accumulation accompanies other forms of accumulation throughout the history of capitalism, see Rosa Luxemburg, *The Accumulation of Capital* (Eastford, CT: Martino Fine Book, 2015). On accumulation by dispossession, see David Harvey, *The New Imperialism* (Oxford: Oxford University Press, 2003). On colonialism as a process of dispossession, see, all by Samir Amin, *Accumulation on a World Scale: A Critique of the Theory of Underdevelopment* (New York: Monthly Review Press, 1974), *Unequal Development: An Essay on the Social Formations of Peripheral Capitalism* (New York: Monthly Review Press, 1976), and *Imperialism and Unequal Development* (New York: Monthly Review Press, 1977). Karl Marx, *Capital. Volume 1* (New York: Penguin, 1990), 874–75, emphasis added.

4. Massimo De Angelis, "Marx's Theory of Primitive Accumulation: A Suggested Reinterpretation," www.researchgate.net/publication/266446934; Louis Althusser and Etienne Balibar, *Reading Capital* (London: Verso, 2009).

5. E. A. Brett, *Colonialism and Underdevelopment in East Africa: The Poli-*

tics of Economic Change, 1919–1939 (New York: NOK, 1973); Richard D. Wolff, *The Economics of Colonialism: Britain and Kenya, 1870–1930* (New Haven: Yale University Press, 1974). As Brett notes, "Independent peasant production and capitalist settler production therefore existed as sharply antagonistic modes, and any effective development of the one precluded an equivalent development of the other in the same social universe" (169).

6. Giorgio Agamben, *Homo Sacer: Sovereign Power and Bare Life* (Stanford: Stanford University Press, 1998).

7. For an elaboration of the effects of the threat of death on the temporal constitution of slave subjectivity, see the last chapter of JanMohamed, *The Death-Bound-Subject*.

8. Martin Heidegger, *Being and Time* (New York: Harper and Row, 1962); Robert Esposito, *Immunitas: The Protection and Negation of Life* (Cambridge: Polity, 2011).

9. Of course, there are exceptions. Consider the cases of Frederick Douglass, Harriet Jacobs, Steve Biko, Nelson Mandela, Mohandas Gandhi, and Martin Luther King Jr. I discuss such figures in *Death-Bound-Subject* and in my current research project, "Thick Love."

10. For more exploration of the theme of agency, see Marilyn Nissim-Sabat's and Lewis R. Gordon's chapters in this volume.

11. Frantz Fanon, *Black Skin, White Mask* (New York: Grove, 2008), 98, emphasis added. For a discussion of the "corps morcelé," see Jacques Lacan, *Ecrits: A Selection* (London: Tavistock, 1977). For a concise definition and related concepts see http://nosubject.com/index.php?title=Talk:Fragmented_body.

12. This poem is available in Richard Wright and Michel Fabre, *Richard Wright Reader* (Boston: Da Capo, 1997). It is also available at http://edhelper.com/poetry/Between_the_World_and_Me_by_Richard_Wright.htm. In the poem the explosion/implosion at one point takes the following form: "Then my blood was cooled mercifully, cooled by a baptism of gasoline. / And in a blaze of red I leaped to the sky as pain rose like water, boiling my limbs."

13. For additional reflection on the theme of social death, see Laura Grattan's chapter in this volume.

14. Richard Wright, *Uncle Tom's Children*, in *Early Works: Lawd Today! Uncle Tom's Children, Native Son* (New York: Library of America, 1991), 324.

15. Toni Morrison, *Beloved* (New York: Random House, 1987), 295. In the second chapter of *The Death-Bound-Subject* I explore at great length the complexity of Wright's gradual discovery of the dialectics of death in the process of writing the stories collected in *Uncle Tom's Children*. The present exploration of these stories must thus be read as a complementary analysis that focuses primarily on the modalities of (dis)possession.

16. The unconscious imperative to live applies, of course, not just to the individual subject but also to a collective subject. The desire to avoid the possible deaths of one's family and community fulfills the same motivational function.

17. Richard Wright, "Down by the Riverside," in *Uncle Tom's Children*, 327, emphasis original.

18. In my forthcoming study of the reproduction of life and death in neoslave narratives, I describe this process as "thick love."

19

Reading Richard Wright beyond the Carceral State

The Politics of Refusal in Black Radical Imagination

Laura Grattan

> I'm a black man in America. . . . I can't secure the safety of my son. I just don't have that power. But what I do have the power to do is say, "You won't enroll me in this lie. You won't make me part of it."
>
> —Ta-Nehisi Coates

> If I were a member of the class that ruled, I would post men in all the neighborhoods of the nation, not to spy on or club rebellious workers, not to break strikes or disrupt unions; but to ferret out those who no longer respond to the system in which they live. . . . The millions I would fear are those who do not dream of the prizes that the nation holds forth, for it is in them, though they may not know it, that a revolution has taken place and is biding its time to translate itself into a new and strange way of life.
>
> —Richard Wright

Ta-Nehisi Coates, when accepting a 2015 National Book Award, declared his refusal to opt into the "lie" of an American Dream whose promise of being or becoming white has been built on a "heritage" of "destroy[ing] the black body."[1] Coates justifies his refusal in his best-selling memoir, *Between the World and Me*. The memoir is named after Richard Wright's 1935 poem of the same title, in which the narrator stumbles upon the charred remains of a lynching and imagines in agonizing detail the scene repeating itself as he is tarred, feathered, and murdered by a drunken white mob. Encounters with violence against black people, not only in the Jim Crow South but also in the industrial North, had led Wright in his literature and activism to refuse to provide relief from what he saw as the "horror of Negro life in the United States."[2] In Irving Howe's words, Wright sought to make "impossible a repetition of old lies" in the white, capitalist United States.[3] Coates contends that today—when police brutality and mass incarceration perpetuate both the nation's antiblack heritage and "the Dream of being white"—writers, protesters, and community activists should find inspiration in Wright's refusal.[4]

This, of course, is controversial. James Baldwin famously maintained that Wright's best-selling novel *Native Son* "betray[ed] a certain thinness of imagination."[5] The central character, Bigger Thomas, was a duplication of the "monster" that white Americans had created and used to reinforce their "nightmare" of black violence. In Baldwin's view, Wright's critique of white supremacy therefore remains "trapped" within white society's image of blackness.[6] His "bitter railing" against the "cage of reality"—that is, the *social* conditions forced upon black people by white categories—fails to recognize what Baldwin calls the complex, *human* realities of black culture: the rich traditions of shared struggle and survival that "create a new way of life."[7]

The dispute between Wright and Baldwin attracted attention from Eldridge Cleaver and Howe (who side with Wright) and Ralph Ellison and Cornel West (who believe Baldwin shows incomparable aesthetic and moral complexity).[8] Both critics and admirers see the refusal to accept the social and political norms of white Americans as tied to a stark choice: either to align oneself with a violent overcoming of the white, liberal, capitalist nation-state, or to withdraw from it. Withdrawal may lead to participation in democratic experiments to enact alternative social and political visions, such as the local projects of the Black Panthers or today's prison abolitionists.[9] However, the most legible forms of withdrawal in today's neoliberal society resemble Coates's advice to his son: to forgo not only *the* Dream but *all* dreams (including legacies of collective black struggle) in favor of the personal existential struggle to live "an honorable and sane life."[10]

This essay argues that Wright's refusal is more complex than both critics and admirers allow, and that Wright struggled lifelong for a "new and strange way of life."[11] Today, refusal commonly means "to reject" and implies direct and even aggressive repudiation of the status quo. Earlier, however, refusal also meant "not to recognize," for example, by withholding allegiance to the nation, disidentifying with a group or its ideals, or opting out of expected norms and practices.[12] In three works written between 1940 and 1945 (*Native Son*, *Black Boy*, and *12 Million Black Voices*), Wright constructs a multifaceted politics of refusal that puts the regeneration of the body and its aesthetic senses at the center of struggles to create "new and strange way[s] of life." In these writings, individual and collective transformation entails varied repertoires of refusal that lessen bodily and psychic attunement to an antiblack social order and that make possible generative practices necessary for black freedom.[13]

Wright thus wrestles with the tension that theorists of radical imagination identify between "the refusal of something . . . which I am henceforth led to reject" and "the possibility of another thing that is in no way certain." He prompts us to ask: What forms of refusal might enable black radicals in conditions of dire uncertainty to generate practices, aesthetic dispositions, and images that "give rise creatively to the newly thinkable"?[14] Wright shows that refusal can be isolating, disorienting, and uncertain. His ambivalence seems crucial to a politics of refusal, because he acknowledges that rejecting or opting out of a given order (however disorderly it is for those living on its underside) is as likely to narrow actors' sense of possibility as to encourage new ways of living. Wright proposes generative practices, such as literature, black folk culture, and collective action, that might enhance the creative potential of refusal. Ultimately, however, he affirms the necessity of refusal even in the face of its unpredictable outcomes. It is in this spirit, I conclude, that today's movements against policing and prisons tie collective refusal to ongoing experiments to enact democracy beyond the carceral state.

Repertoires of Refusal in Wright's Early Literature

In composing his trilogy of books, Wright drew on memories from his early life in the South and his later move to Chicago. Although readers sometimes view *Native Son* as fiction, *Black Boy* as autobiography, and *12 Million Black Voices* as "folk history," each work blends personal experience, social critique, and art. Scholars therefore at times read these works in tandem with each other.[15] *Native Son* has its origins in Wright's biographical experiences, his Depression-era work at the Chicago Boys Club, and the case of serial killer Robert Nixon.[16] *Black Boy* is less an accurate recounting of Wright's youth than a stylized meditation on how black people might develop their aesthetic senses and create meaning out of their lives in the white United States—a meditation that Ellison likens to the blues.[17] Wright's *12 Million Black Voices* narrates the collective history of African Americans from slavery through the Great Migration. Wright, who wrote text to accompany photographs of rural and urban black life from the files of the Farm Security Administration, conveys his identification with black folk life through the use of the collective first-person voice. Houston Baker argues that the work "testifies better to Wright's engagement with the folk than do some of his fictions," while David Bradley observes that *12 Million Black Voices* "stands out as a work of poetry, of passion, of lyricism and of love."[18]

In all three books, Wright depicts the "social death" that has been the "afterlife of slavery" in the United States.[19] (For different takes on the afterlife of slavery, see Jane Gordon's account of *neoslavery* and Abdul R. JanMohamed's discussion of *social death* in this volume.) Wright repeatedly exposes diverse forms of social death: from a slave trade that erased African folkways, to the experiences of families torn apart, first by the traffic in human lives and then by dislocation and alienation in the industrial workplaces and crowded kitchenettes of the nation's northern cities.[20]

Wright also ponders the cultural consequences of social death. The protagonist of *Black Boy* reflects, "I used to mull over the strange absence of real kindness in Negroes, how unstable was our tenderness, how lacking in genuine passion we were, how void of great hope, how timid our joy, how bare our traditions, how hollow our memories, how lacking we were in those tangible sentiments that bind man to man, and how shallow was even our despair."[21] Although critics often read the protagonist literally when he "broods upon the cultural bareness" of black life, Ellison notes that this passage can be read as an "affirmation" of black Americans' "capacity for culture" despite Western society's efforts to destroy black cultural forms and "sensibilit[ies]."[22]

For Wright, social death involves bodily techniques that destroy black peoples' creative emotions and senses, and that situate them in an "emotional no-man's land."[23] *Black Boy*'s protagonist states that the quotidian violence he experienced constituted a "racial attack that went to the roots of [his] life," "corroding and devastating" his emotions and aspirations.[24] Like Wright, the protagonist hopes that literature can "create a sense of the hunger for life that gnaws in us all, [can] keep alive in our hearts a sense of the inexpressibly human."[25] This regenerative work, however, requires what Nicholas De Genova, in analyzing Wright, calls a "remorseless rejection and subversion" of white authority as well as a refusal "to cut a pact with the devil" and accept "a series of compromises which reduce life in some sense to a protracted way of death."[26]

Wright thus affirms refusal as a cathartic rejection of the dehumanizing racism that works itself out in the bodies and psyches of black Americans. As the protagonist of *Black Boy* explains, to survive in the South, most black people developed "a delicate, sensitive controlling mechanism" that taught them "unerringly what to aspire to and what not to aspire to." Even when taunted by the nation's false promises, they were to "keep control of [their] unruly emotions."[27] The possibilities for agency were thus choked. Consequently, "If you act at all," Wright explains in *12 Million Black Voices*, "it is either to flee or to kill; you are either a victim or a rebel."[28] Or as Bigger puts it, "I didn't know I was really alive in this world until I felt things hard enough to kill for 'em."[29]

Some critics read Bigger's violence as evidence of his *ressentiment*, arising from his intense attachment to the white society he hates. Wright, however, prefigures Frantz Fanon's claim that violence can function as cathartic rejection, whereby the oppressed cleanse their bodies of routinized domination. Violence becomes an equalizing force, through which black actors mock the values of white society and affirm their existence as human beings who create their own values—even though they can never be certain about the outcome of their actions.[30]

Arguably, Bigger learns the significance of his violent refusal to accept social death too late, while awaiting the electric chair. But for Wright, the writing of *Native Son* "turned into a way of living." Although Wright understood that *Native Son* would reify white images of black violence, he rejected what he calls his "mental censor . . . draped in white." He says of his decision to create Bigger, "I'd be reacting out of fear if I let what I thought whites would say constrict and paralyze me." He wrote *Native Son* in part "to free *myself* of this sense of shame and fear."³¹ He channeled cathartic fantasies of violence into a "way of living" that allowed him to adopt a "creative attitude toward life." In *Black Boy*, Wright describes writing as a practice by which he could "build a bridge of words between me and that world outside," a world that "seemed unreal" because, in the most violent ways, its terms were not his own.³² Wright thus experienced writing as a world-building practice and viewed his books as "sensory vehicle[s]" that opened "new avenues of feeling and seeing" for his readers.³³ Believing that "the world compels active participation," he thought literature should not only represent the world as it is, but become part of that world—in order to change it.³⁴

Wright intended *Native Son* to assault and disrupt prevailing social sentiment. He understood that "the white superiority complex," like the disposition toward subservience among black people, is bodily and affective: "It's a reaction. It's visual. It's latent. It's olfactory, auditory."³⁵ He had regrets about his first book, *Uncle Tom's Children:* "I had written a book which even bankers' daughters could read and weep over and feel good about it." Knowing the dangers of protest novels steeped in sentimentality—what Lionel Trilling calls white readers' ability to "vicariously suffer in slippers and become virtuous . . . or to feel consciously superior to the brutal oppressor"—Wright "swore to [him]self that if [he] ever wrote another book, no one would weep over it; that it would be so hard and deep that they would have to face it without the consolation of tears."³⁶ Rejecting white, bourgeois mores and withholding recognition of shared humanity on white terms, *Native Son* refuses to let white readers settle into familiar sentiments—pity, guilt, a sense of helplessness—that foster a sense of innocence about the destruction of black life in the United States. Perhaps counterintuitively, Wright saw his refusal to reinforce white sentimentality in *Native Son* as a first step to building a bridge between the white world and the world that might be.

Wright found resources to help build that bridge in the larger literary tradition of black folk heroes who, in Baker's words, "hate and wish to destroy [the] contrived symbols of white culture that insure our victimization." Bigger's traits and exploits call to mind the "timely trickery" of Brer Rabbit, the narratives of ex-slaves who repudiate their masters, the genre of "white woman tales" celebrating enslaved men who humiliate or kill their mistresses, and the figure of the "badman hero" (from Nat Turner to the fictional Shine and Stackolee) who militantly refuses to heed the dictates of white society.[37]

This tradition resonated with Wright's experiences with several black men who also inspired his fictional character. He explains, "The Bigger Thomases were the only Negroes I know of who consistently violated the Jim Crow laws of the South and got away with it, at least for a sweet brief spell."[38] Far from reacting impulsively to the violence of the white South, the Bigger Thomas "type" adopts a "consistent" stance. He adopts what Ellison calls "a criminal attitude."[39] One "Bigger" Wright had met refused to "live without the necessities of life." He bought on credit and never paid bills, because only a "fool" would submit to a world in which "white folks had everything and he had nothing." Another "Bigger" "laughed and cursed and broke" the laws of the Jim Crow South, even though he knew that one day he would be killed for his freedom.[40] According to Wright, the "Biggers" he knew were acutely aware of both the "call of the dominant civilization whose glitter" taunted them, and the meaninglessness of the social death to which they were relegated. "The civilization which had given birth to Bigger," he elaborates, had thus "created no culture which could hold and claim his allegiance and faith, had sensitized him and left him stranded." For this reason, "Bigger Thomas . . . will not become an ardent, or even a lukewarm, supporter of the status quo."[41]

The Bigger Thomas "type" not only rejects white society. He refuses to recognize it. This is a particularly dangerous form of refusal. As the protagonist in *Black Boy* points out, whites would be far more terrified if they confronted "Negroes who made no claims at all than by those who are buoyed by social aggressiveness."[42] According to Wright, because black people have always lived in but are not of the United States, "the very tissue of their consciousness received its tone and timbre from the strivings of that dominant civilization" that disavows them.[43] Bodily and affective nonrecognition therefore evince indifference to white, capitalist ideals that demand allegiance from the oppressed. Like Nietzsche's Zarathustra, who refuses to give any energy to what he hates, Wright argues for a type of refusal that, rather than fueling *ressentiment*, might lessen black Americans' attunement to the glittering lure of the "prizes that the nation holds forth."[44]

Published five years after *Native Son*, *Black Boy* wrestles with the tensions between the arts of refusal and more generative practices that might create "new meanings" and "new way[s] to live."[45] In Ellison's words, the book's drama "lies in its depiction of what occurs when Negro sensibility attempts to fulfill itself in the undemocratic South."[46] Richard—the book's narrator and protagonist, and a stand-in for Bigger—asks how can one "live in a world in which one's mind and perceptions meant nothing and authority and tradition meant everything?"[47] Estranged from a family and community that respond to one despotic authority (white supremacy) by submitting to other dictators (religion and fear), Richard repeatedly acts out and resists punishment, often violently. Regardless if dealing with white society or black community, the protagonist "could not make subservience an automatic part of [his] behavior."[48] He distances himself from black acquaintances who honed routines of subservience: "I never criticized or praised them, yet felt in my neutrality a deeper rejection of them than if I had cursed them."[49] He also finds himself less and less "bound by the laws" of white society. "I was outside those laws," he declares, "the white people had told me so."[50] The "real" Richard Wright of course appreciated the vitality (the "hunger for life") in black culture. He also was ambivalent toward US law—which he abandoned through exile, yet engaged through decades of advocacy against prison and the death penalty. Still, the book conveys Wright's belief that rejecting and withholding recognition from white, capitalist society is "the first step" toward "embracing a creative attitude toward life." By lessening his sensuous attunement to the lure of white capitalist society, the protagonist of *Black Boy* sustained his tenuous desire for "the world to be different."[51]

The young Richard nourishes this desire "for a new way to live"[52] with the generative practices of reading and writing and, ultimately, with dreams of collective refusal and revolution. At a Depression-era relief station in Chicago, Wright observes black men and women who, until then, were strangers to each other "mumbling quietly among themselves" and "exchanging experiences." Across the country, poor and working-class black people previously had "lived as individuals . . . each staunch in that degree of Americanism that had been allowed him." As they began to learn "the sentiments of their neighbors for the first time" and "sense the collectivity of their lives," they recognized their lost faith in a society that "had betrayed them, had cast them out."[53] Through public confessions about their physical hunger, they came to realize that they had been hungering spiritually for the wrong things.

Although Wright interprets this scene at the relief station through the lens of the Communist philosophy that he had embraced in his twenties, he resists an easy leap to class-consciousness. He explains that "these people had not abandoned their past lives by choice," but "simply could not live the old way any longer." He contends that "in them . . . a revolution has taken place and is biding its time to translate itself into a new and strange way of life."[54]

For Wright, the bodily and affective development of revolutionary consciousness begins with the gut recognition by "millions of perplexed and defeated people" that they could no longer enroll in the lies of equal opportunity and social mobility in the United States.[55] He maintains that the gut-level disidentification with a white, capitalist US dream makes evident that a revolution has *already* taken place. Contrary to familiar readings of Wright, he insists that black people must cultivate attunements to "new and strange ways of life" if they are to translate so many moments of gut refusal into revolutionary action.

Wright, who believes in what Baldwin calls the "unspoken recognition of shared experience" in black culture, avers that black culture can enlarge the sensibilities and aspirations of poor and working-class black folks. *Black Boy*'s narrator laments the Communists' obtuse disregard for "the profundity latent in" black folk life and their inability to recognize its usefulness for mobilizing revolutionary consciousness.[56] In "Blueprint for Negro Writing," published several years earlier and reprinted in this volume, Wright similarly argues that black folk culture "creates emotional attitudes which are conducive to action." Black vernacular, folktales, work songs, blues, and so many "whispered words" between parents and children "embod[y] memories and hopes of [the] struggle for freedom." Amid the dislocation and destruction wrought by white supremacy and capitalism, black folk life sustains the "sense of a common life and a common fate . . . a recognition of a value in life as it is *lived*, a recognition that marks the emergence of a new culture in the shell of the old."[57]

In *12 Million Black Voices*, Wright depicts black folk life as a "fragile" yet "feverish" culture of survival carried on in the hidden spaces and hidden transcripts of the white United States. He presents black folk culture as evidence of life *lived* under conditions of physical and social death. A section of the book on life in the North, titled "Death on the City Pavements," contains a series of images of dilapidated housing, crowded kitchenettes, backbreaking labor, and police brutality. The section then switches to images of young bodies letting loose in the "pleasure" of song and dance, and describes the way blues, jazz, and swing partake in a tradition of black cultural forms that have regenerated the senses and nourished hunger for new ways of life. "With death ever hard at our heels," these "'spirituals' of the city pavements" keep alive "a sense of what our bodies want, a hint of our hope of a full life lived without fear . . . a cry of hunger for something new to fill our souls."[58]

Wright contends that the infrapolitical quality of black folk life has the potential to generate ways of life that are not only novel but also strange. "You usually take us for granted and think you know us," he says in a passage directed toward whites. "But our history is far stranger than you suspect, and we are not what we seem." He unsettles his readers with a threat—or a promise—that black life defies the terms of social categorization common in the white United States. In Wright's view, most black Americans, beneath their "outward guise," carry an "uneasily tied knot of pain and hope whose snarled strands converge from many points of time and space."[59] He demonstrates this by mixing accounts of social death with scenes of rebelliousness that are carried in the "embodied memories" of black folk culture: hunger strikes and suicide on slave ships; revolts on plantations; hidden transcripts "that enabled us to speak openly of revolt in the presence of our masters"; and boycotts, strikes, and squatting in southern fields and northern cities.[60]

These strange cultural practices not only lessen snarled attachments to the nation's false promises—embedded in the "words, laws, [and] legal claims" of white capitalist society—but also attune sense and affect toward new ways of life that are not yet legible and in no way certain. Wright insists at one point that black people "must accept the death of our old folk lives" in order to "move into the sphere of conscious history" and must "cross class and racial lines" to become free.[61] This may be one of Wright's less-inspired appropriations of communist thought. However, he does not imply that people can or should replace folk culture with a disembodied form of class-consciousness. He believes, instead, that communist politics should cultivate sense and affect in ways that parallel his own world-building experiences with reading and writing. Communism should be a "way of living" that cultivates the "emotional capacities" and "passional nature" of black people by involving them in a "continuous current of shared thought and feeling circulating through the social system."[62] As Baker, turning Wright's logic on its head, notes: "communism fit Wright's fundamental cultural assumptions . . . born of a black communal or collectivist ethos," which saw group uplift as a condition of individual striving.[63]

At the end of *12 Million Black Voices*, Wright refers to black folk life as a "dark mirror" to the United States' past and its revolutionary future. Revealing the paradoxical underside of the nation's history, Wright prophesies, "If we black folk perish, America perishes." For him, black struggle and survival are central to the possibilities for freedom thus far unrealized in the United States. He declares that although black citizens want a "share in the upward march of American life," their share will not come on terms set—or recognized—by white capitalism: "We ask you to grant us nothing. We are winning our heritage."[64] (For different accounts of Wright's "dark mirror" and how subversive political collectivities are forged in and through black folk culture, see the essays by Perry S. Moskowitz and Lori J. Marso in this volume.)

12 Million Black Voices ultimately strikes an uncertain tone about the creative outcomes of a politics of refusal. Wright notes the "strange moods" of black youth and affirms their refusal to submit to conditions of social death: "Always our deepest love is toward those children of ours who turn their backs upon our way of life" because "those brave ones who struggle against death are the ones who bring new life into the world, even though they die to do so."[65] It is not certain, however, where their refusal of social death will lead. As Wright once said of Bigger's strange moods, "I felt . . . that he carried within him the potentialities of either Communism or Fascism."[66] The story of Bigger shows that those who refuse the status quo, who are "looking and feeling for a way out," are susceptible to other lies that "promise rashly to fill the void."[67] Even communism ultimately lost its luster for Wright. Unable to reconcile his membership in the Communist Party with his vocation as a writer seeking to connect black folk culture and communist philosophy, the protagonist of *Black Boy* admits that he "would never again make so total a commitment of faith." That semi-autobiographical book closes on a chastened note: to build a bridge between himself and the world, the protagonist passionately "hurl[s] words into the darkness and wait[s] for an echo" that may not come.[68]

Wright's disinclination to predict the creative outcomes of refusal leaves his work open not only to critique but also to inheritors, like Coates, who sever refusal from what Robin Kelley calls the "freedom dreams" of past and present collective black struggle.[69] Coates's position resembles that of contemporary Afro-pessimists, who believe slavery's heritage in the United States retains an "absoluteness of power."[70] Black liberation therefore requires, in the words of Frank Wilderson, "a politics of refusal and the refusal to affirm, a 'program of complete disorder.'"[71] Although Afro-pessimists share Wright's sensitivity about the ways white life is predicated on black social death, they insist on the immutable ontology of antiblack racism and lack Wright's appreciation for the paradoxical quality and existential openness of black life in the United States. This appreciation leads Wright to attempt, however uncertainly, to build bridges both with words (to audiences that include both white and nonwhite readers) and with actions (through communist organizing). For Wright, black liberation requires that one engage, in order to transform, the struggle over democracy.

Wright's acceptance of refusal's unpredictable outcomes is a testament to his own appreciation of the obstacles to freedom and world building during the afterlife of slavery. It is also a testament to his understanding of refusal's political quality. Rather than turn to refusal in order to celebrate or deny the agency of the oppressed, Wright depicts refusal as a nonsovereign act the ends of which are always uncertain. This is partly because white supremacy claims a monopoly on fantasies of sovereignty in the United States. Partly, however, it is because Wright locates refusal's political promise in its collective character—that is, in the necessity of forming difficult horizontal relationships with others who hope to build strange and new ways of life together.

The Politics of Refusal in Anticarceral Organizing

To evaluate the political promise of refusal, I turn briefly to recent movements against the carceral state, which connect collective refusal to experiments informed by antiracist social visions. The term "carceral state" refers to the ever-evolving networks of laws, institutions, and discourses that secure order by policing and caging threats to the nation and its citizens. A growing body of research shows that the carceral state, despite its foundations in seemingly race-neutral laws and institutions, functions as a system of racial control.[72] Like Wright, who published *Native Son* to expose the "horrors" of black life in the United States, today's movements against policing and prison refuse to ignore the violence against black bodies that remains the nation's heritage. For example, Claudia Rankine has called protests by the Movement for Black Lives acts of public mourning: activists "refuse to look away from the flesh of our domestic murders" and "insist that we look with [them] upon the dead."[73] They therefore seek to make impossible the repetition of today's lie that the United States, despite periodic white backlash, is becoming postracial. Refusing to relieve us from the responsibility for ending antiblack violence, activists insist, with Coates and Baldwin, that the nation's "innocence constitutes the crime."[74]

Today's anticarceral activists have also begun to adopt criminal attitudes toward the US racialized state and the distorted vision of democracy it serves and polices. Their approach calls to mind Wright's ongoing participation in struggles against an antiblack criminal justice system from the trial of the Scottsboro Boys in 1931 through the postwar death-penalty trials of the Martinsville Seven and Willie McGee. Wright, for example, exposed the shift to "authorized lynching" when he wrote about Willie McGee's trial (in his article reprinted in this volume), "Today, what used to happen outside the law now takes place within the law."[75] Similarly, today's activists insist that carceral institutions "are not broken; they are functioning precisely as designed."[76] Indeed, the architects of mass incarceration had by the 1980s and 1990s used racially coded discourse of "law and order" to justify militarized policing, draconian sentencing, and prison growth as measures to protect law-abiding citizens from the threat of "criminals" envisioned as primarily black and brown.[77]

Abolitionist groups, such as Critical Resistance and the Movement for Black Lives, therefore refuse to recognize laws and institutions that justify violence against black bodies. They will not negotiate with the very state responsible for creating "criminals." For example, they will not compromise with politicians and reformers on measures to build prisons and police forces; on projects that improve health care in prisons but also add prison beds; or on policies that not only educate police on racial profiling but also increase the number of police officers. They cooperate with lawmakers and criminal justice institutions only on reforms that "lead . . . toward the direction of abolitionism."[78] For example, when Critical Resistance Oakland joined a coalition with reform groups to end police use of gang injunctions in 2010, the group also called for "community self-determination" in the form of reallocating funds toward education, after-school programs, and counseling services, and they worked with community groups to build the

Fruitvale Community Garden. They envisioned these efforts as resources to reduce the community's reliance on policing.[79] In other words, anticarceral activists engaged in reform without making a virtue of reformism, which, as Angela Davis puts it, encourages "the stultifying idea that nothing lies beyond" policing and prisons.[80]

Anticarceral activists refuse to recognize any vision of democracy that rests on the bifurcation of "the citizen" and "the criminal" in order to "contain, control, and kill those people representing the greatest threats to [the] state['s] power."[81] Activists therefore publicly act in solidarity with "criminals." This is, in a sense, what Wright did when he chose to tell Bigger's story, despite the "mental censor" of white liberal respectability, which made other "educated black leaders . . . afraid to make known to the nation how *we* exist."[82] Likewise, anticarceral activists, such as Michelle Alexander, argue today that "advocating on behalf of criminals" is necessary to transform the criminal justice system, even if this move risks alienating mainstream allies.[83]

Acting in solidarity with criminals, anticarceral activists eschew recognition of the state in favor of experiments with alternative social and political visions that emerge from the infrapolitical spaces of black life. This work is perhaps most remarkable among those women and queer and transgender people of color who try to resolve gendered violence in their communities without policing or incarceration: for example, by experimenting with difficult practices of community accountability and transformative justice that offer alternatives to carceral institutions.[84] Alexis Pauline Gumbs explains that these practices are rooted in the refusal to "criminalize each other for harmful actions that are already rooted in wider structures of harm." Gumbs employs the African concept *ubuntu*, which means "I am because we are," to elaborate alternative visions of accountability and justice that are rooted in the recognition that "we are all necessary to each other and we are all involved in each other's actions for better and also for worse."[85] Replacing the dire uncertainty of black life in a white democracy with a radical uncertainty of horizontal relationships, anticarceral activists welcome new and strange ways of life.

Notes

I am grateful to Nick Bromell, Melvin Rogers, George Shulman, and the editors for their comments on earlier drafts of this essay.

Epigraph 1: Qtd. in Alexandra Alter, "Ta-Nehisi Coates Wins National Book Award," *New York Times,* November 18, 2015, www.nytimes.com/2015/11/19/us/ta-nehisi-coates-wins-national-book-award.html?_r=0.

Epigraph 2: Richard Wright, *Black Boy (American Hunger): A Record of Childhood and Youth* (New York: Harper Perennial, 2006), 301–2.

1. Ta-Nehisi Coates, *Between the World and Me* (New York: Spiegel and Grau, 2015), 103.

2. Richard Wright, "How 'Bigger' Was Born," in *Bigger Thomas,* ed. Harold Bloom (New York: Chelsea House, 1990), 42.

3. Irving Howe, "Black Boys and Native Sons," in *Critical Essays on Richard Wright,* ed. Yoshinobu Hakutani (Boston: G. K. Hall, 1982), 41.

4. Coates, *World and Me,* 132.

5. James Baldwin, "Many Thousands Gone," in *The Price of the Ticket: Collected Nonfiction, 1948–1985* (New York: St. Martin's, 1985), 71.

6. Ibid., 72–73.

7. Ibid., 72.

8. See the exchange between Howe and Ellison in Howe, "Black Boys and Native Sons," and Ralph Ellison, "The World and the Jug," in *The Collected Essays of Ralph Ellison,* ed. John F. Callahan (New York: Modern Library, 2003); and Cyrus Ernesto Zirakzadeh's chapter exploring their debate in this volume. See also Eldridge Cleaver, *Soul on Ice* (New York: Dell, 1968), 103–7. For West's critiques of Wright and praise of Baldwin, see Cornel West, "Philosophy and the Afro-American Experience," *Philosophical Forum* 9, no. 2/3 (Winter–Spring 1977–78), 117–48; and "Black Strivings in a Twilight Civilization," in *The Cornel West Reader* (New York: Basic Civitas, 1999), 87–118. Richard Wright offers a more favorable view of his own "transformative nonconformism" in his introduction to *Black Power* (New York: Harper Perennial, 2008), vii–xiii.

9. I am indebted to George Shulman for his insights on the differences between today's "Afro-pessimists" (including Coates) and earlier black radicals, who held more nuanced critiques of white intractability that enabled them to affirm transformative visions.

10. Coates, *World and Me,* 97. In emphasizing Coates's account of personal struggle, I do not wish to overlook his appreciation for the possibilities of world building and self-making within black communities such as Howard University. For relevant critiques of Coates, see Michelle Alexander, "Ta-Nehisi Coates's *Between the World and Me,*" *New York Times,* August 17, 2015; Melvin Rogers, "Between Pain and Despair: What Ta-Nehisi Coates Is Missing," *Dissent,* July 31, 2015; and Cornel West, "In Defense of James Baldwin," Facebook post, July 16, 2015.

11. Wright, *Black Boy,* 302.

12. Audra Simpson also revives this older meaning of refusal in *Mohawk Interruptus: Political Life across the Borders of Settler States* (Durham, NC: Duke University Press, 2014). She focuses on strategies of refusal made possible by membership in a sovereign nation that predated Canada (and the United States). I am interested in refusal among those who lack the political means to make similar claims.

13. Drawing on *Moby Dick*'s Ishmael and Strike Debt's Rolling Jubilee, Bonnie Honig argues for forms of refusal that link "unplugging from the system" to efforts to "plug *in* to something else" (see Honig, "Charged: Debt, Power, and the Politics of the Flesh," in Eric L. Santer, *The Weight of All Flesh*, ed. Kevis Goodman [New York: Oxford University Press, 2016], 131–82).

14. Cornelius Castoriadis, *World in Fragments: Writings on Politics, Society, Psychoanalysis, and the Imagination*, ed. and trans. David Ames Curtis (Stanford: Stanford University Press, 1997), 268–69. See also Robin Kelley, *Freedom Dreams: The Black Radical Imagination* (Boston: Beacon, 2002), 9.

15. Houston Baker, for example, reads *Native Son* alongside *12 Million Black Voices* in "On Knowing Our Place," in *Richard Wright: Critical Perspectives Past and Present*, ed. Henry Louis Gates Jr. and K. A. Appiah (New York: Amistad, 1993). Edward Margolies treats *12 Million Black Voices* as an anticipation of *Black Boy* in *The Art of Richard Wright* (Chicago: Southern Illinois University Press, 1969). Robert Stepto views *Black Boy* as an "authentication" of *Native Son* in "Literacy and Ascent: Black Boy," in *Richard Wright: Critical Perspectives*, 226–54.

16. Keneth Kinnamon and Michel Fabre, eds., *Conversations with Richard Wright* (Jackson: University of Mississippi Press, 1993), 30; Wright, "How 'Bigger' Was Born," 24–25.

17. Ralph Ellison, "Richard Wright's Blues," in *Richard Wright's "Black Boy" ("American Hunger"): A Casebook*, ed. William Andrews and Douglas Taylor (Oxford: Oxford University Press, 2003), 46–47.

18. Baker, "On Knowing Our Place," 202; David Bradley, introduction to Richard Wright, *12 Million Black Voices* (New York: Basic, 1949), xix.

19. See Orlando Patterson, *Slavery and Social Death: A Comparative Study* (Cambridge: Harvard University Press, 1985); Saidiya Hartman, *Scenes of Subjection: Terror, Slavery, and Self-Making in Nineteenth-Century America* (New York: Oxford University Press, 1994); Frank Wilderson III, *Red, White, and Black: Cinema and the Structure of U.S. Antagonisms* (Durham, NC: Duke University Press, 2010); and Jared Sexton, "People of Color-Blindness: Notes on the Afterlife of Slavery," *Social Text* 28, no. 2 (2010): 31–56.

20. Wright, *12 Million Black Voices*, 15, 36, 46, 108–11, 123.

21. Wright, *Black Boy*, 37.

22. Ibid.; Ellison, "Richard Wright's Blues," 59.

23. Kinnamon and Fabre, *Conversations*, 45.

24. Wright, *Black Boy*, 265.

25. Ibid., 384.

26. Nicholas De Genova, "Gangsta Rap and Nihilism in Black America: Some Questions of Life and Death," *Social Text* 43 (Autumn 1995): 91.

27. Wright, *Black Boy*, 196, 266.

28. Wright, *12 Million Black Voices*, 57.

29. Wright, *Native Son* (New York: Harper Perennial Modern Classics, 2005), 429.

30. Frantz Fanon, *Wretched of the Earth*, trans. Constance Farrington (New York: Grove, 1963), 43, 56–59, 81. See also Lewis R. Gordon, *What Fanon Said: A Philosophical Introduction to His Life and Thought* (New York: Fordham University Press, 2015), 114–18.

31. Wright, "How 'Bigger' Was Born," 33.

32. *Black Boy*, 297, 384.

33. Wright, "Blueprint for Negro Writing" (1948), in this volume, 222; Wright, *Black Boy*, 249, 252.

34. Kinnamon and Fabre, *Conversations*, 15. I am indebted to Nick Bromell for encouraging me to crystalize this point.

35. Ibid., 100.

36. Wright, "How 'Bigger' Was Born," 37.

37. Baker, "Racial Wisdom and Richard Wright's *Native Son*," in *Critical Essays on Richard Wright*, 69, 74–77. Baker argues that Wright's depictions of black culture in *Native Son* and *Black Boy* are "simply too narrow" to do justice to the "activist strategies" he borrows from national and diasporic black folk traditions.

38. Wright, "How 'Bigger' Was Born," 26.

39. Ellison, "Richard Wright's Blues," 51.

40. Wright, "How 'Bigger' Was Born," 24–25.

41. Ibid., 27, 32.

42. Wright, *Black Boy*, 301–2.

43. Wright, "How 'Bigger' Was Born," 27.

44. Wright, *Black Boy*, 301–2; Friedrich Nietzsche, *Thus Spoke Zarathustra: A Book for None and All*, trans. Walter Kaufmann (New York: Penguin, 1978), 26–27. I am indebted to George Shulman for pointing out this connection.

45. Wright, *Black Boy*, 100, 383.

46. Ellison, "Richard Wright's Blues," 49.

47. Wright, *Black Boy*, 164.

48. Ibid., 196.

49. Ibid., 280.

50. Ibid., 201.

51. Ibid., 297.
52. Ibid., 383.
53. Ibid., 300–301.
54. Ibid., 301.
55. Ibid.
56. Ibid., 335.
57. Wright, "Blueprint for Negro Writing," 216.
58. Wright, *12 Million Black Voices*, 126–30.
59. Ibid., 10. On "infrapolitics" and "hidden transcripts," see James Scott, *Domination and the Arts of Resistance: Hidden Transcripts* (New Haven: Yale University Press, 1992).
60. Wright, *12 Million Black Voices*, 15, 17, 25–26, 40, 87, 144.
61. Ibid., 144, 146.
62. Wright, *Black Boy*, 318, 372.
63. Baker, "Racial Wisdom," 68. See also Wright, *12 Million Black Voices*, 60.
64. Wright, *12 Million Black Voices*, 146–47.
65. Ibid., 136.
66. Wright, "How 'Bigger' Was Born," 32.
67. Ibid., 32.
68. Wright, *Black Boy*, 384.
69. See Kelley, *Freedom Dreams*.
70. Jared Sexton, "The Social Life of Social Death: On Afro-Pessimism and Black Optimism," *In*Tensions 5 (Fall/Winter 2011): 23, 33.
71. Frank Wilderson, "The Prison Slave as Hegemony's (Silent) Scandal," *Social Justice* 30, no. 2 (2003): 26.
72. See, for example, Naomi Murakawa, *The First Civil Right: How Liberals Built Prison America* (New York: Oxford University Press, 2014); Vesla Weaver, "Frontlash: Race and the Development of Punitive Crime Policy," *Studies in American Political Development* 21, no. 2 (Fall 2007); and Michelle Alexander, *The New Jim Crow: Mass Incarceration in the Age of Colorblindness* (New York: New Press, 2012).
73. Claudia Rankine, "The Condition of Black Life Is One of Mourning," *New York Times*, June 22, 2015.
74. On the geography of prisons and the "disposability" of black lives, see Angela Davis, *Are Prisons Obsolete?* (New York: Seven Stories, 2003), 15–16. On racial innocence, see Coates, *World and Me*, 8–9; and Baldwin, *The Fire Next Time* (New York: Vintage International, 1993), 6.
75. Wright, "Behind the McGee Case," originally published in *Le Droit de Vivre*, May 15, 1951, and reprinted in full in this book. Thanks to Tommy J. Curry, who discusses Wright's involvement in the McGee case in his chapter in this vol-

ume, for bringing this case to my attention. See also Philip Dray, *At the Hands of Persons Unknown: The Lynching of Black America* (New York: Modern Library, 2002), 394–405.

76. Erica Meiners, "More than 'Education, Not Incarceration,'" *Abolitionist: A Publication of Critical Resistance* 16 (Spring 2012), 4.

77. See Murakawa, *First Civil Right*; and Weaver, "Frontlash."

78. Critical Resistance, *A World Without Walls: The CR Abolition Organizing Toolkit* (Oakland: Critical Resistance, 2004), 48.

79. See Critical Resistance Oakland, http://criticalresistance.org/chapters/cr-oakland/our-work/; and Stop the Gang Injunctions in Oakland, https://stoptheinjunction.wordpress.com/about/.

80. Angela Davis, *Are Prisons Obsolete?* (New York: Seven Stories, 2003), 20.

81. See Critical Resistance, http://criticalresistance.org/about/.

82. Wright, *12 Million Black Voices*, 136.

83. Alexander, *The New Jim Crow*, 214–17.

84. See, for example, the work of Incite!, www.incite-national.org/; and Project NIA, http://www.project-nia.org/.

85. Alexis Pauline Gumbs, "Freedom Seeds: Growing Abolition in Durham, North Carolina," in *Abolition Now! Ten Years of Strategy and Struggle against the Prison Industrial Complex* (Oakland: CR10 Publications Collective, 2008), 152.

Slavery Continued, Freedom Sought

Wright's Political Intellectual Journey

Jane Anna Gordon

Richard Wright described consideration of how he and others like him could live freely as *"the question of his life."*[1] Part of the second generation to be born "in freedom," when Wright was a child, his parents were "eking out an existence as sharecroppers on land not far from where their parents had involuntarily labored."[2] Facing poverty, segregation, and political disenfranchisement, "just putting together the economic rudiments of survival" was a feat.[3] When economic survival proved elusive, Wright and his brother were briefly institutionalized. There they "spent their time tormented by hunger, working at mindless tasks like picking the grass lawn, which the orphanage could not afford to have mowed."[4] Home was not much better. A domineering grandmother tried to prevent Wright from the reading, writing, and thinking that "he instinctively knew could save him from the bleak circumstances of racism and poverty." His mother was too frail to intervene on his behalf. Instead, she would "beat him to make him conform so he could survive."[5] His Uncle Hoskins, who had the audacity to successfully run a saloon, was "shot by local [jealous] white men . . . [after ignoring their] repeated warnings to stop living so well."[6]

Wright brought an unflinching racial realism and brilliance to his unremitting exploration of freedom. He focused on three defining features of racialized enslavement that persisted in neoslave circumstances. His insights suggest that while nonblack descendants of slaves have become free of the histories of their ancestors, freedom from historical experiences of enslavement remains elusive for African-descended communities. For most black people, "postslavery" is therefore a protracted racialized neoslavery where there is widespread public embarrassment regarding slavery's continued grammar that is not matched by commitment to its actual eradication.

Slavery, Continued

While Wright repeatedly and insightfully stressed the economic legacies of racialized enslavement, he singled out three grammars of enslavement that fundamentally shaped the lives of black persons in the United States before and after abolition.

First, as documented in almost all narratives of racialized enslavement (from those of Ottobah Quobna Cugoano and Mary Prince to Frederick Douglass and Harriet Jacobs), was the complete absence of a relationship between that for which enslaved people were responsible and that for which they were punished. This was especially maddening for the slave and soul-eroding for planters. Under conditions of racialized enslavement, the slave's actual actions were unrelated to the culpability attributed to them. Frantz Fanon described the same phenomenon under colonial conditions: regardless of what one had or had not done, one was always presumed guilty. As the authors of slave narratives observed, this afforded considerable flexibility to those assigning blame: any misbehavior of a master or master's friend or kin could be pinned on a slave, who would then be punished. Many slaves described futile attempts to follow completely arbitrary "rules" that were in fact decrees: their content was constantly shifting while their source was always the whims of any present white person.[7] This produced a pervasive sense of unreality in which one's experience of innocence of wrongdoing was not what the larger white society would acknowledge as reality. At the same time as one knew that what was being treated as true was false, one's survival depended on adhering to "the baroque machinations of an alternate, always changing set of rules."[8]

Second, Wright described a legacy of American enslavement as one of "two races locked in daily combat."⁹ Historically, enslavement grows with expansionary, protracted warfare in which the labor and ransom of the vanquished offset the costs of battle. Indeed, enslavement often was rationalized as an act of mercy, given that the vanquished could simply have been killed. In ancient Athens, *choosing* servitude was seen as indubitable evidence of cowardliness, making the status of a slave deserved. In *The Spirit of the Laws*, Baron de Montesquieu rejected this logic, reminding readers that military triumph did not entitle the victors to the gratuitous taking of lives. Jean-Jacques Rousseau advanced this argument in *On the Social Contract* when he defined enslavement as a protracted state of war. When analyzing racial slavery in the Caribbean, Gordon Lewis demonstrated that it relied on terror or plantation despotism. In a situation in which the enslaved had every reason to despise their masters, threats and actual extreme violence were not the psychological excesses of individual, sadistic masters but indispensable in making the system operate.[10] Wright offers a more recent US example: "To quench all desire for mutiny in us, they would sometimes decapitate a few of us and impale our heads upon the tips of the spars, just as years later they impaled our black heads upon the tips of pine trees for miles along the dusty highways of Dixie to frighten us into obedience."[11]

Third, black people were treated as if they had no kin. While a master or other members of the master's society might acknowledge that a slave had a spouse or child or elderly relative or cousin, the corresponding recognition of wanting to treat such people as priorities and the conditions for doing so were consistently absent.[12] This also had historical precedent. As Moses Finley writes, the "slave was always a deracinated outsider—an outsider first in the sense that he originated from outside the society into which he was introduced as a slave, second in the sense that he was denied the most elementary of social bonds, kinship."[13] Although, typically outside of plantations and mines, such acquired outsiders were assimilated in varying degrees to the culture of their owners' society, David Brion Davis affirms James Vaughan's description of bondage as the "institutionalization of marginality."[14]

Since, for Wright, these three features of slavery continued in neoslavery and postslavery, some explanation of each of these terms is required.

The notion of "continued slavery" refers to instances when practices before and after the abolition of racialized enslavement were literally unchanged. "Post-Emancipation" enslavement persisted in Alabama, Arizona,

Arkansas, Florida, Georgia, Illinois, Kentucky, Louisiana, Mississippi, Missouri, New York, North Carolina, South Carolina, Tennessee, Texas, and Virginia.[15] People remained on plantations, doing unpaid labor against their will, unaware that the arrangement was no longer legal. For them, without transportation and threatened about what would be done to them should they run away, it was as if 1863 never occurred.

Cases of *neoslavery,* in which plantation racial grammars continue but under changed conditions, are far more ubiquitous. For instance, in *Slavery by Another Name,* historian and journalist Douglas Blackmon considers the eighty years following the Emancipation Proclamation to be an "Age of Neoslavery," in which the outlawed institution continued with the "permission of the nation." For many prison abolitionist scholars, among them Dennis R. Childs, the mass incarceration of black people today marks an evolution from people being slaves of individual masters without government intervention to becoming literal slaves of the state.[16]

In so doing, these scholars build on the earlier work of George L. Jackson, who argued in *Soledad Brother* that while chattel slavery involved the "total loss or absence of self-determination," under neoslavery, "chattel slavery [is] updated to disguise itself."[17] Due to our dependence on earning wages, without which we would be exposed "to the elements," we rely on those who can give or withhold employment and who, in determining its character, determine how we spend the majority of our time. If there is any mystery as to whether or not we are neoslaves, Jackson suggests subtracting the cost of one's transportation and meals and shelter from one's earnings. If one cannot afford to travel or relocate when one feels so moved, *one is a neoslave.* Jackson elaborates, "If you're held in one spot on this earth because of your economic status, it is just the same as being held in one spot because you are the owner's property." This economic condition arises whenever a small group of men, exercising their property rights, organize and control the lives of others as if they were inert property. In the case of black neoslaves, who are not only Karl Marx's classic wage slaves, police can beat, maim, and kill them with impunity.

Finally, the term "neoslave" designates a genre of Africana creative writing that Ashraf H. A. Rushdy describes as using contemporary literary techniques to consider the presence of the past in the present.[18]

Scholars rarely use the term "postslavery." When they do, it is simply synonymous for the period following legal abolition (as in Trevor Bernard's

2016 work *Ties That Bind: The Black Family in Post-Slavery Jamaica, 1834–1882*). Elsewhere, as in the explanation of the subtitle of the journal *Slavery & Abolition: A Journal of Slave and Post-Slave Studies*, "postslavery" refers to an object of study: "concerned with the dismantling of the slave systems and with the legacy of slavery."[19]

Drawing on Wright, I will show that while in many human communities life after the abolishment of slavery converges with freedom from its legacies, racialized enslavement casts a long shadow, indeed. As a result, most black people (both those who are and are not descendants of enslaved people) experience a condition that resembles what Achille Mbembe describes as the "postcolony."[20] The term refers not to an ending of colonial conditions but to moral embarrassment over practices that in fact continue and are therefore disavowed as elements of the present. Put slightly differently, there is no postslavery for most black people in places that practiced enslavement. Instead their condition is one of protracted racialized neoslavery in which legacies of racial slavery continue but without a public acceptance of this fact. As a result, we see the three grammars that Wright emphasized alongside a refusal to acknowledge their origins or the meaning of their persistence.

Neoslavery

Wright's early essay "The Ethics of Living Jim Crow" is a guide to a world where legal enslavement is no longer formally permitted, but most of its norms continue. Key among them is the perverse relationship between the actions of a black person and the culpability ascribed to them, usually with social and often legal backing.

The essay begins with a striking example: Wright and his black childhood friends would play-fight, pelleting each other with black cinder that surrounded Wright's home. Wright never realized its disadvantages until his friends and he entered a "war" with the white boys from the other side of the town's tracks. As they "laid down [their] cinder barrage," the white boys responded with broken bottles. Worse still, while the white boys had trees behind which they could hide as well as the embankments of their yards, the black boys had only their homes' brick pillars. When Wright was hit and a gash opened behind his ear, his friends left him while a neighbor took him to the doctor. When he was back at his house, waiting for his mother to return from the white home where she worked, he hoped she would comfort him and tell him how to do better next time. Instead, *she* became furious and quickly blamed him. Rather than expressing indignation at the white boys who had hurt her son by dangerously throwing broken glass, she asked why Wright hadn't hid and why he'd fought at all. To drive the point home she then stripped him naked and beat him, "imparting to [him] the gems of Jim Crow wisdom": "I was never, never under any conditions, to fight *white* folks again. And they were absolutely right in clouting me with the broken milk bottle. . . . She finished by telling me that I ought to be thankful to God as long as I lived that they didn't kill me."[21] The suggestion, of course, was that they would not have been deemed criminal if they had. *Even in death, the fault would have been Wright's.*

In a second "lesson," when hired for an optical company, Wright was asked by his boss about whether he would like to learn the skills of this trade. A month in, Wright asked two nonblack coworkers with whom he got along well about this offer. One grew red and asked if Wright was trying to get smart. When he asked the other, the man replied, "Nigger, you think you're *white,* don't you?" From then on, all friendliness disappeared and the two coworkers sought evidence of Wright's failings. This culminated in a showdown: they charged him with neglecting to call them *Mr.* If he insisted that this was not so, they charged him with calling them liars. Wright concluded quickly that the only response was to concede: "I'll leave right *now.*"[22] When recounting this to black kin at home, rather than sharing his frustration, they called him the fool for attempting "to exceed [his] boundaries."[23] Pursuing a promised opportunity for self-development made *him* guilty. Any and every punishment that followed was merited.

Wright describes the ingenuity required to evade trouble in such circumstances. "Salvaging a shred of personal pride," he tried to avoid degrading norms without appearing to reject them outright.[24] This required feigning mistakes and inabilities, as when Wright pretended to drop a pile of packages so as not to have to say, "Thank you, sir," to a man who removed Wright's hat for him in an elevator when his arms were too full of packages to do so himself. After describing concessions of his friends and families to these "rules," Wright closes the essay by asking how black people discussed these conditions among themselves: "I think this question can be answered in a single sentence. A friend of mine who ran an elevator once told me: 'Lawd, man! Ef it wuzn't fer them polices 'n' them ol' lynch-mobs, there wouldn't be nothin' but uproar down here!'"[25] Wright elaborates in *12 Million Black Voices* that any outright black protest was met by "poor whites ... eager to form mobs."[26] Hysterical, the mobs would seize any black person, "it does not matter who, the innocent or guilty—and, as a token, a baked and bleeding body will be dragged ... throughout the quarters where we black folk live."[27] Sheer terror produced a seeming stasis in what would otherwise have been ongoing race war. Wright described it thus in 1941:

> Two streams of life flow through the South, a black stream and a white stream, and from day to day we live in the atmosphere of a war that never ends. Even when the sprawling fields are drenched in peaceful sunshine, it is war. When we are awake, it is war. When one of us is born, he enters one of the warring regiments of the South. When there are days of peace, it is a peace born of a victory over us; and when there is open violence, it is when we are trying to push back the encroachments of the Lords of the Land.[28]

When commenting on the case of Willie McGee (explored in Tommy J. Curry's chapter in this volume), Wright emphasized that the trial took place in Mississippi, "whose health, educational, cultural, and social standards are lower perhaps than could be found in any part of Europe today."[29] Because no industrialization had taken place since the Civil War, there was nothing "to relieve the sharp master-slave relations, and the domination of whites over blacks [was] complete and unmitigated."[30] Given that blacks outnumbered whites in the state, race relations were "at a pitch just short of daily violence."[31] The whites for the moment held control over the police, the state national guard, the press, radio, church, banking, farming, industry, and the educational system, "allow[ing] expression to *whites only*."[32] Since blacks did not agree to such terms, "a kind of daily race war rages on all levels of life among people who live *side by side as neighbors*."[33] How was stability secured, given that black women labored in white homes while black men worked in white-controlled farms? Wright's answer: "This control is maintained only at a cost of nightmarish tension which suffuses the whole of daily life in Mississippi," through rigid race laws that determine the movement, habitation, and social and economic lives of black people. But these alone did not suffice. Echoing an observation from W. E. B. Du Bois's 1903 classic *The Souls of Black Folk*, Wright wrote, "It is necessary for each individual white man in the community to take it upon himself to act the role of the racial policeman," meeting with violent reprisal any "infraction."[34] When this proved limited and "the Negro population became what the whites called 'intractable,'" public lynchings and other dramatic acts of domestic terror offered reinforcement.

The sense of ubiquitous, unmerited guilt in a context of simmering racial war was exacerbated by feelings of impotence because of an inability to protect others. Wright recounts walking home from the hotel where he worked as a young man with one of the Negro maids who lived nearby. When a white night watchman slapped her butt, Wright turned around amazed. The night watchman responded by pulling out his gun and asking Wright if he had liked what he had seen. When asked a second time, Wright mumbled, "Yes, sir." The watchman asked for a more enthusiastic reply. Ashamed and unable to look at the woman as they walked on, she reassured him: "'Don't be a fool! Yuh couldn't help it!' This watchman boasted of having killed two Negroes in self-defense."[35]

In another instance, Wright reflects on a black woman who was dragged from a car and into a store where Wright worked. Meanwhile, a policeman "twirled his nightstick" out front. After hearing her yells from inside, Wright saw her come out bleeding and holding her stomach. The policeman responded by accusing her of being drunk. When Wright went to the back of the store and saw that the floor was bloody, the boss slapped Wright on the back and explained that this was what they did when "niggers [didn't] want to pay their bills." The son of the boss offered Wright a cigarette and lit a match. Wright observes: "This was a gesture of kindness indicating that even if they had beaten the poor woman, they would not beat me if I knew enough to keep my mouth shut."[36]

Postslave Circumstances

Wright suggested that, after World War II, even Mississippi had been dragged into the twentieth century. The state realized that it was politically costly to continue its lawless buttressing of white supremacy through antiblack racist violence. As a result, "what used to happen *outside of the law* now [took] place with the *sanction of the law*."[37] This evolution from "lawless to legal lynching" was "a moral step forward" since it placed "the actions of Mississippi [and all other US] whites squarely and responsibly before the bar of world opinion."[38] Still, the three core features of slavery and neoslavery that we have examined continued in northern black "postslave" life.

Consider Wright's discussion of housing, in which he describes the anger of even young white boys, who had been "taught—at home and at school—that we black folk are making their parents lose their homes and life's savings because we have moved into their neighborhoods."[39] Warned that they must move as soon as a black person rents a nearby apartment, white renters would hastily abandon their homes. Meanwhile, the property owners "take these old houses and convert them into 'kitchenettes,' and then rent them to us at rates so high that they make fabulous fortunes." Dividing seven-room apartments into seven small apartments, each with a small gas stove and small sink, "the same apartment for which white people—who can get jobs anywhere and who receive higher wages than we—pay $50 a month is rented to us for $42 a week. . . . and [we] are glad to get them."[40] The landlords, who profit from their manipulations of false alarms, create the effects of which they caution. They effectively frame black people with limited options as the "fall guys," building on a readiness of the white public to blame black people for the supposed costs of their mere presence.

The same applied to the purchasing of homes, an experience that Wright knew intimately. The black people who saved wages to make down payments encountered white homeowners who refused to sell and saw their rejection as an act of racial and economic solidarity against "any extension of the Black Belt." Whenever "some shrewd white man, eager for a high profit, decides to sell his home to a black buyer," this black "invasion" is met with violence and flight. Street by street, the white population "falls back . . . leaving its homes empty." Wright notes: "Sometimes the members of a white family will board up their old homestead and move away, but not before they have cautioned their real-estate broker that no black folks should be allowed to . . . dwell within the walls of rooms made sacred to them through long years of intimate living." Real estate brokers are not so romantic. They purchase empty and devalued homes and, claiming to honor previous owners' wishes, immediately "hang up placards, saying: NOW OPEN TO COLORED TENANTS." This development delights black people, who are suddenly able to "find living space, [who therefore] rush to sign leases at exorbitant rentals."[41] Facing frequent housing restrictions, they willingly pay much more for "homes than whites for those of similar value."[42] But again, black people are framed as culpable for producing white economic losses, when, in fact, it is discrimination against them that enables real estate brokers to prey simultaneously on white fear and black desperation.

The same logic followed with paid work. Wright explains that blacks entered industry mainly through two routes: "(1) strike-breaking and (2) when factories and mills expand so rapidly that not enough white workers can be found to work in them." Because the most powerful trade unions barred black membership, when white workers would strike, employers would "send labor agents into the South to fetch us north." While hungry and eager to work, these black men did not want to take the jobs of other men. They did not want to be scabs "snatch[ing] food from the tables of poor white children, for we, of all people, really know how hungry children can be." Nonetheless, white workers were "emphatic in drawing the color line against us." There were no options. "So, trembling and scared," Wright explains, "we take spikes, knives, guns, and break the picket lines. . . . [and] when the work day is over, we find ourselves fighting mobs of white workers in the city streets." Although their refusal to tolerate black membership made them vulnerable to such strategies, most white workers simply hated and accused black people of undercutting their labor power.[43]

While blacks were grateful to be in northern cities, Wright describes their living conditions as places where "simple folk such as we should never be held captive."[44] Black people nonetheless faced a "war" of emotions. On the one hand, the anonymity of city life freed them of the requirement of ongoing public performances of subordination. On the other, the inflated costs of living could be insurmountable as "the city heaps too much responsibility upon us and gives too little security in return."[45] Wright likens the kitchenettes to prison, to a death sentence without trial, and to a "new form of mob violence that assaults not only the lone individual, but all of us, in its ceaseless attacks." Even in times of peace "some of the neighborhoods in which we live look as if they had been subjected to an intensive and prolonged aerial bombardment."[46] Wright writes: "We say, of the North as of the South, that life for us is daily warfare and that we live hard, like soldiers. We are set apart from the civilian population; our kitchenettes comprise our barracks; the color of our skins constitutes our uniforms; the streets of our cities are our trenches. . . . We are always in battle, but the tidings of victory are few."[47]

The unremitting war took a literal toll on black families. Wright reports that the mortality rates of black babies living in unsanitary tenants were so heightened that black people would have become extinct had it not been for constant replenishments from the rural South. "The kitchenette," he continues, "with its crowded rooms and incessant bedlam, provides an enticing place for . . . crimes against women and children . . . throw[ing] desperate and unhappy people into an unbearable closeness of association, thereby increasing latent friction, giving birth to never-ending quarrels of recrimination, accusation, and vindictiveness, producing warped personalities."[48] "The kitchenette injects pressure and tension into our individual personalities," Wright adds, "making many of us give up the struggle, walk off and leave wives, husbands, and even children behind."[49]

Perhaps hardest hit were black women, whose lives were "the most circumscribed and tragic . . . [b]ecause their orbit of life [was] narrow—from their kitchenette to white folk's kitchen and back home again." Anticipating much later work in intersectionality theory, Wright adds: "Surrounding our black women are many almost insuperable barriers: they are black, they are women, they are workers; they are triply anchored and restricted in their movements within and without the Black Belts."[50] "For every 5 white girls between the ages of ten and fifteen who must work, 25 of our black girls must work," he elaborates; "for every 5 white mothers who must leave their children unattended at home in order to work, 25 of our black mothers must leave their children unattended at home in order to work."[51]

The Relationship of Exile to *Fugitivity*

When reading of Wright's departure from the United States to Paris through the lens of protracted racialized neoslavery, one is tempted to draw on Juliet Hooker's (2015) account of Frederick Douglass's outline of a fugitive democratic ethos and to think of Wright as a twentieth-century maroon, fleeing the US plantation to seize whatever illicit liberty he could.[52] As Hooker explains, black fugitive thought embraces and extends Sheldon Wolin's (1994) notion of "fugitive democracy."[53] Wolin argues that democracy is not a form of government but appears episodically when ordinary citizens enact their political potential by identifying shared concerns and pursuing goals collectively and spontaneously. Such moments tended not to appear through institutionalized reform but in revolutionary transgressions that expanded the demos through trampling over existing barriers.[54]

Hooker explains that figures like Douglass developed this view. They suggested that it was liminal subjects and incomplete citizens who were likely, in pursuing their self-determination, to enliven the democratic character of their political "home." For example, in "What to the Slave Is the Fourth of July?" Douglass connects the refusal of tyranny of the Founding Fathers to his own contemporary abolitionist activities. He urges fellow and former slaves to read and interpret the US Constitution themselves, unmediated, through the lens of their own continued unfreedom. Douglass thus "connect[s] the law-breaking of fugitive slaves to the U.S. founding . . . suggest[ing] that [the readiness to reject the following of unjust law] should be seen as constitutive to the praxis of citizenship."[55] Recalling Douglass, Hooker contends that it is historical and contemporary groups "with precarious claims to citizenship" who exhibit "enhanced democratic subjectivities."[56] This would connect resistant slaves and neoslaves to protestors in Ferguson, Missouri, and today's Dreamers, who "enact exemplary democratic practices even as their . . . activism renders them vulnerable to increased state reprisal."[57]

Hooker specifies the key features of black fugitive thought as follows: "(1) taking seriously as political activities the survival strategies of fugitives: secrecy, concealment, flight, outlawry, etc.; (2) a concern with the creation of autonomous, and at times clandestine, spaces where black political agency can be collectively enacted, which is often coupled with a rejection of the strategy of seeking inclusion into existing racial states due to pessimism about their ability to be reorganized on bases other than white supremacy; (3) embracing the intellectual orientations arising from fugitivity, such as 'speaking out of turn' to reveal racial injustice, and imagining alternate racial orders, futures, and forms of subjectivity."[58]

Wright's observations would seem to affirm such an account: "I live in exile because I love freedom, and I've found more freedom in one square block of Paris than there is in the entire United States!" Clarifying that his aim was not to stir dissatisfaction among US blacks or to incite a mass exodus, he explains: "My decision stems from one simple, personal fact: I need freedom. Some people need more freedom than others, and I'm one of them." He then adds, "In short, to me, freedom is equated directly to reality, to life; it's not an abstract dream to be realized, an ideal to be worshipped from afar—but life itself, each moment."[59] In other words, Wright may be enacting the survival strategy of flight and refusing to seek inclusion in a racial state that is unlikely to disavow its white supremacy.

In addition, Wright made specific observations about the United States through his French experiences. For instance, he was struck that poor US citizens were made to feel culpable for their economic destitution. In their context "poverty is something somehow shameful, akin to criminality."[60] This was different from France, where, perhaps because of its feudal heritage, people could be unashamed and might even opt to live modestly. Wright then inverted the question of responsibility: In a world "where two billion-odd human creatures are sunk in an abject poverty from which there is, in the foreseeable future, no hope of redemption. . . . Is it not, perhaps, a crime, to make poor people feel that their poverty is criminal?"[61] These comments suggest that Wright was engaging in a third dimension of black fugitive thought. He was embracing an intellectual orientation rooted in fugitivity that enabled him to imagine alternative racial orders and future forms of subjectivity.

At the same time, as Jennifer Wallach observes, while Wright, like other black Americans living in Paris, sympathized with Algerian struggles for freedom, most did not dare to speak out in fear of being forced to leave. They took seriously *that they remained guests* of the French Republic and therefore could not express themselves in public with the unqualified candor of those who fully belonged or resided in their political homes. This especially concerned Wright, who did not want to return to the United States to raise his daughters amid the "hysterical political climate of McCarthyism," even if he voluntarily expressed to the US embassy concern about Communist influence at the 1956 International Conference of Negro Writers and Artists.[62]

Put differently, while Wright was able to live outside of protracted racialized neoslave conditions—or without racialized culpability, the protracted mundane war of race relations, and the way that both undercut the possibility of moving through the world in and with any relations—*he did so as a foreigner.* Although he would remain outside the United States for the rest of his life, his predicament had all the trappings of a temporary solution, suggesting, as Douglass had, that freedom could not be found in a condition of permanent flight. From this location, he did reconsider questions of democratic practice in expanded terms. For instance, if in his youth he had perceived the advocacy for black rights in absolute terms—if this "fight was not right, then nothing was right"—he described developing a "sneaking sense of futility because . . . there was something basically wrong in a nation that could so cynically violate its own Constitution and democratic pretensions by meting out physical and psychological cruelties upon a defenseless minority."[63] In France, Wright's indignation at the treatment of fellow descendants of racialized slaves turned to pity for a country that, in assaulting black people, was attacking her own ideals and herself. The United States was, he thought, a country where there was little relationship between what was said and what was done.

This taste of individual reprieve, if creating a break from mundane degradation and room for individual self-expression, should not be considered a manifestation of postslavery, however. That feat would be indicated by the absence of protracted racialized neoslave grammars in the lives of the black French. Put differently, Wright, the man and writer, could and did *steal himself away* from US unfreedom, but this fugitive status, for him, remained far short of a normative ideal of freedom. He refused to put up with the existing options in the United States and left its claustrophobic worldlessness for spaces of refuge with other black and white expatriate artists who sought in Paris an established locus for artistic creativity. But surely he would have preferred a set of conditions from which he did not again have to flee; a physical and territorial political home beyond that which he forged in and through the world of letters; standing in the United States, a country which, as Douglass argued, his ancestors had built and should have been able to claim as their own. I take this to be Wallach's meaning when she states that Wright probably never "solved the nagging question . . . of how best to live freely."[64]

The argument that the formal abolition of slavery fell far short of eradicating many features of slavery is not new. After all, in his magisterial 1935 *Black Reconstruction*, W. E. B. Du Bois outlined what a genuine abolitionist democracy would require.[65] Cindy Hahamovitch more recently has documented how varieties of peonage—whether sharecropping, indenture, or guest worker programs—were recognized by those who adopted them as labor regimes most closely resembling enslavement.[66]

This conclusion serves different aims each time it is reached. Du Bois emphasized that the hijacking and abandonment of the project of Reconstruction was a loss to the nation and to the world—not only to black people. Black Power activists have stressed continuities of legal racialized enslavement to draw attention to the limited gains wrought by the civil rights movement.[67]

Wright's work enables us to diagnose the exceptionality of the black postslave condition. US examples demonstrate that even if few human communities have been untouched by forced labor,[68] white descendants of slaves, while struggling with the insecurities of poverty, do not fundamentally lack standing in the nations that they made their new homes. Even with enslaved ancestors, freedom really means freedom. Nonblack descendants of enslaved ancestors live in genuinely postslave conditions in which their actions and their culpability are coherently related, in which the governments under which they live are not only punitive and hostile, and in which laws honor their familial relations and attendant obligations.

By contrast, Wright's diagnoses make sense of the spate of police killings of unarmed black men in 2015 and 2016. In these instances, it did not matter whether the person shot held a concealed or unconcealed weapon; whether he was making a purchase or walking; whether he was wearing particular clothing; whether he was seeking to evade law enforcement. In each instance, their actual actions were irrelevant because, as targets, they were perceived as belonging to a group with which armed, trained policemen were permanently at war. How else to explain the radically different rules that apply when law enforcement officers apprehend (even armed) white men? Lastly, when death was the outcome of police confrontation with black men, authorities did not treat the loss to black family members seriously and instead sought to find fault with *them*. Again, this differed from the respect shown by police to white kin.

Even if it betokens a condition of prolonged, compromised freedom, the appeal of fugitivity in such circumstances is completely understandable. Nonetheless, if Wright abandoned hopes for an actually democratic United States, he never diminished the value of political militancy for black people themselves. During World War II, he celebrated when black people, who had never accepted "external definitions of the reality of their lives," found it possible to act on the basis of perceptions of reality organically tied to their communities.[69] He championed the "seething unrest among Negroes, in the army, the navy, on jobs, in streetcars, in stores . . . [the new] willingness of the Negro to strike back when struck."[70]

Reminiscent of Hooker's vision of fugitive democracy discussed earlier, Wright credited Adolf Hitler with this growing black global consciousness. Because Hitler had compared his own extermination aims with the subjugation of black people in the United States, black people saw their own resistance as tied to that of others who, together with them, constituted a numerical majority. Poignantly, Wright argued that black people now saw their fate as uniquely tied to that of democracy at home and abroad.

However, crucially, their growing volatility and aggression were not stimulated by outside agents and would not be quelled by "throwing" black people "a few bones." Black people were "with complete justification, [taking] matters into their own hands" because they were human beings driven to act by their identification with the ideals of modern Western culture.[71] What they sought, as Wright, was to live as men and women in the only political home they had known.

Notes

1. Jennifer Jensen Wallach, *Richard Wright: From Black Boy to World Citizen* (Chicago: Ivan R. Dee, 2010), 138, my italics.
2. Ibid., 9.
3. Ibid., 13.
4. Ibid., 17.
5. Ibid., 19.
6. Ibid., 20–21.
7. For Prince, the Moravian Church offered a haven because it was a place of fair adjudication: one admitted what one had done to Christ, the ultimate assessor (see Prince, "The History of Mary Prince, a West Indian Slave [1831]," in *Six Women's Slave Narratives,* ed. William L. Andrews, 1–40 [New York: Oxford University Press, 1988]). This need of tyrants for the world to be unpredictable is on ample display in current US politics.
8. This wonderful phrase is Anna Mae Duane's, from feedback she offered on this essay.
9. See Richard Wright, "Behind the McGee Case," in this volume.
10. Gordon Lewis, "The Eighteenth and Nineteenth Centuries: The Proslavery Ideology," in *Caribbean Political Thought: The Colonial State to Caribbean Internationalisms,* ed. Aaron Kamugisha (Kingston: Ian Randle, 2013), 111–34.
11. Richard Wright, *12 Million Black Voices* (1941; New York: Basic, 2002), 15.
12. Consider accounts like that of Harriet Jacobs of being unable to attend her father's funeral that took place within walking distance. Her mistress demanded that she instead do trivial work (see Jacobs, *Incidents in the Life of a Slave Girl* [1861; Mineola, NY: Dover; 2001]).
13. Moses Finley, *Ancient Economy* (Berkeley: University of California Press, 1973), 143.

14. David Brion Davis, *Slavery and Human Progress* (New York: Oxford University Press, 1984), 14.

15. See Tobias "Profit" Smith and Timothy Smith's 2012 documentary *Cotton Pickin' Truth: Still on the Plantation.*

16. See Dennis R. Childs, *Slaves of the State: Black Incarceration from the Chain Gang to the Penitentiary* (Minneapolis: University of Minnesota Press, 2015). For rich discussion of this theme, see Laura Grattan's chapter in this volume.

17. For the complete volume, see http://historyisaweapon.com/defcon1/soledadbro.html.

18. Ashraf H. A. Rushdy, *Neo-Slave Narratives: Studies in the Social Logic of a Literary Form* (Oxford: Oxford University Press, 1999). For exploration of the range of literary techniques employed by Wright, see the chapter by William Dow in this volume.

19. For the scholarly aim and vision of the journal, see www.tandfonline.com/action/journalInformation?show=aimsScope&journalCode=fsla20.

20. Achille Mbembe, *On the Postcolony* (Berkeley: University of California Press, 2001).

21. Richard Wright, *Uncle Tom's Children* (1938; New York: Harper Perennial, 2003), 2–3.

22. Ibid., 7.

23. Ibid.

24. Ibid., 15.

25. Ibid.

26. *12 Million Black Voices*, 43.

27. Ibid.

28. Ibid, 46. Wright writes: "we are unable to establish our family groups upon a basis of property ownership. For the most part our delicate families are held together by love, sympathy, pity, and the goading knowledge that we must work together to make a crop. . . . And we reckon kin not as others do, but down to the ninth and tenth cousin. . . . Our scale of values differs from that of the world from which we have been excluded; our shame is not its shame, and our love is not its love" (ibid., 60–61).

29. Richard Wright, "Behind the McGee Case," in this volume, 156.

30. Ibid.

31. Ibid.

32. Ibid.

33. Ibid.

34. Ibid.

35. Wright, *Uncle Tom's Children*, 13.

36. Ibid., 9.

37. Wright, "Behind the McGee Case," 157.
38. Ibid.
39. Wright, *12 Million Black Voices*, 103.
40. Ibid., 104–5.
41. Ibid., 112.
42. Ibid., 115.
43. Ibid., 119.
44. Ibid., 105. For rich discussion of black movement from distinct rural to urban landscapes and the role of each in forms of emergent political consciousness, see James B. Haile III's chapter in this volume.
45. Wright, *12 Million Black Voices*, 105.
46. Ibid., 114.
47. Ibid., 123.
48. Ibid., 108.
49. Ibid., 109.
50. Ibid., 131.
51. Ibid., 135.
52. While Douglass is often employed today to think about the continued grammar of slavery after its abolition, he was averse to using "slavery" as metaphor and would likely be opposed to my designations of neoslavery and postslavery. Many scholars committed to conveying the historical specificity of transatlantic racialized enslavement share his position. I thank Nick Bromell for emphasizing this and related points regarding Douglass in his feedback on this essay.
53. Hooker, "'A Black Sister to Massachusetts': Latin America and the Fugitive Democratic Ethos of Frederick Douglass," *American Political Science Review* 109, no. 4 (November 2015).
54. Sheldon Wolin, "Fugitive Democracy" *Constellations* 1, no.1 (December 1994): 11–25.
55. Hooker, "Black Sister to Massachusetts," 692.
56. Ibid.
57. Ibid.
58. Ibid. To these, Neil Roberts adds attention to agency where it is supposedly impossible, as in the case of the slave, and to moving beyond static and dualistic conceptions of freedom and its opposite that tend to dominate discussions in Western political thought (see Roberts, *Freedom as Marronage* [Chicago: University of Chicago Press, 2015]).
59. Richard Wright, "I Choose Exile," Box 6, Folder 110, draft, typescript, corrected, n.d., Richard Wright Papers.
60. Ibid.
61. Ibid.

62. Wallach, *Richard Wright*, 161–62. Wallach writes: "Wright, of course, had to remain mute about his intervention when the conference finally opened and a letter was read from the venerable W. E. B. Du Bois who, though invited, was unable to attend because he had been denied a passport. Wright resented Du Bois's claim that the only Americans who were allowed to travel abroad were those who were willing to censor themselves in accordance with government demands" (ibid., 165–66).

63. Wright, "I Choose Exile."

64. Wallach, *Richard Wright*, 179.

65. W. E. B. DuBois, *Black Reconstruction in America, 1860–1880* (1935; New York: Free Press, 1992).

66. Cindy Hahamovitch, *No Man's Land: Jamaican Guestworkers in America and the Global History of Deportable Labor* (Princeton, NJ: Princeton University Press, 2013).

67. The most recent version of this argument is the critical response to claims about Barack Obama's presidency marking a definitive end to structural commitments to antiblack racism and racial inequality in works like Michelle Alexander's *The New Jim Crow* and other critics of mass incarceration, including anarchist ones who reject the many varieties of liberal reformism. In literary theoretical circles, Afro-pessimists have also vociferously articulated the continued afterlife of slavery (see, for instance, Yumi Pak, "Outside Relationality: Autobiographical Deformations and the Literary Lineage of Afro-Pessimism in 20th and 21st Century African American Literature" [PhD diss., UC San Diego, 2012]; Frank Wilderson III, *Red, White, and Black: Cinema and the Structure of U.S. Antagonisms* [Durham, NC: Duke University Press, 2010]; Jared Sexton, "The Social Life of Social Death: On Afro-Pessimism and Black Optimism," *In*Tensions 5 [2011]: 1–47; and Fred Moten, "Blackness and Nothingness [Mysticism in the Flesh]," *South Atlantic Quarterly* 112, no. 4 [Fall 2013]: 737–80).

68. James Walvin, *Atlas of Slavery* (New York: Routledge, 2014); Milton Meltzer, *Slavery: A World History* (New York: Da Capo, 1993).

69. Wright, "I Choose Exile."

70. Ibid.

71. Ibid.

Acknowledgments

Cyrus Ernesto Zirakzadeh and I are grateful to the Richard Wright Estate for five separate permissions. First, for the permission to reprint Richard Wright's "I Have Seen Black Hands," which was originally published on 26 June 1934 in *New Masses*, no. 11. Second, to print "Behind the McGee Case," previously only published in French as "Derrière l'affaire" in the Parisian weekly newspaper of the International League against Racism and Antisemitism (Ligue Internationale Contre le Racisme et l'Antisémitism, or LICRA), *Le droit de vivre* on 4 June 1951. (The typescript carbon version of the English article is held in box 5, folder 82 of the Richard Wright Papers at the Beinecke Rare Book and Manuscript Library at Yale University. We thank Tommy J. Curry for encouraging us to publish it in this volume.) Third, to reprint "Joe Louis Uncovers Dynamite," Wright's first piece of journalistic writing, which appeared on 8 October 1935 in *New Masses*. Fourth, for permission to include "Blueprint for Negro Writing," originally printed in *New Challenge* 2, no. 2 (Fall 1937). Finally, we also thank the Wright Estate for allowing us to use the wonderful, searching photograph of Wright for the cover of this volume. The picture is also housed among the Richard Wright Papers at the Beinecke. We are appreciative of the assistance of the staff at the Beinecke as well as Annie Kronenberg with John Hawkins & Associates for her conscientious help as we sought these rights.

We also thank the University of Illinois Press for permission to reprint Michael S. Harper's "The Meaning of Protest," which was previously published in his *Images of Kin* (Champaign: University of Illinois Press, 1977) and *Debridement* (New York: Doubleday, 1973); the University of North Carolina Press for permission to reprint excerpts from chapter 11 of the second edition of Cedric J. Robinson's *Black Marxism: The Making of the Black Radical Tradition*; Paul Gilroy for permission to reprint excerpts from chapter 5 of his *The Black Atlantic: Modernity and Double Consciousness*

(Cambridge: Harvard University Press, 1993); and Duke University Press for permission to reprint a shortened version of Kevin Kelly Gaines's "Revisiting Richard Wright in Ghana: Black Radicalism and the Dialectics of Diaspora," which first appeared in *Social Text* 19, no. 2 (Summer 2001): 75–101.

We thank the University of Connecticut (UCONN) for supporting our project in multiple ways. Two Scholarship Facilitation Grants covered our reprint costs and allowed us to hire Alexander Trotter, who prepared the book's index. Lindsay Halle, with characteristic ingenuity, handled all of the actual payments that were made with these two grants. The University of Connecticut's Humanities Institute generously footed the bill for a two-day symposium in May 2015 entitled "Lessons in Resistance: Richard Wright as Social Critic and Political Thinker," where many contributors to this volume met each other for the first time and presented initial drafts of their chapters. The Harriet Beecher Stowe Center and Mark Twain House and Museum graciously provided the meeting rooms while Lewis R. Gordon tirelessly transported and fed the symposium's participants. We thank three UCONN political science graduate students for their contributions. Meghan Peterson, who, while completing her own dissertation, prepared and retyped manuscripts and tracked down relevant copyrights. Brooks Kirchgassner helped with editing the chapter abstracts, and Caryl Nuñez assisted us with the preparation of the book's bibliography.

This project began with an informal conversation at the University Press of Kentucky booth at one of the American Political Science Association's annual conferences. Looking through the early volumes in the Political Companion to Great American Authors series, Stephen Wrinn asked me who I thought was missing from the lineup. While there was not yet a volume on Frederick Douglass, Neil Roberts had already agreed to do one, and Nick Bromell had signed up to prepare a book on W. E. B. Du Bois. Wrinn replied enthusiastically at the suggestion of the great Richard Wright. It was my husband, Lewis R. Gordon, who first learned and shared the news of the admiration my then new colleague, "Ernie" Zirakzadeh, had for the work of Wright.

Even though Wrinn and Allison Webster have since left University Press of Kentucky, we are thankful for their shepherding this project through its initial stages of contract. We are also grateful that they left our project in the capable hands of Melissa Hammer, who showed tremendous skill in overseeing the completion of the project. Susan Murray did wonderfully meticulous and thoughtful work as the book's copyeditor, while five anonymous reviewers provided us with galvanizing comments and astute guidance that contributed to the gravitas of the final book.

My own fascination with Richard Wright began at a very early age. When I would do my homework on the burnt-orange rug of my dad's office, sitting heavily and formally bound on the lowest shelf was *Native Son*. Before I could understand the full narrative or its import, I did grasp that it conveyed with gritty and sober depth the actual character of the South Side of Chicago that surrounded me. It was as an undergraduate in Professor Michael S. Harper's "Every Shut Eye Ain't Asleep" seminar that he singled me out, saying, "You, Chicago. You will work on Wright."

This volume is dedicated with appreciation to the memory of Michael S. Harper and the recently deceased intellectual giant of the black radical tradition, Professor Cedric J. Robinson.

Further Reading

Below is a list of primary and secondary writings for readers interested in the politics and political vision of Richard Wright. While by no means a complete record of all the academic work undertaken on Wright and his politics, the selected bibliography should be useful in conveying the range of themes and disciplinary approaches that scholars have pursued and applied when thinking about this seminal writer. For more extensive lists of the writings used in the making of this book, please see the endnotes to the individual chapters.

Writings by Richard Wright

Fiction

Uncle Tom's Children. New York: Harper and Brothers, 1938.
Native Son. New York: Harper and Brothers, 1940.
The Outsider. New York: Harper and Brothers, 1953.
Savage Holiday. New York: Avon, 1954.
The Long Dream. Garden City, NY: Doubleday, 1958.
Eight Men. Cleveland: World, 1961.
Lawd Today. New York: Walker, 1963.

Nonfiction

"Blueprint for Negro Writing." *New Challenge* 2 (Fall 1937): 53–65.
"The Ethics of Living Jim Crow: An Autobiographical Sketch." In *American Stuff: A WPS Writers Anthology*, 39–52. New York: Viking, 1937.
"How 'Bigger' Was Born." Pamphlet and, beginning in 1966, an addendum to Perennial Classics paperback editions of *Native Son*. New York: Harper and Brothers, 1940.

Twelve Million Black Voices: A Folk History of the Negro in the United States. New York: Viking, 1941.

"I Tried to Be a Communist." *Atlantic Monthly,* August 1944, 61–70.

Black Boy: A Record of Childhood and Youth. New York: Harper and Brothers, 1945.

"Early Days in Chicago." In *Cross-Section,* edited by Edwin Seaver, 306–42. New York: L. B. Fischer, 1945.

Introduction to *Black Metropolis: A Study of Negro Life in a Northern City,* by St. Clair Drake and Horace R. Cayton. Chicago: University of Chicago Press, 1970.

Black Power: A Record of Reactions in a Land of Pathos. New York: Harper and Brothers, 1954.

The Color Curtain: A Report on the Bandung Conference. Cleveland: World, 1954.

Pagan Spain. New York: Harper and Row, 1957.

White Man, Listen! Garden City, NY: Doubleday, 1957.

"The Position of the Negro Artist and Intellectual in American Society." Manuscript. 1960.

American Hunger. New York: Harper and Row, 1977.

Conversations with Richard Wright. Edited by Keneth Kinnamon and Michel Fabre. Jackson: University Press of Mississippi, 1993.

Byline Richard Wright: Articles from the "Daily Worker" and "New Masses." Edited by Earle V. Bryant. Columbia: University of Missouri Press, 2015.

Poetry

Haiku: This Other World. New York: Arcade, 1998.

Biographies of Richard Wright

Bakish, David. *Richard Wright.* New York: Frederick Ungar, 1973.

Blyden, Jackson. "Richard Wright: Black Boy from America's Black Belt and Urban Ghettos." *CLA Journal* 12 (1969): 387–423.

Fabre, Michel. *The Unfinished Quest of Richard Wright.* New York: Morrow, 1973.

Gayle, Addison. *Richard Wright: Ordeal of a Native Son.* New York: Doubleday, 1980.

Kinnamon, Keneth. *The Emergence of Richard Wright: A Study in Literature and Society.* Urbana: University of Illinois Press, 1972.
Rowley, Hazel. *Richard Wright: The Life and Times.* Chicago: University of Chicago Press, 2001.
Walker, Margaret. *Richard Wright, Daemonic Genius: A Portrait of the Man, a Critical Look at His Work.* New York: Warner, 1988.
Wallach, Jennifer Jensen. *Richard Wright: From Black Boy to World Citizen.* Chicago: Ivan R. Dee, 2010.
Webb, Constance. *Richard Wright: A Biography.* New York: G. P. Putnam's Sons, 1968.
Williams, John A. *The Most Native of Sons.* Garden City, NY: Doubleday, 1970.

On Wright's Politics and Political Visions
(including books containing chapters devoted to Wright's thinking)

Baldwin, James. *Notes of a Native Son.* Boston: Beacon, 1955.
Brivic, Sheldon. "Conflict of Values: Richard Wright's *Native Son*." *Novel* 21 (Spring 1974): 231–45.
Bryant, Jerry. "The Violence of *Native Son*." *Southern Review* 17 (April 1981): 303–19.
Butler, Robert Olen. *Native Son: The Emergence of a New Black Hero.* Boston: Twayne, 1991.
Cleaver, Eldridge. *Soul on Ice.* New York: Dell, 1968.
Craven, Alice Mikal, and William E. Dow, eds. *Richard Wright in a Post-Racial Imaginary.* New York: Bloomsbury, 2014.
Cruse, Harold. *The Crisis of the Negro Intellectual.* New York: William Morrow, 1967.
Ellison, Ralph. "The World and the Jug." In *Shadow and Act.* New York: Random House, 1964.
Fabre, Michel. *The World of Richard Wright.* Jackson: University of Mississippi Press, 1985.
Gates, Henry Louis, Jr., and K. A. Appiah, eds. *Richard Wright: Critical Perspectives Past and Present.* New York: Amistad, 1993.
Gibson, Donald. "Wright's Invisible *Native Son*." *American Quarterly* 21 (Winter 1969): 728–39.
Gilroy, Paul. *The Black Atlantic: Modernity and Double Consciousness.* Cambridge: Harvard University Press, 1993.

Gloster, Hugh M. *Negro Voices in American Fiction*. Chapel Hill: University of North Carolina Press, 1948.

Haile, James B. *Philosophical Meditations on Richard Wright*. Lanham: Lexington, 2012.

Hakutani, Yoshinobu. *Richard Wright and Racial Discourse*. Columbia: University of Missouri Press, 1996.

Hayes, Floyd W. "The Concept of Double Vision in Richard Wright's *The Outsider*." In *Existence in Black: An Anthology of Black Existential Philosophy*, ed. Lewis R. Gordon. New York: Routledge, 1997.

Howe, Irving. "Black Boys and Native Sons." In *A World More Attractive*. New York: Horizon, 1963.

JanMohamed, Abdul R. *The Death-Bound-Subject: Richard Wright's Archaeology of Death*. Durham, NC: Duke University Press, 2005.

Joyce, Joyce Ann. *Richard Wright's Art of Tragedy*. Iowa City: University of Iowa Press, 1986.

Kent, George E. "Richard Wright: Blackness and the Adventure of Western Culture." *CLA Journal* 12 (June 1969): 322–43.

Kinnamon, Keneth. *New Essays on "Native Son."* Cambridge: Cambridge University Press, 1990.

Macksey, Ricard, and Frank E. Moorer, eds. *Richard Wright: A Collection of Critical Essays*. Englewood Cliffs, NJ: Prentice Hall, 1984.

Margolies, Edward. *The Art of Richard Wright*. Carbondale: Southern Illinois University Press, 1969.

Marso, Lori J. "Solidarity *Sans* Identity: Richard Wright and Simone de Beauvoir Theorize Political Subjectivity." *Contemporary Political Theory* 13 (2014): 242–62.

McCall, Dan. *The Example of Richard Wright*. New York: Harcourt, Brace and World, 1969.

Reilly, John. *Richard Wright: The Critical Reception*. New York: Franklin, 1978.

Roberts, Brian Russell, and Keith Foulcher, eds. *Indonesian Notebook: A Sourcebook on Richard Wright and the Bandung Conference*. Durham, NC: Duke University Press, 2016.

Robinson, Cedric J. *Black Marxism: The Making of the Black Radical Tradition*. London: Zed, 1983.

Smith, Virginia Whatley, ed. *Richard Wright's Travel Writings: New Reflections*. Jackson: University Press of Mississippi, 2001.

Stepto, Robert. "I Thought I Knew These People: Richard Wright and the Afro-American Literary Tradition." In *Chant of Saints*, edited by Michael Harper and Robert Stepto. Urbana: University of Illinois Press, 1979.

Stringer, Dorothy. "Psychology and Black Liberation in Richard Wright's *Black Power* (1954)." *Journal of Modern Literature* 32 (2009): 105–24.

Tate, Claudia C. *Psychoanalysis and Black Novels: Desire and the Protocol of Race*. New York: Oxford University Press, 1988.

Zheng, Jianqing, ed. *The Other World of Richard Wright: Perspectives on His Haiku*. Jackson: University Press of Mississippi, 2011.

Contributors

Tommy J. Curry is professor of philosophy and Africana studies at Texas A&M University. He is author of *The Man-Not: Race, Class, Genre, and the Dilemmas of Black Manhood* (2017) and *Another white Man's Burden: Josiah Royce's Quest for a white Racial Empire* (2018), and editor of *The Philosophical Treatise of William H. Ferris: Selected Readings from "The African Abroad or, His Evolution in Western Civilization"* (2016).

William Dow is professor of American literature at the Université Paris-Est (UPEM) and professor of English at the American University of Paris. He is the author of the book *Narrating Class in American Fiction* (2009), and coeditor of *Richard Wright: New Readings in the 21st Century* (2011) and *Richard Wright in a Post-Racial Imaginary* (2014).

Kevin Kelly Gaines is the W. E. B. Du Bois Professor of Africana Studies and History at Cornell University. He is the author of *Uplifting the Race* (1996), which was awarded the John Hope Franklin Prize of the American Studies Association, and *American Africans in Ghana: Black Expatriates and the Civil Rights Era* (2006), which was a Choice Outstanding Academic Title.

Paul Gilroy is professor of American and English literature at King's College London. He is author of, among other works, *There Ain't No Black in the Union Jack* (1987), *Small Acts* (1993), *The Black Atlantic* (1993), and *After Empire* (2004; published as *Postcolonial Melancholia* in the United States [2006]).

Jane Anna Gordon is associate professor and director of graduate studies of political science at the University of Connecticut. She is author of *Why*

They Couldn't Wait (2001) and *Creolizing Political Theory* (2014), coauthor of *Of Divine Warning* (2009), and coeditor of *Not Only the Master's Tools* (2006), *A Companion to African-American Studies* (2006), *Creolizing Rousseau* (2015), and *Journeys in Caribbean Thought* (2016).

Lewis R. Gordon is professor of philosophy at the University of Connecticut; European Union Visiting Chair in Philosophy at Université Toulouse Jean Jaurès, France; honorary president of the Global Center for Advanced Studies; and honorary professor at the Unit of the Humanities at Rhodes University, South Africa. He is the author/editor of many books, including *Bad Faith and Antiblack Racism* (1995), *Fanon and the Crisis of European Man* (1995), *Her Majesty's Other Children* (1997), *Existentia Africana* (2000), *Disciplinary Decadence* (2006), *An Introduction to Africana Philosophy* (2008), *Of Divine Warning* (2009), *La teoría política en la encrucijada descolonial* (2009), *What Fanon Said* (2015), and *Geopolitics and Decolonization: Perspectives from the Global South* (2018).

Laura Grattan is associate professor of political science at Wellesley College. Her research is at the intersections of democratic theory, grassroots politics, and critical studies of race and culture in the United States. She is the author of *Populism's Power: Radical Grassroots Democracy in America* (2016) and is currently working on a book on radical imagination in movements that are organizing against the carceral state.

James B. Haile III is assistant professor of philosophy at the University of Rhode Island. He is editor of *Philosophical Meditations on Richard Wright* (2012), now in its second, paperback edition, and is currently working on an edited collection on James Baldwin and a book about refiguring the black male literary canon from 1850 to the present. He also runs a speaker series, "Black Aesthetics as Politics," now in its fourth year.

Floyd W. Hayes III is retired senior lecturer and coordinator of programs and undergraduate studies in the Center for Africana Studies at Johns Hopkins University. He is the editor of *A Turbulent Voyage: Readings in African American Studies* (2000), which is currently in its third edition, and author of numerous scholarly articles and book chapters. His research focuses on Africana political philosophy, politics, and public policy. He is at work on a book that examines Richard Wright's social and political thought.

Abdul R. JanMohamed is professor of English at the University of California, Berkeley. He is author of *Manichean Aesthetics: The Politics of Literature in Colonial Africa* (1983) and *The Death-Bound-Subject: Richard Wright's Archaeology of Death* (2005), and is editor of *The Nature and Context of Minority Discourse* (1991) and *Reconsidering Social Identification: Race, Gender, Class and Caste* (2011). He was the recipient of the Frantz Fanon Lifetime Achievement Award from the Caribbean Philosophical Association in 2014.

Lori J. Marso is Doris Zemurray Stone Professor of Modern Literary and Historical Studies and professor of political science at Union College in Schenectady, New York. Her most recent books include *Politics with Beauvoir: Freedom in the Encounter* (2017), *Politics, Theory, and Film: Critical Encounters with Lars von Trier* (edited with Bonnie Honig, 2016), and *Fifty-One Key Feminist Thinkers* (2016). She is also author/coeditor of *Feminist Thinkers and the Demands of Femininity* (2006), *W Stands for Women* (2007), *Simone de Beauvoir's Political Thinking* (2006), and *(Un)Manly Citizens* (1999). Marso won the Susan Okin, Iris Marion Young Award for Feminist Political Theory in 2013 and is currently writing on the films of Chantal Akerman.

Perry S. Moskowitz is a political theorist and doctoral candidate in the Department of Political Science at Johns Hopkins University. He studies the politics of representation broadly, ranging from engagements with early modern political theory and phenomenology, to work on anarchism, film, race, and queer theory. His dissertation explores monstrosity and anarchistic practices of subject formation in early modern political thought.

Marilyn Nissim-Sabat is emeritus professor of philosophy at Lewis University. She is the author of *Neither Victim nor Survivor* (2009) and has written many book chapters and articles for such journals as *The C. L. R. James Journal, Philosophy, Psychiatry, and Psychology* (*PPP*), *American Journal of Psychotherapy, Human Studies, Husserl Studies, Listening*, and *Psychoanalytic Review*. She is a licensed and practicing psychotherapist.

Cedric J. Robinson was professor emeritus of black studies and political science at the University of California, Santa Barbara. He was the author of *Terms of Order: Political Science and the Myth of Leadership* (1980), *Black Movements in America* (1997), *Black Marxism: The Making of the Black Radical Tradition*, 2nd ed. (1999), *An Anthropology of Marxism* (2001), and *Forgeries of Memory and Meaning: Blacks and the Regimes of Race in American Theory and Film* (2007).

Dorothy Stringer is a psychoanalytic critic working on twentieth-century African American and US literatures. She is the author of *"Not Even Past": Race, Subjectivity and Historical Trauma in Faulkner, Larsen, and Van Vechten* (2010), as well as articles on Richard Wright, Junot Díaz, Zora Neale Hurston, and Samuel R. Delany. She teaches at Temple University.

Cyrus Ernesto Zirakzadeh is professor of political science and associate dean for the social sciences at the University of Connecticut. He has written and edited eight books on social movements and political protest, on experiments in participatory politics (sometimes called "small 'd' democracy"), and on politics and contemporary US popular culture. His work also has appeared in a variety of political science and cross-disciplinary journals, among them *Polity, Social Movement Studies, West European Politics, Journal of Theoretical Politics, The Review of Politics,* and *Comparative Studies in Society and History*.

Index

Italic page numbers refer to illustrations.

Aaron, Daniel, 48, 57
Abzug, Bella, 138
Africa, 46, 162, 221, 233; aid as "reparations" to, 163; anticolonial movements in, 11; black radicals' pilgrimage to, 191–92; civilization in, 228; colonialism in, 6; living reality of, 207; Soviet Union's attempt to gain influence in, 188; underdevelopment of, 206
Africana literature and thought, 8, 31, 107
African American(s), 14, 226, 227, 276; farmers, 279; folk culture of, 4; inner life or black interior, 265–69, 270, 274; life in placeless places, 264–66; nature writing and ecoliterature, 13; novelists and poets, 12. *See also* black(s)
Afromodernity, 27–31, 34
Agamben, Giorgio, 296
Agee, James, 227
agency, 32, 38, 90, 101, 113, 206
Aggrey, Kwegyir, 187
Alexander, Elizabeth, 265–66, 270
Alexander, Michelle, 323
Algeria, 8, 100
alienation, 46, 99, 273, 313; of black workers, 54; expressed through misogyny and sexism, 115; haiku moment and, 281; of placeless place, 266, 267; undoing of self-alienation, 89
Allred, Jeff, 227
Althusser, Louis, 295
American Dream, 310–11
American Hunger (Wright), 47, 124, 275, 279; description of Chicago in, 270–71, 272; fate of African Americans in Chicago portrayed in, 282–83; published posthumously in 1977, 45
American Peace Mobilization, 5
American Society for African Culture, 8
Amin, Samir, 294
anticarceral organizing, 321–23
anti-imperialism, 181–82, 192
Arendt, Hannah, 26, 32
Aristotle, 32
Armah, Ayi Kwei, 193–94
Asia, 28, 58, 161, 233–36
atheism, 89
authenticity, diversionary quest for, 182
Awkward, Michael, 111

Baer, Max, 3, 15, 289, 290
Baker, Houston, 264–65, 268, 313, 315, 319–20
Bakhtin, M. M., 227
Baldwin, James, 6, 9, 65, 71, 80, 149; on Bigger Thomas as stereotype,

Baldwin, James *(cont.)*
72–75; "Everybody's Protest Novel," 7; "Going to Meet the Man," 136; literary journalism of, 224; on "Man of All Work," 145; *Native Son* criticized by, 7, 72–75, 145, 247, 311; on violence in black literature, 122; "The White Man's Guilt," 256; on Wright's representative politics, 247, 248, 256–57

Balthaser, Benjamin, 250

Bandung conference (Indonesia, 1955), 8, 160, 167, 233–36

Barbusse, Henri, 219

"bare life" (homo sacer), 296, 298, 300

Baudrillard, Jean, 36

Bearden, Romare, 266

Beauvoir, Simone de, 6, 11, 86, 98; on divisions and commonality among women, 167; on identity of "Woman," 170; meetings with Wright, 160–61, 166; *The Second Sex*, 91–93, 130, 161, 170–76; on women and the patriarchal regime, 110; Wright's influence on, 90–93, 97, 129–30

"Behind the McGee Case" (Wright), 14, 134, 140–43, 155–58

Belgium, 163

Bell, Vikki, 90–100, 101

Bendixen, Alfred, 229–30

Beneduce, Roberto, 7

Benjamin, Walter, 247, 248, 249–50, 254, 255

Bernard, Trevor, 332–33

"Between the World and Me" (Wright), 225, 294, 298, 299

Biko, Steve, 27, 32, 34, 302

Bing, Geoffrey, 191

Black Belt Thesis, 49

Black Boy (Wright), 8, 86–87, 97, 98, 159, 272; critique of the family in, 122; Ellison's reading of, 121; folk culture and the natural world in, 274; on human society as part of the natural world, 277; images of the black feminine in, 109; the individual as representative of a group in, 225; justification of violence in, 141; politics of refusal and, 312, 313–17; republication of (1966), 45; Wright's concept of the human in, 96

Black Consciousness movement (South Africa), 27

black diaspora, global, 7

black feminine, images of, 108, 109–11

black interior, 265–66, 270, 274

Black Lives Matter movement, 16

black melancholia, 29

black men: access to industrial jobs (1940s), 146; economic vulnerability of, 143–44, 145; as emasculated figures, 144, 147; imagined as rapists, 133; vulnerability to sexual violence, 11; white women as rapists of, 134–37. *See also* masculinity, black

Blackmon, Douglas, 332

black nationalism, 15, 45, 46, 71; black intellectuals and, 54–55; Howe's criticism of, 67–68; as product of capitalist development, 59; revolutionary consciousness of, 60

blackness, 34, 148, 165, 255; agency and, 32; authentic embodiment of, 11; emergence from Euromodernity, 29; essentialist understanding of, 182; as ground of politics, 162

Black Panthers, 311

Black Power (Wright), 7, 32, 184, 194, 198, 200, 224; "Black Power" concept of 1960s predated by,

205; black radicalism and diaspora theorized in, 181; *The Color Curtain* compared with, 233; criticism of Ghanaian society in, 191; on diaspora as transnational unity, 193; generic features as travel narrative, 200; literary-journalistic techniques in, 229–33; on pan-Africanism, 183; psychoanalytic theory and, 199

Black Power movement (1960s), 47, 116

"black problem," 30, 38

black(s): alternative institutions and enclaves of, 69, 71; black family, 110, 116, 121, 122; blackness born from Euromodernity, 29; as a collectivity of "we," 168, 250–52, 255, 256; culture of, 215–16; dehumanization of, 30; exodus from the South, 3, 5; extralegal terror against, 2; in industrial jobs, 338; "kindred consciousness" with other people, 4; lived experience of, 14; mass incarceration of, 16, 332; middle class, 49; as outsiders and problems, 31; political consciousness of, 11; poor whites and, 229; racist exclusion from public venues, 72; social position of women compared with, 91–93; as vanguard of American working class, 56; working-class, 48. *See also* African American(s); black men; black women

black women, 108, 144; conditions of life in kitchenettes, 339; enslaved, 172; in *The Outsider*, 111–16; rape and sexual exploitation of, 134, 146–47, 336; in revolutionary Ghana, 160; stereotyped images of, 10, 112; womanist and black feminist criticism, 108–9, 112; as workers in white homes, 156, 335; Wright's images of the black feminine, 109–11

"Blueprint for Negro Writing" (Wright), 14–15, 48, 213–23, 225, 318

Bone, Robert, 45

bourgeoisie, 58, 59, 214

Bracero worker-exchange program, 75

Bradley, David, 313

Brett, E. A., 295

Britain: imperialism of, 184, 295; independence of African colonies from, 163; slave trade and, 186

Browder, Earl, 51

Brown v. Board of Education, 75

Bullins, Ed, 45

Bush, George W., 15–16

Butler, Judith, 110

capitalism, 9, 29, 46, 58, 108, 217, 316; Africa and, 231; black anticapitalist struggle for freedom, 320; circuit of money and trauma, 204; destruction of, 54; Euromodernity and, 30; fascism and, 50–51; gut-level refusal of, 318; Marxist/socialist critiques of, 59, 65; racial segregation and, 229; social consciousness and, 52–53; the United States and, 75–76; withdrawal from struggle against, 311–12; writers' depiction of horrors of, 219

Cappetti, Carla, 228

carceral state and institutions, 312, 321–23

Caruth, Cathy, 200

castration, racialized, 136–37, 143, 145, 147

Cayton, Horace, 6, 225, 228, 229

Cendrars, Blaise, 227

Césaire, Aimé, 6

Chicago, South Side of, 3, 10, 53, 70, 220; celebration of Joe Louis boxing victory in, 15, 289–92; kitchenette apartments in, 269–70, 272, 273; sense of possibility associated with, 76; Wright's depiction of, 64–65, 68, 272

Childress, Alice, 12, 224

Childs, Dennis R., 332

China, Communist, 140

Christendom, 27, 28, 29

Christianity, 40, 56, 184, 187, 302; in Ghanaian politics, 205; Marxism compared to, 58

CIA (Central Intelligence Agency), 8

Cicero, Marcus Tullius, 40

Citizens' Emergency Conference for Interracial Unity, 5

citizenship, 35, 340

civilizations, ancient, 28, 33, 331

civil liberties, 65

Civil Rights Congress, 137

civil rights movement, 75, 342

civil society, 34, 112

Civil War, 156

class, 171, 221, 230

class consciousness, 46, 50, 51, 318

Cleaver, Eldridge, 311

Clifton, Lucille, 275–76

Coates, Ta-Nehisi, 310–11, 311, 321

Coffin Texts, 33

Cold War, 9, 35, 68, 75, 183, 192

colonialism, 6, 8–9, 26, 108, 208; alienating effects of, 188; Bandung conference and struggle against, 233, 234; French colonialism in Algeria, 100; neocolonialism, 189, 199; petite bourgeoisie and, 190; racism and, 233; "rot" of white culture and, 162; "unconscious and unintentional" results of, 161; Wright's opposition to, 160

Color Curtain, The (Wright), 224, 229, 233–37

Communism, 140, 166; black collectivist ethos and, 319–20; Comintern (Communist International), 48, 51; in Germany during Weimar Republic, 51; as obstacle to pan-Africanism, 183

Communist Party USA, 3, 5, 7, 60, 302; activists depicted in *Native Son*, 73; *Daily Worker* newspaper, 4, 225, 238; depicted in *The Outsider*, 114; nationalism and, 55; *New Masses* (party journal), 3, 225; position on fascism, 50–51; Wright's involvement with, 27, 48–50, 70

Congress for Cultural Freedom, 8

connectivity: Bell's explanation of, 93–94; blurred boundaries of identity and, 92, 95; mundane forms of, 98, 100; politics of the human and, 100–102

contradictions, dialectical, 31, 35, 37, 54

Convention People's Party (CCP), 7, 165, 187, 188, 205, 207

Coulthard, Glen Sean, 39

creolization, 28, 29, 30

Critical Resistance, 322

Cugoano, Ottobah Quobna, 330

Cullen, Countee, 6

Curry, Tommy J., 11

Daily Worker (Communist newspaper), 4, 225, 238

Damon, Cross (fictional character), 31, 111–12; black women and, 112–15, 120–21; death as existential tragedy, 41–42; death of, 116; as nihilist-radical, 115; significance of name, 40–41, 56. See also *Outsider, The* (Wright)

Danquah, J. B., 206

Davis, Angela Y., 32, 323
Davis, David Brion, 331
Davis, Rebecca Harding, 227
Day, Dorothy, 227
De Angelis, Massimo, 294
decolonization, 182
defamiliarization, 249
De Genova, Nicholas, 314
demagogy, 80
democracy, 155, 192, 312, 344; anticarceral organizing and, 323; black liberation and, 321; fugitive forms of 339, 343; US racialized state and, 322
Denning, Michael, 64–65
diaspora, African, 181, 182, 186, 192, 194; memorialization of trauma and, 203; as transnational unity, 193
Diawara, Manthia, 162–63, 166
Diop, Alioune, 6, 206
disenfranchisement, 2, 329
Dollard, John, 144–45
double consciousness, 4, 31, 32, 37
Douglass, Frederick, 133, 302, 339, 340, 341, 342
Dow, William, 12
Drake, St. Clair, 6, 228, 229
Du Bois, W. E. B., 2–3, 12, 29, 32, 47, 143; black modernity and, 187; *Black Reconstruction*, 342; Black–White labor solidarity and, 56; literary journalism of, 224; *The Souls of Black Folk*, 335–36; on the "talented tenth," 49
Dulles, John Foster, 234
Dungy, Camille T., 275–77, 282
Dussel, Enrique, 27

Ebony magazine, 225
Edwards, Brent, 182
Egypt, ancient (Middle Kingdom), 33
Eight Men (Wright), 45
Eliot, T. S., 219

Ellison, Ralph, 9, 64, 65, 80, 224, 311, 316; critique of Bigger Thomas, 68–72; *Invisible Man*, 264, 265; reading of *Black Boy*, 121; on *12 Million Black Voices*, 313
Emancipation Proclamation, 332
Engels, Friedrich, 40
Enlightenment ideals, 200
Esposito, Roberto, 297
"Ethics of Living Jim Crow, The" (Wright), 333–34
Ethiopia, Mussolini's invasion of, 291
Eurocentrism, 130, 199, 200
Euromodernity, 9, 26, 34; Afromodernity in, 27–31; emergence of, 27; Wright as Afromodern writer, 34–42
Evans, Dennis F., 239
Evans, Walker, 167
exile: of African revolutionaries, 191, 192; of black radical intellectuals, 11, 182, 183; fugitivity and, 339–44; Wright in Paris, 160, 236, 317, 339, 340; Wright's exile writings, 224, 230, 237
existentialism, 6, 7, 31, 47, 166

Fabre, Michel, 47, 116
Fanon, Frantz, 4, 7, 8, 32, 37, 298–99; *Black Skin, White Masks*, 5–6, 39, 294, 300; on French colonialism in Algeria, 100; on presumed guilt of colonial subjects, 330; on violence as cathartic rejection, 314; on violence of the lumpenproletariat, 53; *The Wretched of the Earth*, 7, 101–2, 163, 300
Farm Security Administration (FSA), 225, 226, 227, 248, 252, 313
fascism, 35, 50–51, 52, 78, 320
Fauset, Jessie, 12, 224, 227
FBI (Federal Bureau of Investigation), 5, 7

Federal Writers' Project, 3
femininity, 160
feminists, 10, 91–92; "personal is political" slogan, 96; in scholarly fields, 206; Third World antiracism and, 166–67; white feminists' exclusionary practices, 108, 111; womanist and black feminist criticism, 108–9, 112
Ferguson, Kathy, 110
Finley, Moses, 331
First Congress of Negro Artists and Writers (1956), 8
folk culture, 4, 13, 16, 215, 216–17; attempt to replicate in the North, 279; death of, 273–74; Mississippi River and, 275; politics of refusal and, 312, 318–19; tricksters and "badman heroes," 315–16; US government failure to help freed slaves and, 280; "white woman tales," 315–16
France, 140, 342; Algerian war and, 7; independence of African colonies from, 163; slave trade and, 186
Franco, Francisco, 237
Franco-American Fellowship, 133
Frazier, E. Franklin, 144
Freedmen's Bureau, 280
Freud, Sigmund, 5
Fruitvale Community Garden, 323

Gaines, Kevin Kelly, 11
Garner, Eric, 26
Garvey, Marcus, 4, 187
gender, 10, 161, 171, 206, 230
Genet, Jean, 130
Ghana, 160, 163–66, 167, 183; Akan culture in/of, 184; as first independent sub-Saharan African state, 198; moral and spiritual decay in, 193; Wright's travels in, 185–94, 230–31. See also Gold Coast

Gibson, Nigel, 7
Gikuyu people, of Kenya, 295
Gilded Age, first, 3
Gilded Age, second, 15
Gilmore, Glenda, 136
Gilroy, Paul, 10, 11, 112, 166–67
Global South, 27, 101
Gold Coast, 12, 46, 181, 184, 188; British neocolonialism in, 189–90; slave trade sites in, 186; Wright's journey through (1953), 185–94, 198, 200, 201, 230, 233. See also Ghana
Gordon, Jane Anna, 13–14, 28, 313
Gordon, Lewis R., 8, 90, 97, 101, 112
Gorky, Maxim, 219
Grattan, Laura, 13
Great Depression, 3, 47, 51, 53, 225, 248
Great Migration (1910–1930), 167, 175, 226, 227, 313; black collectivity and, 250; existential element of, 271; natural world and, 277
Greeks, ancient, 33
Grimke, Archibald H., 135–36
Gumbs, Alexis Pauline, 323

Habermas, Jürgen, 32
Hahamovitch, Cindy, 342
haiku moment, 281–83
Haiku: This Other World (Wright), 281–83
Haile, James B., III, 12–13
Haitian revolution, 6
Hakutani, Yoshinobu, 207
Hale, Grace Elizabeth, 136–37
Hall, Stuart, 80
Hamera, Judith, 229–30
Hamilton, Charles R., 205
Hansberry, Lorraine: "Lynchpoem" (1951), 132
Harlem (New York), 5–6, 48, 65, 68–69, 220

Harlem School, of literary expression, 221
Harvey, David, 294
Hawkins, Wilmetta, 133, 137, 138, 139
Hayes, Floyd W., III, 10, 30, 40, 239
Haywood, Harry, 49
Heard, Alex, 137–38
Hegel, Georg Wilhelm Friedrich, 34, 59, 128
Heidegger, Martin, 296
Hemingway, Ernest, 219
Henry, Paget, 31
Hernton, Calvin C., 142–43
Himes, Chester: *If He Hollers Let Him Go*, 6
historical materialism, 46
Hitler, Adolf, 37, 78, 79, 343
Hodes, Martha, 136
Holocaust, 87, 88
homophobia, 10
homosexuality, 127
Honneth, Axel, 39
Hooker, Juliet, 339, 340, 343
hooks, bell, 111
housing restrictions, race and, 337–38
"How 'Bigger' Was Born" (Wright), 1, 10, 65; analysis of, 35–38, 40–41, 50–53, 64–81, 88–101, 299, 304, 311, 314–317, 320, 323; on blurred boundaries of identity, 92; on workers' consciousness, 51–52
Howe, Irving, 65–68, 70, 71, 72, 80, 311
Hughes, Langston, 12, 224, 278–79
humanness (the human): lived experience of, 87; presence and absence of, 87–88; self-transcendence and, 96
human rights, 215, 230
Humphrey, Hubert, 71
Hurston, Zora Neale, 12, 123, 224; *Their Eyes Were Watching God*, 123

Iadonisi, Richard A., 282
"I Bite the Hand That Feeds Me" (Wright), 225
identities, 160, 171, 281; alienated, 161; disruption of identity categories, 172; distance from African identity, 164; hybrid, 162
identity politics, 91, 93, 307
ideology, 47, 59, 80, 114
"I Have Seen Black Hands" (Wright), 14, 23–25
imaginary, Lacanian, 305
imperialism, 108, 184
Incidents in the Life of a Slave Girl (Jacobs), 295
indirect writing, 38
Indonesia, 160, 237, 238
industrialization, 46, 57, 231
integration, 53, 67
intellectuals, 9, 47, 49, 66; anticolonialism and, 6; black nationalism and, 55, 60; on blacks and universalism, 29–30; Ghana's revolution and, 191; global black diaspora and, 7; Marxism and, 11, 46, 57; at Paris Congress (1956), 159; Parisian milieu of, 200; radicals in exile, 182
International Conference of Negro Writers and Artists. *See* Paris Congress (1956)
International Literature (Communist Party journal), 3
International Trade Union Committee of Negro Workers, 49
intersectionality theory, 339
Island of Hallucination (Wright). *See American Hunger* (Wright)
"I Tried to Be a Communist" (Wright), 124

Jackson, George L., 332
Jacobs, Harriet, 302

James, C. L. R., 11, 47, 182
JanMohamed, Abdul R., 13, 15, 36, 147, 313
jazz and blues music, 56, 71, 313, 318, 319
Jews, Nazi genocide of, 86
Jim Crow system, 2, 10, 13, 76; "bare life" in, 300; Beauvoir's knowledge of, 166; black women's resistance to, 108; emasculation of black men under, 144; fear of death and, 302; homoerotic nature of, 133; literature and, 87; McGee case and, 134; mythology of black men as rapists and, 136, 139; plantation-feudal economy and, 217; resisted by "Bigger Thomas," 36; role of women in the black family and, 109–10; violent responses to, 316; Wright's traumatic experiences with, 116
"Joe Louis Uncovers Dynamite" (Wright), 15, 283–92
John Reed Club, 3, 48
Jones, Claudia, 140
Jones, LeRoi, 45
Joyce, James, 219
Judaism, 56
juvenile delinquency, 225

Kardiner, Abram, 145
Kessel, Joseph, 227
Kierkegaard, Søren, 38
King, Martin Luther, Jr., 39–40
King, Rodney, 15
kitchenette apartments, in northern cities, 172–74, *173*, *174*, 272, 273, 318; compared to prisons, 172, 338; emotional toll of life in, 269–70
Koestler, Arthur, 46
Kolakowski, Leszek, 46
Kotelawala, Sir John, 234

Lacan, Jacques, 298
Lamming, George, 7

Lange, Dorothea, 167
Larsen, Nella, 12, 224
Larson, Pier, 203
Law, Oliver, 49
Lawd Today (Wright), 50, 126
Lead Belly, 4
League of Struggle for Negro Rights, 49
Lee, Russell, 167, 252
Lenin, Vladimir, 31, 46, 49, 214
Le Sueur, Meridel, 227
Lévi-Strauss, Claude, 6
Lewis, Gordon, 331
literature, African American, 120, 248; canon of, 129; Harlem School, 221; psychology and, 12, 198–99; sociology and, 228
lived experience, 10, 174–75, 247; of black workers, 14; Fanon's "Lived Experience of the Black Man," 294, 298; of humanness, 87; transcendence and, 100; of women, 171
London, Jack, 219
Long Dream, The (Wright), 126–29
Louis, Joe: fight with Max Bauer, 3, 15, 289–91; fight with Max Schmeling, 225
Lowrie, Walter, 40
Lukacs, Gyorgy, 46
lumpenproletariat, 40, 53
Lumumba, Patrice, 163
Luxemburg, Rosa, 294
lynching, 2, 135, 294, 300–301, 336; legal and extralegal, 14, 157, 322, 336; stereotype of black men as rapists and, 136. *See also* McGee, Willie, lynching of

Malcolm X, 40, 183
Mamdani, Mahmood, 32
Mandela, Nelson, 302
Mannoni, O., 128

Index

"Man of All Work" (Wright), 134, 143–49
"Man Who Saw a Flood, The" (Wright), 266–69, 277, 279
"Man Who Went to Chicago, The" (Wright), 126
Marcuse, Herbert, 46
Marshall, Stephen, 73
Marso, Lori J., 11, 95, 110, 232, 251, 320
Martel, James, 250
Martinsville Seven trial, 133–34, 322
Marx, Karl, 40, 51, 52, 60, 332; on the bourgeoisie as a ruling class, 59; on primitive accumulation, 294; on religion, 56; on use value and exchange value, 298
Marxism, 6, 7, 11, 50, 184; in Africa, 188; classical and Leninist, 46; Hegel and, 59; intersection with psychoanalysis, 293; Negro writing and, 218–19; philosophy of history, 107; shortcomings of, 57–58; Wright's lifelong engagement with, 9
masculinity, black, 121, 126, 137, 146; black men's internalization of white society's view of them, 144; gender theory and, 147–48; hypersexualization and hypermasculinity, 148; in "Man of All Work," 143. *See also* black men
masculinity, white, 145, 146
mass incarceration, 16, 332
master/slave relationship, 128, 156, 293
Matthews, Herbert, 237
Mbembe, Achille, 333
McCarthy, Joseph, 185
McCarthyism, 341
McDowell, Calvin, 135
McDowell, Deborah, 108
McGee, Willie, lynching of, 11, 14, 137–40, 148–49, 322; false accusation of rape and, 133;

Hansberry poem about, 132; "Man of All Work" and, 143–49. *See also* "Behind the McGee Case" (Wright)
McGuire, Danielle, 134, 139
Merleau-Ponty, Maurice, 46
Mignolo, Walter, 27
Minus, Marian, 5
misogyny, 10–11, 110, 115, 122
Mississippi Delta, 46
Mississippi River: flood (1927), 266–69; meaning in southern culture, 274–75
Mitchell, Thomas W., 280
Mitford, Jessica, 137–38
modernism, transnational, 236, 241
modernity, 9, 128, 176; black modernity, 182, 187–88; dehumanization in, 233; rejection of, 11; tradition of, 165; Western, 183; Wright's qualified embrace of, 160, 162
modernization, 181
montage, literary: Benjamin and Wright on, 248, 249–53; as constellatory method, 253–56
Montesquieu, Baron de, 331
Morgan, Thomas L., 281
Morrison, Toni, 87, 87–88, 207, 295, 300, 306
Moskowitz, Perry S., 12, 168, 320
Moss, Thomas, 135
Movement for Black Lives, 322
Mussolini, Benito, 37, 79, 291
mythic literature, 38–39
mythopoetics, 40

NAACP (National Association for the Advancement of Colored People), 137
Nasser, Gamal Abdel, 234
nationalism, 1, 182, 188; in Negro writing, 216–18, 223; of Nkrumah, 187, 188

Native Son (Wright), 5, 9, 31, 98, 126, 159, 225; on Afro-American geography as placeless place, 264, 265; as autobiography, 313; Baldwin's critique of, 7, 72–75, 145, 247, 311; Ellison's critique of, 68–72; film version of (1951), 7; historical moment during writing of, 75–76; Howe's defense of, 65–68; the individual as representative of a group in, 225; justification of violence in, 141; politics of refusal and, 312, 313, 314–16; public reception of, 64, 79–81; republication of (1966), 45; view of black women in, 122, 124; violence of the lumpenproletariat in, 53; Wright's experience with Communist movement and, 50; Wright's introduction to second edition, 30. *See also* Thomas, Bigger

Natsir, Mohammed, 234

nature, in Wright's work: exploration of political possibility, 263; haiku moment and, 282–83; "nature" of politics, 264–69; as politics of natural disaster, 263, 267; "politics" of nature, 273–81; urban North versus rural South, 263, 271–73

Nazism, 4, 51, 78, 155; accounts of horror under, 87; vision of social order offered by, 53

Négritude movement, 6, 162, 182

"Negro problem," 30

Nehru, Jawaharlal, 234

neoliberalism, 311

neoslavery, 14, 313, 331–32, 333–36

New Challenge (journal), 5, 225

New Deal, 51, 167

New Journalism, 241

New Masses (Communist Party USA journal), 3, 225

Newton, Huey P., 144

Nexo, Martin Andersen, 219

Nissim-Sabat, Marilyn, 9–10, 110

Nixon, Robert, 313

Nkrumah, Kwame, 7, 160, 163, 193, 230–31; authoritarianism of, 188–89; foreigners in government of, 189–90, 191; Marxist politics of, 200, 204; nationalism of, 187, 188; overthrown in coup, 192; tribal customs and religions mobilized by, 165; Wright's meetings with, 165–66, 187, 199–200; Wright's open letter to, 231

non-aligned nations, 233

Norman, Dorothy, 6

North, US America(n), 13, 66, 318–19; death of folk culture in, 273–74; false promise of boundless wealth in, 76; industrialized cities of, 5; urban life versus rural South, 263, 271–73, 277, 338–39; violence against black people in, 311

"Not My People's War" (Wright), 225

Obama, Barack, 1, 15

Outsider, The (Wright), 7, 31, 47, 108, 120, 126, 238; Afromodernity in, 41–42; on black Christianity, 56; critique of Communist movement in, 57; on double vision of blacks, 55; images of women in, 111–16; Kierkegaardian themes in, 40; republication (1965), 45. *See also* Damon, Cross

Padmore, Dorothy Pizer, 6, 7, 191, 192, 201

Padmore, George, 6, 7, 11, 47, 183; black modernity and, 187; Cold War and, 183; Négritude rejected by, 182; Nkrumah's government and, 191; *Pan-Africanism or Communism?* 230

Index 373

Pagan Spain (Wright), 8, 126, 224, 229, 230, 237–41
pan-Africanism, 6, 7, 11, 182, 183, 191
Paris Congress (1956), 11, 159, 161, 166, 175; US embassy concern about Communist influence at, 341; Wright on colonialism and modernization at, 190
Park, Robert, 17
Partisan Review, 225
patriarchy, 110, 111, 115, 145, 160; Europatriarchy, 10; lynching of black males and, 137; universalizing mythology of, 143
petite bourgeoisie, 49, 57, 58, 59, 195, 214
Plato, allegory of the cave, 193, 194
Pochmara, Anna, 252
political consciousness, 11, 13, 183
populism, right-wing, 79
postcolonial scholarly fields, 206
post-Reconstruction period, 2
postslavery, 14, 330, 332–33, 336–39
poststructuralism/postmodernism, 94, 307
Présence Africaine (journal), 6, 159, 206, 225
primitive accumulation, 293, 294, 302, 307
Prince, Mary, 330
prison abolitionists, 311
Proust, Marcel, 219
pseudonyms, 38
psychoanalysis, 12, 46, 170, 198; avoidance of historical questions, 199; intersection with Marxism, 293; trauma theory, 200, 204
psychotherapy, 41
public spheres, 32, 110

race, 171, 230; belonging to humanity and, 165; otherness and, 161
racism, 10, 16, 30, 38, 46, 53, 96; apartheid South Africa, 34; challenge to racist state, 35; as crime against black man's sexual expression, 110; Euromodernity and, 34, 42; existential challenges posed by, 26; existential rebellion of non-European people and, 108; fascism and, 35; in global context, 233; as historical force of oppression, 165; inability to resist, 145; institutional, 94, 269; intersection with patriarchy, 115; Marxist failure to understand, 57; as mediating force, 55; myths at base of, 72; origins of, 28–29; as a religion, 162; social traits fostered by, 127; stereotypes and, 79–80; Wright's family history and, 329
Rankine, Claudia, 322
rape, 110, 113, 149, 303; alleged rape in McGee case, 137–39, 155; of black men by white women, 133, 134–37; of black women by white men, 134, 146, 336; false allegations as justification for lynching, 142, 157, 300–301; stereotype of black men as violent rapists, 132, 140, 148
Rassemblement Démocratique Révolutionnaire, 6
realism, literary, 248
Reconstruction period, 3, 342
"Red Clay Blues" (Wright with Hughes, 1938), 278–80, 281, 283
Reed, Ishmael, 45
Reich, Wilhelm, 51
religion, 112–13, 114, 218, 302; black church, 4; Marx's view of, 56; monotheism, 297; slavery and, 215; Sunday church services of rural blacks, 252; transcendence and, 89; as veil of illusion, 114
"Resolution on the Negro Question" (Comintern, 1928), 48

ressentiment, 90–93, 99, 314, 316
Robinson, Cedric J., 9, 12, 40, 107
Rooney, Caroline, 207
Roosevelt, Franklin D., 51
Rosskam, Edwin, 5, 11, 167, 225, 251, 252
Rousseau, Jean-Jacques, 331
Rowley, Hazel, 240–41
Rushdy, Ashraf H. A., 332
Russia, czarist, 51, 53

Sartre, Jean-Paul, 6, 46, 86, 87, 94; atheism of, 89; intersubjectivity and, 90; Wright in dialogue with, 130
Savage Holiday (Wright), 124
Schmeling, Max, 225
Schocket, Eric, 231
science, 125, 170
Scottsboro case, 4, 48, 214, 225, 322
self-determination, 49, 113, 114, 322, 332, 340
Self-Other dialectics, 39
self-transcendence, 90, 95
Senghor, Léopold Sédar, 6, 162
sexism, 94, 96, 115, 141
"Shame of Chicago, The" (Wright), 225
sharecroppers, *169*, 267, 329
Sierra Leone, 230
Sjahrir, Sutan, 234
slavery, 14, 72, 130, 162, 206, 236, 313; "absoluteness of power" as heritage of, 321; "afterlife" of, 313, 321; capitalism and, 9; condition of diasporic blacks and, 181; continuation of, 330–33; cultural encounter and, 202; establishment of, 295; homoerotic nature of, 133; legacy of psychological trauma of, 198–99, 201; Negro culture and, 215–16; racial theories and origin of, 165, 185; reenslavement through denied land rights, 280; slave narratives, 87, 295, 330; slave revolts and resistance, 319. *See also* neoslavery; postslavery
Slavery & Abolition (journal), 333
slave trade, 12, 184, 186, 199, 202–3, 313
Smith, William Gardner, 191
socialism, 51, 54, 140, 187
sociology, 145, 225, 228, 277
South, US America(n), 2, 121, 133; Confederacy, former, 2; Jim Crow system, 2, 10; mass exodus of blacks from, 3, 5; miscegenation laws, 135; nature in, 276–79; neoslavery in, 333–36; plantation economy of Deep South, 141, 155; rural life versus industrial North, 263, 271–74, 277, 338–39; violence against black people in, 311. *See also* "How 'Bigger' Was Born" (Wright); lynching
South, Global, 294
South Africa, 27
Soviet Union, 140, 188, 192, 231
Spanish Civil War, 238
Stalin, Joseph, 37, 79
Stalinism, 49, 78
Stein, Gertrude, 6, 219
Stewart, Lee, 135
Stringer, Dorothy, 11–12, 231
Strout, Richard, 237
subjectivity, 161, 171, 302, 307; African American, 227; of Afromodernity, 42; appropriation of, 13; democracy and, 340; intersubjectivity, 90; of photographers, 167; of slaves, 293–94, 295–96; sociological models of power and, 93, 96; of women, 170
Supreme Court, US, 133–34

Tenant Leagues, 49
Third World, 47, 160, 162, 166–67, 183

Index

"This Too, Is America" (interview of Wright, 1954), 141
Thomas, Bigger (fictional composite character), 1, 3, 5, 159–60, 247; agency of, 101; attraction to authoritarian ideologies, 78, 79; based on Wright's life experiences, 65, 76; black and white versions of, 77, 78, 92; black folk heroes and, 315–16; Cold War–era appropriations of, 9; crushed by alienation, 10; Ellison's critique of, 70; embrace of impending death by, 307; existential condition of, 7; explosion and implosion of, 299; as "hard" character, 302; as homeless soul of Euromodernity, 35; incorporated into Beauvoir's *The Second Sex*, 91; inner life of, 38; interior monologue on eve of execution, 88; lack of class consciousness, 50, 51–52; as literary archetype, 64; path to self-acceptance and human connection, 88–89, 98, 99–100; politics of refusal and, 316; revolutionary consciousness of, 2, 16; solidarity with "criminals" and, 13; as stereotype held by whites, 67, 72–75; universalism and, 4; Wright's typography of, 35–37. See also *Native Son* (Wright)
Thurston, Michael, 226
Till, Emmett, 133, 139
Tolson, Melvin, 12, 224
totalitarianism, 35, 101
Toussaint L'Ouverture, 6
trade unions, 23–25, 52, 310, 338
"Tradition and Industrialization" (Wright), 190
transcendence, critical theory of, 89–90
trauma, psychological, 200–201, 283

travel writing, 229–30, 241
tribalism, 165, 205
Trilling, Lionel, 315
Trotskyism, 49, 65
Trump, Donald, 16, 37
Ture, Kwame (formerly Stokely Carmichael), 205
Turner, Nat, 316
12 Million Black Voices (Wright and Rosskam), 5, 12, 110, 224, 225–26, 230, 272; blacks as a collectivity in, 168–69; *The Color Curtain* compared with, 233; as folk history, 313; on formation of lynch mobs, 335; "landscape" of politics in, 269–73; on life in North and South, 263; literary-journalistic use of analogy in, 228–29; montage as constellatory method, 253–56; montage as used by Benjamin and Wright, 248, 249–53; "politics" of nature in, 273–75, 277–81; politics of refusal and, 312, 313, 314, 318–21; representative politics in, 248–49, 256–58; *The Second Sex* in conversation with, 161, 170–76; sharecropper portrait in, *169*; "we" and "you" in, 226–28; Wright's relationship to photography and, 167–68

ubuntu ("I am because we are"), 323
Uncle Remus Stories, 275
Uncle Tom's Children (Wright), 13, 47, 53, 74, 293, 306–7; "Big Boy Leaves Home," 50, 300–301; "Bright and Morning Star," 108, 225, 305–6; "Down by the Riverside," 301–3; "Fire and Cloud," 304, 305; "Long Black Song," 303–4; Wright's regrets about, 315
Unemployed Councils, 49

United States, 233, 321, 343; Beauvoir in, 160–61; as country built by enslaved people, 342; as racialized state, 322; racial segregation in, 35; white Left in, 192. *See also* North, US America(n); South, US America(n)
universalism, 4, 16, 30
urbanization, 46, 225, 226. *See also* Chicago, South Side of; Great Migration (1910–1930); Harlem (New York)

Van Peebles, Melvin, 45
Vaughan, James, 331
violence, 54, 67, 93, 208; in black literature and social life, 122; black male vulnerability to, 134, 143; carceral state and, 321–22; as cathartic rejection, 314; against children and women, 99; domestic, 10; gendered, 13; invisible, 204; in the Jim Crow South, 116, 141, 142; of the lumpenproletariat, 53; lynching and sexual violence, 135, 137, 142; mythology of black men as violent rapists, 133; nature and emotional response to, 275; oppressive conditions and, 66; pressures of urban capitalism and, 78; in the public sphere, 110; race relations in the South and, 156; of racist state, 34; sexual, 11; threat of violent death, 294–95; white women as participants in, 139, 140, 146–47; Wright's images of, 107, 120

Walker, Margaret, 111
Wallace, Michelle, 144
Wallach, Jennifer, 341
Washington, Booker T., 71
Wells, Ida B., 135

Wertham, Dr. Fredric, 5–6
West, Cornel, 311
West, Dorothy, 4–5
Western civilization, 46, 47, 254; antiblack racism of, 107; blacks as part of, 168; industrial revolution of, 186; Marxism and, 57; moral and religious hypocrisy of, 183
"What You Know Won't Hurt You" (1942), 225
White Man, Listen! (Wright), 8, 140
white nationalism, 16
whiteness, 129, 136, 141, 254
white(s), 32, 36, 66, 319; antiracism and, 35; black men raped by white women, 134–37; cultural "rot" of, 162; housing and racial policies, 337; landlords/landowners, 268, 278, 279, 280, 281, 337; liberals, 69–70, 323; nationalist consciousness and, 52; Negro writing and, 213, 222; poor whites, 229, 335; unawareness of war on dignity of black people, 107; white women in Wright's fiction, 112, 114–15; working-class, 3, 54
white supremacy, 16, 142, 148, 311, 340; phantasmic modes of representation and, 250; racialized representation and, 248; sexual mythology of black rapist, 133, 139–40; violence of, 2, 336
Wilderson, Frank, 321
Williams, John A., 45
Williams, Sherley Anne, 110
Wolff, Richard D., 295
Wolin, Sheldon, 339
women: divisions and commonality among, 167; identity of "Woman" as false subject, 167, 170, 172; lived experiences of, 171–72; normative categories of sexual difference and, 175–76; patriarchy and, 110; rape

of black men by white women, 133, 134–37. *See also* black women
World War II, 5, 6, 75, 86, 343
Wright, Ellen (wife of R. W.), 161, 201
Wright, Julia (daughter of R. W.), 191
Wright, Rachel (daughter of R. W.), 8
Wright, Richard: African identity and, 201–4; as autodidact, 1, 12; at Bandung Conference (1955), 160; on black diaspora, 181–83, 194; black modernity and, 187–88; on black women, 59–60; book reviews, 6; break with Communist Party, 5, 320; childhood hardships, 329; as Communist Party organizer, 27, 48–50, 70, 318; death of, 8, 163; debate on misogyny in fiction of, 10–11; education of, 2; FBI monitoring of, 5, 7; in Ghana, 7, 160, 163–66; humanism of, 94; images of the black feminine, 109–11; influence on Beauvoir, 90–93; journalistic essays, 12, 224–25; literary legacy of, 120; literary style of, 14; motive for becoming a writer, 86–87; as proletarian writer, 48; protofeminist statements made by, 122–23, 124; self-exile to Paris, 160; sexist and misogynist attitudes held by, 121, 123; slavery and family history of, 203–4; social function as black writer, 4; speech at Paris Congress (1956), 11, 159–62, 175; stereotyped images of black women, 10; as supporter of McGee, 133–34, 141; waning popularity in the United States, 6
Wright, Richard, works of: *American Hunger,* 45, 47, 124, 270–71, 272, 275, 279; "Behind the McGee Case," 14, 134; "Blueprint for Negro Writing," 14–15, 48, 213–23, 225, 318; *The Color Curtain,* 224, 229; *Eight Men,* 45; "The Ethics of Living Jim Crow," 333–34; *Haiku: This Other World,* 281–83; "How 'Bigger' Was Born," 1, 10, 35–38, 40–41, 51–53, 64–81, 88–101, 299, 304, 311, 314–317, 320, 323; "I Bite the Hand That Feeds Me," 225; "I Have Seen Black Hands," 14, 23–25; "I Tried to Be a Communist," 124; "Joe Louis Uncovers Dynamite," 15, 283–92; *Lawd Today,* 50, 126; *The Long Dream,* 126–29; "Man of All Work," 134, 143–49; "The Man Who Saw a Flood," 266–69, 277, 279; "The Man Who Went to Chicago," 126; "Not My People's War," 225; *The Outsider,* 7; *Pagan Spain,* 8, 126, 224, 229, 230, 237–41; "Red Clay Blues" (with Hughes), 278–80, 281, 283; *Savage Holiday,* 124; "The Shame of Chicago," 225; "Tradition and Industrialization," 190; *Uncle Tom's Children,* 13, 47, 53, 293, 300–307; "What You Know Won't Hurt You," 225; *White Man, Listen!* 8, 140; "Between the World and Me," 225, 294, 298, 299. See also *Black Boy* (Wright); *Black Power* (Wright); *Native Son* (Wright); *Outsider, The* (Wright); *12 Million Black Voices* (Wright and Rosskam)
"Wright School," 45

Zinn, Howard, 69
Zirakzadeh, Cyrus Ernesto, 9
zoot-suit riots, 75

www.ingramcontent.com/pod-product-compliance
Lightning Source LLC
Chambersburg PA
CBHW031845220426
43663CB00006B/504